SPECIAL ADVISERS

Viewers of *The Thick of It* will know of special advisers as spin doctors and political careerists. Several well-known ministers have been special advisers, among them David Cameron, Ed Miliband, Jack Straw and Vince Cable. People also know about the public relations disasters involving Jo Moore, Damian McBride and Adam Smith. But what is the reality? What do special advisers actually do in government? Who are they, where do they come from and why are they needed?

This book is the most detailed study yet carried out of special advisers. The Constitution Unit's research team, led by Dr Ben Yong and Professor Robert Hazell, assembled a comprehensive database of over 600 special advisers since 1979. They conducted written surveys and interviewed over 100 special advisers, ministers and officials from the past 30 years. They conclude that special advisers are now a permanent and indispensable part of Whitehall, but are still treated as transient and temporary.

The book concludes with practical recommendations for increasing the effectiveness of special advisers through improvements to their recruitment, induction and training, support and supervision, and strengthening their accountability.

Special Advisers

Who They Are, What They Do and Why They Matter

Ben Yong and Robert Hazell

·HART·
PUBLISHING

OXFORD AND PORTLAND, OREGON
2016

Hart Publishing
An imprint of Bloomsbury Publishing Plc

Hart Publishing Ltd
Kemp House
Chawley Park
Cumnor Hill
Oxford OX2 9PH
UK

Bloomsbury Publishing Plc
50 Bedford Square
London
WC1B 3DP
UK

www.hartpub.co.uk
www.bloomsbury.com

Published in North America (US and Canada) by
Hart Publishing
c/o International Specialized Book Services
920 NE 58th Avenue, Suite 300
Portland, OR 97213-3786
USA

www.isbs.com

HART PUBLISHING, the Hart/Stag logo, BLOOMSBURY and the
Diana logo are trademarks of Bloomsbury Publishing Plc

First published in hardback, 2014
Paperback edition, 2016

British Library Cataloguing-in-Publication Data
A catalogue record for this book is available from the British Library.

ISBN: PB: 978-1-50991-388-6
HB: 978-1-84946-560-1

Typeset by Compuscript Ltd, Shannon
Printed and bound in Great Britain by
Lightning Source UK Ltd

To find out more about our authors and books visit www.hartpublishing.co.uk. Here you will
find extracts, author information, details of forthcoming events and the option to sign up for our
newsletters.

The choice of servants is of no little importance to a prince, and they are good or not according to the discrimination of the prince. And the first opinion which one forms of a prince, and of his understanding, is by observing the men he has around him; and when they are capable and faithful he may always be considered wise, because he has known how to recognise the capable and to keep them faithful. But when they are otherwise one cannot form a good opinion of him, for the prime error which he made was in choosing them.

Machiavelli, *The Prince*, chapter XXII

Preface

This project sprang from the work that we did in 2011–12 studying the new Coalition Government, which led to our book *The Politics of Coalition*. We became curious about the role of special advisers under the Coalition, and that led us to reflect on the growing importance of special advisers more generally. So a new project was born, with many of the same research team. The Coalition Government has now announced its plans for extended ministerial offices (EMOs) with more special advisers, so the subject is very topical.

Ben Yong led the project and is the main author of this book. Two former senior civil servants, David Laughrin and Peter Waller, kindly wrote chapters four, five and six. Another retired senior civil servant, Hilary Jackson, and Brian Walker (ex-BBC) helped with the interviews, came to all our meetings and commented on successive drafts. Anna Sellers very generously turned her LSE Master's dissertation on special advisers' subsequent careers into appendix three. We were also very fortunate in that Sophia Lambert—another retired senior civil servant—was able to do a magnificent job in copyediting our final manuscript.

Between us, the research team interviewed just over 100 people. The breakdown of the interviewees is given in chapter one. They include secretaries of state, Cabinet secretaries, ministerial chiefs of staff, senior civil servants, special advisers from all parties, journalists and other external stakeholders. We are immensely grateful to them for giving up their time and telling us about their experiences of special advisers, good and bad. The chapters are full of quotations from the interviewees to help bring the book alive. We are also grateful to the many interviewees and interested parties who read our chapters in draft, and corrected our mistakes and misunderstandings. Those we can thank openly include Leila Brosnan, Sir Chris Foster, Ian Heggie, Nick Hillman, Darryl Howe, Paul Richards, Sir Adam Ridley, Andy Westwood and various former heads of the Policy Unit.

The collective effort went wider than just the core research team. We benefited from a series of excellent interns—Jeremy Swan, Matthew Honeyman, Daniella Lock and Robin McGhee—who took our research much deeper and wider than we could have managed alone. Ed Lucas and Nitish Verma also helped with copyediting of the final manuscript. Max Goplerud came back from Oxford for a second summer to finalise the database that we compiled of all special advisers between 1979 and 2013, and he is the main author of appendices one and two. Ben Webb has been a wonderful administrator, supporting the project with his usual cheerfulness and efficiency. Likewise Rachel Turner at Hart Publishing, who has looked after us with exemplary tact and skill.

We have received generous advice from several academics, both in the UK and overseas. From Canada, we thank David Brown and Jonathan Craft; from Australia, Andrew Podger, Paddy Gourley, Maria Maley, Anne Tierney and Pat Weller; and from New Zealand, Chris Eichbaum and Richard Shaw. In the UK we would like to thank Professors Ed Page (LSE) and Stephen Hanney (Brunel University). Professors Scott Greer and Holly Jarman (University of Michigan) also offered useful comments on our work.

The project has a webpage, and supporting data and research papers can be found here: www.ucl.ac.uk/constitution-unit/research/special-advisers. Also posted on the webpage is a handbook for special advisers, *Being A Special Adviser*, compiled by Hilary Jackson. This is designed mainly for new special advisers, with a series of practical top tips from current and former special advisers drawn from all three parties.

We are grateful to *Private Eye* magazine for granting us permission to use Richard Jolley's cartoon on special advisers. This is reproduced in chapter one and also adorns the cover of the handbook for special advisers.

Finally, we should thank the Joseph Rowntree Charitable Trust, which generously funded this research project. It was the Rowntree Social Service Trust that funded the first researchers who became special advisers in Harold Wilson's second government, known as the 'chocolate soldiers', so it is very fitting that Rowntree should be supporting work on special advisers 50 years on. We are very grateful to Steve Pittam and Nick Perks and their Trustees.

Robert Hazell
Constitution Unit, School of Public Policy, UCL
Ben Yong
Faculty of Law, Queen Mary University of London
March 2014

Contents

List of Figures and Tables

Figures

Tables

1

Why Study Special Advisers?

BEN YONG

It is not hard to see why Whitehall is so wary of political advisers. They are unelected and unaccountable in any true sense ... Over the past six years it has sometimes seemed like amateur night in Whitehall as party political advisers, inexperienced in government, have put aspirations before realistic programmes and slogans before solid planning. The culture of spin has not been limited to presentation; it has infected the policymaking process itself. (Sue Cameron, journalist)[1]

A good special adviser is gold dust, but they can be an awful nuisance ... many of them treating themselves as unaccountable junior ministers. (Sir Robin Mountfield, former Permanent Secretary, Cabinet Office)[2]

Part of the art of being a special adviser is walking in grey areas. (Former Conservative special adviser)

THIS IS A book about special advisers, temporary civil servants personally appointed by government ministers who often carry out political tasks that career civil servants cannot. Special advisers are called many things: spin doctors, policy wonks, bag carriers, cronies, bright young things. In British politics, everyone has heard of some 'spads'—Alastair Campbell, Damian McBride, Andy Coulson—and indeed some senior politicians (David Cameron, Ed Miliband and Vince Cable amongst others) are former special advisers themselves. There is even a popular BBC comedy, *The Thick of It*, in which the key characters are special advisers.

For much of the twentieth century, and into the twenty-first, special advisers have been seen as a malign development—at best a necessary evil and at worst a waste of public funds, whose potential for shady and pernicious behaviour had to be contained.[3] Stories of internecine bickering and briefing were an integral part

---

[1] Sue Cameron, 'Advisers Have Corroded Trust in Whitehall' *Financial Times* (7 April 2003).

[2] House of Lords Select Committee on the Constitution, 'The Cabinet Office and the Centre of Government' (2010) 72.

[3] Peter Oborne, *The Rise of Political Lying* (Free Press 2005); Nicholas Jones, *Sultans of Spin* (Gollancz 2000); Nicholas Jones, *The Control Freaks: How New Labour Gets its Own Way* (Politico's 2002).

of the Labour years.[4] Special advisers are reported as briefing behind the scenes, poisoning the relationship between ministers and ministers, or as gatekeepers, poisoning the relationship between ministers and civil servants. They are seen as part of a move towards 'Prime Ministerial government'—a concentration of power in the Prime Minister at the expense of the Cabinet. They are perceived as having too much power and as being unaccountable. Special advisers are also often seen as young politicians in waiting, a cadre of insular tribalists, with no experience of 'the real world', symptomatic of the 'professionalisation' of politics at Westminster.[5]

So from the outside special advisers are viewed with hostility and suspicion. But from 'the inside'—in Whitehall—they have become an essential part of the government machinery. They have now been around for over 50 years, with the first official special advisers having been appointed in the 1960s.[6] No Prime Minister or government has seriously considered their abolition. Their number at Westminster has been slowly increasing ever since their introduction (mirroring developments in other countries that follow the 'Westminster model', where governments are also employing greater numbers of political staff).[7] As Lord Turnbull, a former Cabinet Secretary, said, 'ministers, special advisers and officials are three parts of a triangle'.[8]

Yet, in spite of their acceptance within Whitehall and their notoriety outside of it, there is a surprising dearth of solid evidence on who special advisers are, what they do and why they are needed. That is what we want to explore.

I. FOUR KEY QUESTIONS

In this book, we are looking at three 'cohorts' of special advisers: those under the Conservative Governments of 1979–97; under the Labour Governments of 1997–2010; and under the current Coalition Government. We ask four key questions:

1. *Why do ministers appoint special advisers?* The Coalition Government pledged to reduce the number of special advisers. In June 2010, the Coalition appointed 63; by late October 2013, there were 98 special advisers in office. But in fact the number of special advisers has been steadily rising over time. The obvious reason why the number of special advisers

---

[4] See, for example, Andrew Rawnsley, *Servants of the People: The Inside Story of New Labour* (Hamish Hamilton 2000); Andrew Rawnsley, *The End of the Party* (Viking 2010); and Damian McBride, *Power Trip: A Decade of Policy, Plots and Spin* (Biteback 2013).

[5] Anoosh Chakelian, 'Back to Front: From SpAd to Worse?' (*Total Politics*, 28 May 2013), www.totalpolitics.com/articles/370997/back-to-front-from-spad-to-worse.thtml.

[6] There is some debate about the genesis of special advisers. See ch 2; *cf* Andrew Blick, *People Who Live in the Dark* (Politico's 2004).

[7] See ch 8; and *cf* Carl Dahlström, B Guy Peters and Jon Pierre (eds), *Steering From the Centre: Strengthening Political Control in Western Democracies* (University of Toronto Press 2011).

[8] Chris Eichbaum and Richard Shaw, 'Conclusion' in Chris Eichbaum and Richard Shaw (eds), *Partisan Appointees and Public Servants: An International Analysis of the Role of the Political Adviser* (Edward Elgar 2010) 219.

continues to rise is because ministers keep appointing them. So we need to ask: *why* do ministers keep appointing special advisers? Have the reasons for appointing special advisers changed over time? Would Whitehall be better with more or fewer special advisers?

2. *Who becomes a special adviser, in terms of age, skills and experience, and what do special advisers do after they leave government?* There are a number of stereotypes about special advisers: they are all young, inexperienced, politicians-in-waiting; and following government, many become politicians and lobbyists, being part of the network making up 'the Westminster village'. That is the image of special advisers portrayed in the popular media. But there have been few systematic studies of the background of special advisers—or what they do following their time in government.

3. *What are the roles and functions of special advisers?* If ministers keep appointing special advisers, what do they need them for? Government ministers have thousands of officials at their beck and call: what is it that special advisers offer that officials do not? Before questioning the impact and importance of special advisers, we must first establish what it is special advisers do and how they do it. This will help us understand why ministers need them and whether or not special advisers are as powerful as some have suggested.

4. *How can the role and effectiveness of special advisers be improved?* If we accept that special advisers are now a fixture in British government, we should begin to ask how they might be best used by ministers. A great deal of time and analysis has been spent on devising means to constrain special advisers and hold them accountable. That is important. But it is also important to discuss how special advisers can be made more effective, given that virtually all senior ministers now expect to have them when they enter government.

To anticipate our conclusions: ministers need special advisers because they are overloaded and cannot do all that is being asked of them; because they feel isolated in their departments and need aides who share a common commitment; and because special advisers are able to be political in a way that career civil servants cannot be. Our evidence suggests that special advisers are a valuable part of British government and, indeed, almost all ministers now regard them as indispensable. What we have seen, however, is that the arrangements for special advisers remain ad hoc and haphazard, and this impacts on their potential effectiveness. If ministers and governments want more effective special advisers, then they and the political parties need to adopt a more systematic approach to their recruitment, training, support and supervision.

II. SPECIAL ADVISERS: A DEFINITION

We need a definition of special advisers. Technically, they are temporary civil servants, usually paid for out of public funds. But they are also personal appointments of government ministers and leave when the minister leaves, when there

Figure 1.1: *Private Eye* **cartoon (reproduced with the permission of** *Private Eye***)**

is an election or of their own volition. They may be asked to carry out 'political' tasks that career civil servants cannot. They have a particular contract and are subject to a specially drawn-up 'Code of Conduct for Special Advisers'.

We have taken a simple approach to identifying who is a special adviser. If a government has named an individual as a special adviser, then we regard them as one. We have presumed that those named as special advisers by the government also have the characteristics we noted above.

This approach has drawbacks, which we cover in more detail in appendix one. Relying on government statements about who is a special adviser is under- and over-inclusive. It is *under*-inclusive in that it fails to include people who may in effect act as special advisers. Successive governments have made use of individuals to support ministers who are not stated to be special advisers, but may act as de facto special advisers. We cover these de facto special advisers in greater detail in chapter seven.

Our definition is also *over*-inclusive in that it includes individuals whom many would not regard as 'special advisers'. Governments have been inconsistent in who they label as a special adviser. For instance, the Prime Minister's political secretary is not usually understood to be a special adviser. Political secretaries are appointed by the Prime Minister in his or her capacity as Party leader; maintain links between the Prime Minister and the Party organisation; and are paid for by the Party. But Sally Morgan, Tony Blair's Political Secretary, was sometimes listed as a special adviser.[9] By contrast, one of her successors, Joe Irvin, was not listed as a special adviser in the period in which he was Political Secretary to Gordon Brown (2008–10).

We acknowledge these methodological problems, but we have found in practice that the vast majority of the special advisers whom we have examined fall within the definition of those officially stated to be special advisers. Where there are exceptions, we shall make note of them in the text.

III. METHODOLOGY

In order to answer our four key questions, we used a number of methods: a review of the academic and popular literature; the construction of an easily searchable database of all special advisers between 1979 and 2013; surveys and interviews. Here we set out the broad approach we took: there is a more detailed discussion of methodology in appendix one.

Our initial objective was to examine the roles and effectiveness of special advisers under the Labour Governments of 1997–2010 and the Coalition Government (2010–). But midway through the project, we realised that the Coalition cohort of special advisers was too small and too short in terms of tenure to be comparable to those under Labour, and so we chose to extend to the project to cover special advisers under the Conservative Governments of 1979–97 as well.

---

[9] For two conflicting classifications of Sally Morgan, see: HC Deb 20 March 2000, vol 346, col 403W (political secretary); and HC Deb 31 March 2003, vol 402, col 526W (special adviser).

A. Academic Literature, Biographies, Autobiographies, Histories and Periodical Articles

We examined key academic texts and articles concerning special advisers in the UK and political staff overseas, as well as memoirs, biographies, periodical articles and histories of British governments between 1979 and 2013.

B. The Database

No comprehensive list of special advisers from 1979 to 2013 has ever been compiled. This is mostly because data on special advisers is partial or not readily available and is spread out over various disparate sources. It is also because the definition of 'special adviser' has not been consistent over time.

We took our data from various sources: official, periodicals, academic and miscellaneous. The key sources are *Hansard* and Cabinet Office reports. We took these as authoritative. Periodicals such as *Vacher's Quarterly* supplement these official sources. Where an individual is not mentioned in *Hansard* or Cabinet Office reports, then we required verification from two independent sources, preferably from key periodicals.

With the help of our excellent research assistant Max Goplerud, we drew this data together into a single database. The core dataset was coded by entering one 'case' for each special adviser in each year with information including their name, department, minister, government and so on. It covers all 626 special advisers employed between May 1979 and November 2013.[10]

C. Surveys

We carried out two online surveys: one survey focused on all those special advisers who had served under the Conservative Governments of 1979–97 and the other on special advisers who had served under the Labour Governments of 1997–2010. These surveys were carried out over 2012–13 and response rates were relatively high—see appendix one for more information. The questions covered background, roles and skills involved, accountability and performance evaluation.

D. Interviews

Our aim in interviews was to ensure representativeness across a number of different variables in order to get a rounded view of who special advisers are,

---

[10] Note that we are only looking at special advisers who work in Westminster and Whitehall. There are special advisers working in the devolved administrations of Scotland, Wales and Northern Ireland, but a lack of resources and time meant we were unable to examine them.

what they do and where they are most effective. We aimed to get a '360-degree view': we interviewed special advisers, but also ministers, officials and external stakeholders who worked with special advisers. Where possible, we also tried to triangulate: that is, interview special advisers, ministers and officials who had all worked together—although this often proved difficult in practice. We used the database to select special advisers and ministers to interview.

We interviewed key actors across the Conservative, Labour and Coalition administrations. We also made sure to interview across premierships: so, for instance, we interviewed Labour special advisers and ministers who worked in either the Blair premierships (1997–2001, 2001–05 and 2005–07), the Brown premiership (2007–10) or both.

We wanted to capture the experiences of different types of special adviser. Many previous studies on special advisers have focused on those in No 10, but in fact most special advisers have been 'embedded' in departments. So we interviewed special advisers from the Centre (ie, No 10 and the Cabinet Office) and from departments. We also interviewed a varied range of special advisers: those with long and short tenures, and those whose primary function was media, political liaison or policy.

We took a similar approach in interviews with ministers and officials. We interviewed secretaries of state, but also less senior ministers; those ministers who only ever had one or two special advisers and those who had had several. Interviewing officials was less systematic. We often asked ministers and special advisers we interviewed to suggest officials we might interview; and we also made sure to interview not just Cabinet secretaries and permanent secretaries (who by reason of their long tenure meant they could compare special advisers from different cohorts) but also relatively 'younger' members of the senior civil service.

The six members of the special advisers project team (Ben Yong, Robert Hazell, David Laughrin, Peter Waller, Hilary Jackson and Brian Walker) all carried out interviews. Interviews were semi-structured: we had a standard set of questions for each group—special advisers, ministers, officials and external stakeholders. These questions covered recruitment, induction and training; roles and functions; effectiveness and accountability; and recommendations. The number and composition of our interviewees is set out below in Table 1.1.

Table 1.1: Number and type of interviewee*

Type	Number
Special advisers	39
Ministers	27
Officials	23
External satakeholders	13
TOTAL	**102**

* Note: some interviewees were special advisers who had become ministers or officials, and so for the purposes of these tables, they are counted once under special advisers. We also interviewed a number of individuals more than once, but these additional interviews have not been counted.

Finally, it should be noted that the object of our study is the examination of special advisers as a generic group. So while we touch upon the roles and influence of special advisers at the Centre, we are not primarily concerned with the longstanding debates over the 'presidentialisation' of British government or the capacity of the Centre and in particular No 10.[11]

IV. TERMINOLOGY

In this book we have chosen to use the more formal term 'special adviser' over the now common acronym 'spad'; the latter is only used where we are quoting someone. We use the generic term 'minister' to cover all ministers including secretaries of state—in practice the vast majority of special advisers are employed by secretaries of state, but there are certain other ministers who have also had special advisers. Finally, 'the Centre' refers to No 10 and the Cabinet Office, unless otherwise stated.

V. THE OUTLINE OF THE BOOK

Following this introduction, *chapter two* sets out a history of special advisers in the UK and looks at the academic literature on special advisers. Special advisers began as a modest response to the perceived deficiencies of and pressures on British government, but they have become, over time, an established fixture of Whitehall: ministers cannot imagine life without them. Special advisers have often been understood in terms of the 'Whitehall model' of government, where they are seen very much as interlopers in an established system. It is better to place special advisers in a context in which ministers are understood to be 'resource weak': ie, they (including the Prime Minister) are increasingly overloaded; lack the time and expertise to deal with the complexities of government; and need to work through and with others to achieve their goals. Special advisers exist, therefore, because ministers need them, and much of their value lies in their flexibility and relative freedom from hierarchy and neutrality.

---

[11] See most recently Keith Dowding, 'The Prime Ministerialisation of the British Prime Minister' (2012) 66 *Parliamentary Affairs* 617; Richard Heffernan, 'There's No Need for the "-Isation": The Prime Minister Is Merely Prime Ministerial' (2012) 66 *Parliamentary Affairs* 636; Paul Webb and Thomas Poguntke, 'The Presidentialisation of Politics Thesis Defended' (2012) 66 *Parliamentary Affairs* 646; Michael Foley, 'Prime Ministerialisation and Presidential Analogies: A Certain Difference in Interpretive Evolution' (2012) 66 *Parliamentary Affairs* 655; Keith Dowding, 'Beneath the Surface: Replies to Three Critics' (2013) 66 *Parliamentary Affairs* 663.

Chapter three answers question two: who are special advisers? It examines the characteristics of special advisers in all three government cohorts prior to entering government (eg, their political, educational and professional background, and age when appointed) and the characteristics of special advisers while in government (such as their average tenure). It then analyses the process by which special advisers are recruited. From the outside, this process looks ad hoc and haphazard, but there are underlying structural factors and common requirements which mean that particular kinds of individuals tend to be selected. A recruitment cycle is identified, in which the longer governments are in power, the more difficult it becomes to recruit suitable candidates, and ministers are forced by necessity into seeking alternative recruitment pools and holding semi-open competitive interviews. The chapter concludes by noting that recruitment is an ongoing issue and may become even more problematic if the number of special advisers continuesto rise.

Chapters four, five and six broadly answer questions one and three: why do ministers appoint special advisers and what are the roles and functions of special advisers? *Chapter four* looks at how special advisers support ministers generally. Ministers can feel isolated and in need of additional support: they want familiar and trusted associates that they have chosen themselves. Being overloaded, with ever-increasing pressures on their time, ministers also want additional expertise, people who can ensure policy delivery and chase progress. In providing support for ministers, special advisers have three key functions: policy advice, communications advice and political support. These functions are explored in relation to special advisers both in departments and at the Centre.

Chapter five examines the role of special advisers in the-policy making process and the benefits they can bring, particularly in their relationship with officials. On the whole, special advisers do provide significant benefits. Policy making in government cannot be divorced from politics and few civil servants will be as adept as special advisers at understanding the political merits and demerits of different policy options. Special advisers provide other benefits: additional capacity; helping officials understand priorities; challenging departmental orthodoxies; and, alongside their political focus, subject-area expertise. But we found that there were also problems—most notably, the appointment of inexperienced special advisers, the blocking of access to the minister and the tendency to act in haste.

Chapter six examines the most controversial function of some special advisers: communications. It pays particular attention to the 'Campbell revolution' of 1997, which saw a move away from providing information and explanation to persuasion, and in which special advisers played a crucial role. It examines the impact of that revolution, which still reverberates under the Coalition. The chapter concludes that the greater capacity created to present the government's arguments was necessary to deal with a changing and rapacious media, but that this additional capacity brought with it a tendency to pursue internal political arguments through the media.

Chapters seven, eight, nine and ten broadly answer question four: how can the effectiveness of special advisers be improved? *Chapter seven* examines different aspects of the regulation of special advisers—from the regulation of their conduct to the regulation of numbers. There are a number of lines of accountability for special advisers—primarily to their minister and, less clearly, to the government. In practice they are only very loosely managed. Special adviser numbers are subject to a political cap, but this cap is circumvented in a number of ways. Finally there are problems about induction, performance evaluation and management. The chapter concludes by noting that there is often an accountability gap, in that no one can effectively be held accountable for political advisers when things go wrong, but that there is also a responsibility gap, in that no one is responsible for ensuring that things go right. The chapter concludes by suggesting that greater input from the Centre is necessary for dealing with the responsibility gap.

Chapter eight steps back from earlier chapters and examines the comparable international experience of 'political staff'—that is, those individuals personally appointed by ministers to provide political support in Canada, Australia and New Zealand, and there is a short discussion of ministerial *cabinets* on the continent. A number of common themes emerge. The numbers of political staff in those other countries are also generally rising and there are signs of greater centralisation. As in the UK, the rise in numbers brings with it other problems: problems of management and accountability become pronounced; and there is an increasing drive towards professionalisation, or at least attempts to formalise arrangements. Finally, in all jurisdictions surveyed, there are concerns about the appropriate role of special advisers—their purported impact, controversies over their conduct and their potential to distance ministers from their departments.

Chapter nine focuses on effectiveness. This is a multifaceted concept, which is measured by a number of actors, of whom the minister employing the adviser is but one. It includes such matters as the need for clear political objectives and priorities, drive and determination, being good at policy detail and building relationships, having a good media sense, and strong support for the minister. It then discusses possible solutions to enhance effectiveness and the practical difficulties involved in this. The three main means focus on recruitment, training and induction, and support and supervision. Attempts to increase professionalism will require greater centralisation at the cost of ministerial choice in the appointment and use of special advisers. There have already been signs of a move in this direction under both Labour and now the Coalition.

Chapter ten summarises the findings of the book, sets out recommendations and concludes with some thoughts on special advisers as a mini-profession. Special advisers are now considered indispensable by all key actors within Whitehall. The demands on ministers are now so great that they need people who know their minds and to whom they can delegate. Special advisers have a particular authority because they have usually been personally chosen by their ministers and because they are bound by fewer restrictions than other sources of ministerial support.

Recommendations are made to improve the effectiveness of special advisers: they would be more effective if they were more professionally managed in terms of their selection, support and supervision, and development of their professional skills. But this is only likely to happen if the Prime Minister, supported by his or her chief of staff, takes the lead in raising the overall quality threshold.

Appendix one sets out in more detail the methodology behind the database and the collation of background information. *Appendix two* is a more in-depth quantitative examination of special adviser distribution and tenure, broadly confirming that special advisers usually serve one minister and in a single department for a median of 3 years. *Appendix three* examines what special advisers do once they leave government. A relatively high proportion move into public affairs and a high proportion go into the business sector. But the number of special advisers who enter politics following their time in government is, contrary to some perceptions, quite small.

For those wanting more information about any special adviser mentioned in the text, they are listed in *appendix four*, along with brief details of their tenure, the minister(s) they served and in what period. Ministers with special advisers are also listed in this appendix.

The special adviser database, listing all special advisers who were in government between 1979 and 2013, will be posted on the Constitution Unit's website to coincide with the publication of the book.[12]

There is also a companion text to this book: 'Being a Special Adviser', edited by Hilary Jackson. This is a short handbook for new or prospective special advisers, with advice from former Conservative, Labour and Coalition special advisers. This will also be freely available on the Unit's website.

---

[12] See the Constitution Unit webpage, under 'Special Advisers': www.ucl.ac.uk/constitution-unit.

2

Special Advisers and British Government

BEN YONG

THE ROLE AND development of special advisers cannot be understood without talking about the work of British government, and the work of ministers in particular, as well as how these have changed over the years. This chapter will discuss three matters: first, the overall framework of British government and particularly the role of the civil service; second, the emergence and gradual institutionalisation of special advisers; and, finally, some theories put forward to explain the growth and functions of special advisers.

I. MINISTERS, SPECIAL ADVISERS AND WHITEHALL

Special advisers work for senior ministers, and ministers sit at the apex of British government. Ministers are appointed by the Prime Minister and are drawn from Parliament. There is a three-tier ministerial hierarchy: Secretary of State, Minister of State and Parliamentary Under-Secretary of State. There are around 20 ministers in the Cabinet, mostly Secretaries of State, and another 70 or so 'junior' ministers (that is, those below the Secretary of State).[1] Ministers have a bewildering number of roles.[2] As a group, they collectively contribute to and determine the policies of the government as a whole. As individuals, secretaries of state are usually the political head of a Whitehall department, while less senior ministers take responsibility for one or more of the department's many portfolios.

Central British government ('Whitehall') traditionally has had a federal structure. It is organised into a set of departments (or ministries, as they used to be called), each of which is usually responsible for an area of government, and a

---

[1] We do not include Whips here.

[2] Bruce Headey, *British Cabinet Ministers: The Roles of Politicians in Executive Office* (Allen & Unwin 1974); David Marsh, David Richards and Martin J Smith, 'Re-assessing the Role of Departmental Cabinet Ministers' (2000) 78 *Public Administration* 305; Peter Riddell, Zoe Gruhn and Liz Carolan, *The Challenge of Being a Minister: Defining and Developing Ministerial Effectiveness* (Institute for Government 2011).

Centre (here, No 10 and the Cabinet Office) which is relatively weak compared to those in other Western countries.[3] In the UK, departments have always been the powerhouses of policy making, with the Prime Minister having relatively limited resources to achieve his or her goals.[4]

Within a department, ministers have a policy role (setting the agenda, initiating or selecting policies); a political role (defending their department's policies in Cabinet, Europe, Parliament and to the Party or Parties); an executive role (taking executive decisions within their area of responsibility); and a public relations role (overseeing the department's relations with interest groups, the public and the media).[5] Ministers from the House of Commons are also expected to carry out their duties as MPs—defending and promoting the Party, and dealing with constituency business.

Of course, ministers receive support to help them in their various roles. For the Secretary of State, there is the junior ministerial team, but it is not necessarily a guaranteed source of support. Junior ministers are chosen not by the Secretary of State but by the Prime Minister (in the Coalition Government, jointly with the Deputy Prime Minister), often to maintain balance between Party factions, and in any case junior ministers are often too busy with their own portfolios.[6] There are parliamentary private secretaries—MPs who act as the eyes and ears of a secretary of state in Parliament and the Party—but their key function is to help the minister in Parliament, not in the department. Ministers also have the assistance of their parliamentary researchers—a relatively new development—but researchers are only allowed to work on parliamentary matters, not departmental business.[7]

The primary source of support and advice for ministers has traditionally been, and continues to be, the career bureaucracy—the civil service. The average department has hundreds, sometimes thousands of civil servants, all of whom work for the Secretary of State and the ministerial team. In 2012, 422,000 people were employed in the civil service (the post-war high was 751,000 in 1976).[8] The 'Senior Civil Service' (SCS) makes up about one per cent of the total, and there are roughly similar numbers of people working in the one or two grades below them. It is these 10,000 or so officials who work closely with and support ministers in

---

[3] Martin Smith, 'The Paradoxes of Britain's Strong Centre: Delegating Decisions and Reclaiming Control' in Carl Dahlström, B Guy Peters and Jon Pierre (eds), *Steering From the Centre: Strengthening Political Control in Western Democracies* (University of Toronto Press 2011).

[4] Dennis Kavanagh and Anthony Seldon, *The Powers Behind the Prime Minister: The Hidden Influence of Number Ten* (HarperCollins 2008); Smith (n 3).

[5] Marsh, Richards and Smith (n 2).

[6] Chris Mullin, *A View from the Foothills: The Diaries of Chris Mullin* (Profile Books 2009); Kevin Theakston, Mark Gill and Judi Atkins, 'The Ministerial Foothills: Labour Government Junior Ministers 1997–2010' (2012) *Parliamentary Affairs* 1.

[7] Independent Parliamentary Standards Authority, *MPs' Scheme of Business Costs & Expenses* (2013) para 3.4.f.

[8] House of Commons Library, 'Civil Service Statistics' (House of Commons Library 2013).

the key departments and associated central government agencies.[9] Of particular importance to ministers is their 'Private Office', which is staffed by civil servants who liaise with departmental officials on behalf of the minister, handle correspondence and organise the minister's diary.

The respective roles and responsibilities of ministers and civil servants in Whitehall appear quite clear. The *traditional* understanding—sometimes referred to as the Northcote-Trevelyan 'settlement' or 'the Whitehall model'[10]—is that ministers govern, but with the support of the civil service. Civil servants are politically neutral, or non-partisan; they are appointed by open competition and promoted on merit; most are generalists rather than specialists; and they have a strong policy advisory role.

The key principle in this traditional model is ministerial responsibility. Ministers are responsible to Parliament and ultimately the public for what happens in their departments. It is the responsibility of ministers to govern and to implement government policies, with help from the civil service. The civil service is impartial. Its impartiality is demonstrated by service and loyalty to each successive party in government. This does not, however, mean being 'non-political', neutral or independent of the party in government. Heclo captures this in his discussion of 'neutral competence', which he states:

> [It] consists of giving one's cooperation and best independent judgment of the issues to partisan bosses—and of being sufficiently uncommitted to be able to do so for a succession of partisan leaders. The independence entailed in neutral competence does not exist for its own sake; it exists precisely in order to serve the aims of elected partisan leadership ... [It] is a strange amalgam of loyalty that argues back, partisanship that shifts with the changing partisans, and independence that depends on others.[11]

The principles of admission to the civil service by open competition and promotion on merit are intended to avoid a patronage-based system, to ensure impartiality and to allow the civil service to serve administrations of different political complexions. But it also means that officials are not appointed by ministers; in this sense, officials are not beholden to ministers and do not necessarily share their political views.

The Whitehall model conceals a more complex reality. Ministerial responsibility ensures democratic accountability, but it masks the influence that the civil service had and has over the development and implementation of government

---

[9] Peter Waller, 'Workings of Whitehall—An Insight into the Civil Service and How Policy is Developed' (The Whitehall & Industry Group 2012).

[10] Peter Hennessy, *Whitehall* (Pimlico 2001); Vernon Bogdanor, 'The Civil Service' in Vernon Bogdanor (ed), *The British Constitution in the Twentieth Century* (Oxford University Press for the British Academy 2004); Edward Page, 'Has the Whitehall Model Survived?' (2010) 76 *International Review of Administrative Sciences* 407.

[11] Hugh Heclo, 'OMB and the Presidency: The Problem of Neutral Competence' (1975) *The Public Interest* 80, 81–82.

policy.[12] Moreover, the guiding principles of selection on the basis of open competition and promotion on merit say little about what kind of civil servants are best suited to run a modern state: the selection procedures were designed to produce generalists rather than specialists (although, over time, more specialists have been recruited to Whitehall). Ministers are accountable to Parliament and the electorate, but it remains unclear to what extent they have—or should have—control over the civil service. The principles of non-partisanship and selection by open competition and promotion on merit have militated against the direct involvement of ministers in the appointment or removal of officials.

So the Whitehall model sees the key actors in British government as ministers and their civil servants. There has always been the potential for tension between these two sets of actors: between the impartiality of the civil service and pressures stemming from the need for ministers to be responsive to the public.[13] In this model special advisers could be,seen to be an answer to resolving this tension, but they could also be seen as interlopers, threatening the well-established relationship between ministers and civil servants. We return to the Whitehall model and the problems underlying it in section II.

For much of the twentieth century, this 'Whitehall model' was deemed satisfactory by both ministers and civil servants alike. In retrospect, however, the period between the inter-war years and the two decades after the Second World War marked the heyday of confidence in the British civil service and the British state in general. There appeared to be nothing that the civil service could not achieve: win two world wars, manage an empire and establish a welfare state. But as Britain declined politically and economically, and as the makeup of British society changed, confidence in these arrangements began to erode. There was a slow loss of faith in the civil service.[14]

Throughout the 1960s, various criticisms were made, culminating in the 1968 Fulton Report, which was critical of the civil service for its amateurism, which was the result of the meritocratic principles noted earlier. The report called for more infusions of expertise and outsiders, and more systematic training for 'generalist' civil servants.[15] Over the next half-century, successive governments tinkered with the civil service, but in essence it remained the same.

It would be a mistake, however, to lay the blame for the ills of the British state at the feet of the civil service or to see special advisers emerging solely as a remedy to the perceived deficiencies of officials. Successive British governments have come

---

[12] Matthew Flinders, 'The Enduring Centrality of Individual Ministerial Responsibility within the British Constitution' (2000) 6 *Journal of Legislative Studies* 73; Edward Page and WI Jenkins, *Policy Bureaucracy: Government with a Cast of Thousands* (Oxford University Press 2005).

[13] Chris Eichbaum and Richard Shaw, 'Introduction' in Chris Eichbaum and Richard Shaw (eds), *Partisan Appointees and Public Servants: An International Analysis of the Role of the Political Adviser* (Edward Elgar 2010).

[14] These have been discussed in various texts. See, for example, Hennessy (n 10); Colin Campbell and Graham Wilson, *The End of Whitehall: Death of a Paradigm?* (Blackwell 1995); Christopher Foster, *British Government in Crisis, Or, the Third English Revolution* (Hart Publishing 2005).

[15] Committee on the Civil Service, *The Report of the Committee on the Civil Service* (1968).

under increasing pressure as a result of broader changes in politics and society. The British state became increasingly interventionist over time; the late twentieth century saw the growth of a voracious 24/7 media environment[16] and there was a general decline in deference to established institutions. The job of governing Britain became more complex: ministers were expected to be responsible for more and there were also increased expectations about the speed with which they were expected and wanted to respond.

In the 1960s the two main political parties, Labour and the Conservatives, had working groups examining 'machinery of government' issues, running parallel to the public and official critiques of the civil service. Both parties examined models from overseas, in particular, the US system, where entire levels or classes of bureaucracy were staffed with political appointees, and the French system of ministerial *cabinets*, a select group of officials personally appointed by ministers. But in time a more incremental, ad hoc approach was adopted: the addition of a small number of personal appointments as temporary civil servants.

A. The Introduction of Special Advisers

In fact, British Prime Ministers (and some ministers) had long employed 'outsiders' (ie, those who did not belong to the permanent civil service) to assist them while in government.[17] David Lloyd George, for instance, established a Prime Minister's Secretariat of outside advisers ('the Garden Suburb') during the First World War.[18] Winston Churchill had a statistical section attached to his office during the Second World War, consisting of a number of economists led by Professor Frederick Lindemann—a physicist later elevated to a peerage (as Viscount Cherwell) and brought into government.

Many outsiders or 'irregulars' came into government during wartime, bringing in much-needed expertise that the permanent civil service was thought to lack.[19] John Maynard Keynes, for instance, was recalled to the Treasury in 1940 and remained there until his death in 1946.[20] William Beveridge, designer of the welfare state, was a temporary civil servant in both world wars. Ministers have also brought in political aides and policy experts in peacetime as well. Harold Macmillan, for instance, brought in John Wyndham,[21] an aristocrat and close friend, in 1957 to act as his political adviser.[22]

---

[16] See, for instance, Lance Price, *Where Power Lies: Prime Ministers v the Media* (Simon & Schuster 2010).

[17] Andrew Blick and George W Jones, *At Power's Elbow: Aides to the Prime Minister from Robert Walpole to David Cameron* (Biteback 2013).

[18] Andrew Blick, *People Who Live in the Dark* (Politico's 2004) 36.

[19] Hennessy (n 10).

[20] Blick (n 18) 40.

[21] Later Lord Egremont.

[22] Hennessy (n 10) 57.

However, the number of such personal appointments was very small indeed and they were not seen as a fundamental challenge to the Whitehall model in which ministers and civil servants were the dominant actors. It was only in the 1960s and 1970s that the first steps towards the systematisation of personal political appointments were made.[23] Harold Wilson, upon becoming Prime Minister in 1964, appointed a number of experts, such as the economists Thomas Balogh and Nicholas Kaldor, to assist him on economic policy, who were to be known as 'special advisers'. Balogh and Kaldor were the most well-known special advisers of the period, but there were others, such as John Allen and John Harris, who were appointed by ministers for their political nous rather than their technical expertise.[24]

When the Conservatives took power, they continued with Wilson's 'experiment' in appointing special advisers: the Prime Minister, Edward Heath, even established a new unit at the Centre in 1971, known as the Central Policy Review Staff (CPRS, also known as 'the Think Tank'), to provide a long-term strategic focus, briefs to Cabinet and advice independent of departments.[25] But, generally, special advisers were not as prominent as they had been under Labour in the 1960s. It was only under Wilson's second spell as Prime Minister that the status of special advisers was slowly formalised. The number of special advisers reached 30 at any one time and included individuals like Jack Straw and Margaret Beckett who later became ministers, as well as those who had served as assistants in opposition, funded by the Joseph Rowntree Social Service Trust (the 'Chocolate Soldiers').[26] In a 1974 paper, Wilson identified two reasons why he had introduced special advisers on a more systematic basis. The first was ministerial overload:

> [T]he burden of modern government as developed in our country, the immense volume of papers, the exhausting succession of departmental committees, of party gatherings and meetings with outside interests make it almost impossible for him [sic] to carry out his departmental and political responsibilities and at the same time sustain a detailed analysis of all the various political nuances of policy. If he can keep on top of his own department's work he is doing very well, but he finds it increasingly difficult to play a constructive part in the collective business of the Government as a whole.[27]

The second reason was concern about the civil service. The social and educational background of senior mandarins was seen as too narrow, and their commitment to stability and continuity meant that they could be an obstacle to change. Thus, special advisers were a means of addressing these two problems. They were 'an extra pair of hands, eyes and ears', they provided a more politically committed, politically aware point of view and they could facilitate more radical change.

---

[23] Blick (n 18). It would, however, be wrong to treat Balogh and Kaldor purely as experts: they were also both strident Labour supporters.

[24] ibid.

[25] For a history of the CPRS, see Tessa Blackstone and William Plowden, *Inside the Think Tank: Advising the Cabinet 1971–1983* (Heinemann 1988).

[26] Blick (n 18) 149.

[27] Harold Wilson, 'Appendix V: The "Political Advisers" Experiment' in *The Governance of Britain* (Weidenfeld & Nicolson 1976).

The new special advisers were, for the most part, classed as temporary civil servants. They were made part of the civil service, but unlike 'ordinary' civil servants, they were personally appointed by the minister and were expected to leave with the minister—hence the 'temporary' qualification. This peculiar status suited ministers, the permanent civil service and special advisers themselves. Ministers concerned about potential conflict thought that they could impose political discipline via the civil service rules operating at the time; permanent secretaries had a means of control over the new advisers because of the their civil servant status; and special advisers at the time were happy to be classed as civil servants in order to avoid parliamentary scrutiny, particularly from backbenchers suspicious about their patronage and influence.

The ambivalence over the status of special advisers extended to other aspects of their work. Wilson and successive Prime Ministers were unwilling to clarify the terms of employment of special advisers because of the fear of political fallout.[28] As we shall see, the result was that the roles, pay and accountability of special advisers have been perennial issues which have never satisfactorily been resolved. This lack of clarity has contributed to the perceived 'shadowy' nature of special advisers.

Like Heath before him, during his second term Wilson was keen to strengthen the support given to him, and so established the Policy Unit, which, unlike the CPRS, worked directly to the Prime Minister. It consisted of six to eight outsiders or special advisers. Its remit was determined by its head, Bernard Donoghue, a London School of Economics (LSE) academic: it was to examine proposals going to the Prime Minister for their strategic value, cross-departmental implications and political perspective. Wilson described his Policy Unit:

> The purpose of the Policy Unit is not only to bring in experts to extend the range of policy options from which the Government—and in particular the Prime Minister as head of the government—has to choose. The Policy Unit was set up, and its members were selected, to provide a team with strong political commitment to advise on, propose and pursue policies to further the Government's political goals. For policies without politics are of no more use than politics without policies.[29]

B. Excursus: The Changing Centre, 1979–2013

It is not the purpose of this book to examine the role of the Centre—No 10 and the Cabinet Office—or, more specifically, the support given to the Prime Minister. But we would be remiss if we did not briefly discuss the changing Centre, particularly as it is often the location of relatively large numbers of special advisers.

---

[28] Rodney Lowe, *The Official History of the British Civil Service: Reforming the Civil Service, Volume I: The Fulton Years, 1966–81* (Routledge 2011) 219–24.
[29] Wilson (n 27).

The support provided to the Prime Minister since 1979 has evolved in two ways: a personal component specific to the Prime Minister of the day and a general trend that is consistent across time. The general trend, with some noticeable deviations, is towards creating a structure of support that is staffed by politically appointed individuals rather than by career civil servants. The personal element acknowledges that each Prime Minister has particular preferences and priorities, and so organises support accordingly.

Prime Ministers have the support of a large Private Office, which is staffed by civil servants who provide general support and maintain links with key departments (for instance, the Foreign and Commonwealth Office and the Treasury). There is the Political Office, headed by the Political Secretary, which provides the link between Downing Street and the governing political party. More generally, there is the Cabinet Office, headed by the Cabinet Secretary, the most senior civil servant in the service, and staffed by civil servants. The Cabinet Office has traditionally supported the Prime Minister and the Cabinet as a whole, and has served as a coordinating body for the various government departments. But over time, as numbers have risen, staff to the Prime Minister and various units supporting the Prime Minister have spilled into the Cabinet Office. It is worth noting, however, that the Cabinet Office is tiny in Whitehall terms: an 'average' spending department might be 15–20 times bigger than the Cabinet Office. So in 2012, for instance, the Cabinet Office had approximately 1,600 staff, while the Home Office had over 24,000.

So, contrary to popular belief, the Centre has always been relatively weak in comparison with departments. Successive Prime Ministers since the 1960s have therefore sought to strengthen the Centre's policy-making and communications capacities. This objective has become more pressing as Prime Ministers have come to be seen as responsible for the failures and successes of all parts of their government, and as successive Prime Ministers have sought to assert greater control over both the detail of government and perceptions of their government.

This assertion of control has taken a number of forms. Political appointees have 'claimed' certain roles that were historically held by civil servants, the most obvious example being that of 'chief of staff' to the Prime Minister. Prior to the period under consideration, the functions of a chief of staff were shared between the Principal Private Secretary in the Private Office, the Cabinet Secretary and sometimes the Political Secretary. Since 1979, however, successive premiers have appointed outsiders or special advisers as chiefs of staff. Margaret Thatcher appointed David Wolfson, Tony Blair appointed Jonathan Powell and David Cameron appointed Ed Llewellyn, and it is now fairly accepted that the chief of staff role will be held by a special adviser.

In terms of policy capacity, we have already noted the establishment of the CPRS and then the Policy Unit. The Policy Unit has existed alongside the other organisational structures at the Centre fairly continuously from 1979 to the present. It is for this reason that we have set out in Table 2.1 its changing composition over time, illustrating, to some extent, the needs and priorities of different Prime Ministers.

Table 2.1: Size and composition of the Policy Unit and other units in the Centre, 1979–2013

Dates	Head of No 10 Policy Unit	Size and mix of No 10 Policy Unit	Other units	Comments
Thatcher				
1979–82	John Hoskyns	2 (Hoskyns and Strauss); then 3–4	Central Policy Review Staff (CPRS): Robin Ibbs 1980–82; John Sparrow 1982–83	CPRS abolished 1983. Two joined Policy Unit
1982–84	Ferdinand Mount	initially 2, later expanding to 8: including 2 orignally from CPRS, and 2 civil servants	Efficiency Unit: Derek Rayner 1979–83; Robin Ibbs 1983–84	Efficiency Unit under Ibbs was 8–10 people, mainly officials
1984–85	John Redwood	10: 4 special advisers, 3 business secondees, 3 civil servants		
1985–90	Brian Griffiths	8: 6 special advisers, 2 civil servants		
Major				
1990–95	Sarah Hogg	8: 4 special advisers, 4 civil servants		
1995–97	Norman Blackwell	8–9: 6–7 special advisers, 2 civil servants		
Blair				
1997–2001	David Miliband	9–12: mainly special advisers, but included 2–3 civil servants	Social Exclusion Unit: Moira Wallace 1997 Performance and Innovation Unit: Geoff Mulgan 1999	Performance and Innovation Unit became Strategy Unit in 2002. Strategy Unit at its zenith grew to 100 people
2001–05	Jeremy Heywood and Andrew Adonis, joint heads of Policy Directorate	PU merged with civil service Private Office to become Policy Directorate; 6 civil service Grade 7s added to give support	Delivery Unit: Michael Barber 2001 Strategy Unit: Geoff Mulgan 2002–04	Adonis was succeeded as Head of Policy by Mulgan in 2003 and then by Matthew Taylor in 2004. Taylor was Head of Political Strategy 2003–06

(Continued)

Table 2.1: *Continued*

Dates	Head of No 10 Policy Unit	Size and mix of No 10 Policy Unit	Other units	Comments
2005–07	David Bennett	10: 6 special advisers, 4 civil servants	Strategy Unit: Stephen Aldridge 2004–09 Delivery Unit: Ian Watmore 2006–07	Strategy Unit became research and analysis arm of Policy Unit
Brown				
2007–08	Dan Corry	10: 8 special advisers, 2 civil servants; plus 3 CS researchers	Strategy Unit: Gareth Davies 2009–10 Delivery Unit: Ray Shostak 2007–10	
2008–10	Nick Pearce	12: 11 special advisers, 1 civil servant; plus 4 civil service researchers		
Cameron				
2010	James O'Shaughnessy	5: 5 special advisers, plus 5 civil service researchers	Strategy Unit and Delivery Unit both abolished 2010	Cameron had promised to slim down Policy Unit
2011	Kris Murrin and Paul Kirby, joint heads of Policy and Implementation Unit	11: formally all civil servants, but 6 came from outside Whitehall		Performance and Innovation Unit created spring 2011 to serve Prime Minister and Deputy Prime Minister jointly; in addition, Clegg acquired additional Lib Dem special advisers
2013	Jo Johnson MP	8: all special advisers; plus Policy Board of 7 MPs		

Sources: former Policy Unit Heads; JM Lee, GW Jones and J Burnham, *At the Centre of Whitehall: Advising the Prime Minister and the Cabinet* (Macmillan 1998); Constitution Committee, *The Cabinet Office and the Centre of Government* (HL 2009–10), 30.

As can be seen from Table 2.1, newly incumbent Prime Ministers often reduce Policy Unit staff upon entering government, but then expand the Unit over time. Thatcher initially saw little need for special advisers, and so the Policy Unit consisted of only two special advisers in 1979. Both Gordon Brown and Cameron similarly reduced the size of the Policy Unit, but later in their premierships expanded it. Tony Blair was exceptional in increasing the number of special advisers available to him upon entering No 10, but it may be that he and his key staff were more forward-thinking in this respect.

The composition of the Unit has also changed over time. Civil servants have been a relatively small but persistent component of all Policy Units since Thatcher. Blair temporarily merged his Policy Unit with the Private Office to create a much larger Policy Directorate: this was an experiment which did not last. Cameron, on the other hand, chose in 2011 to staff his Policy Unit entirely with civil servants. This was widely thought to be a mistake because officials were thought to lack political nous and/or connections. In 2012 the Unit returned to a traditional configuration, consisting of special advisers and a small contingent of officials.

More recent Prime Ministers have also created a number of auxiliary units upon entering government, reflecting their priorities. Table 2.1 also sets out some of the units, which are normally located in the Cabinet Office (but may be shuffled across government departments, depending on their function). However, it is important to note that these units have generally consisted of officials rather than special advisers.

C. The Slow Institutionalisation of Special Advisers

The title of Wilson's 1974 paper—'The Political Advisers *Experiment*'—highlighted the fact that special advisers were still seen then as a temporary part of the Whitehall environment.[30] And while numbers increased under Wilson and James Callaghan, they declined again under Thatcher. Thatcher was not interested in special advisers or in machinery of government issues.[31] At the beginning of her premiership, the Policy Unit was small, and initially there were only 14 special advisers in total appointed—just over half of what the Wilson and Callaghan governments had had. In 1983, she abolished the Central Policy Review Staff (CPRS) after a damaging leak—but also because the CPRS served the Cabinet rather than her. In spite of her antipathy towards the civil service as a whole, she preferred to rely on the civil servants within her office and on the Cabinet Office in general.

---

[30] Wilson (n 27).
[31] Kavanagh and Seldon (n 4).

Thatcher did, however, over time appoint various ad hoc advisers to support her—such as Alan Walters, an economics professor, as her economic adviser (1981–84; 1989); and former diplomat Sir Percy Cradock (1984–92) as foreign policy adviser.[32] She also retained the Policy Unit, and it grew over time, as a means for her to test the work of departments and provide intellectual justification for Conservative policies. But generally special advisers and the structures at the Centre remained very much in the background during her premiership.

However, while in the early 1980s not all secretaries of state chose to have special advisers, by the end of the John Major Government, it had become standard practice that secretaries of state would have one or two special advisers clearly aligned with the Conservative Party to add the politics to policy making and communication. That was partly because Major was more relaxed about ministers appointing special advisers, but it was also a recognition that media relations had become more important.[33]

The incoming Blair Government in 1997 saw a step change in the use of special advisers, brought about by having spent over 18 years in opposition. Labour had a set of long-held manifesto promises to deliver: they had built up a cadre of experienced people and in particular a sophisticated, tightly run media operation, but there was also suspicion of the civil service, which Labour sometimes—at any rate at the beginning—identified with the Conservatives.

The number of special advisers doubled from 34 to 73, both at the Centre (from eight in 1996 to 18 in 1997) and in departments (from 26 in 1996 to 55 in 1997). Numbers continued to rise over successive Labour governments. Alastair Campbell and Jonathan Powell at No 10 were given explicit powers to direct officials and not just to advise ministers. Advisers in No 10 and the Treasury were used to drive policy and presentation throughout Whitehall, with the clear support of Blair and Brown. Numbers at the Centre continued to rise and various units were also set up at the Centre, including the Delivery Unit, Efficiency Unit and Strategy Unit.[34] The Policy Unit underwent several changes over Blair's two-and-a-half terms in government.[35] Many officials thought there was a diminution of their traditional role in policy making.

Special advisers were also used to strengthen the Government's media and communications capacity.[36] Special advisers had had such a role in the past, but under Labour, this role became far more prominent. Alastair Campbell, Tony Blair's press spokesman, became the Prime Minister's Official Spokesman and was portrayed in the media as having enormous influence over government decision

---

[32] All were appointed as special advisers.

[33] Blick (n 18).

[34] Constitution Committee, *The Cabinet Office and the Centre of Government*, (HL30, 2010) 44.

[35] Patrick Diamond, 'Governing as New Labour: An Inside Account of the Blair and Brown Years' (2011) 9 *Political Studies Review* 145.

[36] Paul Fawcett and Oonagh Gay, 'The United Kingdom' in Chris Eichbaum and Richard Shaw (eds), *Partisan Appointees and Public Servants: An International Analysis of the Role of the Political Adviser* (Edward Elgar 2010) 43.

making. The mass departure of many Heads of Information, the establishment of a Strategic Communications Unit and a Research and Information Office, and the new formalised quota of two special advisers per Cabinet Minister, one of whom usually dealt with the media, only reinforced the view that special advisers were dominant in government (see chapter six for more on media advisers).[37]

Along with the greater numbers and greater influence came increased media scrutiny and, for some special advisers, notoriety. There were cases of well-publicised misconduct by special advisers—notably Jo Moore, who had stated to officials that 11 September 2001 was a 'good day to bury news'—but special advisers were also implicated in unofficial briefings and leaks. There were stories of special advisers in No 10 being more powerful than Labour ministers.[38] It was also the high-water mark of negative briefing and the Blair–Brown internal factionalism that blighted that period of government. Special advisers were prominent in that factionalism and arguably increased it. Several prominent Labour special advisers also went on to enter politics—for instance, Ed Miliband, Ed Balls and David Miliband. The post of special adviser came to be seen as a turbocharged pathway to politics, stoking fears that politics was now a business of a privileged few (see appendix three).[39]

The large increase in numbers led to renewed calls for the regulation of special advisers. Concerns over accountability have been voiced about special advisers from the beginning: their explicitly partisan nature and the personal nature of their appointment by ministers meant that they sat uneasily within the Whitehall model. They raised the fear of patronage, the re-establishment of a spoils system and the 'politicisation' of the civil service. Special advisers were the subject of a number of inquiries by various parliamentary select committees and the Committee on Standards in Public Life. By 2001, special advisers had become subject to at least five separate documents: the Ministerial Code; certain Civil Service Orders in Council;[40] the *Model Contract for Special Advisers*; the *Civil Service Code*; and the *Special Advisers Code of Conduct* (for more on this, see chapter seven).

Both parties in the Conservative–Liberal Democrat Coalition Government came in pledging to reduce the number of special advisers. This was a predictable response of a new government. Various units at the Centre, such as the Strategy Unit, were also abolished. The cap on numbers, together with the fact that Conservative and Liberal Democrat special advisers barely knew each other, meant a step back in their role and influence.

However, it became increasingly clear that a reduced number of special advisers and a pared-down Centre was a false economy. Partly this was because more

---

[37] ibid.

[38] Peter Oborne, 'The Eunuchs of the Cabinet' *The Spectator* (15 December 2001).

[39] For more on this, see Max Goplerud, 'The First Time is (Mostly) the Charm: Special Advisers as Parliamentary Candidates and Members of Parliament' (2013) *Parliamentary Affairs* 1.

[40] Now superseded by the Constitution Reform and Governance Act 2010.

special advisers were needed to deal with the politics of coalition government,[41] but it was also because government was simply too complex—particularly for two political parties who had had little recent experience of being in government. More special advisers were appointed in late 2011 and numbers at the end of 2013 stood at just under 100.

In parallel, Francis Maude as Minister for the Civil Service and a number of other ministers made clear that they wanted to see a greater opening-up of the civil service, whether through more special advisers or time-limited civil servants, to provide greater political drive and support for ministers (see chapter ten). So the potential for advisers to recover ground initially lost under the Coalition was clear.

II. THEORY

It is worth taking a step back and seeing how political scientists have understood special advisers. Section I set out how special advisers have traditionally been understood: they have been located within the 'Whitehall model',[42] in which civil servants are non-partisan; they are generalists rather than specialists; they have life-long career paths; and they have a strong policy advisory role. This model is part of a broader 'Westminster model', a commonly held understanding of British government in which there is a centralised sovereign state and a responsible and collective Cabinet government, underpinned by ministerial responsibility and supported by a permanent, unified and non-partisan civil service.[43]

Political scientists have long argued that these models are flawed.[44] First, they are over-simplistic. For instance, they presume that there is a simple relationship between ministers and civil servants: ministers make policy and officials implement it. But ministers have neither the time nor the expertise to deal with the detail: they may 'steer' officials, but they leave significant areas of policy for officials of varying grades to determine.[45]

Second, these models do not accurately depict practice or do not depict it with adequate detail. We have already noted the realities of policy making in British government, but there are other problems. For instance, the Whitehall understanding of the civil service presumes that there is only one kind of civil

---

[41] See generally Robert Hazell and Ben Yong, *The Politics of Coalition: How the Conservative-Liberal Democrat Government Works* (Hart Publishing 2012).

[42] Page (n 10); Scott L Greer, 'Whitehall' in Robert Hazell (ed), *Constitutional Futures Revisited: Britain's Constitution to 2020* (Palgrave Macmillan 2008).

[43] See generally RAW Rhodes, John Wanna and Patrick Weller, *Comparing Westminster* (Oxford University Press 2009).

[44] See, for instance, RAW Rhodes and Patrick Dunleavy, 'From Prime Ministerial Power to Core Executive' in RAW Rhodes and Patrick Dunleavy (eds), *Prime Minister, Cabinet, and Core Executive* (St Martin's Press 1995).

[45] Page and Jenkins (n 12); Joel D Aberbach, Robert D Putnam and Bert A Rockman, *Bureaucrats and Politicians in Western Democracies* (Harvard University Press 1981).

servant: the career generalist who remains politically neutral and gives policy advice. Yet many academics criticise this view as simplistic. Hood and Lodge, for instance, suggest that there is not one kind of civil servant, but a variety of types with different 'public service bargains' (PSBs) in Whitehall.[46] A PSB is an implicit agreement between the civil service and those they serve, in which there is an exchange involving loyalty, competence and rewards. Hood and Lodge argue that Whitehall has seen the emergence of different kinds of PSBs alongside the traditional PSB, characterised by competence and absolute loyalty on the part of civil servants to ministers in return for rewards. So, for instance, alongside the traditional mandarin are chief executives of delivery units, regulators, tsars, expert advisers and, of course, special advisers. These government officials have different PSBs: for some, competence relates not to policy advice but to ability to deliver and implement (chief executives); for others, there is greater distance from the minister than for the 'traditional' civil servant (regulators), and so on.

Third, these models are, to some extent, normative approaches masquerading as description.[47] Those who adopt them often presume that power lies with specific actors and specific institutions, and that the models as laid out above are fixed. Thus, any movement away from these models is a deviation from the norm or even 'unconstitutional'.[48] Thus, a perennial debate about British government is the extent to which Cabinet government has been replaced by 'Prime Ministerial' government (in which references to special advisers are common).[49] There is also a perennial debate about the fact that special advisers are not appointed by open competition or are politically impartial: they are treated with suspicion and are often seen as evidence of 'politicisation' of the civil service, although what this means is often unclear.[50] The Whitehall model, then, makes villains of special advisers.

It is for these reasons that the approach more appropriate to understanding special advisers is the model that most British political scientists studying executive government now use: the resource dependency model, sometimes called the core executive model.[51] This model sees the modern British state as having moved away from a centralised sovereign state with Cabinet government and

---

[46] Christopher Hood and Martin Lodge, 'From Sir Humphrey to Sir Nigel: What Future for the Public Service Bargain after Blairworld?' (2006) 77 *Political Quarterly* 360; Christopher Hood and Martin Lodge, *The Politics of Public Service Bargains: Reward, Competency, Loyalty—and Blame* (Oxford University Press 2006).

[47] Rhodes, Wanna and Weller (n 43).

[48] See, for instance, Hennessy (n 10).

[49] ibid; Keith Dowding, 'The Prime Ministerialisation of the British Prime Minister' (2012) 66 *Parliamentary Affairs* 617; Richard Heffernan, 'There's No Need for the "-Isation": The Prime Minister is Merely Prime Ministerial' (2012) 66 *Parliamentary Affairs* 636; Paul Webb and Thomas Poguntke, 'The Presidentialisation of Politics Thesis Defended' (2012) 66 *Parliamentary Affairs* 646.

[50] L Rouban, 'Politicization of the Civil Service' in B Guy Peters and Jon Pierre (eds), *Handbook of Public Administration* (Concise Paperback edn, SAGE Publications 2007).

[51] Martin J Smith, *The Core Executive in Britain* (St Martin's Press 1999); Rhodes and Dunleavy (n 44); Robert Elgie, 'Core Executive Studies Two Decades on' (2011) 89 *Public Administration* 64.

ministerial accountability towards a more complex entity governing through and by networks—a 'differentiated polity'. In this model, the British state is now a 'hollowed state', consisting of a weak centre with devolved regions; ministers and departments have hived-off major areas of policy to executive agencies and other bodies like the Bank of England; and they have lost power both to supranational bodies like the European Union (EU) and to the devolved regions. Ministers and officials are still dominant in determining policy, but there are far more actors present in the policy field (international, supranational and devolved institutions, lobbyists, the voluntary sector, think tanks etc) that they must engage with and respond to.

More importantly, the starting point for examining the executive in this model is that the key actors—ministers and officials—operate in a context of *resource scarcity and dependency*. This means that ministers in particular must work or cooperate within networks to achieve their goals. There is no immediate presumption that ministers are powerful—it all depends on the resources they have, which must be determined through analysis. So, for instance, at first glance Prime Ministers may have access to seemingly strong institutional resources (as party leader and as head of government), but they are limited by the scarcity of at least one precious resource: time. As Michael Barber, a former special adviser to Tony Blair, noted:

> There are dozens of people hungry for Prime Ministerial time ... the Prime Minister certainly has extensive power, but the nature of the role in modern Britain has made it harder and harder to use effectively.[52]

Moreover, in practice, the power of the Centre and the Prime Minister has been exaggerated. Much of the time, the Centre works through departments.[53] In their policy areas, secretaries of state are often more powerful than the Prime Minister: they have access to the resources of a line department, which may include a massive budget, thousands of civil servants and departmental expertise, and their remit is smaller by comparison.

But overload—in particular, a scarcity of time—is a problem for all ministers. Ministers are expected to respond increasingly faster to a voracious 24/7 media and they want to give policy and presentation more of a political edge. The work is never-ending and the hours are punishing.[54] Ministers are thrust into office, often with little or no notice, and with little direction or advice.[55] There is rarely

---

[52] Michael Barber, *Instruction to Deliver: Fighting to Transform Britain's Public Services* (Methuen 2008) 305.

[53] Patrick Diamond, *Governing Britain: Power, Politics and the Prime Minister* (IB Tauris 2014).

[54] David Laughrin, 'Swimming for Their Lives—Waving or Drowning? A Review of the Evidence of Ministerial Overload and of Potential Remedies for it' (2009) 80 *Political Quarterly* 339; Anne Tiernan and Patrick Weller, *Learning to Be a Minister: Heroic Expectations, Practical Realities* (Melbourne University Press 2010).

[55] Riddell, Gruhn and Carolan (n 2); Tiernan and Weller (n 54); Gerald Kaufman, *How to Be a Minister* (Faber & Faber 1997).

a formal 'handover' or time for preparation. The work of an MP (or peer) is poor groundwork for running a department. Yet ministers are expected to be—and often think they can be—on top of their departmental brief almost instantly upon appointment.

So, for all these reasons—changes in the state, the external environment, and the expectations of the public and of ministers themselves—special advisers have emerged and become a fixture of British government.

From this, we can see that the benefits of the resource dependency model are threefold. First, it provides a minimalist view of political–administrative relations with less normative baggage attached. Second, it suggests that relationships between actors in the executive are relatively fluid and that the question of power is relational. Finally, this approach is consistent with the discussion earlier in the chapter about the ministerial need for special advisers, and the bewildering variety of roles and functions that special advisers are asked to perform.

Special advisers, then, can be seen as a ministerial response to resource scarcity within the core executive. Shaw and Eichbaum explain in their discussion of ministerial advisers (the New Zealand equivalent of special advisers):

> Ministerial advisers facilitate the exchange of resources: they constitute a resource both in and of themselves (insofar as they possess specialist expertise, knowledge of policy networks and other forms of political capital), and in the sense that they can be strategically deployed to leverage resources elsewhere within and beyond the core executive.[56]

Special advisers, then, may be used to provide or develop new policy,[57] to monitor officials and to ensure policy implementation.[58] They may engage with other members of the executive (eg, No 10) and work through networks (eg, special advisers, officials or external stakeholders) to achieve their minister's objectives.[59] Maley, for instance, has shown how political staff in Australia work together with each other to achieve the needs of their ministers and the government in general.[60] Special advisers may also be used to engage with networks that officials cannot engage with—for instance, Eichbaum and Shaw argue that political staff in New Zealand are vital in negotiating politically sensitive issues in the context of multiparty government.[61] Above all, the roles and functions of special advisers

---

[56] Richard Shaw and Chris Eichbaum, 'Ministers, Minders and the Core Executive: Why Ministers Appoint Political Advisers in Westminster Contexts' (2012) *Parliamentary Affairs*, http://pa.oxfordjournals.org/content/early/2012/11/08/pa.gss080.abstract.

[57] Francesca Gains and Gerry Stoker, 'Special Advisers and the Transmission of Ideas from the Policy Primeval Soup' (2011) 39 *Policy & Politics* 485.

[58] The LSE GV314 Group, 'New Life at the Top: Special Advisers in British Government' (2012) 65 *Parliamentary Affairs* 715.

[59] Colin Hay and David Richards, 'The Tangled Webs of Westminster and Whitehall: The Discourse, Strategy and Practice of Networking within the British Core Executive' (2000) 78 *Public Administration* 1.

[60] Maria Maley, 'Strategic Links in a Cut-Throat World: Rethinking the Role and Relationship of Australian Ministerial Staff' (2011) 89 *Public Administration* 1469.

[61] Chris Eichbaum and Richard Shaw, 'Ministerial Advisers, Politicization and the Retreat from Westminster: The Case of New Zealand' (2007) 85 *Public Administration* 609.

may depend greatly on what their appointing minister needs, and on the nature of the government in office.

This resource scarcity approach can be applied both to special advisers at 'the Centre' and to those in departments: again, there is no immediate presumption that special advisers in the Centre are necessarily stronger than those in departments, although in practice there are likely to be asymmetries of resources and power.[62] Power need not be understood as a zero-sum game; it can be a positive-sum game in which key actors share key resources.[63] So, for instance, getting the No 10 special adviser, the Secretary of State, the departmental special adviser and the Permanent Secretary behind a policy is likely to ensure its successful acceptance and implementation.[64]

Finally, treating special advisers as a type of 'empty' resource explains to a great extent why there is so much variety in how they used: as an 'extra pair of eyes and ears', as confidantes, experts, policy wonks, spin doctors, deliverers, apparatchiks, commissars or bag carriers—and why their roles can change, depending on the minister and the circumstances. This fluidity of role is a key reason for their added value: they are a resource which is not as bound by hierarchy and neutrality in the same way that other means of support are.[65] For instance, special advisers have no line management responsibilities (and, conversely, are only loosely line managed), which means they can provide a concentration of focus in a way that officials cannot. Of course, this fluidity is also what makes it problematic in the eyes of many. We return to this in chapter seven.

III. CONCLUSION

Special advisers began as a modest, ad hoc innovation in part to remedy the perceived deficiencies of the Whitehall model and to respond to intensifying pressures on British government—the media, public and ministerial expectations, and the increased pace of government. But although special advisers were initially a useful ad hoc, supplementary aid to ministers, over time they have become an

---

[62] Thus, we do not see power within the core executive as entirely contingent: it is structured by historical legacies, path dependency and location, and so there are *asymmetries* of power. These asymmetries, however, do not mean that agents—meaning here mostly ministers—are instantly weak or powerful: it depends on other factors. To this extent, we follow Marsh et al's 'asymmetric polity model': see David Marsh, David Richards and Martin Smith, 'Unequal Plurality: Towards an Asymmetric Power Model of British Politics' (2003) 38 *Government and Opposition* 306; and Mark Bennister, *Prime Ministers in Power: Political Leadership in Britain and Australia* (Palgrave Macmillan 2012).

[63] Julia Fleischer, 'Power Resources of Parliamentary Executives: Policy Advice in the UK and Germany' (2009) 32 *West European Politics* 196.

[64] Gains and Stoker (n 57).

[65] Stephen Hanney, *Special Advisers: Their Place in British Government* (Brunel University 1993).

established part of British government: ministers cannot now imagine doing without them.

This is partly because of a decline in trust in the career civil service and its capacity to satisfy ministers' needs—a trend that is seen across Western democracies. But it is also because ministers are 'resource weak': they are increasingly overloaded; they lack time and expertise; and they need individuals that they can trust and be comfortable with. In short, special advisers exist because ministers need them and because other sources of ministerial support lack the peculiar characteristics of special advisers which make them valuable to ministers.

Box A. The rising number of special advisers 1979–2013

Figure 2.1 shows the absolute number of persons working as special advisers in any given year, split into 'Centre' and 'Department'. The bars shaded in black indicate the first year of the Labour Governments (1997.2) and the Coalition Government (2010.2). If, in a given year, a person served in both the Centre and the departments, they are coded as being in the 'Centre'.

The most obvious point to draw from Figure 2.1 is that the number of special advisers doubled under Labour, but there are other points to make. Starting with the Conservative Governments of 1979–97, the main increase was driven by an expansion of special advisers in departments; the Centre remained stable. Under Labour, there was a rise in both categories. Under the Coalition, there was an initial drop in numbers, but in 2012 numbers rose again, but noticeably in the Centre rather than in departments (partly because six Liberal Democrat special advisers were allocated to the Deputy Prime Minister).[66]

We should note that in Figure 2.1 the total number of special advisers in certain years reaches well over 100. That is because we are counting the total number of individuals who worked as special advisers in any one year. We are not counting—as official lists do—the number of individuals who were working as special advisers at any one time.[67]

Figure 2.2 shows the total persons recorded minus the number of leavers. The darker bars indicate the first years of the Labour and Coalition Governments. This gives numbers closer to those reported in official lists.[68]

---

[66] Hazell and Yong (n 41).
[67] See, for instance, House of Commons Library, *Special Advisers* (2013). Current data releases from the Cabinet Office can be found at 'Special Adviser Data Releases' (Cabinet Office, 2012) https://www.gov.uk/government/publications/special-adviser-data-releases-numbers-and-costs.
[68] House of Commons Library, *Special Advisers* (n 67).

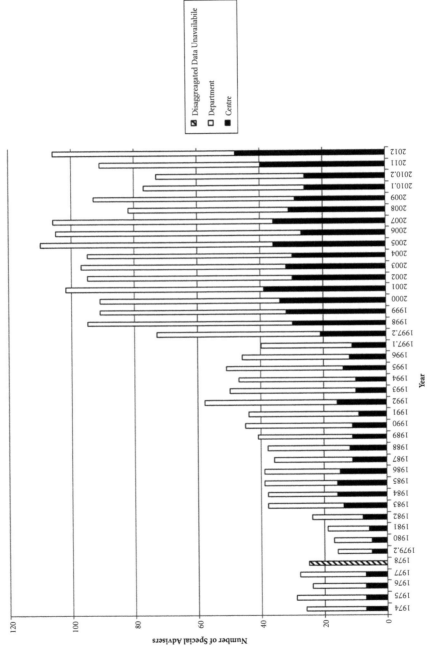

Figure 2.1: Annual number of special advisers, 1979–2013

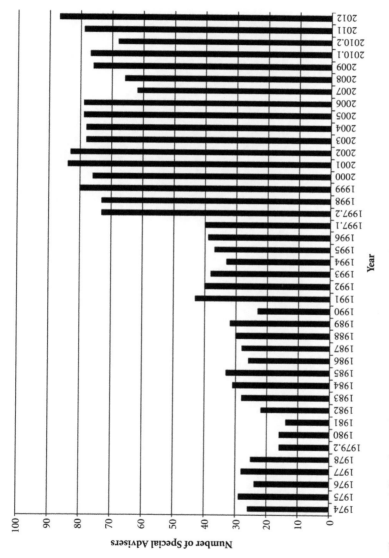

Figure 2.2: Adjusted annual number of special advisers, 1979–2013

3

Who are Special Advisers?

BEN YONG

If you look at Governments, what tends to happen is they come in with quite a lot of ... special advisers, and then they diminish over time. That certainly happened with John Major ... If you're the Prime Minister coming at the beginning, they certainly have more political people, and they then go down ... As they get tired ... fewer political people want to come and attach themselves to a Prime Minister who is clearly on his way out. (Former Labour special adviser)

INTRODUCTION

HOW SOMEONE BECOMES a special adviser comes across as pretty haphazard. Peter Hyman, a key speech writer for Tony Blair, for instance, began as a parliamentary researcher. He described his appointment:

I was not formally offered a job in Number 10. As polling day got closer, I started to think about the future, but like others in the office never dared raise the issue with Tony in case it looked presumptuous. Now I assumed I had a job because I was told there would be an introduction to Number 10 first thing in the morning.[1]

One special adviser who worked for a Conservative Secretary of State in the 1990s told us:

I was simply phoned up ... I'd obviously written something about this which they picked up and I did have a very old personal friend in the department ... One of them had obviously got to [the minister] and said you'll need to bring him in as a special adviser ... and so I got a call ... They said ... come for a very important press conference where [the minister] is going to announce [his] initiative ... And he announced I was appointed. It was about informal as that.

What kinds of people become special advisers and on what basis? Section I provides a broad portrait of special advisers collectively and how they have changed over time. We describe their age, gender, educational and professional background upon appointment. We then set out the average tenure of special

---

[1] Peter Hyman, *1 Out of 10: From Downing Street Vision to Classroom Reality* (Vintage 2005) 66.

advisers in government and their distribution within Whitehall over time. Having sketched the broad characteristics of special advisers seen as a group, we then look in more detail in section II at how they are recruited. We shall suggest that, although recruitment is thought of as an intensely personal and individual decision, there are various institutional incentives and constraints which underlie the recruitment process.

I. SPECIAL ADVISERS: A BRIEF PORTRAIT, 1979–2013

Our analysis here draws on a number of sources: a database, built mostly from collating the responses of ministers to parliamentary questions, Cabinet Office press releases and desk research (using Google, LinkedIn and 'hard copy' sources such as academic texts, biographies and autobiographies). The availability of information on special advisers is uneven and, as a result, our sample sizes differ according to which characteristic we are examining.[2] More details on the varying methodologies are found in appendix one.

A. Numbers of Special Advisers

We begin with numbers. There were 626 special advisers in the period between the May 1979 election and November 2013.[3] We set this out in more detail below in Table 3.1 and further information on numbers of special advisers can be found at the end of chapter two. Table 3.1 shows the total number of special advisers that each government employed during its time in power; obviously, the number in office at any one time was a lot less. To give an idea of the reliability of the data in the figures below, Table 3.2 lists the percentage of each group for whom information was located on age, undergraduate university and pre-special adviser career.

Table 3.1: Number of special advisers by party in government, 1979–2013

Government cohort	No of spads
Conservative, 1979–97	181
Labour, 1997–2010	297
Coalition 2010–13	148 (106 Tory; 42 Lib Dem)
Total	626

[2] See Table 2.2.
[3] See ch 1 for our definition of 'special adviser'.

Table 3.2: Percentages of each special adviser cohort for whom information was located on key characteristics, 1979–2013

Party	Age	University	Career
Conservative	75%	71%	82%
Labour	73%	71%	87%
Coalition	61%	56%	76%

B. Basic Characteristics

i. Age

Special advisers are often thought of as young: John Prescott once referred to special advisers as 'teenyboppers' and the 'beautiful people'.[4] Prescott probably had in mind special advisers like David Miliband (34 at the time) or Ed Balls (then 32). And the youngest ever appointed were in their early twenties: Gavin Barwell under the Conservatives and Spencer Livermore under Labour were both 23 on appointment. But how true is this of special advisers in general?

The graphs below suggest that we are wrong to think of special advisers as particularly young. The *median* age for all special advisers between 1979 and 2013 is 33 years on appointment to government.[5] Generally speaking, those appointed under the Conservative Governments were slightly older, with a median age of 36; under Labour 33; and the current median under the Coalition is 31—so special advisers are getting younger over time. A quarter of all special advisers were below 30. Finally, there are noticeable numbers of special advisers who are over 50 (about 15 per cent for the Conservatives, 11 per cent for Labour and 8 per cent for the Coalition). Advisers who were relatively old upon appointment include John Hoskyns, head of Margaret Thatcher's policy unit (52); Derek Scott, economic adviser to Tony Blair (50); and Chris Nicholson, adviser to Ed Davey, Coalition Secretary of State for Energy and Climate Change (52). Henry Macrory was one of the oldest: he was 62 at the time of his appointment as Conservative Head of Press under the Coalition. It is worth noting that when Prescott made his comments in 1998, he was 60, older than the average MP: Tony Blair was 45 and the average age of an MP at the time was 49.[6]

---

[4] Rod A Rhodes, *Everyday Life in British Government* (Oxford University Press 2011) 216.

[5] We have chosen to use the *median* (ie, the middle number in the list of all ages) rather than the average. This is because there are a number of much older special advisers who pull the average age up. For the sake of completeness, the *average* starting age was 36 years for all special advisers between 1979 and 2013; under the Conservative Governments, the average age was 38, under Labour it was 36, and the current average under the Coalition is 34.

[6] As of 2010, it is now 50: see House of Commons Library, 'Social Background of MPs' (House of Commons Library 2010). It is worth noting that in 2012 the median age of the Senior Civil Service was 49. Earlier statistics on median ages in the Senior Civil Service are

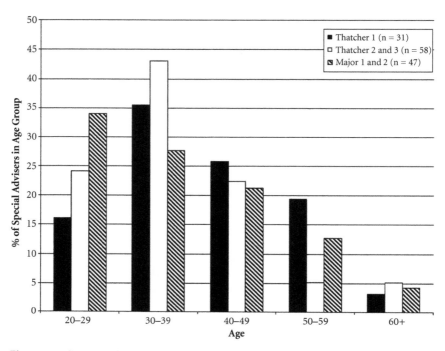

Figure 3.1: Conservative special adviser starting ages by government, 1979–97

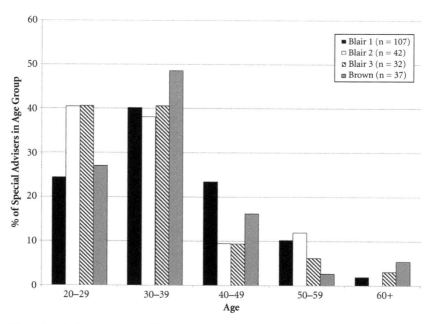

Figure 3.2: Labour special adviser starting ages by government, 1997–2010

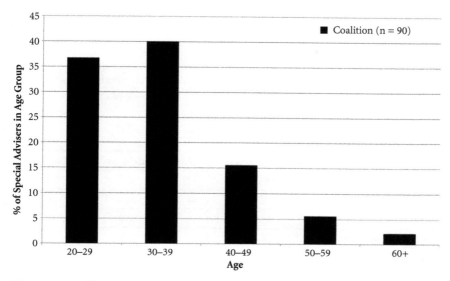

Figure 3.3: Coalition special adviser starting ages, 2010–13

Of course, there is no necessary link between age and effectiveness. Jo Moore was 38 when she made her infamous remarks about 9/11 being a good day to bury bad news and Damian McBride was 35 when he resigned—both hardly teenyboppers.[7]

Other interesting implications emerge from examining the two longer premierships of Thatcher and Blair. As can be seen from Figures 3.1 and 3.2, special advisers become progressively younger the longer their premier remains in office. The similarity between the two premierships suggests that as their time in office continues, governments are unable to recruit older persons to become special advisers: they are forced to look to new, and younger, people to replace the first-generation special advisers. We shall return to this point when discussing recruitment.

ii. Gender

Prominent female special advisers are rare, but prominence and effectiveness may be inversely related. It may be that female advisers tend to keep a lower profile. Perhaps the most obvious example of a strong and high-profile female special

more difficult to determine because of the way that the data has been organised. The median age across the *entire* civil service in 2000 was between 40 and 44: 'Civil Service Statistics 2000' (*National Statistics,* 2000), http://webarchive.nationalarchives.gov.uk/20110426084705/ http://www.civilservice.gov.uk/Assets/css00_tcm6-1085.pdf; 'Civil Service Statistics, 2012' (*Office for National Statistics,* 2012), www.ons.gov.uk/ons/rel/pse/civil-service-statistics/2012/index.html.

[7] See ch 7 for a discussion of special adviser misconduct.

adviser is Shriti Vadera, who worked for Gordon Brown for eight years and who later became a peer and a minister, first in the Department for International Development and then in the Department for Business, Enterprise and Regulatory Reform. But have there been many female special advisers?

For gender, in each government cohort we simply counted the number of female special advisers and divided this by the total number of special advisers in the relevant cohort. The results are given below.

Table 3.3: Special advisers' gender by party, 1979–2013

Party	No of male spads	No of female spads	% Female
Conservative	153	28	15.5
Labour	205	92	31.0
Coalition (Con)	66	40	37.7
Coalition (Lib Dem)	24	18	42.9
Total	**448**	**178**	**28.4**

So the number of female special advisers has been increasing over time, but special advisers as a group remain predominantly male. This obviously reflects 'the gendered disposition of recruitment, resources, relationships and customs of the UK core executive'.[8] It mirrors the situation at Westminster, where women constitute a growing minority of MPs (in 1979, 3 per cent of MPs were women; by 2010 this was 22 per cent),[9] and also in Whitehall, where women made up 35 per cent of the senior civil service as of 2012.[10]

iii. Education

This section analyses the university background of special advisers from all three government cohorts in terms of their first degree. Some caveats are in order, however. First, there are difficulties in establishing how many special advisers did *not* go to university. It is almost impossible to tell whether a university education is not listed because of the fragmentary nature of the data or simply because the person did not attend a university. Second, the sample sizes for subject studied and institution may be different, because sometimes we have found information on university but not subject or vice versa.

Figure 3.4 shows a breakdown of undergraduate institution by party. Most special advisers have studied at what would now be called a Russell Group university (the 24 leading universities in the UK), with approximately 80 per cent of special advisers in each government cohort coming from this background. There

---

[8]   Claire Annesley and Francesca Gains, 'The Core Executive: Gender, Power and Change' (2010) 58 *Political Studies* 909.

[9]   House of Commons Library (n 6).

[10]   'Civil Service Statistics, 2012' (n 6). See also Annesley and Gains (n 8).

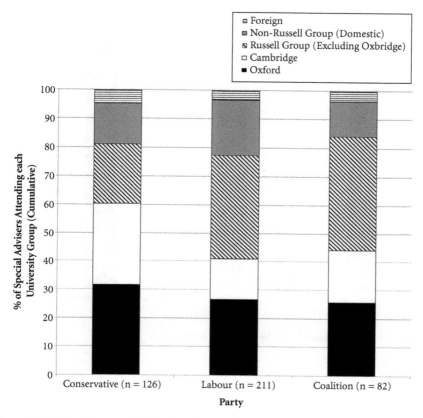

Figure 3.4: University attended for first degree: distribution by party, 1979–2013

is a noticeable drop in those having gone to 'Oxbridge' between the Conservative and Labour Governments, much of this being due to more coming from the other Russell Group universities.

Figures 3.5 and 3.6 break down undergraduate degree by subject. As can be seen, there is a remarkable degree of similarity between the advisers to all three governments: most study politics, history, philosophy, politics and economics (PPE) or economics; only a tiny number have studied one of the 'hard' sciences. Roughly one-third of the special advisers for whom we have university information also have a postgraduate degree of some type, with Oxford, Cambridge and Harvard being the most common sources. Politics and economics are the most common subjects, followed by a Master of Business Administration (MBA) or various business degrees. The figures on university attended and postgraduate education are remarkably similar to those of senior officials in the home civil service.[11]

---

[11] Scott L Greer, 'Whitehall' in Robert Hazell (ed), *Constitutional Futures Revisited: Britain's Constitution to 2020* (Palgrave Macmillan 2008) 262–64.

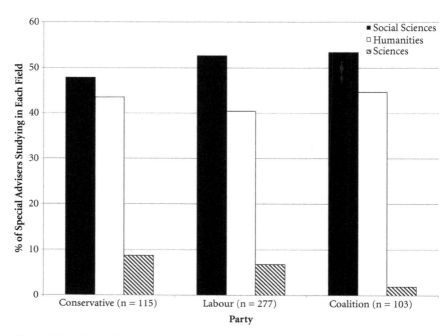

Figure 3.5: Subject distribution by party, 1979–2013

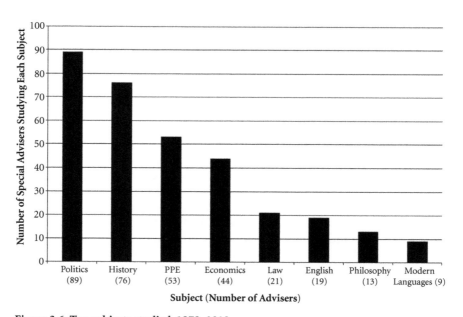

Figure 3.6: Top subjects studied, 1979–2013

iv. Professional Experience

As for age and university, there were methodological difficulties in analysing the career backgrounds of special advisers. We used a mixture of sources, but were unable to find complete information on all special advisers between 1979 and 2013. We also coded for multiple occupations: it would be impossible to limit an adviser's career background to one occupation alone.

Our coding scheme is set out below in Table 3.4; Figures 3.7 and 3.8 show the pre-government career backgrounds of special advisers serving between 1979 and 2013.

Table 3.4: Coding categories for pre-government careers of special advisers

Abbreviation	Explanation
GOV-PB	Government-Public Body: includes positions with local authorities and their executive agencies and commissions, non-departmental public bodies, regulatory bodies, regional bodies, the NHS etc
GOV-CS	Government-Civil Service: includes roles taken in Whitehall with a central government department
ER	Elected Representative: This mostly consists of being a local councillor, though a few exceptions exist
BUS	Business: includes positions taken with investment banks, consultancies, major corporations and public relations firms, as well as being a freelance consultant or working for an association that represents business interests such as the Confederation for British Industry
AC	Academia
ME	Media: includes positions taken with media (print, electronic) organisations
TT	Think Tank
NPS	Non-Profit Sector: positions with NGOs and charities
UN	Trade Unions
POL	Party-Political employment: includes positions such as parliamentary researcher, party central staff and working for a political campaign group such as No2AV
IGO/FG	International Governmental Organisation / Foreign Government: includes positions taken with the World Bank, the European Union, the United Nations and any foreign Governments
PA/COMMS	Public Affairs / Communications practitioner
TECH	'Technical professions': those requiring specialist knowledge but that fall outside the other categories, eg, barristers, solicitors and scientists
OTHER	Individuals in positions falling outside the above categories

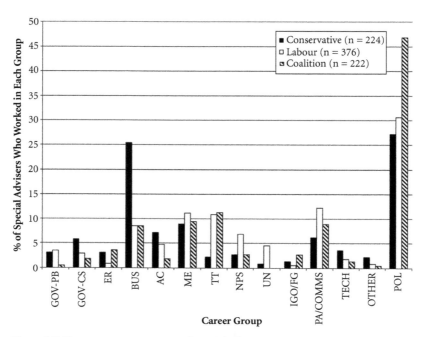

Figure 3.7: **Pre-government careers of special advisers by party in government, 1979–2013**

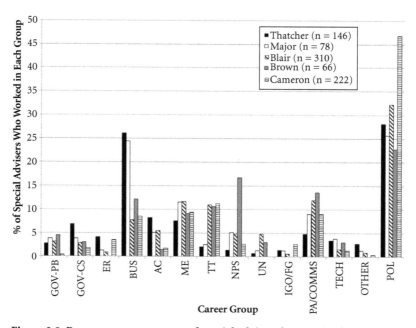

Figure 3.8: **Pre-government careers of special advisers by premiership, 1979–2013**

Figure 3.7 breaks down the pre-government career backgrounds of special advisers according to government cohort; while Figure 3.8 breaks down career backgrounds according to premiership. From these it can be seen that the most common career background of special advisers from all three government cohorts is broadly political. Those having a career in a political party account for one-quarter of all in the total sample.

Figures 3.7 and 3.8 show that the career backgrounds of special advisers—and therefore the recruitment pools—have changed over time. Under the Conservative Governments of 1979–97, for instance, there was an almost equal number of appointments from both business and the party, and small numbers of appointments from academia, the civil service, the media and public affairs. Under Labour and continuing under the Coalition, pre-government career backgrounds shift: the number of appointees from the political parties increases over time; think tanks, the media and public affairs/communications become key recruitment pools, while the numbers of those recruited from business, the civil service and academia shrinks. The Coalition has continued the trends set by Labour.

Some of these shifts reflect the growth of numbers of media outlets, think tanks and public affairs consultancies over the years; that is, they stem from changes in the 'supply side'.[12] For instance, the declining number of special advisers from academia may reflect the increasing professionalisation of university life (such as the pressure to publish): fewer academics may be willing to be seconded into government. But by far the most important change on the supply side was the introduction of 'Short Money' in 1975 (state grants to Opposition parties) and increased funding for MPs. This has led to the employment of greater numbers of party staff and parliamentary researchers, a prime recruitment pool for special advisers.[13]

C. Tenure, Ministers and Departments

In this section, we examine length of service and the number of ministers and departments served. We examine only the tenure of Conservative and Labour special advisers (1979–2010): it is still too soon to examine the tenures of special advisers under the Coalition.

Special adviser tenure in Figure 3.9 below is analysed as a percentage of the total party government special adviser cohort, ie, 1979–97 and 1997–2010. This is because the disparity in absolute numbers between the Conservative and Labour Governments (181 compared to 297) would otherwise make comparison

---

[12] See, for instance Geoff Mulgan, 'Thinking in Tanks: The Changing Ecology of Political Ideas' (2006) 77 *Political Quarterly* 147; Denis Saint-Martin, 'The New Managerialism and the Policy Influence of Consultants in Government: An Historical-Institutionalist Analysis of Britain, Canada and France' (1998) 11 *Governance* 319.

[13] Paul Fawcett and Oonagh Gay, 'The United Kingdom' in Chris Eichbaum and Richard Shaw (eds), *Partisan Appointees and Public Servants: An International Analysis of the Role of the Political Adviser* (Edward Elgar 2010).

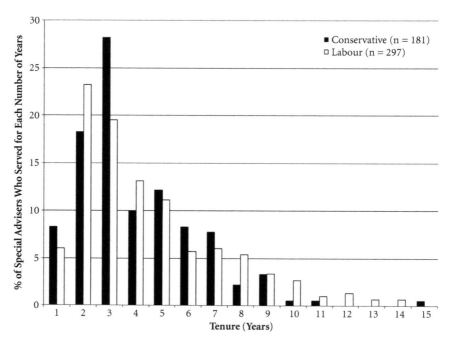

Figure 3.9: Special adviser tenure by party in government (%), 1979–2010

unhelpful. Thus, we see that there are similar distributions for special advisers of both the Labour and the Conservative Governments: a hump for a tenure of around 2–3 years, which decreases slowly to 9–10 years and then stops, except for a few outliers.[14]

Thus, the lifespan of the average special adviser is relatively short: approximately half of special advisers in both cohorts had a tenure of three years or less. This shortness of tenure has implications for recruitment and effectiveness, to which we will return in section II.

This shortness of tenure is understandable as, generally speaking, special advisers are expected to leave with their minister, and three years or less is consistent with some estimates of post-war ministerial tenure at Westminster.[15] But it is

---

[14] It may be that the Labour 'hump' occurred earlier than the Conservative one (two versus three years) because of the difference in lengths of the Labour and Conservative Governments (13 versus 18 years).

[15] See, for instance, Samuel Berlinski, Torun Dewan and Keith Dowding, who suggest that the average ministerial tenure from 1945 to 1997 was 26.9 months: 'The Length of Ministerial Tenure in the United Kingdom, 1945–97' (2007) 37 *British Journal of Political Science* 245, 251. See also Kevin Theakston, Mark Gill and Judi Atkins, 'The Ministerial Foothills: Labour Government Junior Ministers 1997–2010' [2012] *Parliamentary Affairs*, http://pa.oxfordjournals.org/cgi/doi/10.1093/pa/gss054.

worth noting that a quarter of all special advisers (124) remained in post for six years or more and a small number (five per cent, or 23 of a sample of 478) had a tenure of 10 years or more—most of the latter coming from Labour. For instance, Anna Healy, a Labour stalwart, served five ministers in five departments over the entire Labour period (1997–2010), while Andrew Maugham, an economist by training, served one Labour minister—Alistair Darling—in six departments over 13 years.

The surprisingly long tenure of some special advisers should be juxtaposed with the average time in a particular post of senior civil servants. In a recent 2007 study, Greer and Jarman found that the average time in post for civil servants in the home civil service is now very low: few senior civil servants had been in their current position for more than three years (although in a more recent detailed study of one department, the average time in post edged closer to five years).[16] To some extent, then, the similarity in tenure between special advisers and the average time in post of officials calls into question any characterisation of advisers as short-lived actors with shorter time horizons. Indeed, in a number of interviews, some former special advisers—notably those from Labour Governments—spoke of paradoxically representing continuity within a department, because senior civil servants were moved to another job after only relatively short periods (although most civil servants move within the same department).[17]

Two-thirds of all special advisers in both the Conservative and Labour Governments served only one minister. However, there is a wide variation in the distribution of the other third. The Conservative data is more skewed towards special advisers who have a high number of ministers and a low number of departments, suggesting the idea of 'expert' special advisers. By contrast, Labour outliers show more heterogeneity, with high numbers of departments and ministers. So, for instance, Jeffrey Sterling, who was Chairman of P&O shipping (and a part-time adviser), served seven Conservative ministers in eight years, in what was in effect one department (the Department for Industry, later the Department of Trade and Industry). Dan Corry was an economist who served four Labour ministers in six departments for a total of 12 years.

To some extent, special adviser tenure and movement can be likened to the tenure and movement of ministers. In Whitehall there is a great deal of 'ministerial churn', particularly in some departments—for instance, there were six Transport Secretaries of State between 2001 and 2010, and there have been three since 2010.

---

[16] Greer (n 11) 262; Holly Jarman and Scott L Greer, 'In the Eye of the Storm: Civil Servants and Managers in the UK Department of Health' (2010) 44 *Social Policy & Administration* 172, 187.

[17] See, for instance, the comments of Lord Adonis: 'The notion that Britain has a "permanent" and "expert" civil service is largely a misnomer; most career civil servants change jobs every year or two, unrelated to the needs of the state, they mostly possess superficial subject-specific knowledge and frontline experience and few skills beyond those acquired at school and university … Just as officials were getting on top of an individual project or policy issue, they would suddenly disappear, often at a few weeks' notice.'

Andrew Adonis, *Education, Education, Education* (Biteback 2012) 73.

Table 3.5: Distribution of Conservative special advisers, 1979–97

No of ministers	No of departments					Total
	1	2	3	4	5	
1	97	13	7	2		119
2	21	10	5	2		38
3	4	4	3			11
4	3	1	1		1	6
5	1	1				2
6		2				2
7		1				1
8	1		1			2
Total	127	32	17	4	1	181

Table 3.6: Distribution of Labour special advisers, 1997–2010

No of ministers	No of departments						Total
	1	2	3	4	5	6	
1	163	26	8	2	1	2	202
2	18	25	10	7			60
3	7	8	5	4	1	1	26
4	1	1	4	1			7
5					1	1	2
Total	189	60	27	14	3	4	297

But, on the other hand, the tenure of those holding certain major offices—the Chancellor, the Foreign Secretary and the Chief Whips—has remained relatively long over time,[18] and some ministers, known as reliable hands or 'big beasts', remain in government over an entire premiership, moving from department to department.[19] But while the tenure and the path taken in government by special advisers is primarily tied to the fortunes of their minister, it may also depend on a number of other factors, such as diktats from the Prime Minister, the adviser's own value (skill, experience) and the needs of the particular department.

---

[18] Political and Constitutional Reform Committee, *The Impact and Effectiveness of Ministerial Reshuffles* (2013).
[19] Jack Straw or Alistair Darling, for example.

So special advisers are mostly male and highly educated, usually in the humanities or social sciences, and have a strongly political career background.[20] Most are appointed in their early thirties and stay in post for three years or less, serving just one minister.

II. RECRUITMENT: STRUCTURES AND FACTORS UNDERLYING SELECTION

Having painted in broad brush strokes a portrait of special advisers as a collective group, we now examine how they are recruited. To some extent, this section pre-empts the discussion of the next chapter on what ministers want from their special advisers. Here, however, we examine recruitment to help illuminate some of the common characteristics of special advisers that we have already described and to suggest that there are a number of underlying institutional factors which lead to the appointment of particular classes of people.

Various interviewees insisted that recruitment was a very personal matter, emphasising loyalty, chemistry and the needs of the minister himself or herself. And, indeed, as we shall see in chapter four, different ministers want different things from their advisers. Some ministers want someone with strong communication skills, while others want someone with policy expertise, party liaison or a 'safe pair of hands'. This means that the recruitment pools may differ: obviously, ministers wanting someone with communications skills may look to the media, the public affairs industry or the Party, while those looking for policy innovation might look to think tanks or academia. So there was deep scepticism from interviewees about implementing more formalised processes.

In practice, however, there are well-settled means and ways by which ministers select and appoint their special advisers, which, as we have seen in section I, leads to the selection of particular kinds of individuals from particular recruitment pools. Moreover, it is clear from our interviews and data that within a premiership and more generally within a government, there is a recruitment cycle. Here is one former Labour special adviser talking specifically about the Prime Minister and special adviser recruitment, but it applies equally to other ministers as well:

> If you look at Governments, what tends to happen is they come in with quite a lot of ... special advisers, and then they diminish over time. That certainly happened with John Major ... If you're the Prime Minister coming at the beginning, they certainly have more political people, and they then go down .... As they get tired ... fewer political people want to come and attach themselves to a Prime Minister who is clearly on his way out.

---

[20] The vast majority are also white, although this is difficult to quantify. Special advisers having an ethnic minority background include, amongst others, John Taylor, adviser to the Home Secretary (1990–91), Shriti Vadera, adviser to the Chancellor of the Exchequer (1999–2007), Dorothea Hodge, adviser to the Leader of the House of Lords (2005–07), Ayesha Hazarika, adviser to Harriet Harman, Labour Deputy Leader (2007–09), Rohan Silva (2010–13) and Shaun Bailey (2010–), both advisers to David Cameron.

Recruitment therefore differs depending on what stage in the parliamentary term it occurs. We cover the two key stages of the recruitment cycle—at the beginning of a government and during a government—in more detail below.

A. Entering Government

Generally speaking, the broad approach of ministers of all three governments studied—the Conservatives, Labour and the Coalition—was initially to bring with them the party staff they served with in Opposition. For instance, Adam Ridley had been Deputy Head of the Conservative Research Department for a number of years before becoming special adviser to Geoffrey Howe in 1979. Sophie Linden had been David Blunkett's researcher in Opposition since at least 1992: she would go on to be his special adviser for almost eight years. James O'Shaughnessy had been Director of Policy and Research for the Conservative Party for three years before becoming head of the No 10 Policy Unit in 2010.

The reasons for employing staff who had been with their ministers or with the party for several years in Opposition are obvious. There is a shared sense of purpose, forged by years in Opposition, many staffers and MPs have shared offices and crises together, and they have formed a close relationship. Moreover, party-political staffers—be they party staff, 'political advisers' or parliamentary researchers—have greater opportunities to meet with and catch the eye of ministers or ministers-to-be.[21] Trust and personal chemistry can develop. One Conservative Secretary of State told us how he came to appoint his special adviser, who came from the Conservative Research Department:

> We used to have a briefing meeting before ... [X] was so switched on and so amusing. I said 'I like this guy'. So when I got to the Department ... somebody said 'Did I want a special adviser?' and I said 'What about asking [X]?' I didn't interview him. So they rang up and asked him if he wanted to come to me. That's it. And he did.

There were practical reasons why political staffers might be chosen. One special adviser who served under a Conservative Government explained why it was that political staff were a primary recruitment pool of special advisers:

> If they were desk officers [at the Conservative Research Department] advising on a particular area of policy, the Secretary of State ... would have seen them coming back and forth to meetings. Secondly, they knew they didn't really have to train them up. They came fully trained in obvious, basic things like parliamentary procedure, the detail of

---

[21] There are differences between the three groups. Party staff are usually located in party headquarters and are paid for by the party; political advisers (sometimes known as 'pads') are also paid for by the party, but are usually only assigned to or appointed by shadow ministers; all MPs have parliamentary researchers, who are paid for by the Independent Parliamentary Standards Authority (IPSA). There was a noticeable shift towards the recruitment of former parliamentary researchers as special advisers under Labour. For instance, in 1997, just under one-third of all the Labour special advisers brought into government had been parliamentary researchers at some point in time.

policy, also the detail of the Opposition parties' policies ... if you got an adviser who'd been in the Conservative Research Department, you knew that they were able to function at a political level.

Of course, while political staff may be knowledgeable about the Party and Parliament, they may be less so about Whitehall. Still, political staff are an obvious set of recruits. Thus, one former Conservative special adviser, who was not known to her minister before being recruited, drily said to us that she was appointed because 'I was the supposed expert on [the portfolio] in the Conservative Research Department'. This was typical of the replies from Conservative special advisers serving in either the governments of 1979–97 or under the Coalition.[22]

Of course, much depended on the specific minister and the specific context in which they had the opportunity to appoint a special adviser. For instance, a minister might feel that he or she wanted greater impact in communicating with the media, or a minister appointed to a particularly complex portfolio might want to appoint an expert. Here is Michael Heseltine describing how he chose his special adviser upon being appointed as Secretary of State for Defence:

> [I looked] around for the brightest young industrialist who might be persuaded to turn from poacher to gamekeeper and help control procurement. The name of Peter Levene soon surfaced ... We lunched together ... I asked him, on the strength of that lunch, whether he would consider coming to the Ministry as my special adviser.[23]

But, generally speaking, ministers are busy people and they are not trained in human resources management. If they cannot bring with them trusted staff or have need of particular skills, they turn to known and trusted networks, which are almost always party-political. In response to questions about recruitment, ministerial interviewees invariably brought up institutions and individuals, which were often party-poltical in nature: No 10; other ministers; former or serving special advisers; the Party chairman; the Director/Head of the Party policy unit; trusted officials within the Party or even the department; and sometimes heads of think tanks. Lord (David) Young, for instance, when he was adviser to Patrick Jenkin, Secretary of State for Industry, was charged by Jenkin with finding a successor.[24] One Labour minister explained to us how he would go about finding a replacement:

> I would say to my existing special advisers and to colleagues, 'Have we got people who we've really started to respect and to understand are doing a good job somewhere else, who might actually want to be involved with government?' ... [Or] I would look around and see someone who had long standing experience in the Labour movement.

[22] See also Stephen Hanney, 'Special Advisers: Their Place in British Government' (Brunel University 1993) 144.

[23] Michael Heseltine, *Life in the Jungle: My Autobiography* (Hodder & Stoughton 2000) 268–69.

[24] David Young, *The Enterprise Years: A Businessman in the Cabinet* (Headline Book Publishing 1990) 71.

This worked both ways. Another Labour Secretary of State told us:

> There is a pretty close network. Because you are looking for someone who has got party commitment and or affiliation. The word goes out, because they all talk to each other. So someone says, 'Mike is leaving'. So you get people who approach unsolicited saying, 'I understand you are looking for somebody, this is me'.

The result is that while there are a variety of recruitment pools for special advisers, the core pools in all three cohorts are party-political staff, public relations and the media, and to a lesser extent business and think tanks.

B. In Government

Recruitment is not limited to the beginning of a new government—it is in fact an ongoing concern. In 1997, when the Blair Government came in, 73 special advisers were appointed; by 2000, there were 44 new individuals not present in 1997—over half of the initial 'class of 1997' had been replaced, The average number of special advisers leaving annually between 1997 and 2009 was approximately 15.[25] Similarly, the Coalition appointed 63 special advisers upon entering government in May–June 2010; by the end of 2013, it had appointed the same number again as replacements or additional recruits.

Thus, after the first reshuffles or the mid-term, many of the initial wave of special advisers will have left. As before, the first inclination of ministers seeking to appoint a special adviser in this period is to bring with them trusted party staff; failing this, they turn to known and trusted party-political networks.

One recruitment pool, which grows larger as a government progresses, is that of former special advisers. The benefits of (re-)employing someone who had been a special adviser are obvious: they can be trusted and they have a proven set of skills and experience. 'Inheriting' a special adviser has the additional benefit of having an 'old hand' who understands how the department works. One Labour special adviser in government during a reshuffle said:

> I got a call from about four Cabinet ministers within eight weeks … I spoke to three ministers, was offered two jobs and accepted one. It wasn't … so much haphazard as a trawl going round of sympathetic … people who could do the job.

Alternatively, a new minister could simply keep the special adviser already in a department, but there was rarely an expectation that this would happen. One Labour special adviser told us of her experience:

> It was quite difficult because [my minister] was reshuffled out … I thought 'OK, I haven't got a job really'. I didn't want a situation where [the new minister] would take me to one side and say 'I've got somebody else'. I said to [the officials] in the office that I may just want

---

[25] This figure excludes election years. For more detail on the number of special advisers exiting government, see appendix two.

to clear my desk and go ... They were a little bit gobsmacked, because I don't think they realised that's what special advisers have to do. So I came home and got a phone call from [the new minister] in the afternoon saying 'For God's sake come back, don't be so daft. We need you here'. Which was a bit of a relief. I was back at work the next day.

As we have already noted, ministers in the Conservative Governments were more likely to retain the special adviser already in the department than those ministers under the Labour Governments (see Tables 3.5 and 3.6). There may be a number of reasons for such a phenomenon. It may suggest that Conservative ministers wanted expertise and respected continuity—and, indeed, some of those special advisers who remained in departments under the Conservatives despite reshuffles fit the profile of an 'expert adviser'. For instance, Tom Burke was an environmentalist who served three different Conservative ministers in the Department of Environment over six years (1991–97). This can also be seen from an examination of the pre-government careers of special advisers in Figure 3.7: there are far more individuals appointed under the Conservatives who were academics, for instance.

However, it may be because Conservative ministers saw special advisers less as a personal appointment and more as part of the government architecture, or because they did not regard the appointment of special advisers as particularly significant. One former Conservative minister said to us:

When I arrived as Secretary of State ... [in the 1990s], my permanent secretary ... said: 'It has to be decided who is to be your special adviser.' I never had a special adviser in my life. I said rather unctuously: 'I regard you as my special adviser.' He said: 'Your predecessor had [special adviser X] ... I kept him waiting a month, and said 'well, we better have him' ... Previously I had been [a minister in a number of departments] and I didn't have a special adviser to ask for bloody advice.

The number of ministers who served in the Conservative Governments of 1979–97 that we interviewed was small, but this was a response unique to them as a group. There are at least two powerful Conservative politicians who did not appear to have appointed special advisers when becoming Secretary of State:[26] William Whitelaw[27] and Peter Walker.[28] As we shall see in chapter four, senior ministers of later governments were more likely to see special advisers as a vital resource rather than a superfluous burden. By the end of the Blair premiership, a secretary of state not appointing a special adviser would be unthinkable.[29]

---

[26] Hanney (n 22) 111.

[27] William Whitelaw (1918–99): Leader of the House of Commons (1970–72); Secretary of State for Northern Ireland (1972–73); Secretary of State for Employment (1973–74); Home Secretary (1979–83); Leader of the House of Lords (1983–88).

[28] Peter Walker (1932–2010): Secretary of State for the Environment (1970–72); Secretary of State for Trade and Industry (1972–74); Minister of Agriculture, Fisheries and Food (1979–83: note that this was effectively a Secretary of State post); Secretary of State for Energy (1984–87); Secretary of State for Wales (1987–90). Walker did appoint a special adviser in his post as Secretary of State for Energy.

[29] In interviews with former Labour ministers and special advisers, we were told of a single case where a senior minister had queried the need for a special adviser. Ultimately, the minister did appoint one, but this was said partly to be because No 10 did not want to set a 'precedent' of a senior minister without a special adviser.

Many former special advisers are often happy to return: as one former adviser said, 'being a special adviser's a drug'. There have been a number of special advisers who have been called back: Joe Irvin was a former trade unionist who first worked as a special adviser and Chief of Staff to John Prescott (1997–2001), and was later brought back to be Gordon Brown's adviser in No 10 (2007).[30] The Coalition currently has three special advisers who served under former Conservative Governments: Patrick Rock (1987–97 and 2011–), Jonathan Caine (1991–95 and 2010–) and Andrew Dunlop (1986–90 and 2012–).

However, reliance on former special advisers may also indicate weaknesses in core recruitment pools. It was still common in interviews with former ministers and special advisers who were appointed at mid-term or later in a premiership or government for them to mention party-political networks when discussing recruitment and appointment. But it was also evident that for both Labour in the later years and the current Coalition Government, the mid-term stage saw tried-and-tested recruitment pools become shallower. This was partly because the best-qualified candidates had already been selected or had moved on to better jobs. Prospective candidates are also aware of the political cycle as well: fewer people are willing to back a loser or an exhausted government.

That recruitment pools and networks begin to dry up in this stage is indicated in three ways. We can see it first when examining the age of special advisers over a premiership. Recall Figures 3.1 and 3.2: the average age of special advisers upon appointment declines over a premiership, a phenomenon driven by older advisers leaving and younger advisers coming in. This is consistent with the idea that it becomes more difficult for governments as they get older to recruit experienced staff. It mirrors the US experience as well: it is often thought that recruitment is a problem at the beginning of a new administration, but it is more of a problem later.[31] Heclo quotes a US bureaucrat discussing the presidential term and the impact on recruitment of political appointees:

> The most you could ever expect probably is four years [for appointees in a given position] ... you have a real problem, however, when that individual leaves in that third year, because you have a presidential election coming along ... You can fill in the slots, because there will always be folks who will be happy to jump, but they are probably not the ones that you want to take it. Which explains why, during that third year, you have people who are very junior and probably not very skilled ... They are a known quantity, loyal, and they are eager to take the job, even if it is for six months. That is when you pop them in. That third year is probably where you get the greatest quality decrease.[32]

---

[30] Irvin later became Brown's Political Secretary for a further two years (2008–10).

[31] Hugh Heclo, 'The In-and-Outer System: A Critical Assessment' (1988) 103 *Political Science Quarterly* 37. For a recent discussion on the tenure issues of appointees in the US, see David E Lewis, 'Testing Pendleton's Premise: Do Political Appointees Make Worse Bureaucrats?' (2007) 69 *Journal of Politics* 1073.

[32] Heclo (n 31) 50–51.

The drying-up of tried and tested recruitment pools can also be seen in the shift in career backgrounds set out in Figure 3.8, which breaks down pre-government careers by premiership. For instance, there is a noticeable decline in the number of appointees with party career experience under both Major and Brown, both of which followed the long premierships of Thatcher and Blair.

Finally, this phenomenon was also evident from the fact that, in our interviews discussing recruitment with those in government at the mid-term or near the end of a term of a government, a competitive interview process was often mentioned. Ministers in the later years of the Labour Government and in particular the Liberal Democrats under the Coalition have been forced towards more semi-open competitive recruitment processes; they could no longer rely simply on the informality of word of mouth and party-political networks. There is some evidence that this also happened under the Conservative Governments of 1979–97: Stephen Sherbourne, Political Secretary to Thatcher and Chief of Staff to Michael Howard, said in response to calls to increase the number of special advisers: 'You can't have a structure which assumes a calibre which isn't always available.'[33]

For Labour, a shift towards a more formalised process of recruitment began at the end of Blair's first term and gathered momentum over the remainder of his premiership, and continued under Brown. For the Lib Dems, this could be seen as early as late 2011, when they had a semi-open competitive recruitment process in a recent round of recruitment for six special advisers, suggesting that it was a challenge to find sufficiently high-quality candidates.[34] One Labour special adviser appointed in Blair's second term said of the recruitment process: 'there was a lot of interviewing ... I was special adviser to [a number of] different Cabinet ministers, I was also interviewed by another four at various points ... for other special adviser jobs'.

Another special adviser appointed late in the Labour years had applied for the post of special adviser with four different Secretaries of State. For one, she was required to write a two-page essay on the next two years in government, do a live exercise and then an interview. One minister—Jim Knight,[35] Minister of State for Employment—even recruited his special adviser via an advertisement he placed on Twitter in 2009, which read: 'Interested in being my SpAd? DM me on Twitter with why you are the one & if interested I'll give you an email to apply to.'[36] He ultimately appointed a former manager from the National Audit Office and consultant with Ernst & Young.

---

[33] Hanney (n 22) 154.

[34] The Liberal Democrats appointed six special advisers in 2011 to cover key departments in Whitehall: see Robert Hazell and Ben Yong, *The Politics of Coalition: How the Conservative-Liberal Democrat Government Works* (Hart Publishing 2012).

[35] Now Lord Knight of Weymouth.

[36] Posted on 26 June 2009. We are grateful to Lord Knight for tracking down this tweet.

C. Other Structural Factors Impacting on Recruitment

The recruitment cycle, then, explains to some extent why certain classes of people are appointed as special advisers. But we should note that there are other constraints or factors influencing recruitment. One Labour special adviser in No 10 noted the peculiar nature of recruitment to a political party generally:

> In Opposition, it's not actually all that easy to get people to come and work for you. They're paid almost nothing. It's very difficult for them to operate. It's very frustrating being in Opposition. … [Furthermore] recruitment was more recruiting ideologically loyal followers, as it were, not just Labour loyal followers, but New Labour loyal followers. … You're more building a political party than building a cadre of effective administrators.

Bringing staff into government can also be about personal bonds and, sometimes, rewarding loyalty. One former Labour special adviser who was appointed in 1997 said: '[It's] about patronage. If you had earned the loyalty of the politician that you worked for, they batted for you to get into a department.' Put differently, ministers sometimes had motives other than political effectiveness in recruiting staff.

Staffing decisions are not a priority for many ministers or would-be ministers, particularly prior to entering government. For instance, the adviser quoted above went on to say that: 'Politicians … have a superstitious thing about concentrating on government before they actually get into government. It's very hard to make them focus.' Kavanagh and Seldon make a similar point: future Prime Ministers tend to be cagey about appointments: they don't want to reverse decisions or seem foolish, or they may be constrained by the Party.[37] There are also practical constraints. A Conservative special adviser under the Coalition commented:

> [Political parties in opposition] want to make appointments quite discreetly and quite quickly. It doesn't mean they don't look. They go through a search process. They might employ an executive search firm, but they just won't externally advertise. What they don't want is a huge flood of applications … you don't have a great staff. You don't have an HR department. In Opposition you're struggling to manage the people you've got. You don't have the resources to be able to process thousands and thousands of applications.

This mixture of competing motives, over-cautiousness and resource scarcity limits the capacity of governments and ministers to think carefully about the selection of appropriate candidates for government, and to search outside well-trodden networks.

Finally, it is worth noting that we have examined recruitment from the point of view of the employers of special advisers ('demand'), but we should note the motivations of those who would wish to become special advisers ('supply'). The key features of the post of special adviser are important: often intensely political; often all-consuming and involving long hours; an inflexible salary regime;

---

[37] Dennis Kavanagh and Anthony Seldon, *The Powers Behind the Prime Minister: The Hidden Influence of Number Ten* (HarperCollins 2008).

offering little or no career ladder or development; and little job security—being, of course, subject to the tenure of the appointing minister. The characteristics of the job are therefore likely to attract certain kinds of candidate and exclude others. Heclo again is relevant here—he discusses the prime candidates for political appointment in the US:

> Those already located in the Washington area; those young enough to accept the financial and family sacrifices as an investment in future advancement, or those much older who are financially secure and whose children are gone from home; those in major corporations doing business with government (rather than small business entrepreneurs) or those in professions where government appointments provide a marketable expertise; those coming out of policy think tanks or academic schools of thought where advancing the right cause through a stint in Washington helps build credentials.[38]

Transposed to London, it is a description that would fit many potential appointees.

i. The Role of No 10 in Appointment

Finally, there is the role of No 10. The appointment of a special adviser is thought of as a personal appointment, but from our interviews and from documents both historical and contemporaneous, it is clear that No 10 may exercise a strong influence over special adviser appointments in four ways: first, it controls numbers; second, it may act as a feeder; third, it may select a particular individual (or individuals) to be a minister's special adviser; and, finally, it scrutinises and may exercise a veto over proposed appointments.

No 10 may decide if a minister gets a special adviser in the first place. While generally speaking secretaries of state are allowed to have two, it is at the discretion of No 10 if they are allowed more. No 10 also decides if other ministers can have one.[39] So, for instance, under the Coalition, No 10 allowed Michael Fallon, a Minister of State in the Department for Business, Innovation and Skills, to have a special adviser, whereas it did not allow Fallon's predecessor, Mark Prisk, to have one.

No 10 is well placed to act as a feeder given its strong links to the Party. One Conservative special adviser serving under the Coalition told us how No 10 kept an informal list of possible new recruits from the Conservative Research Department, Conservative Campaign Headquarters and those who had worked for shadow ministers. It was not uncommon for a new minister to ask the leadership for suitable candidates. This was particularly so in the years after entering government, when obvious candidates were unavailable and key recruitment pools had been exhausted.

On occasions, however, No 10 might place a special adviser with a minister. Here is Lord (David) Young on his reappointment as a special adviser in the

---

[38] Heclo (n 31) 52.
[39] *Ministerial Code*, para 3.2.

Department of Industry, following the replacement of Keith Joseph with a new minister, Patrick Jenkin, in 1981:

> I was shown into David Wolfson's [Margaret Thatcher's head of the Political Office] room who passed on the request from the Prime Minister that I should continue my work in the Department [of Industry] for Patrick Jenkin as his special adviser ... Patrick had me thrust upon him by the Prime Minister at the very moment he was offered the job [of Secretary of State]. No one refuses in those circumstances![40]

More often than not, however, it was a two-way process. So, for instance, one minister, being given a portfolio he did not expect, appointed the individual suggested to him by No 10: that individual had been the party officer in charge of his new portfolio: 'I would rather have chosen my own person. But I was very new to that brief and the view that I needed support from someone with prior knowledge was a sensible one.'

Finally, No 10 scrutinises special adviser appointments and may exercise a veto over candidates. Various versions of the *Ministerial Code* all state that all special adviser appointments require the 'prior written approval of the Prime Minister'.[41] The criteria by which appointments are scrutinised vary depending on the government and premier involved, but may include political acceptability and competence. Thatcher, for instance, vetoed the suggested appointment of William Hague in 1983, then a 21-year-old researcher in the Conservative Research Department, commenting that 'it would be deeply resented by many who have financial and economic experience'.[42] Recent releases from the National Archives show that Thatcher vetoed at least three candidates.[43]

We were told in interviews that this power had been exercised by later governments. Under Blair, the veto was exercised half a dozen times. In 2010 Andy Coulson blocked Michael Gove's proposal to make Dominic Cummings a special adviser in the Department for Education.[44] One former Labour No 10 adviser told us:

> If [minister X] wanted to recruit someone who was a complete opponent of the Government to be a special adviser, then we were going to make it very, very difficult for him to do that ... [Candidates] weren't vetted for competence in any way. They were only vetted for political danger ... You don't want to have someone who has got a track record as a real troublemaker.

---

[40] Young (n 24) 58–59.

[41] See, for example, para 48 of the 1997 *Ministerial Code*; and para 3.2 of the 2010 *Ministerial Code*. The 1992 *Questions of Procedure for Ministers* had even stronger but perhaps unnecessary language: 'No appointments ... Should be made until the Prime Minister's approval has been secured in each case, and no commitments to make such appointments should be entered into in the absence of such approval'.

[42] PREM/19/1043, 114.

[43] PREM/19/1043 and PREM/19/248. They were William Hague, Simon Burns and David Nicholson, all three of whom later became Conservative MPs.

[44] Alex Barker, 'Exit Coulson, Enter Cummings' (*Westminster Blog [FT]*, 27 January 2011), http://blogs.ft.com/westminster/2011/01/exit-coulson-enter-cummings/#axzz1bi6ctNNP.

Naturally, the power of No 10 to suggest and veto appointments waxes and wanes over time. 'Big beasts' in Cabinet could refuse the 'suggestions' of No 10, while a minister less certain of himself or herself or his or her portfolio might not. And vetoes may not be permanent: Dominic Cummings did later become a special adviser to Michael Gove (in 2011).

CONCLUSION

Special advisers as a group are not as young as might be expected, the median being around 33 years old on appointment. They are mostly male, highly educated, the plurality coming from Oxbridge or more broadly a Russell Group university, usually with a degree in the humanities and the social sciences. Prior to appointment as a special adviser, the largest group worked for a political party or in politics generally; many others came from public affairs and the media, and think tanks. Roughly half remain in post for three years or less, but one-quarter stay for six years or more—a small number having an extraordinary tenure of more than a decade in government. Two-thirds work for a single minister, while the remaining one-third work for multiple ministers.

There are differences between special advisers appointed in the three government cohorts we have examined. For instance, there were fewer special advisers under the Conservatives. Conservative special advisers were slightly older on appointment and tended to come from Oxbridge. They were also more likely to remain within a department in spite of changes in ministers. There were also shifts in the kinds of recruitment pools governments drew upon over time: early Conservative Governments were more likely to appoint those from business, academia and the civil service. Later Conservative, Labour and the Coalition governments were more likely to appoint party staffers, those from public relations, the media and think tanks.

Recruitment, viewed from the 'inside', appears haphazard and ad hoc. But what is striking are the similarities between special advisers under different governments. Those similarities stem from the demands of ministers and governments, from the supply of candidates available and from the conditions under which appointments are made. Ministers from across the political spectrum rely on certain kinds of individuals to do similar sets of tasks and so they will broadly recruit from a core set of networks and pools, a plurality of which are party-political in nature.

Recruitment depends a great deal on when it takes place in the life cycle of a government. Key members of staff are initially transferred across from Opposition into government, but as a Party (or Parties) continues in government, and the initial wave of special advisers begins to leave, new appointments are made via party-political networks and well-understood recruitment pools. As a government enters its mid-point to final years, however, it becomes increasingly difficult to find good-quality candidates, and ministers are forced by necessity into seeking alternative recruitment pools and holding semi-open competitive interviews.

All this suggests four things. First, the personal nature of the appointment (and as a result resistance to the idea of a more systematised recruitment process) has been exaggerated. Many special advisers, especially in later waves of recruitment, are not necessarily well known to the minister, as several of the interviews quoted above show. And the greater reliance on semi-open competitive recruitment processes, particularly in the later years of a government, is inevitably likely to increase that trend.

Second, recruitment is not just an issue at the beginning of a government—it is an ongoing and increasing problem. As we have seen, on average, 15 special advisers leave a year: that means by the mid-term roughly half of those who came in at the beginning of a Government have left and must be replaced.

It follows from the second point that, with the implementation of the proposals to increase the number of appointments of special advisers and/or expert advisers that ministers can make, the recruitment problem may become more serious, and more quickly.[45] More systematised recruitment processes may need to be formalised out of necessity. The Lib Dems, recognising this, have begun a mentoring scheme for potential special advisers by pairing outside policy experts with existing special advisers.

Finally, given the combination of differing motives for recruitment (personal ambition, securing ideological cohesion, patronage) and constraints (personal and practical—eg, candidates imposed by No 10, scarcity of resources for recruitment), it is striking that there were few complaints from our interviewees about special advisers' contribution to the running of government. But the current system means that there are risks that some less well suited in terms of competence or personality can be appointed, and this risk could increase if numbers of special advisers appointments rise significantly.

---

[45] See the discussion of the reforms suggested by the Coalition Government in ch 10.

4

What Special Advisers Do for Ministers

DAVID LAUGHRIN

Couldn't have done the job without them. Completely invaluable. In fact, I was asked for advice by the incoming government by one of their Cabinet ministers and I said: 'The one thing I would say is make sure on day one you have really good special advisers.' (Former Labour Secretary of State)

INTRODUCTION

S PECIAL ADVISERS EXIST to support ministers, so the relationship between them is fundamental to understanding what special advisers do. This chapter covers three elements of this: why ministers need special advisers at all; the roles of special advisers; and the value that they are perceived to add.

We review what ministers, advisers and others have said about the challenges which many ministers appear to face in working solely with civil service support and in dealing with what seems to be an inevitable overload of their time and energy. We show how the growing use of special advisers at the centre of government has developed in practice.

Finally, we discuss the comments made to us about the value of special advisers' work and why they appear to offer ministers something more than they can provide from their own resources or secure from the official machine, both in departments and at the centre of government. We also assess what advantages and risks the growing numbers of advisers have posed.

I. WHY MINISTERS NEED ASSISTANCE

We have seen in chapter two what the early historical impetus for special advisers was and how the development fits into theories about government. The picture is one where new governments—either formed by parties out of office for a long time or attempting to implement significant change to tackle major national problems—feel an increasing need to appoint both experts and political advisers as trusted allies in their missions. Because politics is also a highly competitive profession, even up to Cabinet level, as politicians they also need complete loyalists to help promote their reputation and ambitions in Parliament, the Party and the media. This can be done either in a measured way with integrity or, as has happened from time to time, with skulduggery. In the view of Damian McBride:

> Our political system ... is fuelled by the cut-throat competition to be selected, elected and promoted and the macho bear-pit of parliamentary debate. It encourages vanity, duplicity, greed, hypocrisy and cruelty. It rewards those whose instincts are reactionary and ruthless.[1]

Our interviews did not suggest, however, that many take such a bleak or cynical view. Most emphasised that politicians normally embark on their careers to achieve some political goal, cause or social change that they believe in.

Against that background, we reviewed how the trend to look for assistance from beyond the civil service has developed since 1979. In the early years, the emphasis was slightly more on expert advisers, designed to fill what were seen as gaps in what the civil service could provide. Margaret Thatcher, in a manuscript note recently released in the National Archives, said in May 1979:

> I do not like political advisers as such and have discouraged them. Nevertheless, some Cabinet ministers feel they would like a personal assistant who they know and who can help them tackling that side of their work which is partly government and partly party political ... [As for] Professional [ie, expert] Advisers. I welcome these.

These two motivations—to have near you someone you know and trust, and to have someone with additional expertise to contribute to your thinking—have been common factors across governments of all complexions.

II. SUSPICION AND TRUST

Familiarity and trust is important. In the Westminster system, the political and civil service tribes are kept apart, except when the politicians are actually in government. When out of office for a long time, politicians come to be suspicious of the official machine and think that it must have been brainwashed by their opponents. Civil servants actually strive hard to deliver a changed agenda—Jonathan Powell even thought they might have striven too hard in the early days of the Blair government.[2] But, even so, they may appear to ministers, especially new ones, to be always challenging ideas which perhaps, in the civil servants' eyes, were only half worked up in Opposition. The phrase 'the devil is in the detail' is often on civil servants' lips. Kenneth Baker, a minister who worked closely with Thatcher

---

[1] The most ambitious and unscrupulous may also want to downplay or undermine the work of political rivals on their own side, not just in the official Opposition, as exhibited in extreme form by Damian McBride: see Damian McBride, *Power Trip: A Decade of Policy, Plots and Spin* (Biteback 2013) 414.

[2] Jonathan Powell, *The New Machiavelli: How to Wield Power in the Modern World* (Bodley Head 2011).

in his later ministerial career, used to quote a Lewis Carroll verse to explain what this felt like to a minister:

> I sent a message to the fish, to tell them this is what I wish:
> The little fishes of the sea they sent an answer back to me.
> The little fishes' answer was 'We cannot do it sir, because...[3]

A special adviser from the Coalition implied to us that little had changed over the years. He added:

> The last thing any secretary of state needs is another civil servant. They've got enough of them and that's not really meant as a criticism, it is just you inevitably inherit a policy inertia from a previous government. Though it would be unfair to characterise the civil service as overtly party political, it is perfectly natural that in an environment where you have a persuasive political ideology for 12 or 13 years, people who occupy senior positions or influential positions over certain policy areas who are brought up in a Labour minded environment, let's say pro-EU, for example ... it is perfectly natural that the system will inadvertently encourage people to continue to think in that way.

> One of the clear areas for me and a priority straight away was to help ... address this policy inertia. You were eyes and ears for policy going awry and also the eyes and ears for policy initiatives that you've inherited perfectly innocently that of course are now contrary to Government policy or Government intent. We were a third party, a devil's advocate.

It is not surprising that many secretaries of state prefer to have near them, especially at the beginning of their time in government, devils they know rather than devils they don't know. They have usually chosen them rather than had them imposed upon them—unlike their civil servants and often their departmental junior ministers—and they are likely to have compatible personalities.

III. ADDITIONAL EXPERTISE

Ministers have also felt that they needed to look as widely as possible for the expertise to tackle the formidable problems they face. One former Conservative Secretary of State from the 1980s and 1990s told us that he saw this expert policy work as the most important role of a special adviser and one in which people's own politics were irrelevant to him:

> I decided time and again to bring in people chosen for their expertise and wholly regardless of their politics ... I was simply interested in their expertise in helping me make progress on matters of concern to me.

---

[3] Lewis Carroll, *Through the Looking Glass* (Plain Label Books 2007) 118.

A range of expert appointments has been made over different administrations, including the high-profile examples of Tom Burke on environmental and climate change issues, Michael Barber on improving education, Peter Levene on defence equipment and notoriously Alan Walters on economics.

IV. OVERLOAD

Overload has also been another pressing reason for an extra pair of hands. A special adviser heavily involved in the Thatcher Government was clear that the problem of overloaded Cabinet ministers strongly influenced their resolve to continue the use of special advisers.

This need was compounded as successive administrations faced more and more pressures. In the Blair and Brown Governments, Jack Straw saw the 'overload' that he had first observed as a special adviser to Barbara Castle and Peter Shore in the second Wilson Government take on a new dimension. In a talk he gave in July 2012, he noted that if the pressures in the 1960s and 1970s felt great, they were as nothing compared to those of the late 1990s and early years of the twenty-first century. He reminded his listeners that this was:

> [N]ot because the issues were then less taxing than today: far from it. In many ways they were even more serious ... but what was different was the pace of life and the expectations of the public about their leaders.

Straw suggested that the explanation for the ever-increasing pressures on ministerial time included:

> [T]he revolution in communications, the end of the age of deference, and, bringing the two sets of factors together, a great increase in avenues for holding Ministers to account ... coupled with a powerful shift in the attitude to parliament and politics.[4]

These concerns are echoed by a Secretary of State from the current Coalition Government, who said:

> I feel that the support offered does not always recognise the threat to good decision making that comes from not giving senior people sufficient time to absorb, think about and discuss strategic decisions. Too readily the diary becomes crowded out with a string of meetings, engagements, and paperwork which ranks too much of the business in the same way.

Special advisers can take some of this burden, help prioritise what goes to the Secretary of State, and take on some meetings and some of the preliminary sifting

---

[4] BBC Democracy Live, 'The Rt Hon Jack Straw: Great Offices of State' (2012), http://news.bbc.co.uk/democracylive/hi/house_of_commons/newsid_9688000/9688423.stm.

of options. In the words of one former Labour special adviser who went on to become a Secretary of State, advisers can focus on:

> [A]chieving the objectives, which are to progress the things that your minister wants to progress, win fights in Whitehall, watching their back, stopping small problems turning into big ones, anticipating, being able to be quick to react, to put out fires. Dealing with what appear to be small things that help the minister to do their job. There is some constituency problem or whatever. Just pitching in for whatever was required at the moment.

Special advisers have also taken on an ever-increasing role in dealing with communications, a topic that is covered separately in Chapter 6.

V. POLICY DELIVERY AND PROGRESS CHASING

Ministers are often unused in their previous careers to being at the head of large organisations and unsure about how the levers work in government and how to put policy into practice. As one Minister of State put it to us: 'How do I know that a decision that I have made has actually happened?'

Concerns across the board by the Blair Government led it to set up the Delivery Unit under Professor Michael Barber. As Barber has himself argued:

> The challenge for a Government badgered by a Prime Minister with a 'mandate for reform' is to design an effective reform programme, prepare a strategy to take it forward and seek to motivate a huge, sceptical workforce to implement it.[5]

Of course, all ministers have civil servants in their private offices who act as personal assistants and provide their official link with their department. Private secretaries play an essential role in helping ministers to handle the flow of information and to talk to the right people at the right time. They also keep a weather eye on what is happening on the vast array of issues that cross a minister's desk or find their way into his or her despatch box in any single day. But while ministers' private offices will normally operate progress tracking and bring forward systems to monitor progress, special advisers can more actively pursue issues that they know are of key importance to their boss and can delve further into the machine or probe outside contacts to check the reality of progress and even implementation.

VI. THE WORK OF DEPARTMENTAL SPECIAL ADVISERS

How then have ministers chosen to use their special advisers to meet these disparate needs and how have special advisers gone about the task of delivering the required results?

---

[5] Michael Barber, *Instruction to Deliver: Fighting to Transform Britain's Public Services* (Methuen 2008) 72.

Our surveys of special advisers from the Conservative and Labour Governments in the period covered by this book suggest that the activities and skills of special advisers have not changed much over the years. We asked those surveyed to select the most used and most important of the following list of activities:[6]

— Conveying/clarifying the minister's wishes to/for officials.
— Scrutinising advice from officials and others.
— Keeping officials focused on delivering the minister's policy programme.
— Contributing to the development of policy on cross-departmental issues.
— Developing fresh policy ideas/initiatives.
— Providing technical/expert advice on policy.
— Mobilising support for the minister's policies inside government.
— Mobilising support for the minister's policies outside government.
— Facilitating relationships with stakeholders outside government.
— Negotiating policy details with other special advisers.
— Negotiating policy details with officials.
— Acting as the minister's policy/political 'sounding board'.
— Planning parliamentary tactics.
— Managing presentation of policy.
— Working on the party's election manifesto/campaign.

Of these, conveying messages, keeping officials focused and contributing to policy were high-volume activities for most advisers, and conveying messages, scrutinising advice, keeping officials focused and acting as a sounding board were deemed most important. Some also mentioned the importance of covering things when the minister was abroad on business in Europe or further afield—being the minister's eyes and ears, and even sometimes mouth, when he or she was out of the country.

This does not tell the whole story, however. Even though most advisers used the skills that these activities required, it was clear from our survey and interviews that a degree of specialisation was seen as helpful to advisers and ministers alike. The three key functions undertaken by special advisers over the last two or three decades are best summed up as 'policy advice', 'communications advice' and 'political support'. We have chosen to categorise the work of special advisers by function rather than by 'archetype' (ie, the policy special adviser, the media special adviser and so on) because in the vast majority of our interviews, special advisers usually rejected easy categorisation of their work.

In their *policy* role, which is further explored in chapter five, special advisers bring to their minister expertise and/or practical knowledge of a particular area of policy. They focus on translating innovative ideas for improving outcomes in that area into practical proposals for delivering required improvements either

---

[6] Former Labour special advisers answering this question: n = 96; former Conservative special advisers answering this question: n = 33.

through legislative or other change programmes. As one expert special adviser commented:

> I was able to approach people who civil servants seemed not to be connected with and challenge ideas that had become accepted within the department. I was also able to explain to civil servants more fully what the Secretary of State was seeking to achieve.

In their *communications* role, which is described more fully in chapter six, they ensure that the messages that the minister wants put across to the media and the public get presented in the most effective way, building, reinforcing or recovering the minister's and their government's reputation for competence. Their tasks are to work with the civil service information officers to ensure that the political elements of the communications role are effectively inserted into departmental and government statements and speeches. They develop a range of specialist contacts with the media and party groupings in Parliament and beyond. As one former Labour Secretary of State suggested:

> [T]hey could explain the political rationale, the broader government rationale for what we were trying to do. So the special advisers were actually explaining why we were doing things and not just what we wanted doing. I think that was really important.

Or as one special adviser described the role of an admired colleague:

> Re-drafting press releases, advising on which story was going to go in what paper and so on. It was like watching a very skilled conductor conducting an orchestra. He did it very, very effectively.

In their *political support* role, they are available for a minister right through their long working days to provide support and assistance on whatever needs doing to help their minister achieve his or her political goals. They can turn their hand to anything from dealing with everyday policy crises to more mundane clashes of diary engagements between official and party claims and just giving personal succour to ministers—to be someone with whom ministers can let off steam or from whom they can get frank and private counsel. They also often pick up duties of liaison with the Party in Parliament and more generally. As one Coalition Cabinet minister put it:

> They are invaluable in watching all of our backs because we are always too busy. Having a person who has a second opinion and is talking to a slightly different collection of people and can say: 'Hey, have you thought about that?'

While the media storm over Damian McBride's revelations[7] has focused more on the role of stabbing others in the back than watching ministers' own backs, our interviews suggest that the protection and support role is much more common

---

[7] See, for instance, N Watt, 'Ed Miliband Says He Urged Gordon Brown to Sack Damian McBride', *The Guardian* (22 September 2013); and R Mason 'Douglas Alexander Accused of "Divisive" Leak by Former Spin Doctor', *The Guardian* (22 September 2013).

than the aggression. One special adviser captured this role at the end of the working day:

> Usually it was the only time he could take his bloody shoes off, relax and say: 'What an effing day I've had. That bastard in the house, blah, blah, and my mate let me down. Some of the officials say they want to run riot. And I don't know what my wife's been up to.' Whatever it is, they just want to relax with someone who they can relax with ... It's a lot of that, and that is a terribly personal thing, and you've got to have someone you trust and you like.

Many special advisers end up majoring in one of these roles, but are asked to perform tasks covering all three functions. This short description of a day in the life of an adviser from the last Labour Government gives a flavour of the way that these roles and functions interact.

Box A. A Day in the Life of a Special Adviser

The main thing to understand about the diary of a special adviser is that no day is the same as the last, and every day is subject to unpredictability and change. The days are painted against a broader canvas of the political calendar: the conference season in early autumn, the parliamentary and legislative programme, the 'silly season' in August, May local elections, with the clock ticking ever onwards towards the next general election. Punctuating these political 'seasons' are budgets, autumn statements, spending reviews, major speeches, by-elections, scandals and resignations, and media squalls.

A special adviser's diary is pegged to that of their political boss; one special adviser is with the minister during most, if not all, their ministerial duties. But the adviser's job is to be one step ahead of the minister—with the right briefing note, speech or document at the right time, in the right place. The special adviser works long hours and works closely with the private office (especially the diary manager, driver and principal private secretary) to achieve this.

So the day may start early—5 am or 6 am—to get a full run-down of the day's headlines and news agenda. This can now be done via the Internet or even just via Twitter—unlike in my day, when special advisers would be knocking down the door of newsagents as they opened and carrying huge wads of newspapers around. A trip to the private office at around 8 am would give the adviser a sense of the day's agenda, and any overnight changes. The special adviser would wait for the arrival of the minister and hope for a 15-minute slot in the diary to run through events and responses. Then the day might begin with a series of meetings with officials or departmental 'stakeholders'. The adviser attends, but would not always contribute hugely to these meetings. Instead, they take a note of nuance, body language, action points, and offer a post-match analysis.

The special adviser might then join the minister on a ministerial visit, often involving a train journey; or a trip to 4 Millbank [the broadcasting studios opposite Parliament] for a round of broadcast media interviews. They may sit in the officials' box in the House of Commons if their boss is performing at Oral Questions or in a debate. They may be fielding hundreds of media calls if a story is running hot, giving out the 'line' and quotes on behalf of their minister. They may wander over to Portcullis House [the building next to Parliament where many MPs have their offices and thus the main meeting place between staffers, MPs, journalists and lobbyists]. This is the political bazaar, where rumour, gossip and information are traded over subsidised coffee. Writing speeches, briefings and notes is often conducted in short bursts, or before or after the day's events. I used to joke that I could never begin to write a sentence and finish it before the phone went or someone asked me something.

No special adviser gets a break at weekends—there is usually a campaigning visit, or conference, or speech to attend. The phone never stops, even on public holidays and religious festivals. Sunday is often particularly busy, as journalists want stories for Monday. The only slight relief is Fridays, when ministers tend to be on constituency duties, and the department has a chance to exhale.

Paul Richards, special adviser to Patricia Hewitt at the Department of Health

In the final analysis, therefore, all special advisers, as one minister put it:

[H]ave got to be capable of turning their hand to whatever is the need of the moment. That means coming into work in the morning and doing none of the things that you had thought the night before that you were going to do, because something has blown up, there is a crisis, whatever.

Exactly how ministers use their special advisers, then, can vary widely. Some want experts who will help them push through a new policy; others want a prop with whom they can discuss problems and let their hair down; others want somebody who will keep a close eye on the civil servants; and others want a political adviser who will help them with the Party and the unions—as well as the many who want a mixture of these. So what special advisers do to help their minister will depend crucially on their own minister's methods of working.

VII. VALUE ADDED

So what do ministers and special advisers themselves say about the value that special advisers offer in taking on these roles and moving in a free-wheeling way between them?

A few former Conservative Secretaries of State voiced scepticism about the work of some special advisers, one doubting the need for special advisers at all and another casting doubt on the value of what he called the appointment of 'party apparatchiks':

> I personally don't like that. It creates a grouping of people with very little experience, straight out of university who then get on the candidates list and into Parliament without having actually done anything in the real world and without any street credibility. And I see no grounds for saying that it has improved the conduct and performance of government. My experience working with civil servants is that they will do anything for you within reason; and if it isn't they will tell you so. And you then have [the party machine] to manage the politics. I think that works perfectly well.

But the vast majority of those to whom we spoke took the opposite view. As one former Labour Secretary of State put it:

> If I hadn't had my special advisers I simply would not have been able to cope. If they didn't exist, you would have to invent them. Special advisers had a knowledge of the governing party and its history, the background, the particular political perspectives, the wider political environment. They had links with party backbenchers in the House of Commons and the wider party out there.

These links with party members, the party machine, backbench MPs and party groupings in the House of Commons and the House of Lords can give ministers valuable insights on what issues look like in the political hothouse. It can also give them invaluable channels and levers to use when they are seeking to secure acceptance of a sensitive or controversial issue in the Party and in Parliament, as illustrated below and in the case studies that follow. These channels are not available or often known to civil servants, no matter how switched on the private secretaries and senior officials are.

Box B. Special Advisers and their Wider Political Role[8]

The role of special advisers in supporting their secretary of state in his or her wider political role—and in particular in developing and maintaining links with the political party concerned—is not a particularly high-profile one. For most advisers it is something that they do alongside their main role, whether that is policy advice or communications. But there are times when it is particularly time-consuming.

The most important of these is in the run-up to the Party Conference, given that most members of the Cabinet will give a keynote speech. Departmental officials can help with the factual content of the Secretary of State's speech, but it usually falls to the special adviser to draft the speech and identify new announcements. The special advisers will also seek to

---

[8] I am indebted to Peter Waller and Hilary Jackson for this description.

ensure that their Secretary of State's diary for the conference is well targeted and support is given for fringe meetings as well as the main event. In addition, some special advisers will want to network at the conference on their own behalf, especially if their own long-term ambition is to enter Parliament.

Of equal importance—though every few years rather than every year—special advisers will have a role in the preparation of the party manifesto for the next election. Most manifestos are prepared by a core team, often led by serving ministers, but supplemented by others, including special advisers. The advisers in each department will be expected to come up with new ideas for the manifesto, sometimes checking discreetly with civil servants the practicality of possible options so as to avoid unworkable proposals.

Alongside this, advisers will have a more day-to-day role in political briefing, usually working alongside the Secretary of State's parliamentary private secretary and the relevant whip. This will involve, for example, making sure that backbench MPs or peers are well briefed to support the government in debates, and ensuring that candidates for European or local elections are able to answer questions from a comprehensive policy brief. There are also special interest groups in Parliament with whom the special adviser might liaise, both to ensure they are well briefed and to pick up any concerns about their secretary of state's departmental responsibilities.

Finally, most secretaries of state will have their own programme of political work going wider than their ministerial duties, whether that be appearing on the BBC's *Question Time* or visiting marginal constituencies, and the special adviser will work with the wider party to support such activities.

Obviously, some individual special advisers will have a much larger role in dealing with Parliament where they are in more political roles—for example, the advisers to the Leaders of the House or the Government Whips. There are also some differences between the traditions of the individual parties as to the extent to which they liaise with the backbenchers. The Liberal Democrats have the strongest tradition of internal democracy, and thus more party committees which expect to exert influence over the party frontbench, which can mean extra duties for Liberal Democrat advisers.

On policy development, ministers also saw special advisers adding an extra dimension both in terms of political nous and subject-matter expertise. A Labour minister said:

> I had so many incredibly bright people that I loved working with in the civil service. But very few of them could think laterally in the political sphere. Even some of the very top ones could work out how to fix a problem if you gave them a problem, but wouldn't want to think about the political consequences of that or be able to.

A special adviser said:

> I bring a particular expertise, a knowledge of the Party, the wider movement. You [the civil service] may produce a wonderful policy and I might say: 'You know what, that is all very interesting but it is never going to fly so don't waste your time on it.' We both offer advice to the person for whom we work and in the end he or she decides what is going to happen.

An explanatory role was also cited by a number of those to whom we spoke. One former special adviser outlined this value in some detail:

> You respect the expertise of others while applying your judgement, coaxing people in a particular direction, advising them. Over time, as long as you get the relationship right, people are coming to you and saying: 'Now is this what the Minister is looking for, do you think? What do you reckon about this draft?' 'No, I think you need to change it like that.'

The two case studies below from the period of the Thatcher and Blair Governments illustrate more fully the way in which special advisers can interact with officials to produce results which might have been unlikely to happen without their intervention.

Box C. Two Case Studies
Case Study One: Road Transport Issues

When Norman Fowler was appointed first Minister of State and then Secretary of State for Transport in 1979–81, he appointed the Director of the Oxford University Transport Studies Unit, Ian Heggie, as an expert special adviser. Fowler had been told in Opposition that he would take on the transport role and had brought together a group of transport advisers, including Heggie, to help frame future policy options. Fowler brought Heggie into the department to help him put these proposals into practice.

According to Heggie, the department was seen from the outside as too insulated from external and expert thinking, and some officials were overly focused on traditional public provision. As special adviser, he was able to open up a more effective dialogue with stakeholders such as the National Bus Company—where he had better contacts than the senior civil service did—and where the managers felt that they were competing with private sector coach firms with one hand tied behind their backs. This helped lead to the successful privatisation of National Express and its inter-city coach services. He also helped to draft a consultation document on cycling (despite weak civil service support, because they regarded cycling as low priority).

In addition, Heggie played a key role in the privatisation of road construction sub-units, on which he worked closely with Kenneth Clarke, as Minister of State. Here again there had been some civil service opposition, partly based

---

on a failure to understand how ongoing projects could be passed to a private owner. He knew that this already happened in the private sector when a contractor became insolvent. Some civil servants appeared to prefer a transfer to local government, which would not have brought the dividends gained by privatisation. In private hands, Heggie believed, everyone benefited: the load could be spread and the units' expertise could be used on international and other civil works projects.

The view given to us by officials from the time was different. They suggest that the Permanent Secretary, Sir Peter Baldwin, and other senior officials had rather good contacts with industry, including with the former Labour politician Lord Shepherd, Chairman of the National Bus Company. The civil service team were seen, according to the testimony of civil servants around at the time, as particularly innovative and a breath of fresh air in Whitehall. Led by the 'estimable' Sir Peter, they blazed the trail on privatisation: the National Freight Corporation, Associated British Ports, British Transport Hotels, Sealink and National Express were all moved to the private sector. They actively supported Norman Fowler on the private financing of the Channel Tunnel and on the roadside advertising of motorway service stations. They might not have seen cycling as a priority issue, but this was probably because they saw it more as a local government responsibility.

The special adviser felt he was making a significant impact on innovating policy and providing better contacts. Civil servants saw the adviser more as complementing their own efforts and providing helpful reassurance to Norman Fowler that the plans were sound and based on expert evidence. The special adviser's concerns about cycling—probably far-sighted given recent developments—were then not seen as a priority for central government.

So the precise contribution of different players is hard to determine and the added value of each is difficult to disentangle. The landscape may look rather different from inside and outside the official machine. In the end, it does not matter precisely who had the most influence. For a minister embarking on major new initiatives, the plus clearly came from sound groundwork done in opposition and then, when in government, from advisers from all perspectives delivering similar messages, working constructively together and keeping a range of channels open with the stakeholders involved.

Case Study Two: Farepak Christmas Boxes Collapse

When Ian McCartney was Minister for Trade, he was faced in October 2006 with a public crisis over the collapse of the Christmas hamper scheme run by a company called Farepak. The victims—mainly low earners paying into scheme through the year—had the prospect of a poor Christmas and a lengthy wait for derisory, if any, compensation. By December 2006, however, a fund had been set up for victims of the collapse and £8 million had been raised. Thus, some payouts to the families were possible and all of the hampers that were in stock got distributed.

The fact that there was any good news for these families, and in time for Christmas 2006, was due to the role of McCartney's special advisers in conjunction with the minister, his principal private secretary and officials won over to their cause.

In the words of the Minister's private secretary:

> There were all of these thousands of people, some welfare dependent, that weren't going to get their Christmas savings. They had been saving responsibly to pay their way at Christmas but the system had let them down. Because of their low incomes, many were locked out of mainstream banking and financial products and were now left without a penny in compensation. We were worried that they could end up going without over Christmas or else turning to loan sharks. We knew we had to act quickly and that this was going to be big.

From the Minister's perspective, the priorities had to be:

— to get some money back in the pockets of these families before Christmas—some eight weeks away;

— ensure confidence in the remaining players in the industry or they could also collapse—which would be catastrophic;

— turn a potentially hostile media into a supportive one—it would be easy for them to blame the Government;

— be responsive to Parliament—MPs would rightly be concerned for their constituents and select committees might want to look at policy failures;

— avoid the pressure for a knee-jerk reaction on regulation—the Prime Minister was very keen on keeping 'red tape' to a minimum;

We commissioned urgent advice from officials at the Department of Trade and Industry (DTI) who told us this was 'just a straightforward insolvency of a commercial company. Nothing ministers can, or should, do about it. It's a matter for the Insolvency Service'.

This reflected the formal policy position that the Treasury would expect to see. But the Minister saw the case for something innovative, taking a risk for the public good. The Minister despatched the special adviser and me to see the top officials. We said:

'Hang on a minute, this is no ordinary insolvency—these are people on the breadline—families up and down the country in every constituency. There is no one other than the Government who can clear this up. People will expect it of us: the Government and the DTI will take a huge hit if we fail to act. As for the timing, it couldn't be worse for the families, just before Christmas. What's the media fall-out going to be if we don't act?'

These were people putting aside a few quid each week in order to put food on the table and a few toys in the kiddies' Christmas stockings. Their prospects were bleak. We knew we couldn't give any formal government compensation or intervene in the insolvency process. But there was no way we could walk away either.

We persuaded the Department's Director of Consumer Affairs that we needed to put some official resource into this and he and his team played a full part in helping put together the solution. They attended a Saturday Summit organised by the Minister—bringing together the officials, lawyers, the Administrators of the insolvency, directors of the other Christmas Savings Schemes and representatives of a charity. With the aid of Derek Walpole of the Family Fund, we set up a charitable fund. The Charity Commission pulled out all the stops and processed the application in record time for us so we could be up and running—taking donations within a few days.

Our strategy was to combine the resources of the officials in the DTI, the Minister's private office, stakeholder groups and the special advisers to make things happen. We contacted people like ASDA, Tesco, Sainsbury and Morrisons to ask them to put their hands in their pockets—which they did. While the Minister secured £2 million from HBOS [whose tough line on repayment of Farepak's parent company's debt had been a big factor in the collapse], the policy officials began working out options for a voluntary code and regulatory system. The crucial activity was the special advisers ensuring that we got high levels of parliamentary and media interest—without that there would have been little pressure on the Christmas savings industry, HBOS, many of our donors or even other ministries and ministers.

We had to get a constant flow of media headlines and stories—this was not something that an official DTI press release would be able to achieve. The Press Office worked closely with the special advisers who could add the colour to the story that would excite the media. The special advisers got *The Sun* and the *Daily Mirror* on board and the papers printed things the government was not able to say.

We also needed constant and consistent pressure from Parliament—again officials could only do so much, arranging ministerial statements and so on. But we used the special advisers to provide detailed briefing for the parliamentary party, ensuring they had facts about the impact on their constituents, encouraging them to raise the issues in the House. This ensured that we got a number of heavily attended Westminster Hall debates. Mr Speaker realised the strength of parliamentary interest and was kind enough to allocate a debate on the floor of the House. This put pressure on the remaining companies in the Christmas savings industry.

All that stacked up nicely and it got the Government out of a hole because had that fund not been set up, there would have been a lot of pressure for the

Government to intervene on an insolvency and to regulate the industry—which may have resulted in the industry collapsing and leaving thousands of people without any form of viable savings scheme. It led to the Pomeroy Inquiry into Christmas savings products, the setting up of the Christmas Pre-payments Authority (protecting savings in the schemes) and, of course, to some payment and goods before Christmas. Without the work of the special advisers this would, in my view, not have happened.

This example shows that special advisers were able to add real value by helping everyone think outside of the box. They took on informal, exploratory and unorthodox tasks where official approaches were likely to have floundered. Their flexibility and willingness to take on whatever was needed was critical to the team effort: ministers, an innovative private secretary, officials and special advisers working together to solve a crisis.

VIII. POWER AND INFLUENCE

In our interviews, we also asked ministers and special advisers to comment on the relative power and influence of special advisers in relation to other key players in departments supporting and advising Cabinet ministers. These included the permanent secretary and senior officials in departments, the minister's principal private secretary, parliamentary private secretaries and junior ministers.

Overall, there was a broad consensus that the special adviser role was one which very often exercised significant influence—though rarely absolute power. Our interviewees were clear that special advisers who clearly had the confidence of their ministers could influence significantly the direction of policy, the priorities chosen and the way that they were implemented and presented.

A former Permanent Secretary commented:

I think that often good special advisers were more influential and powerful than junior ministers in a department. This is primarily because they had been chosen by the Secretary of State and junior ministers had not been.

Or as one former Secretary of State put it:

In about half of Whitehall departments the special advisers are more important than the junior ministers. A lot of secretaries of state sideline their junior ministers. Special advisers take their tune from the secretary of state: if the secretary of state is inclusive and collaborative, so will they be; if the secretary of state is close and power hoarding, they follow suit.

Another made clear the close and important relationship between the special advisers, the permanent secretary and the private secretary:

Actually in the end my special advisers worked with the private office and the permanent secretaries on a trusted basis. I think all the way through that two-way trusting was crucial to making it work. If the civil service feared my special advisers as somehow seeking to wrong foot them, or second guess them, or in some way expose them, I don't think we'd have got on in the same way that we did.

Overall, one of the best summaries of the true value of a good special adviser comes from a description by a former minister of state of the best special adviser he had worked with:

> He had a style that was very engaging—people liked him ... You get some special advisers that the civil service doesn't like, because they are very dismissive or superior or they have decided that the civil service are their enemies or whatever. As you do with ministers, you get some like that ... But he wanted to work with civil servants, he wanted the civil service to be a useful resource to the minister, so he wanted it to work. So he had the right approach.

> He was very good at his media work. He was good at pushing his secretary of state and ministers when they needed pushing to do something that they were a bit uncomfortable with. He was discreet. I am not aware of him briefing against people. He was just as useful on policy as well in terms of being able to spot weaknesses in the argument that officials were putting. Just sitting quietly and then asking one or two very perceptive questions at meetings, and spotting trouble, before it really exploded.

IX. SPECIAL ADVISERS AT THE CENTRE OF GOVERNMENT

Power and influence is, of course, often at its most potent at the centre of government, both in the Treasury and in 10 Downing Street and the Cabinet Office. Here those working directly with the Prime Minister, and the Deputy Prime Minister when there is one, have levers to influence the overall impact of their government and the priorities of individual departments.

Some of this has been dealt with in chapter two, but here we examine the work of special advisers at the Centre in greater detail. Most Prime Ministers have felt the need to make personal appointments so that they have had people around them whom they trust to help them pursue their agenda and handle the inevitable crises. This has often—but not always—involved the appointment and utilisation of special advisers.

Perhaps the main point to note first of all is that there has been an increase in the number of special advisers based in the Cabinet Office and 10 Downing Street, as shown in Table 4.1 below. We have sought in our interviews to explore further why the increases have occurred and what the impact of special advisers at the Centre has been.

Table 4.1 Average number of special advisers recorded per year in No 10 and the Cabinet Office over the years of each premiership[*]

	Thatcher	Major	Blair	Brown	Cameron
No 10	10	9	27	23	19
Cabinet Office	1	2	3	4	15
Total	11	11	30	27	34

[*] Note: this table is derived from records of all the separate special advisers listed by parliamentary questions and Cabinet Office data releases in these locations each year. It may slightly exaggerate the number of special adviser posts as new people arrive to replace others, but over time the annual comparison should not be seriously distorted.

A. Overload

Of course, Downing Street is subject to overload pressures even more than the departments of state, as Sir Christopher Meyer described recalling his time as John Major's Press Secretary:

> Nothing, but nothing, prepares you for working in Downing Street in intimate relationship with the Prime Minister. Several things happen to you in shocking velocity. The pressure of events almost suffocates in its intensity. There is little time for reflection. Reflex replaces reasoned thought. You are cut off from the outside world. You function inside a combination of hothouse and bunker ... Exhaustion starts to distort judgment. You keep going on the adrenalin and the thrill of being at the summit of things. In the end the attrition gets to you.[9]

B. Setting the Government's Direction

Against this background, one former Permanent Secretary with experience over a number of administrations defined the job of the Prime Minister to us as 'to set the direction and tone and provide strong leadership for the rest of government'. In Thatcher's time as Prime Minister, he suggested, this could be achieved because of the clarity of her direction and style, and because she had a small group of people around her who shared her political philosophy and whose job it was to make sure that the rest of government understood that. She also had and trusted a party machine that was better funded and staffed than many have been more recently.

But the task of setting and sustaining a coherent and robust strategic grip is never easy and several former senior officials commented in public in the early 1980s, after the demise of the Central Policy Review Staff (CPRS), about what Lord Hunt of Tanworth, a former Cabinet Secretary, described as a 'hole in the centre of government'. He suggested:

> Cabinets are not well placed to exercise this role of continuing strategic oversight alongside the taking of specific decisions. Cabinet ministers are heavily preoccupied with their departmental work and find it difficult to make time to think about the problems of other ministers which do not concern them directly; and of course the more they get involved with their own work the harder it is for them to see the Cabinet strategy wood from the departmental policy trees.[10]

---

[9] Christopher Meyer, *DC Confidential* (Phoenix 2006) 13.
[10] Lord Hunt (who as Sir John Hunt was Cabinet Secretary from 1973 to 1979) in a talk to the Royal Institute of Public Administration in 1983. His comments were echoed at the time by both Sir Douglas Wass and Sir Kenneth Berrill.

Another former Permanent Secretary suggested to us that one consequence of this was that Prime Ministers felt that the overall strategy and media impact of a government did not get the attention it required:

> Modern government after the Thatcher years was more influenced than in earlier days by the increased role of the Prime Minister's office in setting overall agendas. The Blair No 10 approach had been much more interventionist than the Thatcher one, in taking a detailed view on departmental priorities, monitoring delivery, and expecting to be answerable for mistakes and crisis management. This meant the management of the relationship between No 10 and the Secretary of State's office was critical.

C. Step Change: Strategy, Delivery and Media

So, from the Blair premiership onwards, there has clearly been a step change. The immediate staff around the Prime Minister have been required, both by direction from the Prime Minister of the day and by pressures from the media, to focus on both strategy and delivery, while dealing with everyday crises in an era of 24/7 media attention. This pressure seems partly created by the desire of individual Prime Ministers to be seen to be in control of both the priorities and the morning news agenda and partly by the appetite of the media and Parliament for focusing on the Prime Minister's day-to-day role and actions.

Norman Lamont's resignation comment in 1993 reflected his dislike of the latter tendency:

> There is something wrong with the way in which we make our decisions. The Government listens too much to the pollsters and the party managers. The trouble is that they are not even very good at politics, and they are entering too much into policy decisions. As a result, there is too much short-termism, too much reacting to events, and not enough shaping of events. We give the impression of being in office but not in power. Far too many important decisions are made for 36 hours' publicity.[11]

The fear about not wanting to appear out of control was evident when the Coalition attempted to reduce the numbers of special advisers. This was followed by criticism in the media about lack of strategic grip. So the current more 'presidential' expectation of a Prime Minister appears to be one factor in the expansion of special adviser numbers in the Centre. (The point here is not whether Blair, Brown and Cameron have presidential powers, but about how the media and

---

[11] *Hansard* 9 June 1993, col 285.

Parliament come to portray them and expect them to respond.)[12] As one former Minister of State put it to us:

> With the pace at which government now works, the 24/7 media cycle, the volume and complexity of things, we live now in a hyper-connected age. People now expect a response to things very quickly and things can get out of control very, very quickly now.

The increased number of special advisers undertaking this work continued under Brown[13] and, after that initial attempt at reduction, under the Coalition.

D. Variable Geometry

The way in which these extra staff have worked has varied over the years. Since Harold Wilson's time, there has always been a Policy Unit in No 10. Its role has included helping the Prime Minister and the Cabinet formulate an overall strategy for the Government; monitoring implementation of the Prime Minister's key priorities; keeping an eye on what all departments were doing in relation to the Government's mission and reputation; and supplying the Prime Minister with political and media advice.

As already noted in chapter two, the Policy Unit has varied in size from half a dozen to a dozen and a half people, and the mix of staff has varied from all being special advisers to all being officials. Generally the majority of staff has been special advisers. Under Thatcher and Major, civil servants were never more than one-third of the appointments.[14] The argument for including civil servants is their knowledge of Whitehall. Special advisers provide the political drive and party policy angle. The civil servants provide the insider knowledge to connect that drive to the Whitehall and beyond machine, and those in this role have recognised the need to be politically attuned but not partisan.

Peter Mandelson and Roger Liddle argued that the Prime Minister 'has to get personal control of the central government machine and drive it hard, in the knowledge that if the Government does not run the machine, the machine will run the Government'.[15] Patrick Diamond suggests that this was why Blair beefed up the Policy Unit:

> In the Blair era, the Policy Unit comprised 15 senior policy advisers who each oversaw separate policy portfolios covering the major departments of state. Most were politically appointed special advisers, though several were recruited from the permanent civil

---

[12] For a discussion of whether the Prime Minister's role has actually been transformed, see Ana Inés Langer, *The Personalisation of Politics in the UK: Mediated Leadership from Attlee to Cameron* (Manchester University Press 2012); Mark Bevir and RAW Rhodes, 'Prime Ministers, Presidentialism and Westminster Smokescreens' (2006) 54 Political Studies 671.

[13] We were told in an interview with a Brown adviser that the problem was not lack of activity, but the 'lack of policy substance to backfill strategy'.

[14] John M Lee, George W Jones and June Burnham, *At the Centre of Whitehall: Advising the Prime Minister and the Cabinet* (Macmillan 1998).

[15] Peter Mandelson and Roger Liddle, *The Blair Revolution: Can New Labour Deliver?* (Faber & Faber 1996) 235–36.

service, making the body analogous to the *cabinet* system that supports Ministers in the French system.[16]

Diamond goes on to explain:

In day-to-day work, senior policy advisers liaise frequently with ministers and senior officials in their departments, as the link point between the prime minister and the relevant member of the cabinet; they provide written briefings and advice to the Prime Minister on salient issues, pursuing steers on key decisions that would be fed back to ministers and their departments; advisers assist the prime minister in preparing for parliamentary questions and major set-piece events such as public speeches; and they engage in medium- to longer-term strategic thinking about the overall direction of policy and the government's purpose. While the work of Policy Unit advisers has often been depicted as challenging civil service orthodoxy and correcting decision making fallacies, in reality it is more concerned with negotiation, bargaining and forging consensus in Whitehall ... The role of the adviser was often to interpret the Prime Minister's views in terms that the department and ministers could readily understand.

In addition to the Policy Unit, the centre has often also housed other units such as delivery and strategy units, set up because of the difficulty that both policy units and special advisers had in maintaining focus on policy in the medium and longer term, and in avoiding spending all their time on the daily political battles in Westminster and the media. There have also been attempts to counter this by employing 'blue sky thinkers' such as Lord Birt and Steve Hilton to scan the horizon and encourage 'out of the box' thinking.

The reporting lines of these units have varied. Generally, they have reported direct to the Prime Minister and the No 10 Policy Unit has always served the Prime Minister. But the CPRS, at least in theory, served the Cabinet as a whole. The Delivery Unit reported directly to the Prime Minister, but after it moved to the Treasury in 2007, it reported directly to the Prime Minister and the Chancellor of the Exchequer.

The Policy and Implementation Unit, formed in 2011 under the Coalition, reported jointly to the Prime Minister and the Deputy Prime Minister. That was the reason given for its members being all civil servants: the argument being that a political special adviser could not comfortably advise a minister from a different party. But, in fact, half of its members were outsiders and a couple had worked for the Conservatives before the election.[17] The additional work on media management is covered in a later chapter.

---

[16] Patrick Diamond, 'Governing as New Labour: An Inside Account of the Blair and Brown Years' (2011) 9 *Political Studies Review* 145, 148.

[17] Robert Hazell and Ben Yong, *The Politics of Coalition: How the Conservative-Liberal Democrat Government Works* (Hart Publishing 2012) Appendix 7.

E. Finding the Right Levers

Jonathan Powell was recruited as a special adviser by Blair specifically to fill a chief of staff role, where he sought to mediate between the claims for the Prime Minister's attention from the Political Secretary, the Cabinet Secretary, the Principal Private Secretary and the Head of the Policy Unit. His role was to resolve differences for the Prime Minister, funnel all instructions and tell civil servants and political people what the Prime Minister required. Such calls were often prefaced by the clarion call 'Tony wants'. Powell also served as a trouble-shooter.

But even with this role in place—and it has been filled before and since by both civil servants and special advisers—there has sometimes been some confusion about which team is in the lead on which topic and who is responsible for identifying priorities, disseminating decisions and ensuring follow-up to them.

Diamond also notes that, in the Blair years, advisers were encouraged to be highly sceptical of departmental officials, and civil servants 'were often treated as an accident waiting to happen, and were thought largely incapable of producing rigorous evidence-based policy'.[18] He suggests that this did not lead to a productive relationship with the official machine.

Our interviewees unsurprisingly had a variety of views on what worked best. One suggested:

> The right alliance to get things to happen in government is to have a secretary of state, a heavyweight special adviser in No 10 and the permanent secretary all pointing in the same direction. The most successful reform areas were those where we had heavyweight figures who knew the subject but were very adept politically.

This suggested a preference for a 'small and lean' No 10 over a large one:

> If you become too big in Downing Street, you will actually slow the thing down. You won't be able to be as responsive. I think the ideal Downing Street and the ideal Policy Unit would be very light and responsive. I almost think of it like a gear stick. So the Prime Minister touches it and it moves, and then it goes into the transmission. The transmission should be the Cabinet Office.

The complexity of Coalition government has required heavier support in No 10 and the Cabinet Office. This has included support for the Deputy Prime Minister and Liberal Democrat junior ministers in departments to keep track of the compliance of the Government's plans with overall Coalition policy as set out in the Coalition Agreement.[19]

---

[18] Diamond (n 16) 151.
[19] See generally Hazell and Yong (n 17).

F. Ways of Working

Working practices have varied between different advisers at the Centre. Some have chosen to use their special adviser contacts in departments as their main channel of communications. But others have pooh-poohed the idea that there was an effective special adviser network that could work to get things done in parallel with official networks. They suggested that more effective results were achieved by direct contact with principal private secretaries, ministers or permanent secretaries and senior officials. Much depended on individuals' contacts and what worked for them.

G. Quality, Power and Risks

Our interviewees agreed that quality of staffing is key and that both policy and communications skills are needed. Many cited the influence that strong and experienced special advisers could exercise from No 10 if there was confidence that they were truly close to the Prime Minister and knew his or her mind. The name of Geoffrey Norris from the last Labour Government is regularly cited in this regard across our pages.

One with experience of both being a departmental adviser and working in the Centre commented:

> You feel a greater sense of power and being able to effect change at the Centre. In a department you feel it is just one or two politicos against thousands of civil servants. In the Centre there are more advisers in the team and proximity to the Prime Minister to give authority.

Equally, some of our departmental interviewees commented on the frustrations that could be caused if special advisers at the Centre seemed to want to drive the detail of the policy without the necessary knowledge and evidence. Similar frustrations could be linked to the work of the blue sky thinkers. As one departmental adviser put it:

> The other thing that really irritated me was [intervention by] special advisers in Number 10, particularly, or the Treasury, who had no understanding whatsoever of the policy, or the detail. They were trying to impose a particular political solution to a problem that would create other difficulties down the line. They were usually within the orders of their political masters, but operating in a completely evidence free zone and saying, 'We've got to do this policy, we've got to do that thing', and never mind how much it costs, or whether it's effective.

H. Overall Assessment

So the overall impression of the impact of special advisers at the Centre is that it has sometimes worked well to ease the huge burdens on the Prime Minister and the Deputy Prime Minister. They have enabled the Prime Minister and the Deputy Prime Minister to coordinate government strategy, focus on a few key strategic priorities, influence and monitor the delivery of those priorities, secure true inter-departmental cohesion, and respond to increased parliamentary and media pressure. Where the arrangements have worked badly, however, they have got up the noses of ministers and officials. Both have feared a 'ready, fire, aim' approach from people in the Centre more concerned with an immediate issue in the media, with troubleshooting and fire-fighting than longer-term outcomes and strategy. When that happened, the 'hole at the centre of government' identified by Lord Hunt got bigger through the frenetic digging of those within it.

X. CONCLUSIONS

The evidence over the years and from our own interviews clearly suggests that this 'gradual informal emergence of an administrative fixture'[20] is meeting a very real need for additional and different support to ministers from that which the civil service can readily provide. We found very widespread support for the roles and value of special advisers both in departments and at the Centre.

However, there are risks and several important questions raised by the strong evidence we have been given about the importance of this role and its potential for significant influence.

First, there is the issue of how far the role and number of special advisers needs to be controlled and limited to safeguard the value for money for the taxpayer from the public funds used to pay for them. The current limit of two for each secretary of state is under challenge, both from the apparent increasing tendency to evade the limits by use of temporary civil service appointments and from the civil service reform proposals presented by Cabinet Office Minister Francis Maude in July 2013.

Second, there is a debate to be had about whether, if their support is so important to secretaries of state, special advisers should be made available to other levels of minister too, for they too suffer from overload and the need to tap the best expertise available. Most of our interviewees appeared to be reluctant to go down this track. As one former Secretary of State put it:

> Junior ministers should not have their own special advisers save in Coalition. There has to be a single centre of power in the department, and a single line of command from the Secretary of State. Junior ministers cannot set up alternative power centres: that is a recipe for conflict.

But given the evidence presented to us that such conflicts have not appeared to arise when some ministers of state have been allocated special advisers (see appendix two), this is at least a topic for debate. Some better-agreed regime

---

[20] Andrew Blick, *People Who Live in the Dark* (Politico's 2004) 313.

for access to the services of special advisers by all ministers at least seems worth exploring.

Third, there are questions about how, given the importance of the role, the right quality of support is ensured (a subject that is explored further in chapter nine). The process of recruitment can be hit and miss and informal, and there are unclear job descriptions and very limited processes of performance review and accountability. There is no monitoring of the extent to which recruitment mirrors general good practice or may disadvantage women or ethnic-minority staff. Ministers nearly all say that they want the freedom to make their own appointments of people whom they can trust absolutely. However, as one former permanent secretary commented:

> The key question for the future is quality control over appointees. I have no magic solution for this, but it is something that political parties need to think about seriously in Opposition, as to selection, training and preparation.

Fourth, there is a related question of whether the value of good special advisers is worth more than the negative and corrosive influence of those who are less than effective or ethical. A former Permanent Secretary commented, with great concern and force, that a bad special adviser can poison the whole atmosphere, cohesion and functioning at the top of a department. This is a significant downside and suggests the need for extremely alert monitoring, feedback and review.

Fifth, there appears to be further room to explore how special advisers working at the centre of government can be organised so that they help to bring coherence and longer-term strategic planning into the collective consideration of policies. Can the perceived hole in the centre of government be better paved over with the aid of the right combination of the skills and influence of special advisers and civil servants working together?

We explore such issues further in the next and later chapters.

5

Special Advisers and the Policy-Making Process

PETER WALLER

On the whole special advisers are a force for good. When the system works well, you have people who are trusted by the Secretary of State, know the Secretary of State's mind better than any civil servant ever can and can ensure that submissions are put forward which have a good chance of leading to a productive discussion. (Former Permanent Secretary)

INTRODUCTION

A VITAL FUNCTION of all government departments is policy making. While policy delivery is often contracted out to others, most government policy is initiated and developed within the various departments which are dotted along Whitehall and in the surrounding streets.

This chapter focuses on that policy-making function and the role of special advisers in it. It describes how special advisers support ministers by taking an active role in working with officials to develop policy options and ideas. In particular, it looks at the interaction between special advisers and the permanent officials who are the prime movers in developing government policy. Such policy making usually takes place in a rather hidden world, away from the drama of politics in Westminster and in the media. It has thus generated rather fewer headlines and *causes célèbres* than the activities of media advisers, who are the subject of chapter six.

Our research shows that special advisers have become an important player in policy development and that most secretaries of state are now supported by at least one special adviser with a specific remit on policy. Some of those policy advisers—perhaps in numerical terms a majority—focus simply on adding the political gloss to policies largely developed by officials. But some will be heavily engaged in the detailed development of policy and we came across many examples where advisers were core participants in policy thinking well before advice was put formally to ministers for their decision. Indeed, in some areas of departmental policy, special advisers will often have a greater influence on the Secretary of State's eventual decisions than the junior ministers in the department. It is even arguable that a small number of special advisers, especially those working in No 10 on key government priorities, have occasionally had more personal influence on government policy decisions than the relevant departmental secretaries of state.

This chapter examines the relationship between special advisers and officials in policy making in depth, based on the interviews and surveys that we conducted. It identifies how advisers work with officials and assesses the value added of that work. It discusses potential problems in the relationship with officials and how frequently they occur. It also considers how both special advisers and officials interact with third-party stakeholders and lobbyists.

I. OFFICIALS AND SPECIAL ADVISERS: THEIR RESPECTIVE ROLES IN POLICY MAKING

There are roughly 4,000 senior civil servants (SCS) operating in Whitehall and about 100 special advisers—so 40 members of the SCS for every adviser.[1] But special advisers have a much greater impact on policy development than their modest numbers would suggest—the simple fact of their daily interaction with their secretaries of state and the fact that they see almost all papers going to the ministers give them a position of major influence.

The day-to-day tasks of officials and advisers, however, differ markedly. Essentially, on any policy area, the relevant officials do the hard grind of considering the issues in fine detail.[2] Any secretary of state needs officials to work out the practical implications of the aims he or she is seeking to achieve, to identify and work through the potential options for achieving those aims, and to advise on how best to implement them. Officials also need to work out the potential costs of new policies, to consider whether new powers are needed and to manage formal consultation exercises, both externally and within government. In due course, officials have to manage implementation, often including legislation.

There are too few special advisers for them to get involved in the full detail described above. Thus, they are obliged to spread themselves thinly. With at most two policy advisers in a typical department, they have to focus hard on where they can add value, leaving most of the detailed work to officials. But their interventions will often be influential. If an adviser tells an official that something is 'a nice idea but I don't think the Secretary of State will want to go down that road', then the policy option concerned may well be dropped before it gets to the Secretary of

---

[1] See Peter Waller, *Workings of Whitehall: An Insight into the Civil Service and How Policy is Developed* (The Whitehall and Industry Group 2012). The present chapter focuses on the role of the policy-making elite of officials working closely with ministers in the heart of Whitehall. The absolute number of civil servants is far higher, but most of these work in various government delivery functions and are not directly engaged with ministers.

[2] See generally Edward Page and WI Jenkins, *Policy Bureaucracy: Government with a Cast of Thousands* (Oxford University Press 2005).

State. Equally, if an adviser says 'we ought to look closely at the latest ideas from think tank X', officials will respond accordingly.

In making their interventions, most advisers will be focused on the political merits of the policy issues and options being considered. In particular, they will be constantly thinking of the raw politics and how attractive an idea would be once it leaves the closed world of Whitehall and is announced to Westminster and the media. In broad terms, an official will primarily be thinking whether a specific set of potential policy ideas is practical, but the special adviser will be focused on how the Opposition and the media will react to them, and how to present them to the best party-political advantage.

This does not mean that officials and policy advisers live in separate sealed boxes. Officials will invariably have views on how to manage the political aspects, and most senior civil servants have an instinctive understanding of how ideas will be received when they become public. Equally, policy special advisers do not limit themselves to the party-political merits of policy proposals and many will be directly involved in the substance of policy development rather than just the political implications. Like the ministers they serve, advisers will ultimately want policies which achieve the government's underlying objectives as well as being politically attractive in the short term.

It is nonetheless a fair summary to say that special advisers complement the role of departmental officials by adding the political dimension as policies are developed.[3] Working closely with ministers, they identify which policies should be regarded as priorities for officials to develop and update, and as those policies are developed within a department, they consider whether they are being developed in ways that are politically attractive. Policy special advisers will thus be in regular discussion with the relevant officials, explaining and elucidating the political aspects of the proposals to ensure that the options being developed by officials are likely to be politically attractive. They will also be talking to key stakeholders, within the parliamentary and national political Party but also more widely, to see whether those stakeholders are likely to be supportive or dismissive of the emerging ideas. They will be thinking hard about the presentation of the policies and when and how they might best be announced. They will be liaising with special advisers elsewhere in government, both in other departments and especially at No 10, to ensure that emerging proposals will carry widespread support from other ministers with an interest in the policy area. They will be concerned as to whether these proposals are in line with the overall philosophical message that the government of the day is trying to communicate (and, in this sense, doing policy work can merge into communication).

Perhaps most importantly, at least in the priority areas, advisers will often be harrying officials to 'get things done', with an eye to an early announcement and

---

[3] For one view of special advisers in the policy process, see Francesca Gains and Gerry Stoker, 'Special Advisers and the Transmission of Ideas from the Policy Primeval Soup' (2011) 39 *Policy & Politics* 485.

political timetables. This chasing-up by advisers helps officials understand their Secretary of State's key priorities and is reinforced through the daily conversations between ministers and their advisers on how issues are being progressed by officials, following which advisers will check and double-check whether enough progress is being made. This can, of course, occasionally be counterproductive. Whitehall departments have many examples on their record of policies which were announced before they had been fully thought through, leading to legal challenges, U-turns and disappointing outcomes.

One of the special advisers we interviewed summed up the situation as follows:

> What I brought that a civil servant wouldn't be able to in their impartial role was a sense of, politically, what's going to be good and 'What are our main lines of promotion on this?' and also 'What is politically going to be difficult?' and 'What are the arguments we're going to get back?' The Civil Service shouldn't do that, and so that's how I've added value. It worked best for me when we were the political version of what the civil servants were doing. The political part of it is absolutely necessary for a functioning government, whether that's a media appearance or over in Parliament.

In practice, however, the dividing line between what officials contribute to policy making and what ministers and their advisers provide is flexible. If secretaries of state choose to be very hands-on on the detail of policy development, then officials might mutter under their breath about it, but will in practice accept that ministers are fully entitled to get stuck into the detail. In contrast, other secretaries of state may be very hands-off and happy to delegate to their officials—plus junior ministers—issues of quite detailed political judgement. The dynamics of the relationship vary between secretaries of state, and the civil service will change its own ways or working as a new secretary of state arrives.

Such fluidity applies even more so to special advisers. As already noted in chapter two, compared to both officials and ministers—both of whose day is dominated by things that they unavoidably have to do—special advisers have more autonomy as to how they set about the job and there are simply no rules as to how they should allocate their time, provided only that the Secretary of State is satisfied with the results. Box A below suggests the variety which any adviser might encounter in a normal day at the office.

Box A: The Diary of a Policy Adviser

Being the Imaginary Diary Entry of an Imaginary Policy Adviser in the Imaginary Department of Bureaucracy (DB)…

Up at 7 and read the papers on the way in. As expected, yesterday's debate in the House got zero coverage but the Opposition had the better of the debate so zero coverage is good. An interesting report in *The Times* on the potential impact on DB of CLG's new planning regulations. On arrival, I called the official leading on this in the department but she wasn't really sighted on it, so I asked her to look at it and get back to me.

Saw the SoS at 8.30 before she left for Birmingham at 9. There were three submissions in the overnight red box that she wasn't absolutely sure about. I reassured her on the first one as I'd gone through the issues with officials before she got the submission. On the second, we agreed we'd better get the officials up for a discussion later in the week. The third was probably OK, but we agreed I should have a quick word with No 10 before we made the announcement because even though the policy is right, the politics aren't straightforward.

But her big concern was the restructuring policy and whether we would be in time for the announcement next month. Neither of us have much confidence that the officials are giving it the priority it needs so I said I would chase it up with them and she'll mention it to the Perm Sec at her weekly round-up with him.

Did an hour or so of emails and a few calls. Mostly routine but a couple of requests for meetings with companies which I'd better agree to. Rang No 10 as requested and talked them through the upcoming announcement. They were broadly OK and I am fairly sure they were persuaded on the substance. But they are still a bit nervous of the politics so will run it past the PM before finally signing it off.

Then spent two hours in a brainstorming session with the officials leading on the new Departmental White Paper. There are a lot of similar sessions to come as there were lots of good ideas being generated—a few of them mine!—all of which will need to be properly thought through. And then we'll have to work all the ideas into some sort of consistent theme so we have a coherent story to tell rather than a ragbag of unrelated ideas. I've also suggested we have a couple of informal meetings with the relevant think tank because they'll have some ideas as well. Overall the officials understand the challenge of this one pretty well—and I put a quick note to the boss with a thumbs-up on how it is going so far.

In the afternoon, I called up the official leading on the restructuring policy and that was far less encouraging. I just don't think she has understood yet the urgency of the issue and why it is so key to the SoS. I don't entirely blame her as she has got loads of other things on her plate and I am not sure she has got the department's brightest and best supporting her. But we are going to need strong contracting skills if the restructuring is going to work and I'm not sure the department has cottoned on to that yet. I did a quick briefing note for the SoS before her meeting with the Perm Sec tomorrow.

As the boss was out for most of the day, I was able to focus on paperwork more than usual. And there were half-a-dozen submissions to read, all with the usual ridiculous deadlines and all demanding to be in the red box tonight. They were mostly OK, though there were one or two additional questions on some which I suggested to the SoS in a note that she might ask before signing them off. There was also one where I had bigger doubts because they had seemed to overlook a couple of obvious policy options. I rang the lead official and he was OK about it, agreeing to rework the submission and resubmit it by the end of the week. As usual, the deadline of 'tonight' proved to be a bit more flexible in practice.

Took a call from the special adviser at CLG about the newspaper report this morning. He was pretty apologetic about the way it had come out and we worked out a way forward easily enough. We'll need to agree a united front before we approach the Treasury for approval as they'll be worried about the cost. Fed back my conversation to the officials who were pretty relieved and grateful to me for sorting it.

The SoS came back to the office at 6 and we got together with a couple of the junior ministers who were around for an impromptu round table about current issues. Usual mixture of things going well and things not so great. Picked up a couple of action points about briefing backbenchers on the committee of our current bill in the House, but, with a bit of luck, I can get the Parliamentary Private Secretary to do the necessary.

A few more mails and calls and then home at 7 for a rare early night. But read an article in the *New Spectator* about housing policy which made me think a bit and which I'll take up with officials tomorrow.

Above all, how policy advisers spend their time varies both according to the preferences of the Secretary of State and the advisers themselves. Some will spend a great deal of time physically with the secretary of state and attend all meetings when policy is being discussed. All advisers will undoubtedly spend a lot of time reading submissions from officials, if only to check that some key political aspect has not been overlooked. In our surveys of both Conservative and Labour special advisers, 70 per cent of both cohorts said that scrutinising the advice of officials was undertaken 'very frequently'.[4] Others will choose to spend time seeing external stakeholders or discussing issues with advisers in other departments and No 10. On the key priority areas, many special advisers will also have regular meetings with the relevant officials, going into considerable detail.

The respective roles of advisers and officials are summarised in tabular form in Table 5.1 below.

---

[4] Former Labour special advisers answering this question: n = 96; former Conservative special advisers answering this question: n = 33. This can be contrasted with the task of dealing with Parliament and parliamentary questions: only 20 per cent of both Labour and Conservative special advisers thought this was done 'very frequently'.

Table 5.1: The respective roles of advisers and officials

Field of activity	Civil servants	Special advisers	Both
Priority setting	Officials seek to identify the priorities of an incoming Secretary of State, whether from the manifesto (after an election) or from submissions to and discussion with the Secretary of State.	Special advisers help ministers identify key priorities from a political perspective. They will focus on what can be achieved within political timescales, with an eye to the electoral cycle and the Secretary of State's likely tenure. Special advisers also have significant external contacts, notably with the political parties, think tanks and other stakeholders in the work of the Department. They will be a channel for new ideas and proposals.	At this stage, there will be close dialogue between the Secretary of State, special advisers and officials, with numerous meetings. Officials will be seeking to improve the Secretary of State's understanding of the issues confronting the Department—some of which may be politically unattractive but unavoidable. Special advisers will focus on explaining to officials the core values and philosophies of the Secretary of State.
Key priority areas	Officials will develop policy options for key priority areas. In particular, they will manage the policy-making process, including timetabling, consultation, assembling evidence base and identification of options.	Special advisers will get involved in detailed development of key priorities, seeking to ensure that impetus is being maintained. While primarily focused on the politics, they may well generate specific policy ideas and options for consideration. Special advisers are also likely to want to see key submissions in draft and discuss any doubts with officials.	Special advisers will be quite hands-on and work closely with officials. They may well attend the internal meetings organised by officials to develop options and discuss draft submissions, and they will have informal email or oral conversations with those officials to check progress. Special advisers will then invariably attend meetings that the Secretary of State has with officials to discuss the policy options.

(Continued)

Table 5.1: (*Continued*)

Field of activity	Civil servants	Special advisers	Both
Lesser priority areas	Officials will continuously review existing policies and services for incremental change and improvement. They will also seek approval from ministers for potentially contentious decisions that need to be made.	Special advisers will expect to keep a watching brief over non-priority areas to ensure that officials are not missing political implications. They will usually read all submissions to ministers and may decide to comment to the Secretary of State—or talk to officials and ask for a redraft to reflect any concerns.	In non-priority areas, contact between special advisers and officials will be limited and ad hoc. Officials will, however, often seek a steer from special advisers on issues where they are not sure about the Secretary of State's likely reaction or political implications of the issues.
Fresh thinking	Officials will always be seeking out opportunities for worthwhile incremental improvements to existing policies, but will have limited time for 'blue skies' thinking, unless directly requested by ministers.	Most advisers will regard it as part of their role to be 'horizon scanning' and keeping an eye open for new policy thinking whether being promoted by think tanks, the Opposition, interest groups or emerging media lobbies.	Advisers will regularly ask officials for an initial assessment of unconventional policy ideas and may ask for some to be worked up seriously, while other ideas go no further.
Engagement with stakeholders	Officials will know which external stakeholders are most likely to be affected by emerging proposals and are likely to consult them informally to identify the practical impact of new proposals on those affected.	Special advisers have their own networks and will consult with these. Their networks will be more likely than officials to focus on the political attractiveness of emerging ideas, whereas officials are more focused on practicality.	Special advisers and officials are likely to work closely together in this area, though with some degree of overlap.
Drafting of public documents	Officials will expect to draft all consultation documents plus Green Papers and White Papers.	Special advisers will very seldom draft documents themselves. But they will look critically at successive drafts and seek to ensure that the political merits of the proposals or policies are clearly articulated within the wider framework of government policy.	Special advisers will usually be consulted on successive drafts of documents on key issues, largely through internal email. Special advisers might comment extensively and occasionally might offer specific text.

(*Continued*)

Table 5.1: (*Continued*)

Field of activity	Civil servants	Special advisers	Both
Whitehall clearance of policy	Officials will consult other government departments and organise collective clearance through write-rounds or Cabinet Committee meetings.	Special advisers may well discuss contentious policies with special advisers in other departments and in No 10, seeking to encourage support in the write-rounds.	The clearance with other government departments is quite likely to be a joint operation between special advisers and officials, with both operating in parallel to ensure that emerging proposals are likely to find favour both in detail and in political attractiveness.
Presentation of emerging policies	When a new policy or initiative needs to be announced, officials will make recommendations on both the formal announcement and any parliamentary statement. They will also liaise with No 10 on the timing of the announcement. They will usually develop a media plan and arrange interviews with the media.	On any major announcement, the communications special adviser will discuss the handling plan with others in the special adviser network (particularly in No 10) and with the Secretary of State. They may well comment extensively on draft press notices and may take over some of the drafting, especially putting the issue in a political context. They will also identify key press contacts and brief them informally on the political background to the emerging proposals.	In principle, special advisers and the departmental communications team will work closely together on the presentation of proposals, discussing together the handling plan and whether it meets both policy and political objectives.
Parliament and legislation	Officials will prepare detailed briefing and draft speeches for ministers for all parliamentary debates, both in the Commons and the Lords. They will also provide drafting instructions for legislation and then set up Bill teams to take it forward.	Special advisers will review the briefing for parliamentary speaking occasions, often adding attacking points on the Opposition position and attractive political soundbites. They may also talk to 'difficult' backbenchers before debates (though this will often be shared with the Secretary of State's Parliamentary Private Secretary). They will also prepare briefing for the parliamentary party.	Special advisers and officials will discuss informally with each other specific issues as they arise—and how to manage backbench and opposition concerns in the Committee stages.

II. HOW WELL DO SPECIAL ADVISERS WORK WITH CIVIL SERVANTS IN POLICY MAKING?

As the above discussion makes clear, the roles of officials and advisers outlined above should in principle be well understood on both sides and should be complementary rather than conflicting. But the purpose of our research interviews and surveys was to discover how it works in practice and—when practice differs from the theory—what can go wrong and why.

A. Overall views

The great majority of interviewees, whether officials or advisers, were generally comfortable with the way that advisers and officials worked with each other. One former but recent Permanent Secretary commented:

> On the whole spads are a force for good. When the system works well, you have people who are trusted by the Secretary of State, know the Secretary of State's mind better than any civil servant ever can and can ensure that submissions are put forward which have a good chance of leading to a productive discussion. And when you need to lobby other Departments, you can have the Minister, the special adviser and the senior official all working together well as a team. I have seen many occasions when it works well.

Another former official said:

> A good relationship with advisers can help you get things done. For example, we often ran into problems when what our Ministers wanted to do caused issues for other Departments—and their officials were not all that concerned about compromises. Getting the Secretary of State's spads to talk to their opposite numbers often proved the quickest and most effective way to make progress.

This aspect of special adviser work in brokering cross-departmental solutions came up on several occasions. One former senior official commented:

> I can recall many examples of the tight spad network across Whitehall holding together relations between ministers in different departments (not just with the Centre) in ways which added real value, not least because many spads can play quite an autonomous role and may have no great loyalty to Departmental boundaries.

Several advisers in turn stressed the importance of a strong relationship with officials. A Conservative adviser under the current Coalition said:

> The crucial thing is building the relationship with the officials. It is the officials you are going to spend most of your time talking to. Most Cabinet ministers are pretty busy and your ability to sit down and talk to them for any length of time is somewhat limited, whereas with officials you can talk for hours.

But our interviews had some less positive messages about the relationship. For example, one Labour adviser commented on a former adviser colleague:

> One [adviser] I worked with had terrible relationships with civil servants. He just wasn't very emotionally intelligent about how to deal with people, and rubbed them all up the wrong way, and ordered them around in a way that wasn't appropriate.

Another Labour special adviser of long standing said that she had never fully overcome the tendency of officials to exclude her:

> There was always a difficulty about getting access to papers and things. That happened everywhere and was just continuing throughout my career, except for in Number 10 where one was in the system. I was never copied in on things and it was a constant battle. I don't think it was deliberate, I just think that officials regarded you as outside the network.

But it was noticeable from all our interviews that both advisers and officials had the most respect for each other when they both recognised the need to work together constructively. Indeed, in such cases, their respective contributions were not only complementary but also inter-dependent. In developing options to deal with any complex issue—from taxation policy to criminal law, to support for industry or to reform of the welfare state—officials needed a detailed understanding from advisers of the political logic behind the work they were doing and needed to understand what options were 'deliverable' in political terms, while ministers and their advisers needed the input of officials as to whether their political objectives could be delivered through practical and deliverable initiatives.

III. WHERE DO SPECIAL ADVISERS ADD REAL VALUE TO THE WORK OF OFFICIALS?

Our interviews with former advisers contained many views on what they felt that they brought to the policy-making process, often with a recognition of the constraints on officials. One Coalition adviser said:

> The best advisers are the ones that ruffle feathers the most. Because let's face it, there are a lot of people in Whitehall who are paid on a permanent basis to smooth feathers. Therefore, I think challenging thinking at the very heart of the process is something that a spad can provide that nobody else can.

Another Labour adviser went into detail on the value of advisers as 'feather rufflers', also recognising the strengths and weaknesses of officials:

> The area where I think civil servants need help from special advisers is what I would call policy innovation. It's difficult for civil servants to innovate, for very good reasons—not least because I don't think many civil servants are very innovative characters. That's where special advisers come into their own, because they've got different networks, so

they are meeting people from outside government, and they've got different sources of information. They can, in a sense, provide a second opinion. And also because the best ones, I think, are quite innovative. They are entrepreneurs.

And you have tremendous leverage as an adviser because [once you set the ball rolling] you don't do the work, the civil servants do the work. So on one policy area I recall telling Gordon Brown at the Treasury: 'I think we should do something about this. Why don't you mention it in a speech, and announce that we are reviewing the economic incentives?' That intervention didn't take me very long but it acted as the catalyst for a whole shift. Gordon Brown duly included it in a speech and all the work which flowed from it was done by the civil servants. So you pivot the system on the intervention that you make with that authority from the minister. It's an unusually powerful position because very few civil servants actually are in a position to do that kind of pivoting.

Officials saw the value added in similar ways:

The adviser who thoroughly understands the politics and can communicate them to officials is adding clear value. The best were those who had the real trust of their ministers, probably having worked with them a long time—so the best ones tend to be older.

Another official noted that a special adviser could be adding value even if their approach did not make them universally popular:

People sometimes accused my Secretary of State of being indecisive. But I would say that he liked to be confident that every aspect of an issue had been thoroughly tested and thought through before he was ready to make his decision. And he used his adviser to make sure that happened—the adviser was very aggressive with officials in constantly harrying them to make sure everything was really thought through. He was very difficult for officials to deal with but he did the job that the Secretary of State wanted him to do.

Generalisations in Whitehall are difficult as there have been hundreds of special advisers in the period we have studied and no one official knows whether their personal experience of dealing with advisers is representative. In interviews, many officials thought that the majority of special advisers they had encountered had done a perfectly reasonable job in 'adding the politics to policy', but had not made a distinctive contribution to the underlying policy. Other officials were clear that the best special advisers they had worked with had made a substantive difference to the policy itself.

Overall, such a balance is not surprising. It would be equally fair to say that most ministers and most officials fall into the middle ground of competent performance, but with a limited number making a much more decisive contribution to the work of their department—and an equally limited number being rather ineffective. It would be odd if special advisers did not cover much the same range.

IV. INTERACTION WITH THE CENTRE

One important issue in developing policy that all departments find difficult is the relationship with No 10—a relationship which has become more complex under the Coalition with the need to liaise with the Deputy Prime Minister's office and his advisers, alongside the Prime Minister's staff.

Chapter four discussed the role of special advisers in the Centre and so this is not covered in detail in this chapter. But in general terms, most departments—whether that means their ministers, advisers or officials—prefer to develop their emerging policy proposals in house until they are ready for wider clearance and then consult No 10 as part of that clearance. In that context, advisers have a worthwhile and respected role in offering to 'have a quiet word with No 10' to check that the emerging proposals are likely to be well received. In parallel, the advisers at No 10 will be having a similar quiet word with departmental advisers to inquire about progress on issues which are seen by No 10 as core to the government's overall objectives.

However, the advisers at No 10 do not always see themselves as simply there to 'receive and approve' emerging ideas from departments; they also want to drive the agenda.[5] And, over the years, tensions have arisen as differing views on key issues emerge. An example from the Thatcher period was the appointment of Alan Walters as her economics adviser and the way in which he interpreted that role—sometimes in public—as giving him free licence to second guess the Chancellor of the day, Nigel Lawson.[6] The New Labour Government had a significant number of advisers at No 10—for example, David Miliband, James Purnell, Andrew Adonis and Ed Richards—all of whom were determined to drive the agenda, often in ways that drew them into conflict with the parallel Council of Economic Advisers[7] that supported Gordon Brown at the Treasury. Departmentally based special advisers under New Labour therefore often had to manage the development of policy with conflicting messages from the advisers at No 10 and No 11. Our surveys also illustrate that dealing with No 10 and the Treasury became more important over time: under the Conservatives, 40 per cent of those special advisers who responded to the survey said that they had occasional contact with No 10 or the Treasury, while under Labour, 40 per cent of those who responded said that they had 'very frequent' contact with No 10 or the Treasury.[8]

Under the Coalition, however, No 10 is less dominant and the advisers there are less assertive than many of their predecessors. Indeed, in previous research on the Coalition, there was a more common concern than over-interference—the feeling was more that No 10 took an interest in sensitive issues at rather too late a stage.[9] Yet the parallel requirement to consult not only the advisers at No 10 but also those in the Deputy Prime Minister's office has created an additional complexity.

It is impossible, however, to draw any firm conclusions from these examples about the relationship between departmental advisers and No 10 advisers in

---

[5] See, for instance, Andrew Adonis, *Education, Education, Education* (Biteback 2012).

[6] See 'Sir Alan Walters' *The Guardian* (6 January 2009).

[7] The Council of Economic Advisers was widely recognised as a device to enable Brown to have more advisers than he might otherwise have been permitted under the normal rule of two advisers per department.

[8] Former Labour special advisers answering this question: n = 96; former Conservative special advisers answering this question: n = 33.

[9] Robert Hazell and Ben Yong, *The Politics of Coalition: How the Conservative-Liberal Democrat Government Works* (Hart Publishing 2012).

policy making. There is a well-known debate in political circles about whether No 10 should be stronger in relation to departments and whether there should be a fully fledged 'Prime Minister's Department'.[10] But that debate seems unlikely to end any time soon.

V. THIRD-PARTY CONTACTS IN POLICY MAKING

During our research, we carried out interviews with third-party 'stakeholders' and lobbyists, including representatives of companies, trade associations and public affairs consultancies. Contact with such external bodies is a key aspect of the work of both officials and advisers. The purpose of the interviews was to establish the circumstances in which such third parties sought to contact special advisers and whether this was additional to or an alternative to dealing with the relevant officials. A particular issue that we addressed was whether stakeholders found different and confusing messages when talking separately to special advisers and officials. We also wanted to discover the circumstances in which special advisers contacted such third parties and for what reasons.

Overall, the picture which emerged was a benign one, with no real concerns. We began by asking when external organisations decided to contact special advisers. The reason most often mentioned was that special advisers would be contacted when there was a clear 'political' element to the issue concerned which officials might not understand as well. One head of public affairs at a major company told us:

> Spads are often better at spotting political elephant traps than civil servants are; and they can often short circuit issues for business, if, for example, officials are foot dragging or if there is something which doesn't quite fit within a specific official's portfolio. My experience is that the advisers are good at spotting the political and PR aspects of a situation, not only in terms of the impact on government but also the impact on business.

A public affairs consultant commented:

> Where spads are particularly useful is where it looks like an issue may become the subject of public comment, especially where it is cross-departmental. From our perspective, spads can then be an effective way of raising quickly the profile of the issue in Government; and making sure it is understood at a senior level.

We also asked about the balance between dealing with officials and dealing with special advisers. One interviewee responded:

> My initial preference, perhaps reflecting my civil service background, would be to explain our concerns to the officials. But if that did not seem to be working, we would

---

[10] On this, see Peter Hennessy, *The Prime Minister: The Office and its Holders since 1945* (Allen Lane 2000); Dennis Kavanagh and Anthony Seldon, *The Powers Behind the Prime Minister: The Hidden Influence of Number Ten* (HarperCollins 2008); House of Lords Select Committee on the Constitution, 'The Cabinet Office and the Centre of Government' (2010).

contact the spad, drawing their attention to our concerns and asking them to take an interest in the issue. But I didn't like to use spads to circumvent officials if I could avoid it. Not least because we would need a relationship with those officials after the spad had left the scene.

Finally, we probed whether officials and advisors seemed to be working together and in agreement or whether there were cases of differing messages. The general consensus was that officials and advisers tended to work in reasonable harmony:

I don't think the separate conversations we have are contradictory but complementary. The spads are at times able to give you a more coherent account than the civil servants of what the political drivers behind a proposal are. So you can then have a conversation with them about whether there might be alternative approaches to achieving the same political objectives which would work better for the industry. The civil servants are perhaps more proper in the way they approach things and seek your formal views through consultation without the same degree of interaction. With spads you get a better idea more quickly of what the political bottom line is.

VI. SOME SPECIFIC ISSUES IN THE POLICY-MAKING PROCESS

A. Special Advisers and Access to Ministers

One of our research questions was whether advisers can at times block access to ministers. Throughout Whitehall, the freedom for officials to put submissions directly to the Secretary of State and discuss them face to face if necessary is regarded as critical. If an official in charge of a specific area of policy is not present when decisions are taken, there is a clear risk that ministers will not be made aware of an aspect of the issue which might influence their decision. One former official said:

If you have very senior officials in effect reporting through spads, it can be very dangerous. In my experience, spads quite often don't know precisely what the Secretary of State wants. They might often get it reasonably accurate but not wholly right. So you need the meeting with the Secretary of State. It works best when senior politicians speak directly to officials.

The *Code of Conduct for Special Advisers*[11] makes clear that special advisers must not 'suppress or supplant the advice being prepared for Ministers by the permanent civil servants, although they may comment on such advice'. But anyone with connections in Whitehall will have heard of cases where special advisers are seen as a barrier between officials and ministers. And a number of Labour Secretaries

---

[11] Cabinet Office, 'Code of Conduct for Special Advisers' (Cabinet Office, 2010), www.gov.uk/government/uploads/system/uploads/attachment_data/file/62451/special-advisers-code-of-conduct.pdf, para 7ix.

of State were mentioned unfavourably in our research for the way they used their advisers as a barrier to interaction with officials:

> Ruth Kelly had a large team of spads as well as political allies appointed as temporary civil servants; and she was incredibly difficult to deal with in that she spent all her time talking to that closed circle and it was very difficult for officials to get into the room for meetings.

Another former official, referring to Stephen Byers when at the Department of Transport, said:

> The issue isn't just about listening to civil service advice—which secretaries of state are fully entitled not to accept—but about making sure that decisions which are being made are being communicated and acted upon. The problem was that no one in the Department really knew what Byers' position was, because so much was being managed by the spads and being communicated to the media directly without the Department knowing.

Perhaps most famous was the 'closed' approach taken by Gordon Brown, both at the Treasury and at No 10. An official summed it up as follows:

> Gordon Brown operated a 'Court' system in which he wanted to have regular contact with only a limited number of people—who in turn interacted on his behalf with the officials both in Treasury and at the Departments he was interested in. In due course the 'Court' approach was how No 10 operated under him.

That said, the same official also made clear that, in Brown's case, the closed approach did not necessarily mean excluding all officials:

> Frankly I am not sure that Gordon Brown really distinguished that much between spads and officials but simply surrounded himself with a small circle of people whom he saw regularly, whom he had confidence in and whom he trusted to get things done. He'd probably use a spad for the more overtly political stuff but the distinction between spads and trusted officials was marginal.

One of Brown's advisers, Shriti (now Baroness) Vadera, came in for specific criticism from a former official:

> No other adviser in my experience ever really tried to restrict officials' access to Brown in the way that Vadera did. I am not saying that she deliberately tried to restrict access on principle—she just had the view that her view was Brown's view so it did not need to be tested.

In all of these cases, however, it would be unfair to criticise advisers for blocking access if they were simply operating in the way that their Secretary of State preferred. Moreover, our interviews suggested there while there had been problems over access to specific ministers, they were the exception, not the rule. One former Private Secretary, for example, commented positively on John Prescott's working style:

> Prescott liked to hear a very wide range of views and then make a decision. So he tended to have large meetings with plenty of civil servants as well as his spads, spark a debate in the meeting and then come to a decision which we collectively rolled out.

A former special adviser from the last Conservative Government told us how his Secretary of State also wanted meetings with officials and his adviser:

> The Secretary of State liked to hear differing views before deciding his own position. And my role at meetings was to a degree calculated to create space for him to decide his position. There was inevitably on many issues a Departmental orthodoxy, and if you were not careful, that orthodoxy was very difficult to move from. But through my arguing at times strongly against what officials recommended, I could allow the Secretary of State to move beyond that orthodoxy without being so out of line with it that officials would find the outcome unacceptable.

B. Do Special Advisers Prevent or Promote the Politicisation of the Civil Service?

An issue which came up regularly in our interviews was whether having special advisers provided an essential protection for officials by allowing them more readily to side-step overt political activity or whether it diminished the role of officials by discouraging them from offering political advice.

It would be wrong to assume that officials are unable or unwilling to get involved in raw politics. One former Permanent Secretary recalled his experience at the time of the Major Government:

> When I was Principal Private Secretary we only had one special adviser, so I dealt with Central Office direct. Because of the interrelationship of the Secretary of State's official duties and political duties, you had to be very alert to what else was going on in his life. I'd even drink a pint in a Conservative club with him. And in the office we'd get the political people along for the face-to-face briefing alongside the civil servants. Effective civil servants, particularly those who work close to the minister, have to be very politically attuned. That doesn't mean to say they have to be politically aligned.

Another official who had worked at No 10 said:

> The spads I worked with provided a very valuable role right on the dividing line between the role of the civil service in providing advice and the more political issues that ministers are entitled to take account of. Having spads in that role does provide a very helpful benefit to the civil service in allowing them to stay on the right side of what can be a rather fuzzy dividing line. The best spads are able in considering policy to distinguish between the political and practical aspects of policy.

A Conservative special adviser took the same line:

> I am strongly in favour of an independent permanent civil service. And special advisers help you keep that, they help keep the civil servants from delving into the political sphere. They are a firewall for the civil service.

However, one Labour adviser thought that at No 10 at least, the line was much more blurred:

> There are many civil servants that work on a political level. It obviously doesn't mean that they're out campaigning and sticking leaflets through doors, but they actually are

part of the political agenda of the Government and are very happy to be there, and are instrumental in, essentially, supporting the Prime Minister of the day's agenda. Number 10 is like that.

And another, who had moved with Gordon Brown from the Treasury to No 10, said:

> The Treasury had quite a few officials who were good [at taking on the political agenda], and they tended to cluster with us and come with us to Number 10. But there were some civil servants who were very prissy, who didn't like the idea of engaging, who were much more rigid about saying: 'Well that is a party political matter.' Then they would just keep quiet. But people who work at Number 10 have to be prepared to live in a frenetic party-political world as well as a world in which they are trying to make policy.

A former Permanent Secretary thought that ministers were at some risk of losing something by not always regarding their officials as a source of political insight:

> Those people that have gone through fast-stream, classic working in private office I think get to see politics close-up. A lot of people have joined because they're politically aware, politically interested and very capable of thinking politically.

> Are ministers taking advantage of this? I suspect that there has been an element to which ministers have turned to special advisers, so it's a bit of chicken and egg. Ministers simply ask special advisers for political advice, so they're not asking their civil servants political questions. But if they asked the questions the right way they would get real benefit. Officials can get into the world of 'Here are the pros and cons of this policy, here are the things which if I were attacking I'd go for', which is perfectly legitimate and perfectly right for civil servants to do.

So the picture which emerges is an uncertain one. The rules on political engagement exist, but the precise line is blurred. Some officials—and very often the most successful ones—know how to be helpful to the politicians and their advisers without technically crossing any lines. The wiser ministers and advisers know how to get strong political input from officials without asking them to breach the rules.

But a further observation on our research is that no one appeared to have concerns about the politicisation of decisions as such. There was widespread acceptance that politics and policy making were indivisible, and that decisions could not be taken in a political vacuum.

C. More Haste, Less Speed

A consistent and understandable concern from both ministers and advisers about their officials is a perceived lack or urgency in policy making. Officials tend to see the announcement of a new policy as the end point of the numerous building blocks in policy making—notably evidence gathering, option development, consultation and decision—and the timetable is dictated by how long the various building blocks might take. But ministers and advisers often want to fix the timing of any announcement first usually for electoral considerations and make the preparatory work fit the announcement timetable.

John Williams, the special adviser to the Labour Cabinet Minister John Hutton,[12] explained the point in a talk to senior civil servants at the Business Department shortly after Hutton became Secretary of State in 2007.[13] He said that the Secretary of State moved to a new Department in the expectation that he would be there for 18 months at most.[14] And both he and Hutton wanted to make a genuine difference. Thus, their priorities would be determined by what could be achieved in that period.

This desire for speed is understandable. In part it is driven by the demands of the media, which demands instant answers from politicians about deep-seated problems. Moreover, we live in an age in which political parties seek to compete against each other rather more on their competence in managing public services than on their underlying ideology. Therefore, no politician can readily accept that decision making in government cannot or should not be accelerated. Special advisers are accordingly encouraged by their secretaries of state to harass and chase officials to prepare and implement decisions more speedily. One interesting decision of the current Coalition Government—though strongly opposed by many external stakeholders—has been to abandon a long-standing commitment to a 12-week minimum period for government consultations essentially to reduce the time it takes to get decisions made.[15]

However, problems can equally arise when decisions are taken too quickly.[16] The Major Government undoubtedly made serious mistakes in privatising the railways because of its desperation to complete the task before the 1997 election.[17] The Labour Government's proposal for new nuclear power stations was delayed for roughly 12 months because the High Court decided in a judicial review that too many corners had been cut in the consultation process.[18] Indeed, a possible underlying cause of many of the problems which all governments have faced with implementing IT projects is that they have wanted results too quickly. None of these problems can be laid directly at the door of special advisers, but it was clear from our research that the default position of many special advisers involved in policy making is 'we have to get this sorted now'.

---

[12] Now Lord Hutton.

[13] The author of this chapter was present.

[14] In the end, Hutton had four Cabinet posts in just over four years between 2005 and 2009. He was in the Business Department for 15 months.

[15] Cabinet Office, 'Consultation Principles' (5 November 2013), https://www.gov.uk/government/uploads/system/uploads/attachment_data/file/255180/Consultation-Principles-Oct-2013.pdf.

[16] See generally Anthony King and Ivor Crewe, *The Blunders of Our Governments* (Oneworld Publications 2013).

[17] See Christian Wolmar, *Broken Rails: How Privatisation Wrecked Britain's Railways* (Aurum 2001).

[18] 'Nuclear Row "was Misleading"' *BBC News* (15 February 2007) http://news.bbc.co.uk/1/hi/uk_politics/6364281.stm.

D. Inexperience

Senior officials in Whitehall have a certain minimum level of competence. They will have been recruited through a formal process which would have been specific about the qualities and experience being sought. They will have agreed job descriptions and annual targets, and improvement plans if they are thought to be underperforming.

None of those elements of formal personnel management applies to ministers or their advisers. There is no rigorous recruitment or appraisal of performance and there are no explicit job descriptions or agreed objectives. Ministers thus live in a more brutal world under which they can rise quickly but then be dispatched even more quickly, whether by the electorate at a general election or by Prime Ministers between elections. Special advisers are arguably even more exposed as they can lose their jobs overnight when their minister goes, regardless of how they have personally performed.

So we were keen in our interviews to find out how officials felt about the inevitable variability in the background, competence and behaviour of advisers. The main concern that arose was that a limited number of advisers were simply too inexperienced to add real value to the policy process. One official commented:

> The least worthwhile advisers are the young party apparatchiks, who to be honest bring negative value rather than added value. That doesn't mean they shouldn't be there and I recognise that they have to learn their trade—but they really don't add much.

A former Permanent Secretary also noted:

> Where it works least well is where the spad is primarily concerned with the reputation of the minister. I remember a discussion where I pointed out to ministers that on any given issue there are three 'brands' in play—the personal brand of the minister, the brand of the governing party and the brand of the department—and problems arise when those three brands are not aligned and a spad is giving total priority to the first.

A representative of a trade association said about his main potential contact in the Coalition Government:

> He was a nice enough guy and I have no reason to think he didn't really support his Secretary of State as the Secretary of State wanted. But he was never a figure of substance. He was too junior and he wasn't of sufficient calibre. He was a former research assistant and had been appointed out of loyalty. As a result, we went to private office and to officials much more than going through him.

One recent example of some of the problems caused when special advisers lack sufficient experience is Adam Smith, the special adviser to the then Culture Secretary Jeremy Hunt in the spring of 2012. The underlying issue here was that the Secretary of State had a formal decision to make about the potential takeover of BSkyB by News International which made it wholly inappropriate for the Secretary of State to be drawn into being seen as supportive of any particular party involved. But Smith allowed himself through texts and emails to be seen as clearly supporting News International, without apparently any reference back to the Department or even to the Secretary of State. Given that any special adviser is seen as representing the view of his or her Secretary of State, it was inevitable that Smith had to resign when the extent of his support for the News International position became public. There seems little doubt that Smith meant to support his Secretary of State loyally, but it is hard to imagine that a more experienced adviser would not have seen the potential pitfalls of his activity—or at least kept the Department in touch with those activities so that the pitfalls could have been pointed out to him in good time.

VII. SOME CONCLUSIONS

Our interviews for this chapter were extensive and wide-ranging. Our interviewees, whether officials, advisers or external stakeholders, had considerable experience and many, especially officials, were able to look back at the development of special advisers over many years—indeed, in some cases, over several decades.

We are confident, therefore, that our conclusions are soundly based. There might be a slight distortion in that they draw on the incidents and examples that interviewees remembered most vividly, while the numerous everyday humdrum interactions will be largely forgotten. But our research suggests a fair degree of consensus.

A. Do Special Advisers Add Real Value to Policy Making in Whitehall?

The focus of this chapter is primarily on whether advisers bring benefits through their relationship with officials, rather than the undoubted support they offer direct to ministers as discussed in the previous chapter.

The absolutely clear conclusion has to be that special advisers offer significant benefits. Ultimately, policy making in government cannot be divorced from politics and ministers need to take account of raw politics in the decisions they make. But, however good individual officials might be in venturing political advice alongside policy advice, very few civil servants will be as adept as special advisers at understanding the political merits and demerits of different policy options. Officials will seldom have a strong sense as to whether particular ideas will be received well or badly by the massed ranks of the political parties, whether in Parliament or in the constituencies. Moreover, busy ministers simply do not have the time to sit back and think through the political issues on their own. So the additional capacity provided by special advisers is essential in terms of ensuring that ministers are better able to take account of both policy and politics in their decision making.

In parallel, officials are likely to provide better advice to ministers the more they understand ministerial priorities and philosophies. Many ministers are far too stretched to provide more than a broad indication of their priorities to the numerous officials in their departments. Thus, a key and highly valuable part of the adviser role is to help the departmental officials better understand ministerial priorities in greater depth.

In addition, we found significant evidence that special advisers add value through the simple act of challenge to the prevailing departmental orthodoxies. While officials always offer options to the secretary of state on any given issue, there is almost always a single recommendation from the bureaucracy and recommendations tend to be based on consensus. Advisers are often those best placed to challenge the consensus—and many do so to considerable effect.[19] Related to that, most officials we interviewed recognised that many advisers could drive the agenda effectively and there was a recognition that the first generation of advisers under new Labour had been noticeably effective in doing so.

Finally, a significant number of policy special advisers—though certainly not all—bring valuable subject-area knowledge to their areas of activity. The area of energy and climate change, for example, has had input from a succession of advisers who had significant experience of working in those areas. The Department for Education also has a long tradition of bringing in external expertise, sometimes as special advisers and sometimes as temporary civil servants. A number of special advisers have been professional economists. Such people can bring real subject-area knowledge alongside the political focus. And Whitehall would be weaker without them.

B. But What are the Problems?

Based on our interviews, three types of problem can arise from the employment of advisers in policy making:

— *Inexperienced advisers*: clearly, every career—whether politician, adviser or official—has to start somewhere. But the apprenticeship before becoming an adviser is usually shorter than the apprenticeship of politician or officials, so some special advisers are undoubtedly appointed who are too young and inexperienced for the roles they are being asked to perform. This does not mean that such special advisers necessarily cause problems; indeed, they might be incredibly supportive of their ministers. But advisers who lack experience can often be over-focused on the short term and create additional work, for example, by constantly wanting things redrafted without being able to say how they should be redrafted (or, as in the case of Adam Smith, by serious misjudgements over the way they

---

[19] For more on the value of challenge in decision making, see the Whitehall and Industry Group Report *Searching for the X Factor: Decision Making in Government and Business* (London 2011).

manage policy issues). There is no doubt from our interviews that most officials preferred advisers to be people of real substance.

— *Blocking access to the minister*: this was a far less regular concern from our interviews, but a more serious one on the relatively rare occasions when it happened. It must be acknowledged that this was a result of the way that some ministers put a barrier between themselves and officials rather than the fault of the advisers themselves. However, there was a consistent concern among officials that higher numbers of advisers would increase the risks of direct access for officials being compromised.

— *More haste, less speed*: this is an intractable problem. Ministers and their advisers will be driven by political timetables and the need to be seen as responding quickly and effectively to events. Officials will equally inevitably be concerned to ensure that the downsides of potentially new policies have been fully identified and considered alongside the upsides, and will seldom want to cut corners with the risk of the policy unravelling. Ministers and advisers will always be acutely conscious of the limited time before the next election, whereas officials will be less keen to charge ahead with something that an incoming government is likely to want to reverse.

VIII. MOVING FORWARD

None of our interviewees—whether officials, advisers or others—had major improvements to suggest. The current proposals for extended ministerial offices divided opinion, but without any suggestion that it was seen by anyone as much more than an incremental development. Yet, nor was there any significant appetite for more radical reform from advisers or officials.

The recurring theme which did come up in conversations was a consistent view that the system as a whole would benefit if ministers (and the political parties) took more care over special adviser appointments. There was ready recognition that the appointment remained a very personal one and it was unlikely that ministers would want their freedom to make their own appointments reduced, but it was widely thought that ministers would get better results from thinking more deeply about the support they were looking for. The more expert and experienced the advisers appointed for the tasks required, the better the outcomes. This theme is taken up in later chapters.

6

Special Advisers and Communications

PETER WALLER

> As a columnist or as a BBC political correspondent, I did not make a single call to a departmental press office. To find out what was really happening about policy making, it was necessary to get to the special adviser. (Political journalist)

> There was no intention in Blair's time—or now with the Coalition in my opinion—to provide an information service that better informs the public. They want an information system that persuades the public. (Former senior official)

INTRODUCTION

OF ALL THE activities of special advisers in the last 20 years, it is undoubtedly their communications role that has proved the most controversial. While those special advisers focusing on policy attract limited attention, the media advisers have not only delivered the story, but have at times become the story.[1]

Indeed, many of the memoirs written by Whitehall insiders—particularly from the New Labour period—portray a world in which politicians and their media advisers appear to be focused almost exclusively on how the media will respond to a particular government announcement or internal argument.[2] Most of the relatively small number of special advisers who have become household names—Alastair Campbell, Charlie Whelan, Damian McBride, Jo Moore and Andy Coulson—have predominantly been associated with the communications function rather than Whitehall policy making.

This chapter seeks to explain why that happened and also to describe the day-to-day role that media special advisers play in supporting their secretaries

---

[1] See the research by Daniella Lock which suggests that 25 out of 26 allegations of misconduct against special advisers since 1997 have involved media advisers:
www.ucl.ac.uk/constitution-unit/research/special-advisers/special_advisers_and_public_allegations_of_misconduct_1997_-_2013.pdf.
[2] See, for instance, L Price, *Where Power Lies: Prime Minister v the Media* (Simon & Schuster 2010); A Campbell, *The Blair Years: Extracts from the Alastair Campbell Diaries* (Arrow 2008); D McBride, *Power Trip: A Decade of Policy, Plots and Spin* (Biteback 2013).

of state in particular and the government as a whole. It does not seek to be a comprehensive history of the various scandals which have afflicted communications advisers, but it does seek to show that it is in this area of activity that the rise of the special adviser has most changed how government works, and considers whether that is cause or effect.

I. MEDIA ADVISERS: WHAT DO THEY ACTUALLY DO?

Before discussing the evolution of media advisers, it is worth outlining what they would normally be expected to do on a day-to-day basis. Their role can be broadly split into a strategic role and a tactical role.

A. Strategy...

The *strategic* role is about seeking to convey a sense that the Secretary of State has an overall agenda for the relevant department and its activities. *Internally*, it will involve working with the Secretary of State and the private office to ensure that the balance of the Secretary of State's time is focused on key priorities, and seeking to ensure that a coherent political theme is getting across to the media whether through speeches, announcements, articles or interviews. The strategic aim will be to portray the Secretary of State as knowing what he or she wants to do and is actively delivering that agenda. In parallel, the media adviser will want to ensure that officials are thinking about the presentational aspects of new initiatives from the outset rather than at the end of the process. *Externally*, the strategic role will involve informal but regular discussions with specific political journalists who are interested in the activities and career of the Secretary of State and with other journalists who have an interest in the relevant department or particular newsworthy aspects of its business.

B. ... and Tactics

The *tactical* role will be more focused on day-to-day issues and will be split between proactive and reactive work. *Proactively*, the role includes informal briefing of the media on upcoming issues, sometimes to 'test the water' and gauge the reaction to specific new ideas. For major policy announcements from the department, it will involve discussion with the Press Office of the detailed media plan, and with No 10 to make sure that departmental announcements fit within the overall presentational timetable. Media advisers will also scrutinise draft press departmental releases to seek the maximum political as well as factual impact. Advisers will also want to ensure that any speeches by the Secretary of State contain strong political messages. They will also arrange briefing for individual journalists who will be particularly interested in a story—and a regular mid-week question for any media adviser will be 'what do we have for this week's Sunday papers?'.

In *reactive* mode, media advisers will keep a close eye on announcements by the Opposition parties and be considering what the Secretary of State should do to respond. Most importantly, all media advisers have to be ready to respond immediately to 'events'—things that happen in the world which require a reaction from government. Moreover, in a 24/7 world, the voracious appetite of the media for stories can all too readily mean that stories can themselves become rolling news events. So an early morning comment on a departmental policy by an Opposition politician on the *Today* programme might gather speed on the lunchtime news, be on the evening news headlines and still be running strong on *Newsnight*. Thus, throughout the day, the media adviser will be considering whether a particular story is best handled by a ministerial comment or interview, or whether it might be best to say nothing and let a negative story fizzle out.

Many media advisers will speak loftily about the importance of the strategic function, but on most days in the life of most media advisers, the immediate and responsive agenda is highly likely to crowd out any time for strategic thinking. It is usually on the days when the unexpected happens that the adrenalin surge is at its strongest—and when, as with Jo Moore, there is the highest risk of a thoughtless email.

II. GOVERNMENT AND COMMUNICATIONS: THE ORIGINS OF 'SPIN DOCTORS'

All governments have always had to pay attention to how they are perceived if they are to fulfil the ultimate political test—re-election. An early example of a political media adviser goes back to the Harold Wilson Government, when Joe Haines, his Press Secretary (a former journalist with the pre-Murdoch *The Sun* and later a columnist at the *Daily Mirror*), was a prominent member of what was known as 'Wilson's kitchen cabinet', a small group of advisers who sought to influence how the Government was regarded by the media.[3] There is little doubt that Haines was a prototype 'spin doctor', ready to present each and every issue to Wilson's advantage, and to some extent feeding Wilson's view that the media was broadly hostile to him.

But those were still relatively innocent days in that the kitchen cabinet was a small team in No 10 rather than having much to do with the formal Government Information Service (GIS).[4] Indeed, until the 1980s, the basic view

---

[3] See generally J Haines, *Glimmers of Twilight: Harold Wilson in Decline* (Politico's 2004); B Donoughue, *Downing Street Diary: With Harold Wilson in No 10* (Jonathan Cape 2005).

[4] The GIS (renamed under the Blair Government the Government Information and Communications Service (GICS)) was the umbrella body for civil servants working on government press relations and communications. It was a largely devolved structure under which individuals would regard themselves as working overall for the GIS (and getting centralised elements of professional support and guidance), while working day to day for a specific department.

of communications taken by the GIS was limited but straightforward. If a department wanted to inform the public of a decision or the issue of a report of some kind, it issued a press release, probably (in the case of a major or controversial issue) after a parliamentary statement. If journalists wanted to ask factual questions or get more detail, they contacted the relevant departmental Press Office, whose staff would answer questions as best they could, checking the detail with the relevant officials. But if the media wanted to ask about the politics of the issue or to debate the underlying policy considerations, that was largely for ministers, not civil servants. As such, the minister would hold a press conference, would agree to be interviewed by radio or television or would be invited to write an article for or be interviewed by the press. The underlying ethos in Whitehall at the time was thus that the function of those employed by the GIS was primarily about information and explanation, but not *persuasion*, the latter being a task reserved for the politicians.[5]

The approach described was not static and was moving forward as the demands of the media grew. The first permanent civil servant dealing with communications to become a household name in his own right was Bernard Ingham,[6] when he became Margaret Thatcher's press spokesman. Ingham conducted his daily press briefings to the press lobby in a distinctly more aggressive manner than his predecessors, being ready to comment extensively on internal government arguments and debates and making clear what Mrs Thatcher's views were. His approach was an example of politicians using the press not simply to inform or explain, but as a way of influencing policy battles within government which had not yet been resolved. Ingham became increasingly controversial as his role developed. It was regularly reported in the press that he had gone beyond the limits of what was acceptable for a civil servant, notably when he lambasted members of the Cabinet who had fallen out of favour with Thatcher.[7] But he retained the support of Thatcher until he retired simultaneously with her departure from Downing Street. In practice, retirement was his only option—it would not have been acceptable for him to return to a conventional civil service role.[8]

It is interesting that Ingham behaved much as a special adviser might today be expected to behave—and he clearly thought it entirely legitimate for an official to

---

[5] One exception was public information campaigns—seat belts, fireworks and so on—but such campaigns were restricted almost exclusively to areas where there was no political controversy.

[6] On Ingham, see P Hennessy, *Whitehall* (Pimlico 2001).

[7] Most notably when he allegedly described one of Thatcher's Secretaries of State, John Biffen, as a semi-detached member of the Cabinet. In response, Biffen allegedly described Ingham as the 'sewer and not the sewerage'. See 'Obituary: Lord Biffen' *BBC News* (14 August 2007), http://news.bbc.co.uk/1/hi/uk_politics/6945600.stm.

[8] In marked contrast to Ingham, Ian Macdonald, the Ministry of Defence (MOD) spokesman during the Falklands War, became famous for his dull and monotone recital of factual information at live press conferences—an approach which symbolised a focus on information, without any sense of persuasion. See 'Ian McDonald: Face of the Falklands' *Channel 4* (1 February 2007), www.channel4.com/news/articles/uk/ian%2Bmcdonald%2Bface%2Bof%2Bthe%2Bfalklands/263753.htm.

behave in that way. But he was himself instinctively distrustful of special advisers. Howell James, a special adviser on communications to several governments, told us: 'I think when I first arrived in the Cabinet Office in 1984, Bernard Ingham regarded it as an extremely dangerous precedent.'

During this period, special advisers in government were not often focused directly on communications work. Compared to the balance since 1997—when most departments have an adviser leading on media work—the smaller number of advisers under the Conservative Governments of 1979–97 were focused primarily on policy, and communications was a secondary aspect of their role. Indeed, one senior Cabinet minister whom we interviewed from that period told us that he considered that it was for 'ministers and only ministers' to seek to persuade the public and media of the merits of the government's position.

But that was even then a minority view. Under the Major Government, there was both a steady increase in the absolute number of special advisers and an increase in the number of such advisers who saw communications as a key part of their role. One special adviser from that era, working for one of John Major's 'bastards',[9] told us that he was primarily focused on policy, but acknowledged that he did go further:

> Press was not the focus of my job. But there were times under Major when I did work with my Secretary of State to get his Euro-sceptic message across in the press. There wasn't something we could remotely ask the Department to do. The Secretary of State was generally a very loyal minister, and on all policy issues we had a straightforward and workmanlike relationship with No 10. But he did feel we had to get his message across on Europe regardless of that.

The quote demonstrates the use of a special adviser to brief the press in order to advance internal arguments which had not decisively been resolved within government. But it was little different from the approach of Ingham a decade previously.

III. THE CAMPBELL REVOLUTION

By 1997, special advisers were being used for an increasing amount of communications work. But the game changer in the use of special advisers for communications was undoubtedly the appointment by the incoming Prime Minister Tony Blair of Alastair Campbell as his Chief Press Secretary. Campbell was effectively placed in charge of communications across the whole of government, directing

---

[9] A term used by Major to describe three Cabinet ministers who were strongly opposed to his relatively conciliatory policy on the EU and who had no hesitation in making those views known to the press, even if off-the-record. Paul Routledge and Simon Hoggart 'Major Hits Out at Cabinet' *The Observer* (25 July 1993), www.theguardian.com/politics/1993/jul/25/politicalnews.uk.

both media advisers and the departmental press teams.[10] And from that point on, it became the clear expectation that every department would have a special adviser with a focus on communications, a development which has never been reversed and seems unlikely to be reversed in future. By giving Campbell (together with Jonathan Powell) the power to issue instructions to civil servants, Blair made clear that his two key special advisers were there not just to advise, but to run things.

Campbell's views had been shaped by his own experience as a political journalist on the *Daily Mirror* and his conclusion on joining Blair's support team in Opposition that any effective politician had to set the agenda with strong, consistent and daily messages to the press—or else the press would impose its agenda on the politicians. He had been both influential and successful in shaping the media strategy of New Labour in Opposition, the high-water mark of which (even if its actual importance might be disputed) was persuading the News International newspaper group to back Labour at the election rather than continuing their traditional support for the Conservatives.

It quickly became apparent, therefore, that Campbell brought with him into government an approach that was markedly different from what Whitehall had previously expected of communications staff. In particular, he emphasised that it was the role of the GICS[11] not just to convey the basic facts about government policy (together with some limited explanation), but much more aggressively to promote what the government was doing and to persuade the press—and through them the public—of its merits. He also wanted a change in pace, recognising that the sheer number of media outlets was growing fast with the explosion of the Internet and 24-hour media channels. This was all a significant step forward from the more limited 'announce and explain' ethos (combined with 'defend if necessary') of the government communications service in a previous generation. But his approach was not unreasonable—it would be difficult to argue that the growth in media demands did not require such a change of pace from Whitehall.

Nonetheless, it was a challenge for the established press officers in Whitehall to understand the nature of the change being sought. Within days of the May 1997 election, Campbell recorded the reaction in his own diaries:

> I had the first formal heads of information meeting ... There was definitely a culture gap. I said things that I felt were blindingly obvious. E.g. about planning of events coming up and they didn't seem to get it. I said it was important to think about backdrops so that they helped communicate a message ... and you'd have thought I was asking the earth.

> What was clear was that the [departmental press heads] had very little clout within departments. They were a pretty dull and uninspiring lot. They felt a bit bruised by some

---

[10] See B Franklin, 'The Hand of History: New Labour, News Management and Governance' in S Ludlam and M Smith (eds), *New Labour in Government* (Palgrave Macmillan 2001).

[11] The previous GIS had '*and Communications*' added to its title in November 1997, becoming the GICS from that point.

of the stuff in the papers, but anyone would think they had been a great success story which we were trying to destroy.[12]

In organisational terms, there were two aspects to the challenge. First, the new Labour administration brought with it into government a new generation of media special advisers who assumed from the outset that they would be in direct contact with journalists rather than leave such contact to the departmental press offices. Second, there was an explicit challenge from Campbell to the existing press office leaders essentially to 'step up your performance or go'—and a significant number went.[13]

One former government press officer, who had been at No 10 under the Major Government, told us that he understood the need for change:

> The almost total clear-out over the next year was not necessarily a bad thing. Some of it was personal antipathy, some of it was about a feeling that we were not professional enough. If we were not prepared to learn fast then we were out. There had been some institutional resistance to new ways of working after 18 years of Conservative Government. But Campbell was one of the more sensible ones, not wanting to throw out everyone and prepared to accept people who changed their ways.

The Mountfield Report,[14] an early official review of the communications function under the new Labour Government, recognised that the Government Information and Communications Service (GICS) was not initially fit for purpose in a more media-obsessed stage. So the initial view taken by Whitehall's senior mandarins was very much that ministers were entitled to be concerned about the service and therefore entitled to make changes and, indeed, to insist on some significant turnover of press office staff.

But change was anything but smooth. Across Whitehall, there were numerous battles between the incoming communications advisers and the existing press teams and a fair amount of bad blood, some of which was enthusiastically reported by the press. Much of it was caused by the incoming generation of media advisers continuing as they had in Opposition in dealing direct with the media, giving limited attention to written press releases and concentrating on informal background briefing, which was aimed much more at winning an argument than at putting information on the public record.

Such advisers were unsympathetic to the formal disciplines of departmental press teams, who were used to clearing precise wording for any press briefing or announcement with their secretaries of state and having a written press briefing plan. Thus, it was uncomfortable for them when they found that the special

---

[12] A Campbell, *Power and the People: The Alastair Campbell Diaries Volume Two* (Arrow 2011), entry for 12 May 1997.

[13] Cabinet Office (Office of Public Service), *Report of the Working Group on the Government Information Service*, 1997. This was informally known as 'the Mountfield Report', the chair of the group being Sir Robin Mountfield.

[14] ibid.

adviser had already been pre-briefing selected parts of the media by talking to their close contacts in advance, often without any reporting back. Such pre-briefing had been common practice before, but it had invariably planned and agreed explicitly between ministers and the press office. The briefing from special advisers was, however, often off-the-record and without any formal authorisation. One press officer head who stepped down from her job in the first few months of the new Labour Government was understood to have made clear that she was leaving because 'the special advisers have taken over three-quarters of my job'.[15] One former Labour Cabinet minister we interviewed told us that such press briefing was entirely reasonable in that ministers needed to float new policy ideas in the media to gauge reactions, but also needed to be able to deny the idea was a serious one if the reaction was negative. However, such an approach inevitably made departmental press offices look flat-footed and uninformed.

Added to this was a view from the new Government that existing press officers were bound to be emotionally tied to the outgoing Conservative Government, which had been in power for the last 18 years. Therefore, there was an assumption that officials would not be sympathetic to what the new Government was trying to do. One former press officer told us:

> Generally in 1997, the new Government were distrustful of the civil service. We were seen as part of the defeated enemy. And the media advisers were used to having enormous access to power in the shadow cabinet. It was clear that the new ministers wanted that access to continue and it was up to Whitehall to fit in with that.

This assumption about long-serving officials having a Conservative bias was not unique to the Whitehall media officials; the new Labour Government had the same view of most Whitehall policy officials. But on the policy side, it would not have been practical for a Secretary of State with one or two special advisers to achieve results without going through officials, so the two groups had eventually to learn to work together. In contrast, on the media side, it was possible for a large part of the communications effort to bypass the departmental press office. So, in a number of cases, communications special advisers simply briefed journalists on their own with little engagement with officials.

One official told us of the atmosphere in one of the departments where relationships were at their worst:

> The [department concerned] was antagonistic from the very first day. The incoming Secretary of State was suspicious of the Department, which was a bit of a tragedy because they were delighted to have him. His media adviser came from a very narrow background in that he had been a Labour Party officer his whole life. The Secretary of State would listen only to the special adviser who despised civil servants, particularly the press office, and bullied them remorselessly. His temper was a byword. If you wanted

15 Franklin (n 10) 139.

not even to disagree but simply to express even a different point of view, you were quite likely to be sacked on the spot.

That said, it is clear that some of the Government's concerns about the limitations of the existing communications teams in Whitehall were justified. A journalist we interviewed was clear about the limited value (as he saw it) of the departmental press officers:

> As a columnist or as a BBC political correspondent, I did not make a single call to a departmental press office. To find out what was really happening about policy making, it was necessary to get to the special adviser who knew in much more depth the policy and political thinking behind the policy.

> [The truth is] you can't extract the political thinking from the policy. It is utterly perverse for each Whitehall department to have this massive press office while the minister has only about two advisers whom all the senior journalists are dependent on ... I've yet to meet a civil servant who understands the relationship between government and the press.

In the same interview, however, he also noted how the media's interest in Whitehall had changed, reflecting to some extent the fact that there were fewer specialist journalists covering politics, so more stories were written by the political correspondents:

> There is a much greater obsession with tactics and strategy. Strategy has been magnified because the media has got so much more interested in process which is so much the story now. [Because they are focused on such an angle] special advisers have become more central to ministers and to journalists.

In broad terms, therefore, the breakdown in communications between Government press offices and special advisers was a reflection of the fact that the two sides were in practice pursuing rather different objectives. The GICS members continued to see their role as primarily to convey information and to explain what the Government was seeking to achieve, whereas the special advisers were seeking to influence how positively the media would report the story and whether it would show the Government in a good light.

In principle, of course, these two functions are compatible and do not need to conflict. In our various interviews, it was said repeatedly that Alastair Campbell himself well understood the dividing line between what officials could reasonably be asked to and what was only appropriate for political appointees. Thus, his focus was primarily on ensuring that departmental press teams were proactive, professional and energetic in promoting what the Government was doing. But his approach was nonetheless undermined by three factors.

First, Campbell had set a tone which, once set, was difficult to turn round. An impression had been created that few if any of the departmental press teams were competent. Many of the more senior press heads had departed, with a significant loss of expertise. Campbell's own relationship with the media had also become fractious and argumentative, making it difficult for him to get good press for what he was doing, with every argument being regarded simply as 'spin'.

Second, as already noted, individual secretaries of state and individual special advisers were rather less fair minded (or perhaps less competent) than Campbell and simply sidelined their official communications team rather than seeking to persuade them of the need to improve their performance. So several departments had long-standing and bitter disputes between the advisers and the press teams, which steadily undermined Campbell's approach.

Third, while media advisers rightly regarded it as part of their legitimate role to advance the personal image and profile of their Secretary of State, this all too easily translated into a feeling that the advancement of one career was in part best achieved by the failure of others. So the unity of purpose which had sustained Labour in its days of Opposition prior to the 1997 election was replaced by the notorious disunity between the Blair and Brown camps which followed the election victory and undermined the Labour Government for most of Blair's period at No 10.

The history of this disunity has, of course, been well documented in the numerous books and memoirs of that period and needs no repetition here.[16] But it was a war which was fought in large part through informal briefings by special advisers to the media, which was more than willing to report the tension between Blairites and Brownites. The fact that there were now at least 30 communications special advisers in Whitehall, all with strong links to favoured journalists, created the ideal conditions for journalists to get numerous stories which made great copy for them and which were intended by the advisers to advance their faction in the internal struggles within the Government.[17]

Ironically, therefore, the additional communications capacity which had been created in Whitehall through the appointment of so many media special advisers ended up at times creating an impression of government disunity rather than successfully promoting the Government's achievements. To a degree, it could be argued that this was displacement activity, in that the Conservative Opposition at the time was too preoccupied with its own inquest into its loss of office to be able to put real pressure on the new Labour Government, so the media found internal dissent within that Government a much more relevant and interesting story. The Alastair Campbell diaries reflect the daily frustrations he felt that so many stories were appearing in the media which were aimed at stoking the fires of internal Labour Party politics—a frustration that increased because, despite his efforts, he seemed to be able to do little to prevent it from happening.

---

[16] See, for example, A Rawnsley, *Servants of the People: The Inside Story of New Labour* (Hamish Hamilton 2000); A Rawnsley, *The End of the Party* (Viking 2010); L Price, *The Spin Doctor's Diary: Inside Number 10 with New Labour* (Hodder & Stoughton 2005); Price (n 2); A Darling, *Back from the Brink: 1000 Days at Number 11* (Atlantic Books 2012); McBride (n 2).

[17] Damian McBride's memoir, *Power Trip*, published in 2013 (see n 2) made it graphically clear that, at least at the time, he regarded negative briefing on possible rivals to Gordon Brown in the 2007 Labour leadership campaign as entirely legitimate, even unexceptional.

One official described the atmosphere at the time to us as follows:

> Special advisers became entrenched as the chief media advisers, if not the people doing the functional stuff, almost everywhere. Journalists quickly learned to go to officials for the formal line to take but to the special advisers for the truth. And special advisers were much more likely to trade information: 'I'll tell you a secret if you slant your story in a particular way.' They would then trawl the department for secrets and were likely to come up with amusing quotes about the deficiencies of colleagues.

It would be a mistake to suggest that the result of Campbell's approach was wholly anarchic, and there is little doubt that some departmental press officers and special advisers worked together perfectly well. Departmental press offices also continued to deal with the endless stream of routine press releases and information campaigns with little attention from the media advisers.

However, the number of *causes célèbres*—Charlie Whelan, Jo Moore,[18] Martin Sixsmith[19] and so on—continued to grow. As a result, a review was established in 2003 under the chairmanship of Sir Robert Phillis effectively to go over the same ground as had previously been covered in the Mountfield Report. The subsequent report[20] was open about the difficulties that had been encountered, while acknowledging that the GICS needed further evolution and greater responsiveness.

Slowly the lessons were being learnt and matters gradually improved. There was a greater willingness by press officers to accept that they had to widen their traditional role and become more engaged with promoting the Government, and the increased scrutiny of the activities of special advisers—combined with the development of the special advisers' code—led to a reduction in the number of problem cases. Campbell himself departed from No 10 in 2003 to be replaced by David Hill, still a long-term Labour supporter, but someone who was much less divisive. The former Conservative special adviser Howell James returned to Government as Permanent Secretary for Government Communications and restored calm in place of the earlier febrile atmosphere.

The disputes between Blairites and Brownites continued, however, until Brown eventually succeed Blair in 2007. A final scandal then emerged in 2009 when Damian McBride, one of Brown's special advisers at No 10, was discovered seeking to fabricate false rumours about Conservative backbenchers.[21] But, by and large,

---

[18] Discussed in detail in ch 7.

[19] Sixsmith was Head of Communications at Stephen Byers' department and was thus an official rather than a special adviser. But, as he had been brought into Government after leaving the BBC and was not a career civil servant, the distinction was never that clear, not least because a number of new appointments were made to departmental press offices in this period of people with journalistic backgrounds and who were often portrayed as Labour-sympathising spin doctors.

[20] Communications Review Group, *An Independent Review of Government Communications* (2004). This was often known as 'the Phillis Report'.

[21] Melissa Kite, 'Gordon Brown Aide Damian McBride Resigns over "Smear Campaign" Emails' *Daily Telegraph* (11 April 2009).

the second half of the Labour Government was quieter in terms of disputes than the first few years.

Inevitably, views on whether the Campbell revolution was justified differed. A former Conservative Cabinet minister from the Major Government was clear in his view:

> The appointment of Alastair Campbell has done the reputation of the body politic no good whatsoever. Putting someone who is in effect a politician in that role is simply wrong. You suspect he is going to lie. I know that is an overstatement. But you can expect a civil servant to respect the truth and know where the boundaries are, whereas a party apparatchik will simply try and present everything to his party's short-term advantage.

That politician also cast doubt on the functional effectiveness of the increased focus on media management, commenting:

> The truth is that governments are always unpopular, especially in mid-term. But we now have the great growth in media advisers. If the object is to make the Government more popular, I don't think that it has achieved its objectives. What is the evidence to show it has made a difference? The fact is they spend a lot of time on press manipulation and it makes absolutely no difference.

But a journalist put the contrary view:

> The best special advisers—and I accept the quality varies—give their secretaries of state policy advice with political awareness of the dangers and opportunities; and then go on to give journalists an insight into that thinking in ways which civil servants cannot. That is where they add value.

Our own view of the New Labour period is mixed. The 13-year Governments of Blair and Brown coincided with the explosion in media outlets and the expectation that news stories needed to be generated on a daily basis—and if the Government did not supply such news stories, then the media would generate them and the Government would be forever on the back foot.[22] Therefore, a more proactive agenda was both necessary and justified.

However, Campbell's approach changed the boundaries round what a government could and could not legitimately do in presenting its case. Our interviews with officials suggested that, having drawn a new line, Campbell himself largely kept within it, though the lead-up to the Iraq War caused many to doubt that. But other special advisers crossed the new line and used their access to the media to over-sell the message, and in doing so to fight internal Labour Party wars. Because Labour at that point was so factionalised, Campbell was unable to control such behaviour. The Labour Party is still suffering from the scars of that period, as the reaction to the publication of Damian McBride's memoirs in September 2013

---

[22] See generally J Curran and J Seaton, *Power without Responsibility: Press, Broadcasting and the Internet in Britain* (7th edn, Routledge 2009).

demonstrated.[23] Public confidence in the accuracy of what politicians—and even government departments—tell them has far from recovered.

New Labour's media strategy as run by so many media advisers was intended as an essential component of a branded and marketed political package—and one in which the Government deliberately took the offensive rather than waiting for criticism and responding to it. But it was subject to diminishing returns and was arguably counterproductive for the government by the end. In June 2007, shortly before he retired as Prime Minister, Tony Blair complained that the political media culture had created 'damage [that] saps the country's confidence and self-belief; it undermines its assessment of itself, its institutions; and above all, it reduces our capacity to take the right decisions, in the right spirit for our future'.[24] But while admitting that his government had spent 'an inordinate amount of time wooing the media' at the beginning, he accepted no blame for himself or his special advisers. The blame of course could never be laid solely at the hands of advisers because it is ultimately ministers who appoint them and who must if necessary constrain their activities. Even if, as McBride claimed, Gordon Brown did not know of his precise activities, it is hard to justify ministers giving their advisers such free rein.

IV. MEDIA ADVISERS AND THE COALITION

A new challenge came with the election of the Coalition, a type of government of which no Whitehall officials had previous experience.[25]

The Coalition's initial position on special advisers was essentially to keep the status quo, except in numbers. The incoming Prime Minister made clear that he was going to restrict the number of advisers overall and that they were to behave well in future, with a clear message that briefing by advisers against each other (or their ministers) would not be tolerated. But in practical terms, there was no fresh attempt to redefine what media special advisers should be doing.

That said, the incoming Government brought additional travails for the departmental communication teams. In particular, Francis Maude, effectively the minister for civil service reform and government efficiency, made clear that he regarded most of the departmental expenditure on paid publicity (such as information campaigns) as ineffective, expensive and ripe for heavy cutting. This was backed up by a new review, conducted by Matt Tee, the Government's new

---

[23] N Watt, 'Ed Miliband Says He Urged Gordon Brown to sack Damian McBride' *The Guardian* (22 September 2013); and R Mason, 'Douglas Alexander Accused of "Divisive" Leak by Former Spin Doctor' *The Guardian* (22 September 2013).
[24] P Wintour, 'Blair: Media is Feral Beast Obsessed with Impact' *The Guardian* (13 June 2007), www.theguardian.com/politics/2007/jun/13/media.television.
[25] The nearest equivalent to a coalition since 1945 was the Lib-Lab pact in 1977–79. This was more than 30 years earlier and was thus an entirely different generation.

Permanent Secretary for Government Communications.[26] The departmental communication heads (who normally managed both the press office and the paid publicity teams) found themselves obliged to cut back staff and resources heavily on that latter side of their activity—the side that had generally been least affected by the Labour incursion into traditional press office territory.

On the press side, the first couple of years of the Coalition saw quite harmonious relations between the media advisers and the press teams. Indeed, as made clear in an earlier book on the Coalition,[27] the first two years of the Coalition saw something of a resurgence in conventional government disciplines and outbreaks of bad behaviour were relatively few. There was also some recognition that the Coalition Government required both parties to do reasonably well—and the Conservatives, for example, noticeably avoided seeking to exploit the Liberal Democrats' difficulties over tuition fees.

That said, there were various allegations in the press about 'bad mouthing' by advisers of public officials, with the advisers at both the Department for Communities and Local Government and the Department for Education being accused. These allegations were denied at the time and no 'smoking guns' were ever identified, though the same issues resurfaced at the Education Department when it was alleged that special advisers were using a Twitter account @toryeducation to denigrate opponents of their agenda, something which was not formally confirmed or denied.[28]

In parallel, the No 10 press operation was going through its own travails. The appointment of Andy Coulson, a former tabloid news editor, as the Prime Minister's Head of Communications was forecast by numerous commentators to be likely to end in embarrassment and duly did so, though essentially for reasons of Coulson's previous behaviour as a newspaper editor rather than on account of his performance at No 10.[29] He was succeeded by Craig Oliver, but the general impression was that the No 10 operation had become less effective since the days of Campbell, rather as Cameron's No 10 was seen by policy officials as rather weak compared to its predecessors, even though perhaps more harmonious.

However, the key distinguishing feature of the Coalition Government press operation was that it had overtly to operate as a coalition. In the first 18 months, this was relatively straightforward as both of the Coalition partners had a vested interest in demonstrating that the Coalition could be made to work harmoniously. The Conservatives were particularly keen to emphasise the benefits of their

---

[26] Cabinet Office, 'Review of Government Direct Communication and COI' (18 March 2011), https://www.gov.uk/government/news/review-of-government-direct-communication-and-coi. This was informally known as 'the Tee Report'.

[27] R Hazell and B Yong, *The Politics of Coalition: How the Conservative-Liberal Democrat Government Works* (Hart Publishing 2012).

[28] J Doward, 'Michael Gove Advisers Face Claims of Smear Tactics Against Foes' *The Observer* (2 February 2013).

[29] 'Andy Coulson Resigns: As it Happened' *The Guardian* (21 January 2011).

decision to go for a full-blown Coalition rather than a minority government, and the Liberal Democrats needed to demonstrate that the Coalition Government could be a strong and united government.

Even the media, in its constant struggle to identify and promote stories of Whitehall conflict, found it difficult initially to identify major rifts. And it was often remarked that the key battles within government which it did identify were the traditional ones between the Treasury and spending departments—which were as likely to be 'blue on blue' arguments as 'blue on yellow' (ie, battles between Conservative ministers rather than between Conservatives and Liberal Democrats).

That said, the honeymoon period was never likely to last—and did not. The 'no change' outcome of the referendum on the voting system was accompanied by bitter attacks by the Liberal Democrats on what they considered to be the underhand tactics of some Conservative ministers. As some of the fault lines between the two parties widened—notably on Europe, the proposed reforms to the National Health Service and constitutional reform—the honeymoon evolved into something much more closely resembling a marriage of convenience. Moreover, the closer the parties got to the 2015 election, the more they moved from wanting to demonstrate the togetherness of the Coalition towards demonstrating the distinctiveness of the two parties.

In the words of a Liberal Democrat special adviser:

> It is the job of all media advisers to put announcements within the framework of the Government's overall approach. But within a Coalition I need to make sure I get the Lib Dem perspective across on any given announcement, just as I know the Tories' advisers will be doing from their perspective. It isn't often going to be possible to give a single account because in a Coalition there will always be two points of view and a compromise. And the closer to an election, we will want to focus more on the differences than the similarities.

And one less happy feature of the Coalition was the growth of negative stories coming from the Government about the civil service. One former senior Government press officer commented:

> The stubborn failure to stimulate growth and all that goes with it is very difficult for the political guys. The tension now is that we are beyond the mid-term and the Government is in a difficult position—lack of growth—the comms are very difficult so now the civil servants are being blamed for not being very good. The political people are saying, the civil servants are rubbish and it's their fault our message isn't getting through.

V. SOME CONCLUDING REMARKS

A key theme in our research was to discover how effective advisers are in their role, but measuring the effectiveness of media advisers is not straightforward.

Part of the difficulty in assessing their effectiveness is that there are four potential judges, with conflicting criteria:

—   The Secretary of State, whose key criterion will be first and foremost the impact of the media adviser on their personal media profile and image. They will expect their special adviser to make them look competent and forward thinking. They may well want their adviser to use briefing of the press to enable them to win internal Whitehall battles—for example, the numerous stories that appear about ministers fighting off impossible Treasury demands for cuts during spending rounds. Provided a media adviser is promoting the interests of the Secretary of State, other concerns will be second order. Both Gordon Brown, in respect of first Charlie Whelan and then Damian McBride, and Stephen Byers in respect of Jo Moore, were clearly satisfied with their advisers until forced to accept they had gone too far.

—   No 10, whose focus will usually be on whether the government as a whole is getting its message across. No 10 will positively not want to see individual ministers fighting battles with each other in the press. Indeed, Prime Ministers normally prefer the profile of individual members of the Cabinet to be roughly equivalent—and well below their own profile.

—   Departments, which will generally want media stories to be balanced—and without surprises. They will generally not be enthusiastic about kites being flown in the press by media advisers on an unattributable basis, even more so if they are not aware that it is going to be happening. Departments may well be uncomfortable about the benefits of policies being over-sold.

—   Journalists, who will invariably be looking for good stories which will usually mean being given some form of private scoop—for example, 24 hours' prior notice of what might be in a future announcement—or being given some inside gossip about who is up and who is down in Cabinet infighting. Journalists will play to the vanity of advisers by encouraging them to see their role as providing good stories.

In practice, most media special advisers would like to be well regarded by all four of these stakeholders, but most will acknowledge that the secretary of state who employs them is first in the list. As we have seen, however, some of the most difficult examples of advisers' behaviour have occurred where they have been promoting their secretary of state at the expense of others.

Turning to the effectiveness of media advisers as a group, there will never be complete agreement on their value. Some politicians and commentators will always look back to a perceived golden age when ministers paid little attention to the media and made decisions on merit without fear or favour of how they might be reported. Others will argue that politics is about battles not only between ideas and policies, but between individuals desperate to gain and retain public office, so any means of winning those battles is legitimate if it secures that objective.

In the same way, some will regard the explosion in media outlets over the last 20 years, and the constant demand for immediate new and juicy stories, however trivial, as a curse. Others will accept and embrace the pressures of the media, and will see it as providing numerous opportunities to get their message across to as a high a percentage of voters as possible—recognising in particular that most voters no longer hear the candidates and debates in person.

So media special advisers do seem to have found their place within this world. The Campbell revolution described above was a game changer in bringing about a new mindset in Whitehall about the need for and value of proactive communications. Having significant numbers of advisers whose focus is not only on explanation but also on persuasion and advocacy has provided the capacity for that to be pursued without obliging civil servants to compromise their focus on hard facts and straightforward justification for developing government policies.

It is clear in that sense that the revolution has succeeded and will not be reversed. Ministers will still want support—and the dedicated resource provided by media advisers—to cover the still-burgeoning number of media outlets. And politicians will continue to want to use the media to get their arguments—and their personal profile—across to the voters.

But, like most revolutions, the Labour media revolution was not bloodless and had its casualties. The official departmental communications and press office teams have felt themselves under sustained attack for more than a decade. As one of our interviewees speaking of life under the Coalition put it:

> Morale amongst comms staff is very poor. They are usually a pretty uncomplaining lot. But there have been huge job losses. The mantra of 'more for less' combined with poor promotion prospects doesn't help. Worse is the general feeling that the war against them will never end. It's not now (as it was in 97) of having to prove yourselves to a sceptical new master, it's the feeling that without a clear idea of what to replace it with, the Government would like everyone to leave.

Moreover, this is not just a question of the morale of government communications teams. The focus on better, more persuasive and more rapid communications is entirely understandable and justifiable. But, however much politicians choose to blame the media for distorting their message, they must also share responsibility for an aggressive attitude towards the media which often puts surface gloss before substance. When Alastair Campbell created additional capacity in the system to present the Government's arguments aggressively, he also inadvertently created the capacity to wage internal arguments through the media. He thus created the conditions which in due course would lead to the resignation of a special adviser for suggesting fabricating stories to discredit opposition politicians, surely a low-water mark in any account of political warfare in the last 30 years.

The fact that such abuses have been identified and publicised is itself a positive. And since the low-water mark established five years ago, the tide has perhaps come back in to provide a better balance. But it is hard to be confident that the tide will not reverse again so long as politics remains a competitive business between individuals just as much as between parties.

7

The Regulation, Accountabilities and Responsibilities of Special Advisers

BEN YONG

> In theory ministers are in charge of disciplining and the like, and that means that
> nobody is in charge. Ministers don't do it, they don't like doing it. I've had per-
> sonal experience of there being complaints to me about special advisers, where
> I've gone to the minister concerned and said: 'This is a problem. This special
> adviser's not behaving properly and not treating people in a way that we would
> expect civil servants to treat people.' The minister has said: 'That's very tough;
> can you sort it out, please?' (Former Cabinet Secretary)

INTRODUCTION

IN HIS BOOK *Power Trip*, Damian McBride describes how in 2005 he used
leaks against Charles Clarke, then Home Secretary and an opponent of
Gordon Brown's succession to the premiership:

> I orchestrated what looked like a briefing war between Charles and Tony Blair's anti-
> social behaviour guru, Louise Casey; each of them in turn appearing to goad the other by
> making some new announcement ... or appearing to claim advance credit for something
> the other was planning to announce ... There was already plenty of ill-feeling between
> them, but the Sunday briefings made it both public and self-fulfilling, contributing to
> Tony Blair's sacking of Charles in May 2006 ...
>
> And did [the] ends justify the means? Well, Charles Clarke and others would disagree,
> but they weren't my concern. Keeping Gordon [Brown] in No 11 and getting him into
> No 10 was my job, from where—in my mind—he could do what was best for Labour
> and the country.[1]

McBride's comments are a visceral reminder of the world of politics and raw
ambition within which special advisers and ministers work. Special advisers are

---

[1] Damian McBride, *Power Trip: A Decade of Policy, Plots and Spin* (Biteback 2013) 192–93. Note
that this set of events appears to have taken place after McBride shifted from being a civil servant to
becoming a special adviser.

civil servants, but of an odd sort: they are not appointed by open competition, but rather personally by ministers, and their tenure is limited to that of their ministers or to the day following a general election. So they are in practice very much temporary civil servants. However, unlike other civil servants, they are entitled to operate with party-partisan sympathies to support their minister, and in this respect the measure of their effective support for ministers is political. In pursuit of their goals, ministers and their special advisers may push at the boundaries of what is deemed acceptable within government. Over time, explicit frameworks have been put in place to make clear what these boundaries are. The history of special advisers is, in part, a history of the grafting of expectations onto an office with deliberately fluid requirements.

In this chapter, we ask within what frameworks special advisers are required to operate and the extent to which these frameworks are realistic or effective. We remind ourselves of the constitutional context in which special advisers work and then examine questions of loyalty, discipline and the cap on numbers. We then shift from accountability to a matter of responsibility, asking who is responsible for the induction, training and performance evaluation of special advisers.

I. SPECIAL ADVISERS: A DISCIPLINARY PROBLEM?

In our interviews with various Westminster and Whitehall actors, most stressed that there had rarely been disciplinary issues concerning special advisers or conflicts between special advisers and civil servants.[2] Nevertheless, the nature of the party-political battle in which they are engaged and the typical temperament of the politically committed mean that the temptation for special advisers to stretch a point is often present. There have been at least 26 public allegations of misconduct by special advisers between 1997 and 2013.[3] These ranged from bullying to briefing against individuals.[4] Three well-known cases are those of Jo Moore and Damian McBride under Labour, and Adam Smith under the Coalition.

Briefly, Damian McBride was an official-turned-special adviser who was accused of planning to smear Opposition politicians by disseminating rumours about their private lives and Adam Smith was accused of having too close a relationship with Rupert Murdoch's media company NewsCorp at a time when his minister, Jeremy Hunt (Secretary of State for Culture, Media and Sport) was

[2] See the LSE GV314 Group, 'New Life at the Top: Special Advisers in British Government' (2012) 65 *Parliamentary Affairs* 715.
[3] See Daniella Lock, 'Special Advisers and Public Allegations of Misconduct 1997–2013' (The Constitution Unit, 2013), www.ucl.ac.uk/constitution-unit/research/special-advisers/special_advisers_and_public_allegations_of_misconduct_1997_-_2013.pdf.
[4] See, for instance, James Cusick, '"Dump F***ing Everyone": The Inside Story of How Michael Gove's Vicious Attack Dogs are Terrorising the DfE' *The Independent* (15 February 2013).

acting in a quasi-judicial capacity in determining whether or not NewsCorp should be able to take over the broadcasting company BSkyB.[5]

The case of Jo Moore may be exceptional, but it illustrates the importance of personal relationships and of being aware of the boundaries between civil servants and special advisers. It also illustrates the latent ambiguities of the special adviser role and of the responsibilities of key actors for special advisers. The case is therefore set out in more detail below.

Jo Moore was one of two special advisers to Stephen Byers, the Secretary of State for Transport, Local Government and the Regions (DTLR). She was 36 when first appointed as a special adviser and was relatively experienced in media handling. She had been Labour's Head of Press for four years (1993–97) and had worked at a lobbying firm for two (1997–98) before being appointed by Byers as a special adviser in the Department for Trade and Industry (DTI) in 1999. Byers was a Blairite minister who had previously been Chief Secretary to the Treasury (1998) and Secretary of State for Trade and Industry (1998–2001). Following the 2001 general election, he was appointed to DTLR.

As a special adviser, Moore was primarily concerned with media relations. There were bad relations between herself and DTLR press officers, who were all civil servants. Ms Moore was alleged to have engaged in bullying behaviour and of lacking an understanding about the political impartiality of the civil service. In this context there had been a number of leaks by the latter intended to undermine Moore.

On 11 September 2001, Moore sent an email suggesting that it was 'a very good day' to 'get out anything we want to bury'. Her email was leaked by DTLR officials and by early October, it had become news. As a temporary civil servant, Moore was subject to disciplinary action by Sir Richard Mottram, Permanent Secretary of DTLR, who was responsible for the conduct of all civil servants in the department. Moore was issued with an official disciplinary warning and a personal reprimand from Byers. Mottram had discussed Moore's conduct with Byers prior to reprimanding Moore.

Mottram later stated publicly in a select committee inquiry that Moore's action was not behaviour which should result in resignation, but he also admitted that, as Moore was a personal appointment of Byers, the decision to dismiss Moore had to be a political matter, not solely one for him. Byers apparently did not want to dismiss Moore; it is unclear if No 10 also had some involvement in the decision retain her.

In October 2001 it was further reported in the press that Moore had asked DTLR press officers to brief the media against Bob Kiley, then Transport Commissioner for London. This request breached the then *Code of Conduct for Special Advisers*, which stated that special advisers could not ask officials to violate

---

[5] On Damian McBride, see McBride (n 1); on Adam Smith, see 'Adam Smith, Jeremy Hunt, and the Fall of the "Spad"' (Channel 4 News, 24 May 2012), www.channel4.com/news/adam-smith-jeremy-hunt-and-the-fall-of-the-spad.

civil service impartiality. The press officers involved refused to carry out her request. Mottram was again put in a difficult position. On the one hand, he had a special adviser whose alleged actions were clearly inappropriate and were prompting some of his department's officials to leak information to the public in order to discredit her. On the other hand, as Permanent Secretary, it was also important for him to maintain a good relationship with his Secretary of State, Stephen Byers. As a result, Mottram chose at this point to manage Moore himself rather than directly to confront Byers again.

In late November 2001, Martin Sixsmith became Director of Communications at DTLR. Sixsmith had been a BBC journalist for 17 years, but left to join the civil service in 1997 as Director of Communications in the Department for Social Security. He was aware of the troubled relationship between Moore and certain press officials in DTLR, but appeared unable to prevent matters escalating.

On 14 February 2002, there were press reports that Moore had suggested that inconvenient news on rail statistics could be announced on the day of Princess Margaret's funeral. Sixsmith (apparently) sent round an intra-departmental email blocking this. This later email was then leaked and led to the resignation of Moore on 15 February. Sixsmith left DTLR a couple of months later, his position having become untenable. In May 2002, Byers resigned as Secretary of State, having been plagued by various controversies.

The case was examined in detail in an inquiry carried out by the Public Administration Select Committee (PASC) in 2002.[6] In its report, PASC was critical of the leaks and misinformation about Moore's activities, stating they were 'a very serious breach of civil service principles',[7] and recommended, amongst other things, that the Government should review the system by which disputes were handled between ministers, special advisers and career civil servants. A later recommendation in 2003 by the Committee on Standards in Public Life led to the *Ministerial Code* being amended to make clear that ministers were personally accountable for the management and discipline of their special advisers.[8] However, as temporary civil servants, special advisers remain subject to disciplinary action by their department's permanent secretary.

II. THE CONSTITUTIONAL AND REGULATORY CONTEXT

The 'Whitehall model' discussed in chapter two remains the broad context in which special advisers are understood to operate. In this model, ministers are

---

[6] Public Administration Select Committee, *'These Unfortunate Events': Lessons of Recent Events at the Former DTLR* (2002). Much of the description of the Moore case in the text has been taken from this report.

[7] ibid 22.

[8] Committee on Standards in Public Life, *Defining the Boundaries within the Executive: Ministers, Special Advisers, and the Permanent Civil Service* (2003) 49. See the *Ministerial Code* (Cabinet Office 2010) https://www.gov.uk/government/uploads/system/uploads/attachment_data/file/61402/ministerial-code-may-2010.pdf, para 3.3.

responsible to Parliament for all that happens within their department, and career civil servants are non-partisan and responsible to ministers. It is a model whose simplicity is belied by the complexity of what it covers.

Special advisers operate within at least five different frameworks. The most important is the 2010 *Ministerial Code*.[9] This is a political framework with a long history, enforced by the Prime Minister. It was initially meant to govern procedural matters, but over time has become a code of ministerial ethics. In relation to special advisers, it reaffirms ministerial responsibility, making clear that ministers are ultimately responsible for the work and conduct of their special advisers, and that the Prime Minister has a right of veto over special advisers' appointment and continued employment. It also sets a maximum of two special advisers per Cabinet minister.

Next there is the *Code of Conduct for Special Advisers*.[10] This draws on Harold Wilson's initial specification of the roles of special advisers, set out in the 1970s, but was publicly introduced in 2001. It sets out the basic responsibilities and roles of special advisers, including guidance on their relationships with the career civil service, the media, the government party and involvement in politics (at the local and national levels). The *Model Contract for Special Advisers*[11] then sets out the basic terms and conditions of employment for special advisers and includes the *Code of Conduct for Special Advisers* in a schedule.

Special advisers are also civil servants (albeit temporary ones), and so they are subject to the *Civil Service Code*.[12] The *Code* has four key values—integrity, honesty, objectivity and impartiality—the latter two from which special advisers are exempt.

Finally, the Constitutional Reform and Governance Act 2010 (CRAG) put the status of both the civil service and special advisers on a statutory basis. There are requirements that a Code of Conduct be published and that a report on special advisers be laid before Parliament annually. In short, with the enactment of CRAG, special advisers were finally recognised as an institution of British government.

The multiplicity of frameworks reflects the fact that, as set out in chapter two, special advisers were an ad hoc incremental experiment inserted into the Whitehall machinery which has slowly become institutionalised over time. Special advisers were inserted into most of these frameworks, or aspects of them, in response to various events or controversies involving special advisers, or pressure from the media, PASC and the Committee on Standards in Public Life.[13]

---

[9] *Ministerial Code* (n 8).

[10] *Code of Conduct for Special Advisers* (Cabinet Office 2010), https://www.gov.uk/government/uploads/system/uploads/attachment_data/file/62451/special-advisers-code-of-conduct.pdf.

[11] *Model Contract for Special Advisers* (Cabinet Office 2010), https://www.gov.uk/government/uploads/system/uploads/attachment_data/file/62452/special-advisers-model-contract_0.pdf.

[12] *Civil Service Code* (Civil Service 2010), http://resources.civilservice.gov.uk/wp-content/uploads/2011/09/civil-service-code-2010.pdf.

[13] For more information, see House of Commons Library, 'Special Advisers' (House of Commons Library 2013).

The sum effect of the frameworks, however, is to create a set of constraints around special advisers: they are defined more by what they are not and what they cannot do than by what they are and what they can do. So, for instance, they are exempted from the *Civil Service Code* in relation to objectivity and impartiality. The *Code of Conduct for Special Advisers* sets out that they are expected to observe the central values of the civil service, but they have no line management powers over other civil servants and no power to authorise expenditure. The *Ministerial Code* sets out limits to numbers. The broad impression is that special advisers are anomalous, represent a potential danger to the existing system and must be contained.

III. ACCOUNTABILITY: THEORY AND PRACTICE

Who is responsible for special advisers and their work? The starting point is the constitutional convention of ministerial responsibility. Ministers are responsible to Parliament for the work of their department, which includes the work and conduct of their special advisers. This is recognised in the 2010 *Ministerial Code*, which reads:

> The responsibility for the management and conduct of special advisers, including discipline, rests with the Minister who made the appointment. Individual Ministers will be accountable to the Prime Minister, Parliament and the public for their actions and decisions in respect of their special advisers. It is, of course, also open to the Prime Minister to terminate employment by withdrawing his consent to an individual appointment.[14]

It was useful to formalise this principle. A minister personally appoints a special adviser and determines what they will and will not do. But that is not the end of the matter. As one former Cabinet Secretary we interviewed said:

> In theory ministers are in charge of disciplining and the like, and that means that nobody is in charge. Ministers don't do it, they don't like doing it. I've had personal experience of there being complaints to me about special advisers, where I've gone to the minister concerned and said: 'This is a problem. This special adviser is not behaving properly and not treating people in a way that we would expect civil servants to treat people.' The minister has said: 'That's very tough; can you sort it out, please?'

> It's not part of their training to give feedback and to manage people, so ministers have turned out to be pretty hopeless at this process. Indeed, I have therefore stood in when the situation has got bad and had words with special advisers to say: 'This can't go on; you can't carry on like this.' Really there's no backing to me doing that. I have no legal force; I'm just doing it on the grounds of I think it's the right thing to do. Because there's no backing to it, it has limited effectiveness.

---

[14] *Ministerial Code* (n 8) para 3.3.

Most ministers are not skilled managers and many are unable to exercise a management role because of demands on their time. Some ministers are also unwilling to step in because their advisers are only doing what their minister wants them to do. Moreover, the key regulatory frameworks with most immediate relevance to special advisers—the *Code of Conduct* and the *Model Contract*—are not set by ministers themselves, but are non-specific to any one government. Therefore, ministers will rarely be familiar with the key frameworks governing the work of special advisers. And, of course, some special advisers may lack the time, experience or inclination to be concerned about the boundaries that should be maintained between their role and that of civil servants. The result is that it is civil servants who are left to ensure that special advisers are aware of these frameworks, and in some cases to 'police' the work of special advisers.

However, certain civil servants have formal responsibilities over special advisers: in particular, it is the Permanent Secretary who investigates and makes recommendations to the minister where concerns about special adviser misconduct have been raised.[15] This follows from the status of special advisers as temporary civil servants. The *Model Contract for Special Advisers* makes it clear that misconduct within a department is dealt with in accordance with the department's disciplinary procedures—for which the Permanent Secretary is ultimately responsible.[16] Similarly, the *Code of Conduct for Special Advisers* states that, where career officials have concerns about special advisers' requests, they can raise this with their line manager, the special adviser concerned, the Minister's Principal Private Secretary or the Permanent Secretary.[17]

This line of responsibility can put the Permanent Secretary in a difficult position. On the one hand, permanent secretaries are expected to maintain a good working relationship with their minister, but on the other hand, they may be expected to answer before parliamentary select committees questions about special advisers in their department, when this is more appropriately the responsibility of a minister. An example of this occurred in 2012, when Jonathan Stephens, then Permanent Secretary of the Department of Culture, Media and Sport (DCMS), was asked repeatedly by the Public Accounts Committee about Adam Smith, special adviser of Jeremy Hunt, and his role in the sale of BSkyB to NewsCorp.[18] But the basic principle remains: once a permanent secretary has investigated an allegation, it is then for the minister to take action in the light of that.

We have considered who is responsible for the work and conduct of special advisers, but what about the responsibilities of special advisers? Special advisers are one of the very few personal appointments that ministers make upon entering

---

[15] See House of Commons Library (n 13) and *The Government's Response to the Ninth Report of the Committee on Standards in Public Life* (2003).

[16] *Model Contract for Special Advisers* (n 11) para 16.a.

[17] *Code of Conduct for Special Advisers* (n 10) para 8.

[18] 'Permanent Secretary "Stonewalls" MPs over Jeremy Hunt' (*BBC News*, 26 April 2012), www.bbc.co.uk/news/uk-politics-17858198. The transcript can be found here: www.publications.parliament.uk/pa/cm201012/cmselect/cmpubacc/c1947i/1947i.htm.

government, and so in practice the primary loyalty of a special adviser is to his or her minister. However, both as members of political parties and also as civil servants, they also have a duty to 'the Government' as a whole. One small change that David Cameron made to the *Ministerial Code* in 2010 was to a provision on special advisers: 'All special advisers must uphold their responsibility to the Government as a whole, not just their appointing Minister.'[19] That was no doubt to address potential issues arising from being in a coalition, but the tension between serving the minister and serving the government is built into the Whitehall model. The New Labour years are thick with stories of special advisers briefing against other ministers,[20] but this had happened under earlier governments as well.[21] Indeed, the primary loyalty of special advisers to their minister has historically impeded the effectiveness of special advisers to work as a network across government.[22]

We have already seen the views of Damian McBride, and one former permanent secretary was blunt: '[Special advisers] are defenders of their minister that brought them in. They do all they can to bolster their minister; they don't really have allegiance to the Government.' Most special advisers we interviewed finessed the point: to serve the minister was to serve the government, playing down the possibility of conflict. Here is Michael Jacobs, a special adviser to Gordon Brown:

> [S]pecial advisers should have the same relationship with their ministers and the Government as a whole as ministers have, which is that ministers are semi-independent. That is, that they are pursuing the interests of their Department, as they define them, and to some extent themselves, but they are also responsible to and working for the government as a whole. That is a tension of which all ministers will be aware, because ministers are powerful political individuals in their own right and special advisers are the sub-units of ministers. They are not independent figures in their own right; they belong to the ministers and they are appointed by ministers.[23]

This tension occasionally came up implicitly in discussions of effectiveness: a poor special adviser was a poor 'team player'. A former Labour special adviser commented:

> [T]he effective special advisers were the ones that you felt were part of a broader special adviser team, and even though there would be disagreements on things ... there was no problem with dealing with them and ... therefore, it was easy to communicate.

---

[19] *Ministerial Code* (n 8) para 3.3.

[20] See Lance Price, *The Spin Doctor's Diary: Inside Number 10 with New Labour* (Hodder & Stoughton 2005); Andrew Rawnsley, *The End of the Party* (Viking 2010); and McBride (n 1).

[21] Blick gives the example of John Harris, who served Labour ministers between 1964 and 1970: Andrew Blick, *People Who Live in the Dark* (Politico's 2004) 110–17.

[22] Rodney Lowe, *The Official History of the British Civil Service: Reforming the Civil Service, Volume I: The Fulton Years, 1966–81* (Routledge 2011) 223.

[23] Public Administration Select Committee, *Special Advisers in the Thick of it* (2001) 29–30.

A former Coalition special adviser made the same point in answering questions about ineffective special advisers:

> Well, special advisers who wouldn't communicate with other special advisers. Who would work in that rather bunker-like mentality, just with their minister. That would be very unhelpful to the teamwork, and it would be quite destructive. Because they would be operating entirely independently of the overall picture.

But the question of loyalty applied equally to those in the Centre as to those in departments, because what was in 'the Government's' best interests was at best ambiguous. One former Coalition special adviser said:

> The other thing that really irritated me were special advisers in Number 10, particularly, or the Treasury, who had no understanding whatsoever of the policy, or the detail, and were trying to impose a particular political solution to a problem that would create other difficulties down the line. They were usually within the orders of their political masters, but operating in a completely evidence-free zone and saying, 'We've got to do this policy, we've got to that thing', and never mind how much it costs, or whether it's effective.

The *Ministerial Code* states that the Prime Minister can terminate employment by withdrawing consent to an individual appointment.[24] We are not aware from interviews that this power has ever been exercised in relation to an incumbent special adviser.[25] However, it is clear that Cabinet Secretaries have been involved in dealing with special advisers accused of misconduct as 'emissaries' of the Prime Minister. Prime Ministers are also seen as a means by which special advisers can be held accountable—for instance, in 2011, David Cameron was asked by the then Cabinet Secretary Sir Gus O'Donnell to restrain special advisers in the Department for Communities and Local Government (DCLG) who had briefed against Jenny Watson, Chair of the Electoral Commission.[26]

This tension between loyalty to the minister and loyalty to government is inevitable and cannot be resolved. The tension between the Centre and departments, and between the Prime Minister and Cabinet is a product of the structure of Whitehall itself. It is a key reason why historically Prime Ministers have been wary of increasing special adviser numbers, particularly in the departments.

Finally, it is worth noting that special advisers have rarely appeared before Parliament. In terms of accountability, it is the minister, and not his or her special adviser, who is accountable to Parliament.[27] Although career civil servants appear

---

[24] *Ministerial Code* (n 8) para 3.3.

[25] Damian McBride may be an exception.

[26] See David Singleton, 'David Cameron Rebuked by Gus O'Donnell over Special Advisers' *PR Week* (3 March 2011), http://www.prweek.com/news/1058054.

[27] Note that in 2005, the Osmotherly Rules, which regulate the appearance and conduct of career civil servants before select committees, were revised to include special advisers—in effect recognising that the Government, rather than Parliament, would determine who would appear before a select committee: see Cabinet Office, *Departmental Evidence and Response to Select Committees* (2005), https://www.gov.uk/government/uploads/system/uploads/attachment_data/file/61192/guide-deptal-evidence-and-response-to-select-committees.pdf, para 44.

regularly before select committees, there have been few occasions when incumbent special advisers have done so.[28] Alastair Campbell, for instance, appeared before the Foreign Affairs Select Committee to discuss his role in the decision to go to war in Iraq.[29] But this was the exception to the rule, with most attempts to invite incumbent special advisers being rejected by governments.[30] In spite of this, select committees, and in particular PASC, have been instrumental in persistently drawing attention to special adviser numbers, conduct and utility.

IV. POLICING THE BOUNDARIES BETWEEN SPECIAL ADVISERS AND CAREER CIVIL SERVANTS: POLITICISATION AND THE CAP

In the Whitehall model, the presence of special advisers raises fears of 'politicisation'. But what does this mean? 'Politicisation', Professor Scott Greer states, 'rivals "presidentialism" and "modernisation" among the most useless words in the study of British government.'[31] However, we venture to define it as it is commonly understood. We should recall first that the career civil service is meant to be 'politically impartial': this means being appointed by open competition and promoted on merit rather than personally appointed and 'giving one's cooperation and best independent judgment of the issues to partisan bosses—and of being sufficiently uncommitted to be able to do so for a succession of partisan leaders'.[32] In this context, politicisation has at least two meanings: politicisation as participation in political decision making; and politicisation as partisan control over the bureaucracy.[33]

The first refers to career officials becoming too closely identified with a particular politician or agenda: classic examples of this would be the civil servants Charles Powell and Bernard Ingham, who became closely identified with Margaret Thatcher and her policies. Politicisation as partisan control over the bureaucracy means 'the substitution of political criteria in the selection, retention, promotion, rewards and disciplining of members of the public service'.[34] More crudely, this may mean patronage or, more subtly, 'appointing people with well-known partisan connections or who are unlikely to be acceptable to a future

---

[28] See, for example, Committee on Standards and Privileges, *Premature Disclosure of Reports of the Foreign Affairs Committee* (1999), before which Andrew Hood appeared.

[29] Foreign Affairs Committee, *The Decision to Go to War in Iraq* (2003).

[30] See, for instance, Public Administration Select Committee, *The Attendance of the Prime Minister's Strategy Adviser before the Public Administration Select Committee.*

[31] Scott L Greer, 'Whitehall' in Robert Hazell (ed), *Constitutional Futures Revisited: Britain's Constitution to 2020* (Palgrave Macmillan 2008) 126.

[32] Hugh Heclo, 'OMB and the Presidency: The Problem of Neutral Competence' [1975] *The Public Interest* 80, 81–82.

[33] Luc Rouban, 'Politicization of the Civil Service in France: From Structural to Strategic Politicization' in B Guy Peters and Jon Pierre (eds), *Politicization of the Civil Service in Comparative Perspective: The Quest for Control* (Routledge 2004).

[34] Peters and Pierre (n 33) 2.

alternative government' or appointing those 'with well-known commitments to particular policy directions that may render them unacceptable to a future alternative government'.[35]

Special advisers, because of the nature of their appointment and their partisan functions, are often thought to indicate 'politicisation' in both senses. But the *Code of Conduct for Special Advisers* suggests the opposite: special advisers protect the civil service from the 'taint' of politicisation—that is, too close an involvement with ministers and their political ends:

> The employment of special advisers adds a political dimension to the advice and assistance available to ministers while reinforcing the political impartiality of the permanent Civil Service by distinguishing the source of political advice and support.[36]

It is worth noting that all Western democracies have some degree of politicisation—appointment by political criteria rather than by merit alone—in their bureaucracies.[37] As we shall see in chapter eight, UK ministers are allowed to personally appoint very few staff in comparison to other Westminster systems, let alone continental systems.[38] And as former Cabinet Secretary Lord Wilson noted, the total number of special advisers at any one time (between 70 and 100) is small compared with the 4,000-odd members of the Senior Civil Service.[39] Special advisers may have influence over ministers and the direction of policy, but this needs to be understood in context.

However, because of their ambiguous status and their potential to affect the career civil service, special advisers have been subject to intense scrutiny and efforts to ensure that the boundaries between them and civil servants are clear. So, for instance, very few special advisers have been able to become civil servants, and vice versa.[40]

Similarly, the *Code of Conduct for Special Advisers* is very specific on the appropriate relationship between special advisers and career officials. One key means to ensure that further 'politicisation' does not take place has been parliamentary

---

[35] Richard Mulgan, 'Politicization of Senior Appointments in the Australian Public Service' (1998) 57 *Australian Journal of Public Administration* 3, 7.

[36] *Code of Conduct for Special Advisers* (n 10) para 1.

[37] Peters and Pierre (n 33); Rouban (n 33).

[38] Public Administration Select Committee, *Politics and Administration: Ministers and Civil Servants* (2007).

[39] Committee on Standards in Public Life, *Reinforcing Standards: Review of the First Report of the Committee on Standards in Public Life* (2000) 74.

[40] Special advisers who have become civil servants following their time in government include Edward Troup, James Howell and Peter Levene under the Conservatives; and Will Cavendish, Tony Grayling and Justin Russell under Labour. It should be noted that the appointment (with the approval of Margaret Thatcher) of Michael Heseltine's special adviser, Peter Levene, as Chief of Defence Procurement was highly controversial at the time: see Richard Chapman, *The Civil Service Commission 1855–1991: A Bureau Biography* (Routledge 2004) 77–79. Special advisers who were once officials are perhaps more common, but include Peter Barnes, Alan Kemp and Sir Adam Ridley under the Conservatives; Dan Corry, Torsten Henricson-Bell, Jonathan Powell and Anna Turley under Labour; and Chris Nicholson and Rohan Silva under the Coalition. It should be noted, however, that it appears rare for a *serving* official to become a special adviser, the key exception being Damian McBride.

insistence on transparency and/or calls to limit the number of special advisers in government. Since the formalisation of the status of special advisers in 1974, Opposition parties have persistently asked successive governments parliamentary questions about the names and number of special advisers in post. However, the patchy nature of this approach means that there has never been a complete and consistent set of annual statistics. The 2010 CRAG Act now requires that the Government place an annual report before Parliament about special advisers serving in government.[41] While the Coalition Government initially produced quarterly reports of special advisers in post, by the end of 2013, it had defaulted to publishing one report per year. This patchy reporting has made it difficult for the public and Parliament to track the numbers and roles of special advisers in government. We return to the need for more effective transparency in chapter ten.

As for numbers of special advisers, the 2010 *Ministerial Code* states:

> With the exception of the Prime Minister and the Deputy Prime Minister, Cabinet Ministers may each appoint up to two special advisers (paid or unpaid). The Prime Minister may also authorise the appointment of one special adviser by Ministers who regularly attend Cabinet. Where a Minister has additional responsibility additional advisers may be allowed. All appointments, including exceptions to this rule, require the prior written approval of the Prime Minister.[42]

This 'cap' on numbers is not a legal requirement, but a political one. It has been kept in place by successive Prime Ministers fearful of a public outcry over increases in the number of special advisers and because they have accepted that to allow too many personal appointments might create more trouble than they are worth. Indeed, the limit of two special advisers per secretary of state was imposed by Prime Minister Wilson in 1975 in order to block the appointment of a third special adviser by one particular minister.[43] But it has loosened over time, with ministers attending Cabinet also being able to appoint a special adviser.

There are two points to make about the cap. The first is that there have been a number of exceptions to the broad principle of one or two special advisers per Cabinet minister. Prime Ministers and Chancellors have always had more special advisers: under the Conservative premierships, Prime Ministers typically had 10 special advisers and the Chancellor between three and five; under Labour, Blair had well over 20 special advisers at No 10 (more if the Cabinet Office were included) at any one time, and Brown's Treasury had an average of 10. The latter was mostly due to Brown's desire to operate a rival policy unit in the Treasury; he avoided the informal cap of two special advisers by having them both assigned to 'junior' ministers[44] and listed under the 'Council of Economic Advisers'. This

---

[41] CRAG 2010, s 16.

[42] *Ministerial Code* (n 8) para 3.3.

[43] Blick (n 21) 152.

[44] Nicola Murphy, for example, was special adviser to three Chief Secretaries in Brown's Treasury in the period 2001–06. That made her almost unique: under Labour (and indeed under the Coalition so far), it was unusual for a special adviser to *remain* in a department and serve different ministers—and

pattern continues under the Coalition, with PM David Cameron having an average of 18 special advisers per year, DPM Nick Clegg 14 and Chancellor George Osborne around four.[45]

To some extent, additional special advisers at 'the Centre' (if we here include the Treasury) are justified: central departments are relatively small compared to line departments, and yet the former have an across-government remit. But there have been other exceptions, usually connected to the importance of the portfolio or policy area. Certain ministers such as Michael Heseltine and David Blunkett had numbers of special advisers higher than the number allowed by the cap: they were 'big beasts', but they also had important portfolios. Similarly, some junior ministers who did not attend Cabinet also had special advisers—for instance, Lord MacDonald of Tradeston (Minister of Transport in the Department for the Environment, Transport and the Regions, 1999–2001) and Richard Luce (Minister of Arts in the Cabinet Office, 1985–90). Again, this arose from the particular portfolios they had—both portfolios later became separate departments in their own right (for a more detailed discussion of this, see appendix two). That there were such exceptions to the broad principle was recognised in later versions of the *Ministerial Code* under Blair and Brown.[46]

By November 2013, the Coalition had eight departments (other than No 10, the Cabinet Office and Treasury) with more than two special advisers (the Department for Business, Innovation and Skills; the Department for Communities and Local Government; the Department of Energy and Climate Change; the Department for Education (DfE); the Department for Work and Pensions; and the Foreign and Commonwealth Office, the Home Office and the Leader of the Lords) at any one time—nearly half of all line departments. This was partly because these departments included special advisers allocated to ministers attending Cabinet, and partly because of the Coalition itself: ministers from *both* parties arguably need special advisers to deal with the 'politics of coalition', which often requires more negotiation.[47] One Coalition special adviser said to us:

> It's a shame that we had such a strict rule about how many special advisers we have, not least because we have this extra function that no other special adviser ever had, which is the cross-Coalition function, which nobody, despite all the polls suggesting a hung Parliament, nobody really quite got.

to serve *three* different ministers in the same post was very unusual indeed. It should be noted that this was a practice under Conservative Chancellors too: Nigel Lawson noted that in his time there were three special advisers appointed to the Treasury, one each for the Chancellor, the Chief Secretary and the Financial Secretary to the Treasury: 'In fact these labels meant little. The three special advisers formed a team responsible to the Chancellor, and other Treasury Ministers used whatever time could be spared.' Nigel Lawson, *The View from No. 11: Memoirs of a Tory Radical* (Corgi Books 1993) 25.

[45] Clegg has gained more special advisers over time: this is to assist him in taking an overall view across government.
[46] See, for instance, the 2001 version: *Ministerial Code* (Leeds University 2001), www.leeds.ac.uk/law/teaching/law6cw/min-7.htm, para 50.
[47] Robert Hazell and Ben Yong, *The Politics of Coalition: How the Conservative-Liberal Democrat Government Works* (Hart Publishing 2012).

BIS, for instance, since 2012 has had four special advisers: two Liberal Democrat advisers attached to the Secretary of State, Vince Cable, and one for each of the Conservative ministers, David Willetts and Michael Fallon.

All this illustrates that the cap is a political one rather than being strictly legal and, as such, is malleable according to the context. As one former Cabinet Secretary said:

> The numbers is always a battle between Number 10 wanting to try and stick within a certain number, mainly for the political reason … It's just … self-imposed … There's always arguments about: 'Can't we have some more?'

The second point is that the cap has been circumvented by appointing individuals as time-limited civil servants. The Civil Service Recruitment Rules have a number of exemptions to the broad principle of appointment by open competition, which allow for the appointment of individuals to the civil service for a time-limited period where there is a pressing need.[48] We refer to these time-limited civil servants, often personally appointed by the minister, as 'policy advisers' to distinguish them from special advisers, who are also temporary civil servants.[49] They are also known colloquially as 'pads', but this is Labour terminology.[50] Reports in 2013 from both the Institute for Government (IfG) and the Institute for Public Policy Research (IPPR) have noted the use of such policy advisers by ministers.[51] The use of policy advisers under the Coalition has been openly discussed in the media.[52]

It is clear from our interviews that several such policy adviser appointments took place under the Labour Governments of 1997–2010—reaching a peak under the Brown premiership of 10–20 pads at any one time—and have continued under the Coalition. Certain departments (Defra, DfE, and the Home Office) had a 'culture' of appointing civil servants on short-term contracts, although in many

---

[48] *Recruitment Principles* (Civil Service Commission, April 2012), http://civilservicecommission. independent.gov.uk/wp-content/uploads/2012/11/Recruitment-Principles-April-2012.pdf, 9–10. At the time of writing, these recruitment principles are being reviewed by the Civil Service Commission.

[49] The qualifying phrase 'personally appointed by the minister' is important. Most individuals appointed under the exemptions to the Recruitment Rules do *not* involve the minister and are appointed by a department to meet a pressing need.

[50] Note that this terminology is potentially confusing, because currently Labour shadow ministers have *political* advisers who also refer to themselves as 'pads'. But political adviser 'pads' should be distinguished from policy adviser 'pads' as we are describing them: the former are paid out of party funds and may or may not sit in a department when their minister is in government; the latter are paid out of government money, are always located in a department and, most importantly, are classified as civil servants.

[51] Institute for Public Policy Research, *Accountability and Responsiveness in the Senior Civil Service: Lessons from Overseas* (2013) 26, 113; Akash Paun, *Supporting Ministers to Lead* (Institute for Government 2013), www.instituteforgovernment.org.uk/publications/supporting-ministers-lead, 11–12.

[52] See, for example, Daniel Martin, 'How Cameron Put 26 Aides on Public Payroll: PM in New Row over Civil Service "Jobs for the Boys"' *Daily Mail* (9 November 2010); Richards Alleyne, 'Government Politicising the Civil Service by the Back Door with Expert Advisers' *Daily Telegraph* (20 February 2013), www.telegraph.co.uk/news/uknews/9882131/Government-politicising-the-Civil-Service-by-the-back-door-with-expert-advisers.html.

cases it was because the department needed particular expertise or to deal with particular interest groups.

The numbers, role and work of policy advisers are murky at best. Some interviewees stated that policy advisers did follow the *Civil Service Code* and remained politically impartial. Other interviewees said that policy advisers were special advisers in all but name, being treated as such by both the minister and those around the minister. One former Labour special adviser said: 'Occasionally they'd be described as "secret spads" because they didn't count formally and weren't on the radar, but they worked in exactly the same way with the same level of ministerial patronage and trust.'[53]

There are a number of obvious issues about such appointments. While they may appear to have been made for the purpose of a pressing need, and the individuals appointed usually had some form of expertise, the appointment of short-term civil servants by ministers suggests 'politicisation' or patronage. Moreover, while the Civil Service Commission's Recruitment Principles do allow for exceptional time-limited appointments, the Commission's direct scrutiny of such appointments is limited.

The selection of someone with party-political affiliations may suggest a lack of professional competence,[54] but it need not necessarily be so. Take, for instance, the example of Tim Leunig. He was a Liberal Democrat who made very public critical remarks about Conservative ministers at a Liberal Democrat conference two weeks prior to his appointment in 2011 as a policy adviser at DfE, where he works for David Laws, the Liberal Democrat minister.[55] But he was also an academic economist at the London School of Economics (as well as the chief economist at Centre Forum, the key Liberal Democrat think tank).[56] So he could be considered to have expertise required by the department.

The problem is rather a lack of transparency, accountability and preserving the integrity of the civil service as a whole from the perception of politicisation. Leunig is again a good example: publications such as *Vachers Quarterly* and public relations firms had Leunig listed as a special adviser;[57] it was only when the Secretary of State, Michael Gove, answered a direct parliamentary question that it was clarified that Leunig was in fact classified as a 'policy adviser' on civil service terms.[58] There is also an issue about a potential political appointee being given

---

[53] As far as we are aware, Labour political advisers in time-limited positions left their posts when the Coalition Government was formed in 2010.

[54] Rouban (n 33).

[55] Daniel Boffey, 'Controversial New Adviser's "Tactless" Jibes Stir up Trouble for Michael Gove' *The Observer* (14 October 2012).

[56] 'Dr Tim Leunig' (London School of Economics 2012), www.lse.ac.uk/economicHistory/whosWho/profiles/tleunig@lseacuk.aspx.

[57] *Vacher's Quarterly June 2013* (Dod's Parliamentary 2013); and see, for instance, the Good Relations Political Communications document on the UK Government: 'The UK Government' (Good Relations Political Communications 2013) www.goodrelationspolitical.co.uk/wp-content/uploads/2013/03/GRPC-UK-Gov-April-2013.pdf.

[58] HC Deb 30 October 2012, col 203W.

line management duties over other civil servants—something that special advisers are strictly forbidden to have.

One former Permanent Secretary said to us that he had made use of the exemption rules and appointed individuals as short-term civil servants to meet a minister's needs:

> I've done that and others have done that. I'm not very proud of it ... So, you'll find permanent secretaries being quite pragmatic, trying to observe the rules, but also trying not to make an issue over what is, effectively, one or two people. When [Minister X arrived at my department, the permanent secretary at Minister X's previous department] rang me up and said: 'X will arrive with a small retinue of people.' He said: 'I strongly advise you to accept those arrangements and not disturb them, because once you've done that, X will be a complete delight to work for.' Indeed, he was a complete delight ...

> I'm not happy about it because it is a sort of circumvention of the rules. It's finding ways around it when, actually, there is nothing disreputable about it. We should just be open about it really. So, it comes back to the argument about what ministerial offices can be ... I just want to say that there is nothing wrong with a minister having an office, whatever you call it, a Private Office, which consists of civil servants, expert policy advisers and pure political advisers. Having a group of people like that, not too large but who the Secretary of State trusts, will make the department work better.

In short, the unrealistic cap has caused ministers and their senior officials to use other, less transparent means to secure support. In this light, the push in recent years by the Institute for Government, the IPPR and the current Coalition Government to expand the number of personal appointees is recognition of a justifiable desire for more support rather than thoughtless aggrandisement.[59]

There were very clear splits amongst our interviewees on the cap. Almost without exception, ministers and special advisers from the pre-1997 Conservative Governments whom we interviewed thought that there were too many special advisers and that one per Cabinet minister was sufficient, though some thought there should be no limit on the number of non-partisan policy experts who might be appointed. But ministers and special advisers from later governments thought the current cap was either just right or should be dropped. Many interviewees from the Governments following 1997 thought that there was too much emphasis on numbers: what mattered was whether the support to ministers was adequate or not.

Officials we interviewed were sympathetic to ministers' concerns, but they often questioned any significant increase in numbers because of potential management issues. One former Permanent Secretary said:

> My experience is that there is no magic number of special advisers ... If you did have a huge increase, and I'm afraid I don't know when you cross the line, you're effectively changing the system, aren't you? You're having a different system. But the difference

---

[59] Paun (n 52); Institute for Public Policy Research (n 51); Cabinet Office, 'Civil Service Reform Plan: One Year On' (Civil Service Reform 2013), http://my.civilservice.gov.uk/reform/civil-service-reform-one-year-on. On the 'extended ministerial office' or 'EMOs' concept, see chs 9 and 10.

between every secretary of state having two and every secretary of state having three is actually not very significant in terms of the way government functions. Successive Governments have got themselves into all sorts of difficulties by having artificial limits. They always now set the limits below the previous Government and they always find it almost impossible to stick to it. I just think it's silly. It's not about the numbers so much as how they operate and behave.

A younger, but highly experienced official who had been Principal Private Secretary to three Secretaries of State said:

It is an issue of balance. If numbers are small you can get a close team working together in reasonable harmony. If you had half a dozen, you risk getting rivalries emerging and differing views between the advisers. And there would be competition for the Secretary of State's time.

Such discussions usually led to a debate about the appropriateness of adopting a ministerial *cabinet* model of government, to which we shall return in chapter eight.

V. RESPONSIBILITY FOR EFFECTIVENESS: JOB DESCRIPTIONS, INDUCTION AND TRAINING

So far we have considered mostly to whom special advisers are accountable; and we have established that special advisers are understood to be primarily responsible to their ministers, and to the Prime Minister and the government as a whole. But what of the responsibilities of ministers and governments to special advisers?

If special advisers are to be more effective, we should recognise that some responsibility must lie with their masters. We have already seen that there are weaknesses in how special advisers are disciplined and policed, but there is another issue. If ministers and governments are accountable for the work and conduct of special advisers, in what ways do they ensure a minimal level of effectiveness? We have already discussed the problem of recruitment in chapter three: here we shall talk briefly about induction and training.

Special advisers across the political spectrum all told a similar story of entering government: disorganisation. One former special adviser who worked for one of the pre-1997 Conservative Governments said: 'I was shown up to an office, and I'd never had my own office before, and there was just an empty desk in it and a telephone. That was it. I didn't have a clue what to do.' A former Coalition special adviser told of his less than happy experience:

It's understandable that first day in government, there's a lot going on … Their [officials] priority is naturally the Secretary of State and getting him comfortable … But I would have hoped that they knew that he was going to have come with special advisers … but not even to talk you through the logistics of the office, here's the stationery cupboards, here's how the printer works, here's your phone number. Silly little things but they make … hitting the ground running difficult … They gave us a great big file of 'Here's a description of the [department]', which frankly is not particularly useful … it was chaotic from the start.

Formal induction was uncommon. Much of this was to do with the speed with which special advisers and their ministers enter government, and the expectation that they will indeed hit the ground running. There is little time for new special advisers to be given any formal induction. Of those Labour special advisers (n = 96) who answered the Constitution Unit survey question 'When you first commenced employment as a special adviser, were you required to participate in an induction programme?', the vast majority (86 per cent) said 'No'. Numbers were similar for those Conservative special advisers (1979–97) who answered the Constitution Unit survey question (90 per cent, n = 32). This was confirmed in interviews with special advisers from all three Parties. Under the Coalition, new special advisers were often given a bundle of papers, which would include the *Civil Service Code*, the *Code of Conduct for Special Advisers*, the *Model Contract for Special Advisers* and documents relating to pension schemes—but little else.

It was also rare for special advisers to be given any job description, other than that set out in the *Model Contract for Special Advisers*. Like almost everything about special advisers, whether or not there was a job description depended on the minister. Many special advisers came in with their minister, having worked with them in Opposition. More often than not, however, ministers did not think to give their special advisers job descriptions, either because they did not know themselves what a special adviser should do or could do, or because they did not know what they as ministers would be doing in their new position. The comments below are the answers of former special advisers and ministers from all three political parties responding to questions about whether they have been given or drafted job descriptions:

> None. None whatsoever. Diddly squat. I had to sort of learn from day one. Make it up as I go along … To be honest I don't think [the minister] was really clear what he wanted me to do initially, so that wasn't very helpful' (Labour special adviser)

> It was simply bumping into things … I don't think I was a very effective special adviser first time around. I think there were a combination of reasons for that, not least of which was I was inexperienced and there was no one telling me how to do the job or indeed what the job was. (Labour special adviser)

> When I was first appointed as Secretary of State, I knew nothing about spads at all because you don't have them in Opposition … I had heard of the term, but I really did not know what they did. (Coalition minister)

The overwhelming response about what induction should include, both in interviews and surveys, was an introduction to the civil service and often more specifically an introduction to the department. Two Coalition special advisers told us of their experiences:

> I can remember when I was appointed … I came up to London in jeans and a jacket to have lunch with [the minister] to discuss what I was going to do next. And I left that lunch in jeans and a jacket, walking into Number 10 as a special adviser and then into the department. Nothing had prepared me between 12 and 2 for what to do that afternoon.

I was then introduced to everyone in the department. I have no idea what I said or who half of them were and, what a principal private secretary was.

Nobody really describes to you how the civil service works ... I was literally racking my brains to remember what I had learned during A-level politics, to remember what, when somebody said to me 'Hi, I'm a grade seven', whatever that meant.

Interviewees noted that in practice it was often the Principal Private Secretary who would organise some form of induction, but this was almost always ad hoc.

There was a similar issue about on-the-job training. In the survey of former Labour special advisers, 94 per cent reported receiving no further training (n = 96) while in government. But there was great ambivalence about further training, with over two-thirds either not knowing whether it would be of benefit or arguing that it would be of no benefit (71 per cent, n = 89). The numbers for former Conservative special advisers were similar: virtually all (97 per cent, n = 32) received no further training and, again, two-thirds were ambivalent about its potential benefits.

Generally speaking, ministers we interviewed saw little need for performance appraisal. They worked with their special advisers on a daily, sometimes hourly basis, so formal appraisal would be an artificial exercise. One former special adviser, later a Secretary of State, explained why formal appraisal was unlikely:

It is not my ambition in life to be a manager in that sense. In politics you are managing things, issues, idea, beliefs. You try and make sure that we would get on and do it. So I didn't worry about that a great deal ... The truth about secretaries of state ... indeed any minister is you don't get any performance feedback. The Prime Minister either carries on with you in the job or one day taps you on the shoulder and says ... 'Thanks very much, but...' So how do you know whether you are doing a good job? ...

The main source of information [for any special adviser] about how you are doing it is going to be your Secretary of State really. If he or she is happy you are doing a good job, it doesn't really matter what anybody else thinks I would say. Have there been occasions when you have said: 'Would I be able to have some training on this?' To be perfectly honest, I don't think I ever stopped and thought, or actually had time to stop. It is a pretty full on, very all-embracing job.

A former Labour special adviser disagreed. He noted that at least one special adviser he knew was hopeless, but there was no way of removing that person. He stated:

There is no one to tell you if you are doing things wrong. A formal appraisal process, preferably run by the Political Office in No 10, would be useful. It would also give No 10 a means of removing poorly performing spads.

In the course of the Coalition Government, there have been the first attempts at performance appraisal. This has been carried out from the Centre, with the respective chiefs of staff of the Coalition Parties overseeing the appraisals.[60]

---

[60] Public Administration Select Committee (n 23).

Take-up was not 100 per cent first time round. A second round of appraisals was initiated in early 2014.

One key reason for the lack of systematic training (induction, on-the-job training and performance appraisal) for special advisers came from the nature of their work. There is no reason why special advisers could not call for additional training—and, indeed, in our interviews we were told that attempts to provide training opportunities for special advisers in the Brown premiership were welcomed and quite popular. But, generally speaking, special advisers did not pursue training opportunities because they had little time to stop and consider their own impact and effectiveness. Sixty- to seventy-hour weeks were not uncommon.[61] One former Labour special adviser commented that on becoming a special adviser, his life was put on hold:

> Your personal space disappears. This almost has to happen, because you're at the beck and call of your minister. But it meant there was little time for personal development. I usually worked from eight in the morning until ten at night, and on weekends. I didn't have a holiday in the entire time I was a special adviser. Part of it was bad workplace practices. If the minister said, 'we can do that this weekend', then everyone had to work in the weekend.

Another former Labour special adviser said:

> It never feels that you really have any time to sit and learn. You have to learn on the job because you're doing what you need to do and what your ministers want you to do. But then circumstances take over and you run on a media story or whatever is happening or events elsewhere that you have absolutely no control over. So, there doesn't seem to be too much time to sit and think really.

The lack of induction or any further personal development or training is an illustration of how special advisers fall into a 'responsibility trap' between the civil service and the political parties, where neither feels responsible for the support, training and supervision of special advisers.

VI. CONCLUSION

For the most part, the key actors in Whitehall—ministers, civil servants and special advisers—find ways and means to work together, but in government there is always the potential for friction and conflict. This is because the key actors all have different goals, values and modes of operating. As such, there have been for some time a number of regulatory frameworks which govern the conduct of special advisers and their work. These frameworks have evolved and been modified over time in response to incidents, controversies, Prime Ministerial equivocation, and

---

[61] Even 'part-time' special advisers under the Conservative Governments of 1979–97 might work 40 hours: Stephen Hanney, 'Special Advisers: Their Place in British Government' (Brunel University 1993) 269.

public and parliamentary pressure. These frameworks provide some measure of clarity on the boundaries of what special advisers can and cannot do.

What is stark, however, is the role of the minister as the key principal within these frameworks: it is the minister who almost always personally appoints the special adviser; it is primarily to the minister that a special adviser is accountable; and it is the minister who is personally responsible for the work and conduct of special advisers. In the big controversies surrounding special advisers, discussions usually founder on this point: the ministers are expected to take responsibility, but are either unable or unwilling to do so. There is therefore often an accountability gap, in that no one can effectively be held accountable when things go wrong. However, there is also a responsibility gap, in that no one is responsible for ensuring that things go right or for improving the performance and effectiveness of special advisers.

If there is to be any serious improvement, action must come from the Centre. This would not be unprecedented: as we have seen in this chapter and in chapter three, Prime Ministers have historically maintained control over numbers, vetoed appointments and informally policed the conduct of special advisers. We return to these issues in chapters nine and ten.

8

The Comparative Experience of Political Staff: Westminster Jurisdictions and Ministerial Cabinets

BEN YONG

INTRODUCTION

Aᴸᴸ WESTERN DEMOCRACIES have political staff: personal appointments created to give the executive branch an additional means of control over public policy, increase policy capacity and avoid ministerial overload.[1] The question is therefore not whether there should be political staff, but rather what their appropriate role and the extent of their influence should be. What has been the experience of other countries and what lessons can the UK learn from them?

'Political staff' is the umbrella term we use in this chapter to describe those individuals personally appointed by a minister, whose primary loyalty is to the minister who appointed them and who are generally exempted from the rules of the career bureaucracy. This is in contrast to the 'career bureaucracy' (the civil or public service) who are usually appointed and promoted on merit, and remain in post regardless of a change in government, and who are expected to be politically neutral in their dealings with successive governments.

We have chosen to look at three Westminster democracies—Canada, Australia and New Zealand—because all three countries have inherited the 'Whitehall model' discussed in chapter two.[2] That is, they share with the UK a particular view of political-administrative relations, but they have also moved some distance away from the UK in terms of their use of political staff.

We shall end with a short discussion of ministerial *cabinets* because references to *cabinets* were common in the interviews that we conducted in the course of this project. Ministerial *cabinets* are frequent in European administrations, and Commissioners in the EU's European Commission also have them. A *cabinet* is an

---

[1] Luc Rouban, 'Politicization of the Civil Service' in B Guy Peters and Jon Pierre (eds), *Handbook of Public Administration* (Sage Publications Ltd 2003) 203.

[2] RAW Rhodes, John Wanna and Patrick Weller, *Comparing Westminster* (Oxford University Press 2009).

office of staff personally chosen to support the minister in his or her work in a government department, providing advice, counsel and expertise.

A caveat: the information available on political staff in most countries remains limited, although in recent years there has been some comparative work.[3] Systematic studies of recruitment, composition, influence and impact are rare: like most work on executive government, studies of political staff are often hampered by issues of access and a dearth of official information. Thus, it is more common to see studies dealing with particular incidents involving political staff which have become public. Such studies should, however, be treated with some caution.

I. CANADA

Canada has a Westminster system at the federal level. The Prime Minister, as the leader of the political party, chooses members of the Cabinet and provides overall direction for the government. Canadian Cabinets are comparatively speaking large, often having between 30 and 40 ministers, in order to ensure regional representation. There is a two-tier ministerial hierarchy: ministers and ministers of state. They are in turn supported by parliamentary secretaries, who have much the same role as parliamentary private secretaries in the UK.

Canada also has a federal career bureaucracy—the Canadian Public Service—which operates along traditional Westminster lines.[4] Departmental permanent heads are known as deputy ministers and are appointed by the Prime Minister on the advice of the Clerk of the Privy Council (the head of the Canadian Public Service), rather than by the relevant departmental minister. The great majority of deputy ministers have been career public servants.[5] Canadian public servants are generally appointed and promoted on merit, and are expected to serve successive partisan governments with political impartiality.

---

[3] But see now Organisation for Economic Co-operation and Development (OECD), *Ministerial Advisors: Role, Influence and Management* (OECD Publishing 2011); Chris Eichbaum and Richard Shaw (eds), *Partisan Appointees and Public Servants: An International Analysis of the Role of the Political Adviser* (Edward Elgar 2010); Akash Paun, 'Supporting Ministers to Lead' (Institute for Government 2013), www.instituteforgovernment.org.uk/publications/supporting-ministers-lead; Institute for Public Policy Research, *Accountability and Responsiveness in the Senior Civil Service: Lessons from Overseas* (Cabinet Office 2013).

[4] Appointments to and promotions within the Canadian Public Service are governed under the Public Service Employment Act 2003.

[5] Jacques Bourgault, 'Canada's Senior Public Service and the Typology of Bargains: From the Hierarchy of Senior Civil Servants to a Community of "Controlled" Entrepreneurs' (2011) 26 *Public Policy and Administration* 253, 262.

A. 'Exempt Staff'

In Canada, political staff are more commonly known as 'exempt staff'. They are so called because, although they are employed under the Public Service Employment Act 2003, they are explicitly not part of the Canadian public service and are exempt from the authority of the Public Service Commission (PSC), the body that oversees appointments to and promotions within the Canadian career bureaucracy.[6]

Canadian ministers normally have a ministerial office with a number of exempt staff, headed by a chief of staff. Exempt staff are appointed by the minister, but chiefs of staff must be approved by the Prime Minister's Office (PMO), and in some cases the chiefs of staff are assigned by the PMO rather than ministers doing the recruiting themselves.[7] More generally, there are guidelines set by the Treasury Board on ministerial offices, including size and exempt staff positions.[8] Exempt staff are paid out of public money: each minister is allocated funds (determined by the Prime Minister) for his or her staff. This funding also pays for public servants seconded from the minister's department to serve as departmental liaison.

Exempt or political staff have long existed in Canada, but their numbers increased over the twentieth and into the twenty-first centuries.[9] The numbers underwent an exponential increase under the Pierre Trudeau administrations of the 1970s and 1980s, and then again when the Conservatives gained power in 1984 after a long period of Liberal Governments.[10] The concern then was that the Conservative Government would find itself 'in office but not in power': it was thought that political staff would ensure an appropriate level of responsiveness from the bureaucracy.[11]

Since then, there has been the occasional attempt to reduce numbers, but in practice numbers have continued to rise. In 1990, ministerial staff totalled 460 (of which almost 100 were in the PMO); by 2007, there were 513 (with 83 in the PMO).[12] The most recent report on exempt staff, compiled by the Federal House of Commons Library in 2008, listed close to 600 for roughly 60 ministers.[13] However, these high numbers are misleading: the function of many individuals classified as

---

[6] In practice, deputy ministers determine appointments and promotions within a department.
[7] Personal correspondence with David Brown.
[8] Treasury Board of Canada Secretariat, 'Appendix A: Exempt Staff Position Structure' (*Policies for Ministers' Offices—January 2011*, 2011), www.tbs-sct.gc.ca/pubs_pol/hrpubs/mg-ldm/2011/pgmo-pldcm12-eng.asp#tocAppA.
[9] See generally Liane Benoit, 'Ministerial Staff: The Life and Times of Parliament's Statutory Orphans' in *Restoring Accountability: Research Studies, Volume 1 Parliament, Ministers and Deputy Ministers* (Commission of Inquiry into the Sponsorship Program and Advertising Activities 2006); and Peter Aucoin, 'Canada' in Eichbaum and Shaw (n 3).
[10] Aucoin (n 9) 71.
[11] Benoit (n 9) 160.
[12] Aucoin (n 9) 73. Note that the PMO consists solely of the Prime Minister's political staff; the Privy Council Office (PCO) provides public service support to the Prime Minister and the Cabinet.
[13] Alex Smith, *Ministerial Staff: Issues of Accountability and Ethics* (Library of Parliament 2008).

'exempt staff' is to provide administrative support rather than partisan advice.[14] So the number of exempt staff involved in the processes of media management, policy making and providing partisan advice is less than the reported numbers.

B. Roles, Functions and Influence

In spite of the large numbers of exempt staff in the Canadian system and of concerns about their potential impact, there is very little publicly available data on them and their roles: successive governments have not published information on exempt staff, nor have they been under significant pressure to do so. There is very little material about recruitment and the overall composition of exempt staff. They are often perceived as young, often being former party political staffers,[15] but there are as yet no systematic studies of exempt staff and their career paths.

Exempt staff have been most discussed in academic literature about the Canadian core executive and usually in the context of a debate about 'court' government (ie, government by the Prime Minister and a carefully selected group of courtiers) or the centralisation of Canadian government.[16] Exempt staff are seen to be extensions of prime ministerial power (since almost one-fifth are located in the PMO). They are rarely treated as a subject of discussion in themselves, and departmental exempt staff are not discussed at all.[17] The focus remains on the growth of centralised executive power and the perceived lack of accountability.

However, it is possible to glean from official reports what exempt staff do. The key guidance document for members of the executive states that 'ministerial "political" or "exempt" staff provide advice that can address the political aspects of the Minister's functions but do not play a role in departmental operations.'[18] They may review briefings and advice, assist the minister in developing policy, prepare speeches, liaise with other ministers and the party or be an expert in a particular field. The Treasury Board Secretariat also provides a useful outline of exempt staff positions in the executive guidance document *Policies for Ministers' Offices*. Exempt staff within a minister's office typically include a chief of staff, directors of policy, communication and parliamentary affairs, and a number of policy advisers.[19]

---

[14] See Treasury Board of Canada Secretariat (n 8). This sets out the exempt staff structure in a ministerial office and includes 'private secretary', 'support staff' and 'driver'.

[15] Benoit (n 9); Ian Brodie, 'In Defence of Political Staff' [2012] *Canadian Parliamentary Review* 33.

[16] Aucoin (n 9); Donald J Savoie, *Court Government and the Collapse of Accountability in Canada and the United Kingdom* (University of Toronto Press 2008).

[17] But see now Jonathan Craft, *Institutionalized Partisan Advisors in Canada: Movers and Shapers, Buffers and Bridges* (Simon Fraser University 2012); and Brodie (n 15).

[18] Privy Council Office, *Accountable Government: A Guide for Ministers and Ministers of State*, http://pm.gc.ca/grfx/docs/guidemin_e.pdf.

[19] Treasury Board of Canada Secretariat (n 8).

How these official descriptions play out in practice is unclear. Benoit, for instance, argues that 'there remains no absolute consensus ... as to what constitutes the appropriate role of exempt staff in the policy development process'.[20] Traditionally it has been understood that exempt staff add a 'political angle' to policy advice, but there have been criticisms that the balance between the public service and exempt staff has now shifted, to the extent that governments are now less inclined to take or listen to the advice of public servants.[21]

The better access to ministers that exempt staff enjoy and their role as gatekeepers in the ministerial office has also led to concerns about the ministerial–public service relationship, and the extent to which staff 'advice' to public servants becomes 'direction'. Exempt staff 'do not have the authority to give direction to public servants, but they can ask for information or transmit the Minister's instructions, normally through the deputy minister'.[22] But in practice, this line may be difficult to draw.

C. Accountability

The key executive guidance document for Canadian ministers, *Accountable Government*, states that: 'Ministers and ministers of state are personally responsible for the conduct and operation of their offices.'[23] In practice, however, there is an accountability 'vacuum', with ministers tending to claim that they are accountable only where they had personal knowledge of the actions of their exempt staff.

There have been a number of controversies involving exempt staff. The most well known is the sponsorship scandal which occurred during the Liberal Government (1993–2006). A number of lucrative contracts under a federal sponsorship programme intended to promote national unity were awarded without going through a proper bidding process. The Gomery Commission,[24] which was established to report on the scandal, found that the minister then responsible for the programme and his political staff had had direct input into the selection for sponsorship, which amounted to inappropriate political encroachment into the administrative domain. Public servants had been excluded from the process.

Following the sponsorship scandal and the formation of the Stephen Harper minority Government, exempt staff were made subject to the Conflict of Interest Act 2006 and the Federal Accountability Act 2006. There have been calls to

---

[20] Benoit (n 9) 236.
[21] See generally the work of Donald J Savoie, *Breaking the Bargain: Public Servants, Ministers, and Parliament* (University of Toronto Press 2003); and Savoie (n 16).
[22] Privy Council Office, *Accountable Government: A Guide for Minsters and Ministers of State* (Government of Canada 2011) 46, at http://www.pm.gc.ca/grfx/docs/guidemin_e.pdf.
[23] ibid 28.
[24] Commission of Inquiry into the Sponsorship Program and Advertising Activities, *Restoring Accountability—Recommendations* (Commission of Inquiry into the Sponsorship Program and Advertising Activities 2006).

introduce a code of conduct for exempt staff, but this has not yet happened. However, the key guidance document for ministers, *Accountable Government*, was redrafted in 2006 to make more explicit the respective roles of exempt staff, their relationship with public servants and the personal responsibility of ministers.[25] The Gomery Commission also recommended induction and on-the-job training for exempt staff, and in recent years this has begun to take place.[26]

II. AUSTRALIA

Australia at the federal level (ie, the Commonwealth) also has a Westminster political system: the government is formed from the party or parties which can command the confidence of the lower house. There is a two-tier hierarchy of ministers: Cabinet ministers and those outside Cabinet, all of whom are based in Parliament House. In addition, there are parliamentary secretaries, the most junior political tier.

The Australian Public Service (APS) is a career bureaucracy that is non-partisan and is selected and promoted on merit. Since 1984, the heads of department—departmental secretaries—have been appointed by the Prime Minister on fixed-term contracts (although the majority of those appointed remain career public servants).[27] The APS is geographically separated from ministers, with ministers and ministerial advisers residing in Parliament House and the departments spread over the city of Canberra. Every minister's private office has at least one Departmental Liaison Officer (DLO), who is a public servant seconded from the minister's department, but the majority of those working in the private office are the minister's political staff.

Ministerial advisers—the Australian term for political staff—are now an institutional feature of Australian federal government.[28] Although there had been some advisers to ministers under previous governments, the Gough Whitlam Labor Government of 1972 moved to increase substantially the numbers of ministerial advisers. Labor had spent 23 years in opposition and was wary of public servants. The 'Whitlam experiment' continued under following governments, and the number of ministerial advisers has increased steadily over time.

---

[25] Aucoin (n 9) 86.

[26] Benoit (n 9) 241–46; Brodie (n 15) 36. Carlton University in Ottawa now offers a Master's degree in Political Management, geared specifically at improving the quality of political staff in all parties. See 'Clayton H. Riddell Graduate Program in Political Management' (Carleton University), http://carleton.ca/politicalmanagement.

[27] Andrew Podger, 'What Really Happens: Department Secretary Appointments, Contracts and Performance Pay in the Australian Public Service' (2007) 66 *Australian Journal of Public Administration* 131.

[28] See generally Anne Tiernan, *Power without Responsibility: Ministerial Staffers in Australian Governments from Whitlam to Howard* (UNSW Press 2007); and Maria Maley, 'Australia' in Eichbaum and Shaw (n 3).

But it was only when Labor returned to power in 1983 that advisers were organised on a more systematic basis. Labor had initially intended to create a political tier within the executive, with both partisan advisers and a layer of personal APS appointments (five per cent of the Senior Executive Service, the equivalent of the British Senior Civil Service), but instead the Members of Parliament (Staff) Act 1984 (MOP(S) Act), was passed. This institutionalised ministerial advisers and put all staff employed by all parliamentarians and their employment on a statutory footing.[29] Prior to this, political advisers had been appointed to the APS using the Public Service Act temporary employment provisions. The MOP(S) Act was enacted to avoid the need to use the Public Service Act to appoint staff for parliamentarians, but, more importantly, it provided for the appointment of political staff and allowed public servants to temporarily disengage from the APS to become ministerial advisers.

The number of ministerial advisers has increased steadily over time. In 1983, ministerial advisers numbered just over 200, under Paul Keating (1991–96) over 350, and near the end of John Howard's premiership (1996–2007) over 460. The Labor Government in 2007 reduced ministerial advisers to 1996 levels, but a 2009 Senate review of government staffing recommended that numbers increase to deal with ministerial workload.[30] By 2012, there were 423 'government personal employees' (the current terminology used by the Commonwealth Department of Finance to indicate those employed as advisers to ministers).[31] However, like the Canadian case, these reported numbers need to be treated with caution, because they also include staff carrying out purely administrative tasks. A more careful analysis would suggest that there were in fact 338 staffers in 2012 exercising roles similar to UK special advisers.[32]

All members of the Australian federal government have ministerial advisers. Generally speaking, there is a standard allocation of staff: Cabinet ministers have nine ministerial advisers, non-Cabinet ministers six and parliamentary secretaries two, while the Prime Minister, the Deputy Prime Minister and the Treasurer all have greater numbers (for instance, Prime Ministers have had on average 30–50 ministerial advisers).[33]

---

[29] Members of Parliament (Staff) Act 1984 (Cth).

[30] See Senate Committee on Finance and Public Administration, 'Review of Government Staffing' (2009) www.aph.gov.au/binaries/senate/committee/fapa_ctte/estimates/bud_0910/finance/tabled_documents/review_govt_staffing.pdf.

[31] Commonwealth of Australia, 'Annual Report 2011–12' (*Members of Parliament (Staff) Act 1984 Annual Reports*, 2012) 40, www.finance.gov.au/publications/mops_annual_reports/2011-2012/docs/MOPS_Annual_Report.pdf.

[32] This figure is arrived at by including all those employed by the categories 'senior staff', 'media adviser', 'adviser' and 'assistant adviser' and excluding the categories 'executive assistant/office manager' and 'secretary/administrative assistant'.

[33] See Senate Committee on Finance and Public Administration (n 30).

A. Ministerial Advisers: Roles, Influence and Staffing Issues

Maria Maley argues that ministerial advisers have at least three functions.[34] First, they help ministers to perform their jobs. Ministers suffer from overload: ministerial advisers help ministers to concentrate on what is important, via gatekeeping and communicating priorities to the APS. They also provide political support, which the APS cannot do. Second, they help ministers steer departments and policy. There was a concern that ministers were too dependent on the career bureaucracy, but that the bureaucracy was also insufficiently responsive. Advisers provided an alternative source of advice; they could also, by providing direction and clarification, ensure greater responsiveness on the part of the APS. Ministerial advisers may also be involved in generating ideas, policy development and implementation. Finally, advisers help coordinate activity, either within the department or across departments. In particular, ministerial advisers manage conflict and ensure policy coherence across government.

It is the greater contact and proximity to the minister that gives ministerial advisers their power and influence. A common criticism of advisers is that there is now an over-emphasis on responsiveness over neutral competence in Australian government. There are regularly voiced concerns about the 'politicisation' of policy making and the marginalisation of the APS,[35] but whether these criticisms are valid remains unclear.

Information on the background of Australian political staff is thin. Reports suggest a mix of former political party staff (from the Australian states, territories and the Commonwealth), journalists and public servants (seconded from departments under the MOP(S) Act).[36] Initially a large proportion of those appointed as ministerial advisers came from the APS, but over time the number of APS recruits appears to have declined.[37] Career officials who have become ministerial advisers have been successfully integrated back into the APS following a change of government, although there may need to be a period of 'decontamination'.[38]

Under the Howard Government (1996–2007), a Government Staffing Committee (GSC) was established. This was a product of the need to ensure centralised control over political staff, but it was also because of increasing numbers. The GSC consisted of the Deputy Prime Minister, the Special Minister of State (who deals with electoral, financial and oversight issues) and the Prime Minister's chief of staff, amongst others. This arrangement continued under both the Kevin Rudd and Julia Gillard Labor Governments. The GSC determines overall staffing numbers, remuneration and performance issues, as well as senior

---

[34] Maley (n 28).
[35] For the most recent example of this, see David Crowe and Annabel Hepworth, 'Business Declares War over Ministerial Staffers "Costing us Billions"' *The Australian* (21 September 2012).
[36] Anne Tiernan and Patrick Weller, *Learning to Be a Minister: Heroic Expectations, Practical Realities* (Melbourne University Press 2010).
[37] Institute for Public Policy Research (n 3) 73–74.
[38] ibid 73.

appointments, particularly at the chief of staff level.[39] The current Tony Abbott Government has faced accusations of 'obsessive centralised control', with one-third of all proposed staffing appointments by ministers apparently being vetoed by its appointment panel.[40]

High numbers and concerns about the conduct of ministerial staff (and in particular their relationship with the APS) led to attempts to introduce more systematic training under the first Rudd Government, which was elected in 2007. Ministers attended presentations on ministerial staff, their role and expected behaviour; there were mandatory inductions for ministerial staff (which included the roles and responsibilities of the APS) and there were also opportunities for on-the-job training, although the take-up rate was not high. A 2009 *Review of Government Staffing* recommended the appointment of a full-time adviser to assist the Government with issues of ministerial staffing, including staff training and support, and ensuring best office practices.[41]

There are also suggestions of high rates of attrition because of the gruelling working hours.[42] The 2009 *Review* stated that it was typical for chiefs of staff and media staff to work 60–70 hours a week, with many regularly working in excess of 80 hours a week, including weekends.[43]

B. Accountability

There have been a number of controversies involving ministerial advisers in Australia. The most well known of these is the 'Children Overboard' affair in 2001, which led to a long debate about the appropriate role of ministerial advisers. This took place in the context of a federal election, when it was alleged by the incumbent Howard Government that asylum seekers on a boat had thrown children overboard. Subsequently it was determined that no such event had occurred, but a Senate investigation found that at the heart of the controversy were the various interventions of the incumbent Government's ministerial advisers and the inability of officials to communicate directly with ministers.[44] The key ministers involved denied that they had been told by their advisers about the concerns of officials from the Ministry of Defence. The Government refused to allow the relevant ministerial advisers to appear before the Senate investigating committee.

---

[39] Maley (n 28) 100–05.

[40] '"Control Freak" Peta Credlin Accused of Pulling Coalition Strings' *Sydney Morning Herald* (4 December 2013) www.smh.com.au/federal-politics/political-news/control-freak-peta-credlin--accused-of-pulling-coalition-strings-20131204-2yqte.html.

[41] Senate Committee on Finance and Public Administration (n 30).

[42] Tiernan (n 28) 9.

[43] Senate Committee on Finance and Public Administration (n 30) 12–13.

[44] Select Committee for an Inquiry into a Certain Maritime Incident, *A Certain Maritime Incident* (2002).

It remains unclear whether such controversies are representative of ministerial advisers as a group.

Historically, very little information was available publicly about ministerial advisers, and by common agreement between the political parties they are not called before Parliament.[45] However, the first Rudd Government instituted a number of reforms as a result of ongoing publicity about ministerial advisers. A code of conduct governing advisers' behaviour was introduced in 2008.[46] This stated, amongst other matters, that advisers should make themselves aware of the APS code, that staff did not have the power to direct public servants and that executive decisions were for the minister alone. The chief of staff in a minister's office was given the power to impose sanctions for violations of the code, but they must act on the advice of the GSC.[47] Since 2008, the Commonwealth Government's Department of Finance and Deregulation has published annual reports on numbers, roles and expenditure relating to ministerial staff under the MOP(S) Act.[48]

III. NEW ZEALAND

New Zealand (NZ) has a political system broadly similar to other Westminster democracies: an executive drawn from and accountable to Parliament, and a permanent bureaucracy which serves successive governments with political impartiality. There is a two-tier executive of ministers and associate ministers. Individuals may have cross-cutting responsibilities: they may be a minister in one department and an associate (junior) minister in another. But there is also a key difference between NZ and other Westminster democracies. The electoral system has been one of proportional representation since 1996. This has had a profound impact on government in NZ.

A. Ministerial Advisers

Political staff—or 'ministerial advisers' as they are known in NZ—are considered 'state servants'. They are appointed by ministers but employed by the Executive Government Support Unit within the Department of Internal Affairs. Political staff have existed since at least the 1980s, but there was an expansion in numbers at the beginning of the twenty-first century. At the beginning of the Labour-led government in 1998, there were 39 ministerial advisers; by 2006, this had

---

[45] Maley (n 28) 107.
[46] '*Code of Conduct for Ministerial Staff* (Minister for the Public Service and Integrity 2008), www.smos.gov.au/media/code_of_conduct.html.
[47] Maley (n 28) 109.
[48] The Department of Finance publishes annual reports on the MOP(S) Act, which are available at: www.finance.gov.au/publications/mops_annual_reports/index.html.

increased to 53.[49] Every ministerial office has at least one ministerial adviser, with the Prime Minister's Office having significantly more.

There were four reasons for the expansion of political staff. The first was the shift to a system of proportional representation, which in turn produced regular multiparty government. Ministerial advisers help ministers negotiate the proliferation of political relationships. The second reason suggested was the use of New Public Management (an initiative to introduce market-orientated management into the public sector) to restructure NZ's state services into separate vehicles of policy and delivery. This has arguably required ministerial advisers to act as agents of their ministerial principals to supervise delivery. A third reason suggested is that Labour spent almost a decade out of power in the 1990s: the expansion of political staff may have been a response to concerns by the Party about the NZ public service. A final reason is that policy making may simply be more difficult: as in the UK, political staff are needed to manage the increasing demands of government.[50]

B. Roles, Functions and Influence

Under the 1999–2008 Labour-led Government, ministerial advisers from the main party were usually recruited from the party's political staff and/or they were known personally by the recruiting minister. Candidates were often vetted by the Prime Minister's chief of staff.

Ministerial advisers have a number of roles in NZ government. In relation to the executive, they draft speeches, initiate policy, convey the minister's wishes, read and comment on advice, and may assist with intra-Cabinet negotiation and coordination. They help to draft official information requests and parliamentary questions, and assist in intra- and inter-party negotiations.[51] NZ ministers surveyed in a study by Eichbaum and Shaw valued advisers not so much for a shared political disposition, but rather for political negotiating skills and knowledge of the processes of executive government.[52] In addition to providing political support in relation to multiparty government, ministerial advisers were seen by ministers as a check on departmentalism and an alternative source of policy advice. Ministerial advisers who were surveyed saw themselves as adding value under conditions of multiparty government—not just within the executive, but also in terms of garnering support and putting together policy coalitions within Parliament.

As in other jurisdictions, there are questions about the impact that ministerial advisers have on the relations between ministers and public servants. However, a

---

[49] Chris Eichbaum and Richard Shaw, 'Ministerial Advisers, Politicisation, and the Retreat from Westminster: The Case of New Zealand' (2007) 85 *Public Administration* 609, 611.

[50] Chris Eichbaum and Richard Shaw, 'New Zealand' in Eichbaum and Shaw (n 3) 116–19.

[51] Chris Eichbaum and Richard Shaw, 'Minding the Minister? Ministerial Advisers in New Zealand Government' (2007) 2 *Kōtuitui: New Zealand Journal of Social Sciences Online* 95.

[52] Eichbaum and Shaw (n 50) 120.

survey of NZ public servants undertaken by Eichbaum and Shaw suggested that a majority of officials did not think ministerial advisers 'politicised' government processes or were a threat to the public service itself.[53] Indeed, with the advent of proportional representation, ministerial advisers were seen by officials as essential to ensuring that the public service did not have to deal with the political relationship management issues that multiparty government produces. That being said, there was some concern about 'administrative politicisation'; that is, restricting public service access to ministers or the prohibition of unwelcome advice.[54]

C. Accountability

As NZ ministerial advisers are state servants, they are subject to the state servants' code. They are also expected to follow the Department of Internal Affairs' own code of conduct; that is, because they are employed by the Executive Government Support Unit within the Department of Internal Affairs. Elements of both codes are clearly inconsistent with the functions of ministerial advisers—for instance, the provision that employees should provide honest and impartial advice to ministers.[55] However, there is no specific code of conduct for ministerial advisers in NZ.[56] This may be because, with the smaller number of political staff in NZ, it has been possible to avoid the controversies that have taken place in Australia and Canada. It may also be because proportional representation and multiparty government may require political staff to act in a more constrained manner in relation to other actors, both in the executive and in the legislature.

IV. A SHORT NOTE ON MINISTERIAL *CABINETS*

References to ministerial *cabinets* (pronounced to rhyme with 'matinee') in our interviews were common. This should not be surprising—suggestions to adopt a *cabinet* system have been a staple since the 1960s. There were divided views:

> I am not in favour of *cabinets*. Our system has enough treacle in it already but *cabinets* would create more. In my current job, I am dealing with one issue where the relevant *cabinet* is telling us one thing and the relevant Commission Directorate saying the direct

---

[53] Eichbaum and Shaw (n 49).

[54] ibid.

[55] Eichbaum and Shaw, 'New Zealand' (n 50) 139.

[56] A short statement on political staff was inserted in the most recent version of the NZ *Cabinet Manual* Paragraph 3.5 (http://cabinetmanual.cabinetoffice.govt.nz/, accessed 30 November 2013):

    A Minister may involve political advisers in policy development and other areas of work that might otherwise be performed within the Minister's department. The Minister and the chief executive must establish a clear understanding to ensure that:

    — departmental officials know the extent of the advisers' authority; and

    — proper accountability exists for results and financial requirements under the Public Finance Act 1989.

opposite. I have no idea which view will win out. There is too much risk of losing the joined-upness of the current Whitehall system. You can't afford the political level and the official level having different views. (Senior civil servant)

It would be honest of us to come out with a French-style *cabinet* system with a mixture of civil servants and outside people. But we are a deeply conservative people and it won't happen. (Former Labour Secretary of State)

I think Labour in '97 should have brought in the *cabinet* system ... I've seen the European style in action, and I don't think you can do that in Britain now. But I think it would have been the right thing. (Former No 10 Labour special adviser)

It has also been common in various UK reports on special advisers and civil service reform to raise the possibility of shifting to a *cabinet* model, only then to dismiss the idea quickly. Here is a 1986 select committee report on ministers and the civil service:

There was clear agreement ... that some form of *cabinet* system could and even should be introduced in this country. We want to ... dispose of the word *cabinet*, primarily because it is too easily confused with the word 'Cabinet', but also because we do not wish what we are to recommend to be seen ... as a copy or even an adaptation of any of the existing continental systems. What we are proposing is more an expanded private office than a *cabinet* ... We propose to call it a *Minister's Policy Unit*.[57]

Almost 30 years later, the Institute for Public Policy Research stated in a government-funded report:

We recommend ... 2. *Providing Secretaries of State and Ministers who run Departments with an extended office of Ministerial staff* that they personally appoint and who work directly on their behalf in the department. Ministerial staff should comprise a mixture of officials, external experts, and political advisers. We do not recommend a *Cabinet* model made up exclusively of political appointees.[58]

So while *cabinets* are often associated with special advisers and support for ministers, they are usually seen as an option to be avoided. Why are they regarded with such ambivalence?

It is best to begin with a definition because there seems to be some confusion over what *cabinets* are. A *cabinet* consists of a number of staff personally chosen by a minister and whose service in that *cabinet* terminates upon that minister's departure. The primary function of a ministerial *cabinet* is to support the minister in his or her work in a government department. They provide policy advice, political counsel and logistical support for ministers.[59]

The number of staff in a *cabinet* differs, depending on the country or institution. In France, for instance, *cabinets* can be between 10 and 20 staff, with

---

[57] Treasury and Civil Service Committee, *Civil Servants and Ministers: Duties and Responsibilities* (1986) para 5.28, emphasis in original.

[58] Institute for Public Policy Research (n 3) 5, emphasis in original.

[59] Robert Elgie, *Political Institutions in Contemporary France* (Oxford University Press 2003) 147–48.

the Prime Minister having as many as 50, whereas *cabinets* in the European Commission are limited to six.[60] But that is still larger than the average two special advisers personally appointed by any one UK Cabinet minister.

The composition of *cabinets* is perhaps misunderstood. Under the French system, for instance, *cabinets* traditionally consist mostly of civil servants. Rouban reported that in the 2000s, two-thirds of all *cabinet* staff came from the French civil service.[61] France is not necessarily representative, however. In Belgium half of all *cabinet* staff are civil servants, with the others coming from think tanks, interest groups and so on.[62] Generally, it appears quite common for *cabinets* in French-inspired systems to have at least half of a typical *cabinet* composed of civil servants.[63] Similarly, in the European Commission, which has drawn heavily on the French tradition, Commissioners' *cabinets* are mixed, half now being required to come internally from the Directorates-General (the EU's functional equivalent of government departments), the other half being secondments from national administrations and from the private sector.[64] This has benefits: by virtue of their composition—often consisting of a plurality of career officials—*cabinets* may be able to use departmental machinery more effectively than 'outsiders' might.

Even though the *cabinet* dissolves upon the dismissal of the minister, it is also common in these systems for civil servants in the *cabinet* not to lose their job in the bureaucracy, though clearly their role may change. In France, for instance, there is no US-style wholesale purge of such appointees, but there may be a 'reshuffle' of *cabinet* staff depending on their known political allegiances—those officials known to be in sympathy with the outgoing party may be transferred to 'less sensitive jobs', but are still employed at senior levels within the civil service.[65] This is partly possible because the political–administrative divide is more blurred in France. French politicians, for example, commonly begin their careers as civil servants: nearly every President, Prime Minister and most ministers have a civil service background.[66]

The following point is worth emphasising: in continental Europe (or at least, in French-influenced governmental systems), it is mainly civil servants who staff *cabinets* and support the minister, not those from 'outside' the career bureaucracy

---

[60] Paun (n 3) 9; Antonis Ellinas and Ezra Suleiman, *The European Commission and Bureaucratic Autonomy: Europe's Custodians* (Cambridge University Press 2012) 95.

[61] Luc Rouban, 'Public Management and Politics: Senior Bureaucrats in France' (2007) 85 *Public Administration* 473, 488.

[62] Guido Dierickx, 'Politicization in the Belgian Civil Service' in B Guy Peters and Jon Pierre (eds), *Politicization of the Civil Service in Comparative Perspective: The Quest for Control* (Routledge 2004).

[63] Sylvia Horton, 'Contrasting Anglo-American and Continental European Civil Service Systems' in Andrew Massey (ed), *International Handbook on Civil Service Systems* (Edward Elgar 2011) 40.

[64] David Spence, 'The President, the College and the Cabinets' in *The European Commission* (3rd revised edn, John Harper Publishing 2006) 65.

[65] Michael Duggett and Maneuline Desbouvries, 'The Civil Service in France: Contested Complacency?' in Massey (n 63).

[66] Luc Rouban, 'Politicization of the Civil Service in France: From Structural to Strategic Politicization' in Peters and Pierre (n 62) 84.

like the majority of special advisers in the UK. But from this it can be seen that the Napoleonic system presumes quite a different approach to the political–administrative boundary from the Whitehall model, in which elected officials (politicians) and unelected officials (civil servants) are kept separate—and any blurring of this boundary is impermissible or is to be regarded with suspicion. In the UK, very few individuals have made the jump from being special advisers to becoming civil servants, and civil servants who become special advisers do not return. Whitehall is not yet used to dealing with a large number of civil servants returning to the fold following this kind of personalised appointment.[67] Damian McBride notes in his memoir how Ed Balls explained to him the consequences of leaving the civil service and becoming a special adviser: '[Gordon] doesn't understand what you'll be giving up. You'll never be able to go back to the civil service. Whatever career you thought you were going to have, that will be over.'[68]

The problem becomes more pronounced when noting that in the British system, there tend to be long periods of single-party government before a change in government. Thus, *cabinets* raise the spectre of 'politicisation' of the civil service in the UK context and of difficulties in times of political transition. This explains, to some extent, concerns over the Coalition Government's introduction of Extended Ministerial Offices (EMOs) in 2013. Under this initiative, Cabinet ministers may personally appoint or select all staff within an EMO, which may include civil servants, special advisers and external appointees (with the status of time-limited civil servants).[69]

But perhaps the primary reason why the idea of *cabinets* is regarded with ambivalence in the UK is their potential impact on the relationship between the minister and the career bureaucracy. The advantages of the *cabinet* system are that it provides a small, easily manageable and personally loyal team for the minister to draw upon for support; they can counterbalance a minister's (or Commissioner's) shortcomings and strengthen their performance; and they can coordinate and mediate between departments or (in Brussels) the European Commission's equivalent, the Directorates-General. But these very same qualities can be a disadvantage too. Commission *cabinets* have been criticised for having 'shielded Commissioners from their services, usurped the responsibilities of Directors General [the heads of Directorates-General] and questioned proposals without consulting the responsible officials in the services'.[70] Indeed the *chef de Cabinet* (the Chief of Staff of a *cabinet*) is empowered to speak and negotiate directly on behalf of the Commissioner. More recent scholarship suggests relations between Commission *cabinets* and the services are now more cordial than much

---

[67] See the discussion of politicisation in ch 7.
[68] Damian McBride, *Power Trip: A Decade of Policy, Plots and Spin* (Biteback 2013) 167.
[69] EMOs are discussed in more detail in ch 10.
[70] Spence (n 64) 69.

of the literature suggests.[71] However, it is worth noting that the Commission's Secretariat-General now enforces a rule that:

> [I]ncoming *cabinets* agree a written concordat with the Director General of the services for which they are about to assume responsibility. These agreements set out commitments covering how information is to be communicated between the *cabinet* and the DG, how often meetings are to take place between *cabinet* members and officials, and who are the approved contact people in the DG.[72]

Similar criticisms are made of *cabinets* in national systems. In France, for instance, *cabinet* members can issue instructions and direct career officials, and represent and speak for the minister both inside and outside the ministry. This power and overlap of administrative responsibilities creates the potential for conflict. Indeed, there are criticisms that policy is increasingly made in ministerial *cabinets* rather than the departments.[73] The No 10 Policy Unit, perhaps the closest that the UK government ever came to a *cabinet* structure (particularly under Tony Blair), was often criticised on this basis.

V. CONCLUSION

Examining the experience of other countries may throw a light on UK practice, but also offer possible visions of the future. The three Westminster jurisdictions examined have all seen the expansion of political staff in the last 30–40 years. Political staff were introduced into these jurisdictions for particular local reasons, but there are some commonalities—partly because all three countries have drawn on each other's experiences. Political staff were often introduced, or their numbers greatly expanded, by incoming governments who had spent a long time out of power. More generally, there appears to have been a decline in trust in the career bureaucracy and a search for more alternative sources of policy advice. The growing complexity of government and the rise of the 24/7 media have also been identified as drivers.

There are a number of common features concerning political staff in all three countries. There is the issue of transparency. At a very basic level in all three countries, the role and functions of political staff are little understood by the public, and this has been hindered by limited publicly available information.

The power and influence of political staff has been an issue in all three jurisdictions. Most commonly, this is seen at 'the Centre', with successive governments strengthening capacity over communications and policy advice. More generally, political staff are closest in proximity to and have the most contact with ministers, which gives them their power and influence. There is the perception that—rightly

---

[71] Hussein Kassim et al, *The European Commission of the Twenty-First Century* (Oxford University Press 2013) 197–209.
[72] ibid 205.
[73] Rouban (n 61) 493; Institute for Public Policy Research (n 3).

or wrongly—political staff generally 'politicise' the workings of government, either through the insertion of partisan individuals into the career bureaucracy or through the marginalisation or the exclusion of the career bureaucracy from access to the minister. In both Canada and Australia, the minister's office now consists almost entirely of political staff rather than those from the career bureaucracy. In this respect, the UK has not yet followed Australia or Canada, although the new EMOs are potentially a step in this direction.

A number of controversies in both Canada and Australia point to the potential for the misuse of power and influence, but there is no firm evidence that misuse is systemic. And then there is accountability. If political staff do exercise power and influence, how is this to be checked? Governments in these countries have resisted parliamentary attempts at scrutiny, but concerns about accountability have led to the introduction of codes of conduct for political staff or calls for their introduction. In this respect, the UK leads the way: it has long had a public code of conduct for special advisers and, unlike the other countries examined, parliamentary scrutiny of political staff in the UK has meant that there are relatively detailed—albeit patchy—records of those serving as special advisers over a long period of time.

The number of political staff in Australia and Canada are much greater: 200–300 in Canada and 340 in Australia, compared with 100 in the UK. As numbers have increased in Australia and Canada, management problems have become more pronounced, as have accusations that political staff create a barrier between minister and the career bureaucracy. Improving the recruitment, induction, training and management of political staff is a recommendation that has been made in both countries as a result. But the implementation of such reforms has been difficult, mostly because of limited time and the rushed, ad hoc nature of politics generally. The UK is only beginning to address these issues, but they are likely to intensify as numbers rise.

Ministerial *cabinets*—a group of staffers personally chosen by the minister—are another institutional form of ministerial support. They are often seen as 'continental' rather than 'Westminster' in nature. There are two points of difference: first, while *cabinet* staff are personally appointed by the minister in many countries, a plurality tend to be officials from the career bureaucracy—they are not 'outsiders', but are in fact consummate insiders; and, second, *cabinets* often have greater autonomy and power to direct career officials than political staff in Westminster countries.

Cabinets have been the subject of some criticism: they are accused of distancing the minister from his or her department, marginalising career officials who are not in the *cabinet* and becoming the centre of policy development to the detriment of the department. Like other forms of ministerial support, then, *cabinets* are often regarded as a threat to the career bureaucracy's relationship with the minister.

But perhaps regardless of organisational form, country or institution, some of the lessons about effectiveness and ineffectiveness are the same. Ministers have seen the personal appointment of staff as providing a valuable resource for them, and to secure greater responsiveness from the bureaucracy. At the same time, such personal appointments also have the potential to cause friction between the minister and career bureaucracy, and the personalised nature of such staff and proximity to power may lead to concerns about inappropriate influence. Various regulatory frameworks and ad hoc responses have drafted and published, but the very political nature of the work of political staff means that the potential for controversy is high. This is a price that has to be paid for the advantages that political staff bring.

9

Improving the Performance of Special Advisers

ROBERT HAZELL

I do think they need to professionalise a bit more and become more hard-nosed about who they pick as their special advisers, and they need to work out what job role they want. It's still a bit amateurish really. (Senior civil servant)

I. DEFINING EFFECTIVENESS

MEASURING THE EFFECTIVENESS of special advisers depends on what they are appointed to do. As we have seen in earlier chapters, they have multifarious roles: they may be appointed primarily as policy experts, as media advisers, for liaison with the Party or as a personal assistant and loyal friend (see chapter four). In these roles they will be representing their minister's views to the civil service, to other ministers, to No 10, to the media, to the Party, to parliamentarians and to interest groups. The work involves being the minister's eyes and ears in the department and outside, being a progress chaser, troubleshooter and fire-fighter, providing moral support to the minister and generally watching his or her back.

To a degree, the effectiveness of any special adviser can only be judged by the minister for whom they work. It is ultimately a personal appointment, which depends crucially on retaining the minister's trust and confidence. When special advisers depart, it is almost always either because the minister loses his or her position or because the special adviser decides to move on. While a handful of advisers have also departed on the grounds of conduct (eg, Jo Moore and Adam Smith), it is uncommon for a minister to remove an adviser simply on grounds of not being up to the job.

It is clear, therefore, that the great majority of ministers have been satisfied with the performance of their advisers—or at the very least have valued the strengths of their advisers more than any perceived weaknesses. But measuring advisers' effectiveness cannot simply be an issue of the relationship between adviser and minister. Our research therefore sought views from a wider range of sources than ministers: we interviewed officials, other special advisers, politicians, lobbyists and journalists, all of whom had different perspectives on what makes special advisers effective or ineffective. From those interviews, we obtained a more balanced and rounded view of how well special advisers perform their different roles and how they might improve their performance. This chapter opens with a summary of those interview findings, and then goes on to discuss the suggestions made by our interviewees of ways in which the performance of special advisers might be improved. In one of those interviews, one former Labour special adviser accepted the value of a more rounded view:

> It is all very well if your political patron says you are doing a good job … But actually, you need the civil servants also. Part of your value is whether the civil servants think that you are contributing, rather than just if your political boss thinks you are contributing.

II. EVIDENCE OF EFFECTIVE SPECIAL ADVISERS

Most of our interviewees spoke of special advisers in very positive terms: they perform an indispensable role; they are committed and hard working; and they definitely add value to the political and policy process. Ministers are so pressured in modern politics that they could not operate without them. A few special advisers were singled out for special praise. The most frequently mentioned was the long-serving Geoffrey Norris (who worked for Tony Blair in No 10 from 1997 to 2007, for Gordon Brown in No 10 from 2007 to 2008 and then for Peter Mandelson in BERR/BIS from 2008 to 2010):

> Geoffrey Norris over time developed a great deal of knowledge and experience and commanded the respect of both Tony Blair and then Peter Mandelson. And he was also shrewd and wise enough not to get in the way of ministers working with officials. He could give genuinely good advice about what Mandelson was thinking—but would then often suggest a meeting with Mandelson to ensure we were on the right lines. (Senior official, BIS)

What qualities make for an effective special adviser? Summing up the answers from our interviews, we can depict effectiveness in the qualities listed in Table 9.1.

For more detailed guidance, see the handbook *Being a Special Adviser* (London, Constitution Unit, 2014).

We will expand on eight of the most important qualities in the following paragraphs.

A. Close Relationship with the Secretary of State

First, an effective special adviser must have a strong and close personal relationship with his or her secretary of state. Whether dealing with civil servants,

Table 9.1 The 'perfect' special adviser

Characteristic	Description
Strategic	Focused on the minister's key priorities, not trying to get involved in everything.
Political	Adding the party political dimension as gleaned from Parliament, the Party and the media agenda with other political intelligence.
Professionally experienced	In policy development or media handling, as well as in politics.
Creative but practical	Governments start with manifesto commitments, but may need new policy ideas as Parliaments progress or an election gets nearer.
Cooperative	With the civil service and other colleagues, working with, not against them.
Analytical	Government is complex and technical, and solutions are not easy.
Efficient	Commenting quickly and clearly on papers, parliamentary questions etc avoids creating a blockage or holding up business.
Open	With the civil service and with junior ministers. Sharing knowledge and information leads to better advice and decision making.
Challenging	Constructive questioning of accepted wisdom but never bullying.
Flexible	The day-to-day business of government is unpredictable. Special advisers have to be ready to provide support on the unexpected as well as the planned.
Loyal and trustworthy	Loyal to the government as a whole as well as their secretary of state, trustworthy and discreet.
Informed and outward looking	Aware of what is happening inside and outside Whitehall and accessible to outside interests and expertise.
Committed	Ministers work a 15–18 hour day. Special advisers must be ready to do the same.

Parliament or journalists, an adviser is representing his or her immediate boss. His or her value is inevitably undermined if he or she is not seen to be reliably reflecting the views of the secretary of state. This does not mean that the adviser must automatically be able to predict his or her boss's views on every single issue, but an adviser who is not perceived as having a very close relationship rapidly loses credibility.

B. Clear Political Objectives

Second, any adviser—like any secretary of state—is most likely to be effective if he or she can articulate clearly the political objectives they are pursuing, whether to Whitehall officials or to the media. Officials do not have daily access to the secretary of state and do not necessarily know what the minister's concerns are on any given issue, so the adviser is a vital intermediary. In a similar way, media advisers need to be able to articulate to journalists not only what policies are being proposed, but why. And all special advisers need to maintain strong links with the Party.

C. Clear Priorities

Third, effective special advisers need to be able to prioritise ruthlessly. They cannot give every subject area in a department equal attention, so they must be able to judge which issues require significant input, which can be the subject of light touch supervision and which just have to be left to one side. Media advisers similarly need to focus on the political priorities, letting the departmental press office manage routine press issues. Advisers who try to do everything risk doing nothing well. This means knowing when not to intervene as much as when to do so:

> In giant political and administrative machines, it is not possible to stop every policy you believe to be undesirable or even damaging, whatever your authority. As a No 10 adviser, husbanding finite time and goodwill, there was a price to trying to stop the pet projects of ministers and colleagues, however wrong-headed I conceived them to be.[1]

D. Drive and Determination

Fourth, advisers generally and policy advisers in particular need considerable personal drive and commitment, and have to demonstrate that commitment by their personal engagement in key issues. There is little doubt, for example, that Geoffrey Norris drove industrial policy throughout the Labour Governments of 1997–2010, whether working in No 10 or in the business department. Similarly, Andrew (now Lord) Adonis, made a strong personal impact on education policy before himself becoming a minister. In both cases, it was clear that they were speaking on behalf of their ministers, but their personal and sustained attention to the subject matter made a considerable difference.

---

[1] Andrew Adonis, *Education, Education, Education* (Biteback 2012) 75–76.

E. Good on Policy Detail

Fifth, the most effective policy special advisers are those who are ready and willing to get stuck into the substance of any policy issue. This does not mean that special advisers always need to be policy experts, but it does mean that advisers need to understand the substance of the issues that their ministers and officials are grappling with. Under Labour, Shriti Vadera was well respected as a special adviser at the Treasury—whatever the concerns about her personal style—for her willingness to engage with the detail of complex financial and commercial issues. Under the Coalition, Chris Nicholson, the special adviser at the Department of Energy and Climate Change, is similarly respected for his skills as an economist with long experience of dealing with energy issues.

F. Challenging Conventional Wisdom

Sixth, special advisers need to be able where necessary to have the self-confidence to challenge conventional wisdom. Officials will almost inevitably begin a re-examination of any policy issue by defending what they are currently doing, especially if the policy has already been agreed by the current government. But a good adviser will be sufficiently robust and intellectually competent to challenge the prevailing orthodoxy: 'the best special advisers added value by challenging received departmental wisdom and exposing the political realities or unrealities of suggested lines of policy' (MOD official). 'Special advisers can and do drive policy down paths that officials would not incline to take, or even see' (former Permanent Secretary).

G. Media Sense

Seventh, effective media advisers need to have a strong sixth sense in order to anticipate how the media might react to different news stories and events. Media reaction to a new policy proposal may quickly determine whether a policy flies or rapidly loses credibility. Being able to present a new policy persuasively is a critical skill. But so too is the ability to judge when a policy, however sensible it might seem in Whitehall, will be trashed by the media or is unlikely to attract popular support or compliance. An effective communications operation from any government will need to minimise the number of U-turns under pressure from a hostile media.

H. Good at Building Relationships

Eighth, special advisers are likely to be most effective where they are capable of developing positive relationships with others, whether these are officials, third parties or the media. Here are third-party descriptions of a pair of advisers, one in the Home Office and the other in No 10, who both knew how to manage relationships:

> So, someone like Ed Owen for example was very highly respected. He was trusted by backbench MPs, he was trusted by junior ministers and he was trusted by his secretary of state. As a consequence, people confided in him and provided him with information and asked him for help. (Labour special adviser)

> He was very, very good at managing stakeholders and representing the Prime Minister and me … Keeping people on side, giving them an outlet, someone to talk to, being responsible and responsive. (Former Labour Secretary of State)

Finally, it would be wrong to finish such a list of qualities without returning to the issue of personal support for the minister. One Labour Cabinet minister characterised this very concisely.

> [Looking after me] is an indefinable quality, but a crucial one. Always watching out for me, so that I wouldn't make a mistake in losing my temper, or become over-aggravated with the bureaucracy, which was easy to be aggravated with. Or stopping me making a mistake by taking on too many challenges at once, which I was inclined to do; or getting on the wrong side of Downing Street unnecessarily.

And here is a Conservative minister saying something very similar:

> It has to be someone you can trust 100 per cent. And they have to know you well. To know how you think. And to know how you are likely to react to emerging issues, good or bad. You can't yourself deal with everything all the time. So your special advisers need to take some of the load off you, be able to tell officials and others how you will react to issues and to be looking out on your behalf for things which could become a concern. Spotting bear traps. Trust is the most important attribute.

III. INEFFECTIVE SPECIAL ADVISERS

However, the interviews also threw up examples of ineffective special advisers, who through their lack of knowledge or lack of skill proved poor performers. Sometimes they performed so badly that their performance was deemed counterproductive. Common themes that recurred in the interviews to explain this poor performance were the inexperience of some special advisers, excessive zeal in promoting their minister's interest against those of the government or the department, unacceptable or aggressive behaviour, and secrecy or lack of communication. These failings are illustrated below with quotations taken from our interviews in order to show that these criticisms of ineffective special advisers are shared by ministers as well as officials, and indeed by other special advisers.

A. Examples of Ineffectiveness

i. Inexperience

Most special advisers are not as young and inexperienced as their public image might suggest. As we saw in chapter three, the median starting age for all special advisers between 1979 and 2012 was 34, but this age is coming down. Those appointed under the Conservatives (1979–97) had a median age of 37, under Labour (1997–2010) it was 33 and the median starting age under the Coalition has been 31. People notice when special advisers are too young and inexperienced, as the following comments show (and the last two come from special advisers themselves):

> X was really too young and inexperienced for the role so never really brought much weight to it. He improved towards the end but he was still too lightweight. (Senior official)

> Sometimes you just wish there was some more weight there. Some older, wiser heads amongst the young, enthusiastic crop. (Special adviser)

> I am struck at how young the spad network is and how inexperienced. (Another special adviser)

ii. Overstepping the Mark

Overstepping the mark can take a variety of forms. The most notorious examples involved media advisers such as Jo Moore and Damian McBride (see chapter six).[2] However, examples mentioned in our interviews illustrate other ways in which special advisers can exceed their authority: by giving instructions to officials; by blocking access to ministers; by freelancing—promoting their own policy ideas without checking with the minister; and by briefing against other ministers.

iii. Giving Instructions to Officials

> Jo Moore was a catalyst which highlighted a big problem. Stephen Byers was incapable of taking a decision. She was his henchman not only on the information side but in the Department. She would demand of the Perm Sec that certain officials would get moved and others promoted … She was ruthless, she wasn't under control because Byers didn't want it. He gave her the licence, she took it, and at some point it was bound to run out of control. (Senior official)

---

[2] Public Administration Select Committee, *These Unfortunate Events: Lessons of Recent Events at the Former DTLR*, HC 303, July 2002; Damian McBride, *Power Trip: A Decade of Policy, Plots and Spin* (Biteback 2013).

The above view was supported by other officials. It illustrates a common difficulty with special advisers overstepping the mark: they may be licensed by their ministers to do so.

iv. Restricting Access to Officials

> If you have senior officials in effect reporting to spads—as officials at the Treasury clearly reported direct to Vadera—it can be very dangerous ... With Vadera it was much more 'I control access to Brown' and she behaved accordingly—even preventing access to ministers. So she became in effect just too powerful. The whole idea of having neutral civil servants depends on officials getting direction from ministers, not advisers. (Senior official)

v. Freelancing

> Those spads who are 'freelancing' with their own agendas make life difficult for their minister and for officials. Officials are there to enable the PM and government to deliver its agenda, not the private agenda of an unelected special adviser. (Labour special adviser)

vi. Briefing against Other Ministers

> Politics is a team game. The spad has got to be part of your team, but they've got to be integrated into a bigger team. I think the good spads knew that, and the ego spads made that more difficult. (Former Labour Secretary of State)

> Too much politicking and briefing against colleagues, especially in the Brown government. (Former Labour special adviser)

As we noted in chapter seven, there will always be tensions between special advisers promoting the narrow interest of their secretary of state and serving the government as a whole. The 2010 *Code of Conduct for Special Advisers* inserted a new provision that they are there 'to serve the Government as a whole and not just their appointing Minister'.[3] David Cameron reminded all special advisers of this at their first collective meeting. The Coalition has certainly seen less of the internecine warfare which was so debilitating under the Brown and Blair Governments. The Centre imposed tighter discipline from the start:

> He made that very clear and he's made that clear on other occasions as well. The golden rule that we operate is that you just wouldn't ever brief against a colleague. (Coalition special adviser)

---

[3] Cabinet Office, *Code of Conduct for Special Advisers* (2010) para 2.

When we first met [in a group meeting for all the special advisers] it was a very inspiring meeting, that spads are the glue of government and that no kind of Coalition backbiting or undermining would be tolerated whatsoever. (No 10 special adviser)

Although there has been less briefing against colleagues, personal attacks against the Government's critics have continued under the Coalition. As part of our background research, we did a trawl for all media allegations of special adviser misconduct between 1997 and 2013. We found 26 instances, with media special advisers being implicated in all but one case. The type of misconduct most frequently alleged was personal attack. This is prohibited under the *Code of Conduct for Special Advisers*, which instructs special advisers to 'observe discretion and express comment with moderation, avoiding personal attacks'.[4]

vii. *Arrogant and Bullying Behaviour*

Some of these episodes can be attributed to arrogant behaviour by special advisers on a power trip. Arrogant behaviour is not ineffective per se, but it is rarely the most effective way to get the best out of civil servants:

You get a lot of arrogance … carry-over from the ministerial power kick that happens because you're suddenly in charge. People are opening doors for you, you're being driven about, you've got boxes and diary secretaries. (Liberal Democrat special adviser)

The real menace is the arrogance of the team of advisers and others around the PM in Downing Street—a nightmare. (Former Labour special adviser responding to our survey)

But the civil service had a separate and more specific complaint about unacceptable and abusive behaviour. This was a theme which cropped up several times in our interviews:

Treating junior staff badly would be a classic [complaint] … in a way that no one would tolerate in any standard business environment. (Former Cabinet Secretary)

X modelled some of the worst New Labour spad behaviours—flash and arrogant, shouted at people and behaved badly but got away with things because [the Secretary of State] would back him whatever. (Senior official)

Abusive behaviour is not confined to men. Gordon Brown's adviser Shriti Vadera was said to reduce junior members of staff to tears, and shouted at people so much she was dubbed 'Shriti the Shriek'.[5]

---

[4] ibid para 12. Paragraph 6 also prohibits the 'preparation or dissemination of inappropriate material or personal attacks'. For the analysis, see Daniella Lock, 'Special Advisers and Public Allegations of Misconduct 1997–2013', https://www.ucl.ac.uk/constitution-unit/research/special-advisers.

[5] 'Shriti Vadera's fierce reputation earned her the nickname "Shriti the Shriek"' *Daily Telegraph* (15 January 2009); 'Not for Nothing is Baroness Vadera Known as "Shriti the Shriek"' *Daily Telegraph* (24 September 2009).

I can remember one meeting in which she came in late, left early, and … just fired a volley of abuse at the civil servants. It was right out of [the satirical television series about the inner workings of government] *The Thick of It.* (Labour special adviser)

Nor is the bad behaviour confined to some Labour special advisers, although they appear to have been particularly bad. Tensions and hostility towards officials have also featured under the Coalition government, as this Coalition special adviser observed:

The most ineffective special advisers, I think, are those who seek to work against the civil service. Who brief against them, and who constantly gossip about them, and blame them for everything that is going wrong. It is very unhelpful and destructive and causes a lot of disillusion within the civil service. Especially when those officials are trying very hard to deliver a particularly difficult programme under 33 per cent cuts.

A senior official under the Coalition commented in similar terms:

What's concerning is not the level of relentless hostility from spads, but the fact that halfway through the Parliament it's getting stronger. Too many spads see themselves as engaged in jihad against the public sector … That makes it almost impossible to build or maintain relationships.

The Department for Education hit the headlines when Michael Gove's adviser Dominic Cummings was named in an internal grievance report involving a DfE senior official who complained of bullying and intimidation.[6] It was not the first time that Cummings had been in the news. His appointment had initially been blocked by Andy Coulson in No 10 as too high risk.[7] Gove's advisers overstepped the mark in other ways. In 2011 they were criticised by the Information Commissioner for using private email accounts to conduct official business.[8] In 2013 they were in the news again, as being behind @toryeducation, a pro-Gove Twitterfeed which fiercely attacked his opponents.[9]

---

[6] The complaint described a 'macho culture of intimidation, favouritism and "laddism"' in the communications department, with Cummings singled out as 'widely known to use obscene and intimidating language'. James Cusick, '"Dump F***ing Everyone": The Inside Story of How Michael Gove's Vicious Attack Dogs are Terrorising the DfE' *The Independent* (15 February 2013).

[7] 'Andy Coulson, Director of Communications, Blocked Cummings' Appointment as a Government Adviser on the Basis that He Might Be Too Independent and a Disruptive Force' *The Guardian* (11 October 2013).

[8] Information Commissioner decision FS50422276, 1 March 2012; 'Education Department "Deleted Email Exchanges" with Michael Gove Adviser' *The Guardian* (3 March 2012).

[9] Toby Helm, 'Are Dark Arts Spinning Out of Control in Michael Gove's Department?' *The Observer* (3 February 2013); 'Michael Gove's Officials Act to Clean Up Abusive @toryeducation Twitter Feed' *The Guardian* (16 February 2013).

viii. *Poor Communication*

Poor communication was a particular problem in some departments where the special advisers acted as a barrier between their minister and officials rather than as facilitators:

> Special advisers who wouldn't communicate with other special advisers. Who would work in that rather bunker like mentality, just with their minister. That would be very unhelpful to the teamwork, and it could be quite destructive. (Coalition special adviser)

> No one in the department really knew what Byers' position was, because so much was being managed by the spads and being communicated to the media directly without the department knowing the line. If the spads don't communicate within the department, then you have chaos. (Senior official, DTLR)

Sometimes when special advisers acted as a barrier, it reflected their ministers' own wishes and operating style. Brown, Byers, David Blunkett and Ruth Kelly were all mentioned as ministers who gathered a coterie round them and kept the civil service at bay. If their special advisers guarded them in their bunkers, it was what their ministers wanted.

Poor communication could also be a problem between special advisers in different departments, and particularly with No 10:

> One of the advisers was very counterproductive, in terms of deliberately trying to fan differences between No 10 and the Department. Basically the objective was to keep [the departmental adviser] out of meetings, as far to the side as possible ... Often the relations are actually better between the spad at the centre and the officials. (Labour special adviser in No 10)

Sometimes special advisers do not deliberately block, but just hold things up:

> In my experience, some spads are just blockages in that they want to see absolutely every-thing—but don't actually have any real views when they do see things. (Senior official)

IV. POSSIBLE SOLUTIONS VERSUS THE REALITY OF MINISTERIAL CHOICE

We have set out at some length these extracts from our interviews in order to demonstrate that there are real problems in terms of the inexperience of some special advisers, plus overstepping the mark, unacceptable behaviour and lack of communication. But it is one thing to expound the problems caused by ineffective special advisers; quite another to devise workable solutions. When we discussed possible solutions, our interviewees were divided: some proposed various forms of intervention or improvement, discussed below. But most recognised that within the current system, there is little that can be done to improve the performance of special advisers without constraining ministerial choice. Also, ministers will be reluctant to see any restrictions over their selection of advisers or the way that they use them. If they want a 'bag carrier' more than a policy expert, that is still regarded as their prerogative; although under the Coalition, the Centre will not allow ineffective special advisers in key departments or policy areas. But otherwise ministers have the right to retain advisers even when others regard them as sub-optimal or positively dysfunctional. It is a highly personal relationship, as our interviewees confirmed:

> There is no standard model and the most effective advisers are those who can tune exactly with their ministers and the needs of the time. So success is not age, or particular expertise. It is about the chemistry of the core relationship. (Special adviser)

> You do have to work these things around the personality of the minister. (Labour special adviser)

> If you're a minister coming into government, you clearly want to take someone in with you you absolutely trust. And the people you completely trust may not be the people who fulfil. (Special adviser)

Most of the proposals that were made for improving the effectiveness of special advisers involve greater professionalisation and greater centralisation to ensure that the improvement happens. In an ideal world, ministers would take greater responsibility for improving the recruitment, support, supervision and performance management of their special advisers, but most ministers have shown little aptitude or willingness to do so, and that is unlikely to change. Ministers are also likely to resist any changes which reduce their freedom of choice and flexibility. We recognise the resistance that there is likely to be to any centralisation of the recruitment and management of special advisers.

However, it is important to rehearse the different options because these were all suggestions discussed in our interviews. There is a connection here with the debate about how to increase ministerial effectiveness: a growing debate, but one still in its infancy.[10] Attempts were made before the 1997 and the 2010 elections to prepare shadow ministers for the realities of governing, and some limited induction training was provided to new ministers in 2010.[11] There have also been some experiments in providing ministers with 360-degree feedback on their performance as a limited form of appraisal. These initiatives would have been unthinkable a few years ago. So suggestions for improving the effectiveness of special advisers which are regarded as visionary or impracticable now might seem less heretical in five or 10 years' time. And if the Coalition Government's plans for extended private offices lead in time to a further increase in the numbers of special advisers or other outsiders, the need for more effective recruitment, induction and support and supervision will only grow.

---

[10] Peter Riddell, Zoe Gruhn and Liz Carolan, *The Challenge of Being a Minister: Defining and Developing Ministerial Effectiveness* (Institute for Government 2011); Zoe Gruhn and Felicity Slater, *Special Advisers and Ministerial Effectiveness* (Institute for Government 2012).

[11] Peter Riddell and Catherine Haddon, *Transitions: Preparing for Changes of Government* (Institute for Government 2009).

V. RECRUITMENT

Recruitment is the biggest single determinant of the calibre of special advisers. Apart from the veto which can be exercised by No 10, there is no quality control of any kind. Ministers are free to choose whom they like. Chapter three showed a lot of variation in terms of how systematically ministers approach the task. On the formation of a new government, ministers will typically bring with them into government their opposition policy adviser or parliamentary researcher, with no competition. When appointing or replacing special advisers mid-term, some ministers will interview a few candidates in a closed competition, while others will see just one. The pool is limited, depending largely on whom ministers happen to know, or know of if they care to make inquiries. When we asked special advisers how they had been recruited, they spoke of learning about vacancies by word of mouth, on the grapevine. There is no advertising or open competition; the Cabinet Office says that open competition is not feasible because of the need for a close relationship of trust between minister and special adviser.[12] The following quotations illustrate the range of different practice and different attitudes amongst ministers about how systematic they wanted to be:

> [It's] all about patronage. If you had earned the loyalty of the politician that you worked for, they batted for you in order to get you into a department. (Labour special adviser)

> I generally thought that they all took recruitment quite seriously, not in the sense of having a formal process, but certainly in the sense of seeing more than one candidate and thinking hard about their choice. (Labour special adviser)

> The second time around was a more systematic process ... [the minister] chose to do a fairly formal process whereby we had a two-stage interview ... we all had to submit a short statement, in effect: 'This is our pitch for the job.' (Special adviser)

Some special advisers were critical of the haphazard nature of the recruitment process and of the tendency of many shadow ministers automatically to bring their opposition researcher with them into government. Of the Labour special advisers recruited on formation of the new Government in 1997, 21 had been parliamentary researchers and 14 were taken by their minister into government. This did not impress some special advisers, who felt the skills required in government were very different from those working in opposition:

> My reservation for what happened was that most just took their parliamentary researcher across with them, now that is not what I think [should happen] when a special adviser comes into government ... (Labour special adviser)

---

[12] Lord Irvine's appointment of his old friend Garry Hart was the subject of a legal challenge by two lawyers who argued that it was discriminatory to restrict the field to people already known to the Lord Chancellor. The challenge was unsuccessful: see *Coker and Osamor v The Lord Chancellor and the LCD* [2001] IRLR 116.

Parties need to think more carefully about recruitment of advisers. I was appointed mainly because of my policy expertise, and this could usefully become a more important recruitment criterion. (Labour special adviser)

However, some parliamentary researchers made the transition very successfully. Jack Straw's researcher Ed Owen was regarded as a highly effective special adviser, as were Blunkett's advisers Conor Ryan and Sophie Linden, and Blair's speech-writer Peter Hyman.

VI. RECRUITMENT BY A GOVERNMENT MID-TERM

It is helpful to think separately about the recruitment of special advisers by a new government when first entering office and subsequently. Subsequent appointments will be in ones and twos, but cumulatively their numbers can be as great as or greater than the total number of special advisers appointed by a new government when coming into office. Chapter three showed that the median tenure is two to three years. The Coalition appointed 63 special advisers upon entering government in May–June 2010; by the end of 2013, it had appointed the same number again as replacements or additional recruits.[13] For these subsequent appointments, ministers will have the support of the Whitehall machine if they care to use it. If they wanted to be more systematic and professional in their search for a new special adviser, they could:

— insist upon a job description and person specification;
— require some element of competition, even if it is a closed competition;
— invite others to be part of the selection process by doing an initial sift or being on the interview panel;
— include tests as part of the selection process (writing a brief, drafting a speech etc);
— insist upon advertisement and open competition.

These steps are set out in roughly ascending order of thoroughness and logistical complexity: open competitions, which attract large numbers of candidates (as these posts would), can be burdensome to administer. But it is to be hoped that ministers might at the least pursue the first two. Having a job description would require the minister to articulate what he or she wants his or her special adviser to do: to be a policy expert—and in which policy fields? A media expert? A link with the party? In addition, the person specification would help to identify what skills and experience are necessary to perform the role. Even experienced ministers can get this wrong. One senior Labour Cabinet minister appointed two generic special

---

[13] Cabinet Office, *Special Adviser Data Releases: Numbers and Costs*, 10 June 2010 and 25 October 2013, https://www.gov.uk/government/publications/special-adviser-data-releases-numbers-and-costs-october-2013.

advisers who told us they floundered when it came to press work because neither had media experience.

The two biggest steps forward would be job descriptions with person specifications and open competition. In government, the Liberal Democrats have developed job descriptions and person specifications when recruiting new special advisers. Open competition is still a step too far as a universal requirement because ministers may have someone in mind or prefer to run a closed competition. But it should be allowed if ministers want an open competition. The Commons Public Administration Select Committee has twice recommended that 'special adviser posts should be publicly advertised and the Minister given the final choice between suitably qualified candidates'.[14] The Cabinet Office says that open competition is not needed because special advisers are specifically exempt from the civil service requirement for fair and open competition.[15] However, just because open competition is not necessary does not mean that it is precluded. The Cabinet Office's second argument is that it is very difficult to advertise for positions which require such a close relationship of trust and confidence. But in other walks of life, such positions are advertised all the time: for housekeepers, personal assistants and parliamentary researchers. In earlier research on special advisers, Stephen Hanney found that one-third of the latter were not personally known to the minister on appointment.[16] And some ministers have advertised: for example, Jim Knight when Minister for Employment advertised for a special adviser on Twitter.[17] He said to us: 'I think it is shocking that ministers don't advertise. Because as ever, with any employer, you are just missing out on a lot of potential talent.' The most prominent minister who has advertised is Jack Straw. He ran an open competition when in Opposition, which attracted 200 applications, and resulted in the recruitment of Ed Owen, then an unknown journalist on the *Stockport Messenger*. In government he used headhunters to find a new special adviser when he was Foreign Secretary, but he also ran closed competitions. His example makes the point that ministers should not be compelled to advertise, but if they want to, they should be helped by the government machine.

VII. RECRUITMENT BY A NEW GOVERNMENT

As noted in chapter three, recruiting a whole cohort of special advisers when a new government first enters office is harder to get right. The rush of business as a new government tries to hit the ground running leaves no time for advertising

---

[14] Public Administration Select Committee, *Special Advisers: Boon or Bane?* HC 293, March 2001, para 55; Public Administration Select Committee (n 2) para 68.
[15] Information from interviews. For the exemption, see *Code of Conduct for Special Advisers* (n 3) para 3.
[16] Stephen Hanney, 'Special Advisers: Their Place in British Government' (PhD dissertation, Brunel University, 1993).
[17] See ch 3.

or open competition. In practice, a team of special advisers has to be appointed in the first few days, and most of those will have been chosen by their ministers while in opposition. So the recruitment choices are effectively ones made in opposition, not in government. And if the recruitment process is to be improved, it has to be done by the opposition, with the Leader and his or her chief of staff asking the shadow Cabinet to think hard about their choice of advisers, and using the implicit threat of a No 10 veto to raise the quality threshold.

The political parties are a step ahead of practice in government, with both Labour and the Conservatives using open competition to recruit political advisers (often called 'pads' within the Labour Party) to work for the Party. The Conservatives have advertised for political advisers to work in the Conservative Research Department, reporting to the Deputy Political Director, and Labour has advertised for political advisers to members of the Shadow Cabinet, working under the direction of the Senior Political Adviser.[18]

These political advisers are seen as special advisers in waiting. The difficulty is that working as an adviser in opposition offers only limited training for working in Whitehall, as many of our interviewees told us:

> People assume that because you did a job that sounds similar in opposition, and you come in as special adviser, they sound like similar jobs. But of course they're completely different ... running a shadow Secretary of State's office, where they might have two, two and a half people working on policy and media, and then going into a Department with thousands of civil servants and agencies are just completely different things. (Special adviser)

Another difficulty is that ministers may be appointed to a different portfolio from the one which they shadowed in opposition. For example, in 1997, 40 per cent of ministers in the incoming Cabinet had portfolios which they had not been shadowing in opposition.[19] They then have the dilemma: do they stick with the adviser they have come to know and trust or do they switch to the adviser who was shadowing their new portfolio? A third difficulty is that many members of the Shadow Cabinet have just one political adviser (paid for out of 'Short Money', state funding to support the Opposition's work in Parliament), while in government Cabinet ministers can expect to have two special advisers. This difficulty will be compounded if, following the Coalition's initiative, ministers want to have extended ministerial offices with additional advisers. Where will they come from and how will they be selected?

The recruitment pools for special advisers are relatively limited. Chapter three showed that the proportion recruited from the political parties (from Party headquarters or working as an MP's researcher) has increased over time, with think tanks, the media and public affairs also becoming important recruitment pools

---

[18] See, eg, the Conservative advertisement for political advisers in May 2012 and the Labour advertisement in September 2013 for a political adviser to the Shadow DEFRA Secretary.
[19] Riddell and Haddon (n 11) 31.

(the last two reflecting an increase in media work by special advisers). If their numbers are to be further increased, the recruitment pools need to be expanded. If ministers decide they want additional policy expertise rather than more media special advisers, they will need to recruit more actively from universities, think tanks, non-governmental organisations (NGOs) and consultancies as sources of policy expertise. Another big source of policy expertise is the civil service itself, which is not normally seen as a pool from which to recruit special advisers; but our survey of Labour special advisers suggested that one-fifth of special advisers had previously worked in the civil service at some point in their careers. Jonathan Powell, with his Foreign Office background, is just one high-profile example.

More professional recruitment of special advisers will happen only if the Prime Minister's chief of staff wants to make it more systematic and more rigorous (and, in coalition, the Deputy Prime Minister's chief of staff). One way of making it more systematic would be to maintain a central list of people who were interested in being special advisers and who had undergone an initial sift and interview to ensure their suitability (rather like the A-list of potential Party candidates). Ed Llewellyn (David Cameron's Chief of Staff) already maintains a list of possible candidates on an informal basis. When a vacancy arises, ministers could be referred to the list if they are short of ideas. Recognising the need to widen the pool, the Liberal Democrats have started a mentoring scheme, pairing outside policy experts with existing special advisers to give them the necessary political and parliamentary expertise.

So long as ministers remain free to appoint their own, one way of ensuring the selection process was more rigorous would be to use the Prime Minister's veto to achieve this by requiring minimum selection standards (job description, person specification or an element of competition). The veto has occasionally been used to weed out people with insufficient experience: William Hague was vetoed by Margaret Thatcher when proposed as a special adviser to Geoffrey Howe because he was aged only 21.[20] Tony Blair vetoed half a dozen candidates during his premiership. But this was to exclude people regarded as potential troublemakers rather than on the ground of insufficient experience. The situation is similar under the Coalition: as mentioned above, Dominic Cummings was vetoed as too risky when first proposed by Michael Gove, but in 2012 his appointment was allowed. Under the Coalition, the chiefs of staff of the Prime Minister and the Deputy Prime Minister interview all prospective special advisers, and candidates have occasionally been rejected.

[20] National Archives PREM/19/1043.

VIII. INDUCTION AND TRAINING

The lack of any proper induction or training was the biggest single complaint we heard from special advisers. In particular, new special advisers wanted a crash course in how Whitehall works:

> I think some training in how the civil service/departments work and some training in parliamentary procedures/processes would have been helpful. I had only rough knowledge gleaned from my degree upon which to draw. (Labour special adviser)

> The biggest challenge for those new to government is probably the actual mechanics and process of how government and the civil service work. You cannot learn this from a book outside government. If advisers have little familiarity with the Party, then induction is needed into the party and political elements of the role. (Labour special adviser)

The demand for training is not new. In 2002 the Commons Public Administration Committee recommended that:

> The Government should ensure that all special advisers receive induction training within three months of taking up the role ... The induction training for special advisers should cover: the structure and work of the relevant department; the scope and meaning of the various Codes of Conduct to which special advisers are subject; the implications of their status as temporary civil servants (including the business appointment rules process, and their obligations under public records and access to information legislation); the nature of their accountability to ministers (and ministers' accountability to Parliament); the role of permanent secretaries in managing the work and reputation of the department as a whole; and where to seek advice and support on propriety issues. This would ensure that all special advisers and their ministers have a shared understanding of what is expected and appropriate behaviour for special advisers.[21]

The Government responded laconically: 'The Government agrees.' But 10 years on, training remains almost non-existent. There is a half-day induction session in No 10, with talks by the Chief of Staff, the Director of Communications and by the Cabinet Office on propriety, and that is it. New special advisers are given the *Code of Conduct for Special Advisers*, shown their office and left to get on with it. Departments will generally organise briefings with senior officials on different policy areas, but no one tells special advisers about the inner workings of the government machine—Cabinet committees, EU councils, legislation and the rest. In 2010 it was left to the Institute for Government to provide some more imaginative induction training in the absence of any proper provision from Whitehall.

Everyone agrees on the need for training, especially at the start. But who should provide the training, and what should it consist of? Who provides the training and how it is delivered depends on the aim of the training and its content. What our interviewees wanted most was training about Whitehall and how it works: in our survey of Labour special advisers, calls for an induction about the civil service

---

[21] Public Administration Select Committee (n 2) para 45.

were overwhelming. That is mainly knowledge- rather than skills-based training. As such, it could be done largely online and in modular form so that new special advisers could access it as and when they want.

The obvious central department to pull together such training is the Cabinet Office, perhaps working in partnership with a body like the Institute for Government, to build on the good work it has already done. Towards the end of the last Labour Government, Joe Irvin organised quite a lot of training when he became Brown's Political Secretary, working with the National School of Government (the chief training establishment for civil servants, now abolished). A lot of material already exists, along with factual guides such as the Cabinet Manual (setting out the main laws, rules and conventions affecting the conduct and operation of government) and the more detailed guides to Whitehall for people like fast-stream civil servants.[22] The Constitution Unit of UCL has produced its new handbook, *Being a Special Adviser*.[23] It needs supplementing with a range of additional material: video clips of talks by former special advisers (the most popular session at the Institute for Government induction event), by the Cabinet Office on ethical conduct and by others with whom special advisers will interact the most—the Principal Private Secretary, Parliamentary Private Secretaries and the No 10 Policy Unit. Within departments there needs to be separate and tailored induction training about the work of the department, which can largely take the form of face-to-face sessions with the Principal Private Secretary, the Director of Communications, the parliamentary liaison team etc.

It is one thing to identify a need for training and suggest who should provide it, but quite another to make it happen. Following the abolition of the National School of Government and the fragmentation of training budgets, it may not be easy for the Cabinet Office even to provide the basic induction training suggested here. An organisation such as the Institute for Government would be an excellent partner, building on the induction training it provided in 2010 and making a bridge from the training it has already provided for shadow ministers and their staff. Having an independent partner might also help get over any anxieties that the civil service was trying to 'house train' special advisers.

A final difficulty is persuading special advisers to attend. The start of a new government is frenetic and it is very difficult to find any spare time. Attendance at the No 10 induction session in 2010 was poor. It will only improve if the Prime Minister's chief of staff makes attendance compulsory, and ministers agree. This would require a change in the leadership role of the chief of staff, which we explore in the final sections of the chapter.

---

[22] https://www.gov.uk/government/uploads/system/uploads/attachment_data/file/60641/cabinet-manual.pdf; Paul Grant and Christopher Jary, *Understanding British Government* (National School of Government 2011), required reading for the Understanding Government course procured through Civil Service Learning.

[23] This is available at the Constitution Unit website (under 'outputs'): www.ucl.ac.uk/constitution-unit/research/special-advisers.

Providing induction training for special advisers who join a government mid-term is easier in some respects and more difficult in others. It is easier in that there may be less of a frenetic rush, so that a newly appointed adviser should find it easier to take some time out, but it is harder to lay on training courses for advisers appointed in ones and twos. So the induction training from the Cabinet Office will perforce be largely online, and in modules which the new recruits can download as and when they want. Filming all the induction training provided at the beginning of the government would be a sensible investment for subsequent recruits. Within departments, there will need to be separate and tailored induction training of the kind provided to the first special advisers. One simple thing that all replacement special advisers should ask for is a meeting with their predecessor and a handover document or a handover period in which they work alongside their predecessor to learn the ropes. Handover meetings have even taken place between special advisers of different parties, with some outgoing Labour special advisers in 2010 briefing their successors about the strengths and weaknesses in their new department.

IX. SUPPORT AND SUPERVISION

Special advisers do a very demanding and stressful and high-profile job, which can sometimes leave them feeling exposed and uncertain what to do. They have had no formal structures of support or supervision, but under the Coalition, that has started to change. They receive little or no feedback as to whether they are performing well or badly, or how they could improve. This section considers what support systems are available and possible supervisory mechanisms, both for supervising their day-to-day work and when things go wrong.

In terms of practical support, special advisers are given a personal assistant or private secretary, but this person is rarely senior or experienced enough to offer advice on how the department works. So one way of improving their support would be to upgrade this post to middle-ranking civil servants such as a Higher Executive Officer (HEO) or a Senior Executive Officer (SEO) or their equivalents, or possibly to allocate fast-streamers on rotation as part of the wider training that fast-streamers receive. When they need advice on how to act, special advisers will normally turn first to the principal private secretary and in more serious cases to the permanent secretary. There has been no formal mentoring system for special advisers, but some informal mentoring goes on. This could be formalised; it would help if every new special adviser was paired with a more experienced one to whom he or she could turn for help and advice.

The other potential source of ongoing advice and support is from No 10 or the Cabinet Office. On Fridays, special advisers are brought together in a weekly or fortnightly meeting convened by the chief of staff in No 10 (under Labour, the convenor was the head of the Policy Unit). Under the Coalition, all the special advisers meet together as well as holding separate meetings in their respective party groups. There have also been meetings just of media advisers. Views about the utility of these meetings varied:

> I knew people who were special advisers in 1996, in the Conservative Government, and they felt very, very isolated from each other. I was very keen to avoid that. If you are a special adviser, you need to know what is happening across government, what the Government's and Party's positions are. (Labour special adviser)

> We meet as a team once a week. That is very important, and a useful exchange. We are very supportive to each other. It is about making sure that people feel part of a team, feel informed, and in the loop. (Liberal Democrat media special adviser)

> As Liberal Democrat and Conservative spads, we have a Friday meeting. The effectiveness of which is extremely limited, if I'm honest. It's just too many people. It's done as running through what's coming up and some main issues … useful if they need to tell us all something as one. (Conservative special adviser)

> Those must be some of the most expensive meetings in terms of manpower and the most under-utilised in terms of the Centre being able to communicate to this group of people who are open and willing to carry messages across government. Completely under-utilised. (Conservative special adviser)

> The limitation on discussing important or sensitive issues in such large gatherings is fear of leaks. The size of the meeting also means these are not occasions when special advisers can raise individual difficulties. In the past these have been taken to the Political Secretary or his equivalent: 'So people who had problems, I think the Political Secretary would be the person they would probably come to.' (Former No 10 adviser)

Under the Coalition, the support and supervision arrangements have improved. The Conservatives and Liberal Democrats have both appointed a Deputy Chief of Staff with specific responsibility for supervising the other special advisers. They in turn have enlisted senior special advisers to help manage different teams: the media special advisers, the Policy Unit, or for the Liberal Democrats the half-dozen 'cross-departmental' special advisers. The Coalition has also introduced appraisals for the first time, once in 2011 and again in early 2014. The 2011 appraisals were optional; not everyone took part because of difficulties about disclosure and who would have access to the appraisal reports. The second round will draw upon feedback from ministers, the Permanent Secretary, the Principal Private Secretary, No 10/the Cabinet Office, the whips and the Party.

This is a big step forward from the previous absence of any feedback or appraisal system, and it begins to suggest an answer to the question of who is responsible for special advisers in HR terms. Previously, special advisers operated in a twilight zone where no one was responsible. Some argued that the permanent secretary should be made formally responsible, but since special advisers' pay and related matters are decided centrally, it would be better for the HR matters to be handled centrally as well. This could also provide an answer to who should take responsibility when things go wrong. We repeat here the comment of a former Cabinet Secretary, first quoted in chapter seven:

> In theory ministers are in charge of disciplining and the like, and that means that nobody is in charge. Ministers don't do it, they don't like doing it. I've had personal experience of there being complaints to me about special advisers, where I've gone to the minister concerned and said: 'This is a problem. This special adviser's not behaving properly and not treating people in a way that we would expect civil servants to treat people.' The minister has said: 'That's very tough; can you sort it out, please?'

The Cabinet Secretary could not do anything because formally only the minister is responsible for appointing, disciplining or dismissing his or her special adviser (see chapter seven). However, there is a secondary line of responsibility to the Prime Minister, who has to approve the appointment of special advisers and can disapprove them. In practice these decisions are taken on advice from the chief of staff. They could be delegated to a deputy chief of staff, made responsible for better personnel management and supervision of all the special advisers:

> Ultimately the problem with this group is that they don't have any career structure, there's no accountability. What I would like to see is a post of Chief Political Adviser in No 10, whose job was to be the senior spad, and reporting to the Prime Minister directly … That person would be in charge of the appraisal and the behaviour, and ensuring a Code of Conduct of all the spads working within government. They would be setting them objectives, they would be getting feedback from the Department, the Secretary of State, other Secretaries of State about their behaviour. (Former Cabinet Secretary)

Under the Coalition, this has started to happen. The chiefs of staff have called in errant special advisers to rein them in. But the formal disciplinary power remains with the Secretary of State: in practice, disciplinary action can only be taken if the Secretary of State consents.

So special advisers are beginning to take more responsibility for the conduct of their colleagues. Legislation in 2010 gave them the legal authority to manage other special advisers.[24] And they are certainly capable of managing other advisers, as these two extracts from our interviews show:

> There was definitely a hierarchy [in the Treasury]. Ed Balls was the boss, Ed Miliband was the deputy boss. They divided policy between them, so your line manager was one of them, depending on which policy area you had. (Labour special adviser)

> Jonny and I meet on a weekly basis. He is my line manager, I run through my work programme, he runs through the things he needs to get me up to speed on. It is standard management practice, and quite efficient. (Liberal Democrat special adviser)

---

[24] 'A special advisers code may permit a special adviser to exercise any power … in relation to another special adviser': Constitutional Reform and Governance Act 2010, s 8(6).

X. CONCLUSION: THE NEED FOR GREATER PROFESSIONALISM

Any concerted attempts to improve the recruitment, the induction and training or the support and supervision arrangements for special advisers will have to come from the centre of Whitehall, and so will inevitably involve a degree of centralisation. Such attempts are likely to be resisted as bureaucratic attempts to impose standardisation on a group of personal appointees whose whole strength is their close personal relationship with ministers, their heterogeneity of skills and experience, and their willingness to challenge Whitehall orthodoxy. But, as with any process of change, it is a question of balance, how skilfully the change is managed and by whom.

If attempts to improve the effectiveness of special advisers are led by the civil service, by permanent secretaries or the Cabinet Secretary, they are doomed to fail. The quotation above from the former Cabinet Secretary shows that the civil service recognises this. Any initiative must come from special advisers themselves, and in particular from the Prime Minister's chief of staff as the chief special adviser, and the Prime Minister's deputy chief of staff. Through the Prime Minister's veto the chief of staff controls the recruitment of all other special advisers, and through the same levers, he has the capacity to improve recruitment processes, and the support and supervision of special advisers if he wishes to do so. Induction remains better suited to the civil service, plus other training providers, but the Cabinet Office needs a push from the chief of staff if it is to organise a better package of induction training.

Special advisers are now an established feature in Whitehall. There are almost 100 of them and their numbers may well increase further. They constitute a mini-profession, with their own code of conduct and regulatory framework. As other professions have grown, their members have recognised the need to become more professional in developing their professional skills, their professional standards, their individual conduct and the collective regulation of their conduct. Whether ministers and their special advisers are ready to accept the need for greater professionalism and greater centralisation is an issue to which we return in the final chapter.

10

A Profession Comes of Age

ROBERT HAZELL

> Government is a machine, but it is a machine which needs driving. And it can only be driven by ministers and special advisers (directed by ministers). It needs and wants political direction. (Former head of No 10 Policy Unit)

THIS CHAPTER BEGINS by summarising some of our main findings in response to the questions we posed in chapter one. These were: why do ministers appoint special advisers? What are their roles and functions? Who becomes a special adviser? And how can their role and effectiveness be improved? It does so by tracing the rise of special advisers, their main characteristics, the roles they perform, and their successes and their failures. It then sets those findings in a broader context by linking them to current debates about the support needed for ministers, and the Coalition Government's proposals for extended ministerial offices. If extended ministerial offices lead to a further increase in the number of special advisers, then the political parties and Whitehall will need to grasp issues about their recruitment, support and management, career structure and professional development which have been ignored for too long.

I. THE EVOLUTION OF SPECIAL ADVISERS

It is 40 years since special advisers started working as an identifiable cadre in Whitehall. Since then their numbers have more than doubled, and are still rising (see Figure 2.1). They have not mostly been as young as is popularly conceived, with the median age between 1979 and 2013 having been around 34 years on appointment. But they are growing younger, with the median starting age of the Coalition cohort being 31. They are mostly highly educated, coming from Russell Group universities, with a third having a postgraduate degree.

Conservative special advisers (1979–97) were fewer in number, slightly older on appointment and tended to include more policy experts, remaining within the same department in spite of changes of minister. Under Margaret Thatcher, they were more likely to be appointed from business, academia and the civil service. Under John Major, and then Labour and the Coalition, they were increasingly recruited from political party staffs or the public relations industry, the media and think tanks. Policy experts were supplemented by people whose expertise lay primarily in media and communications. The doubling in the numbers of special advisers under Labour was primarily due to a big increase in media advisers. Under the Coalition, the numbers have increased by a further 50 per cent, primarily because of the additional demands of coalition management.

Recruitment depends on when it takes place in the life cycle of a government. At the start of a new government, a whole tranche of advisers transfers across from opposition into government. But half of the special advisers remain in post for three years or less, so as many new appointments are made during the life of a government to replace those who have left. New appointments tend to be made via party political networks. As a government enters its final years, it becomes increasingly difficult to find good-quality candidates, and ministers are forced to seek alternative recruitment pools and hold semi-open competitive interviews. This suggests that the personal nature of the appointment may sometimes be exaggerated. Special advisers in later waves of recruitment are not necessarily well known to their minister.

II. THE BENEFITS AND ACHIEVEMENTS OF SPECIAL ADVISERS

Despite their modest numbers, special advisers have had a big impact on Whitehall. Their biggest impact has been in media management, with the communications revolution ushered in by Alastair Campbell (see chapter six). Government communications were raised to a completely different level. But special advisers have also had a big impact on policy. It is invidious to select only a few cases and impossible to disentangle the respective contributions of the special adviser and of the minister. However, just to highlight a few examples, these might include the 1970s legislation on sex and race discrimination (strongly influenced by Anthony Lester, special adviser to Roy Jenkins); the influence of Alan Walters on monetary policy under Thatcher; the contribution of Adam Ridley to Geoffrey Howe's tax reforms in the early 1980s; the changes to defence procurement introduced by Peter Levene under Michael Heseltine; the peace talks in Northern Ireland which led to the 1998 Belfast Agreement (in which a key role was played by Jonathan Powell under Tony Blair); Labour's industrial policy (Geoffrey Norris, working for Blair and Peter Mandelson); the creation of academy schools (of which Andrew Adonis was the architect when he was in the Policy Unit); the radical welfare reforms of the Coalition Government (in which Philippa Stroud has played a major role under Iain Duncan Smith), and the contribution of Chris Nicholson to environmental policy (and of Tom Burke during earlier administrations).

Our interviewees were all agreed that special advisers had become indispensable to the working of modern government (the only dissenters being a couple of Conservative ministers from the 1980s). This was for many reasons, but the single most important one was ministerial overload. The demands on ministers are so great that they cannot be everywhere at once and they need more people to whom they can delegate. These must be people whom they can trust to know their minds and represent them in their absence. Absences include the growing number of ministerial trips to Europe and further afield. The greatest value of special advisers is to be the minister's alter ego, giving a steer to officials in the department, briefing the press and meeting with outside interest groups. Although these functions overlap with those of officials (see chapter five), special advisers have a particular authority because they have been personally chosen, and through regular proximity have far more opportunity to get to know the minister's mind, and because they are bound by fewer strictures than other sources of ministerial support.

Under Labour, some special advisers became particularly powerful, with Jonathan Powell, Alastair Campbell, Andrew Adonis and Ed Balls being prominent examples. They all worked in the Centre. But even in departments, some of the Secretaries of State whom we interviewed ranked special advisers as more important than their junior ministers when we asked about the circles of power and influence around them:

> Special advisers very close to the centre of power, along with the permanent secretary. I would say most senior civil servants and special advisers are pretty equivalent. The permanent secretary is more important; junior ministers some way down the list. (Labour Secretary of State)

> Well, you see [special advisers] far more than you see your junior ministers ... you see them on routine things and things that have to be done all the time. However, a wise Secretary of State will never exclude junior ministers from decision making, and indeed will make that collaborative. (Another Labour Secretary of State)

This may be a startling finding for some readers. It can be explained by the fact that secretaries of state have chosen their special advisers, but not their junior ministers, who may have been wished upon them.[1] A second factor is the one mentioned above: junior ministers may see the secretary of state fairly infrequently, and certainly much less than the special advisers.

A second surprising finding is how isolated ministers can feel:

> Ministers can feel very isolated in their Private Offices. They need a friend whom they can trust, who will find out what is going on in the department. (Conservative special adviser)

> A lot of commentary on Spads seems to overlook how isolated the Secretary of State is. Whom can he really consult? It is not always the Permanent Secretary: in our case we were debating whether we wanted to get rid of him. (Labour special adviser)

The civil service, looking up to politicians as their political masters, do not always appreciate how lonely and exposed they can feel. Ministers are only human and need emotional as well as logistical support. Special advisers are better placed to

---

[1] Chris Mullin's diaries depict vividly the lowly life of a Parliamentary Under-Secretary: Chris Mullin, *A View from the Foothills* (Profile Books 2009).

provide this. At the end of a bad day, or in a media firestorm, special advisers stick with them and help them back on to their feet. It is not always so easy for the civil service to do so, while remaining suitably impartial: sometimes the ministerial setback has nothing to do with the department.[2]

III. INCREASING NUMBERS OF SPECIAL ADVISERS

We saw in chapter eight how much greater are the numbers of political staff in Australia and Canada. Their total numbers increased in the late twentieth century to 600 in Canada and 450 in Australia, compared to around 100 in the UK. But with some of those being in administrative and support roles, the numbers of policy staff equivalent to special advisers may be 200 in Canada and 350 in Australia. These are still much larger figures than in the UK, so if the numbers of special advisers in Whitehall continue to increase, Australia and Canada offer one possible vision of our future.

On the whole, it is not an encouraging picture. The overseas experience suggests that when the minister's office is staffed wholly or largely by political staff, there are greater barriers between the ministerial office and the department, and concerns of undue politicisation. Both countries have seen a serious account-ability gap, with worse scandals than in the UK, with ministers not accepting responsibility for their staff's behaviour when things go wrong. In Canada, many of the political staff are young and inexperienced. In Australia, despite their large numbers, the names and roles of individual advisers are not published.[3] A 2009 review in Australia recommended a full-time adviser who would be responsible for the supervision, training and support of political staff.[4] In both countries there appears to be more central control by the Prime Minister's Office, with the PMO in Canada directly assigning some staff rather than leaving ministers to choose. In Australia the chief of staff to the new Prime Minister Tony Abbott is reported to have tightened the centre's grip, intervening in staff appointments to a third of the Cabinet.[5]

How far down this road is the UK likely to go? Most of our interviewees did not support a cap on the numbers of special advisers and many supported an increase. These views were expressed not just by ministers and special advisers, but also

[2] Examples include ministers afflicted by personal scandals, such as Peter Mandelson, David Blunkett or Chris Huhne.
[3] But there is a detailed annual report about numbers and functions: see www.finance.gov.au/publications/mops_annual_reports/2011-2012/docs/MOPS_Annual_Report.pdf, at 20.
[4] Senate Committee on Finance and Public Administration, 'Review of Government Staffing' (Estimates Review of Government Staffing, 2009), www.aph.gov.au/binaries/senate/committee/fapa_ctte/estimates/bud_0910/finance/tabled_documents/review_govt_staffing.pdf, at 25.
[5] 'At least a third of Tony Abbott's 19 member Cabinet have had senior staffing appointments either knocked back or imposed upon them by the Peta Credlin-led appointments panel, known as the "star chamber".' 'Control Freak Peta Credlin Accused of Pulling Coalition Strings' *Sydney Morning Herald* (4 December 2013).

by civil servants. They particularly emphasised the need for additional advisers under the Coalition in order to help broker deals between the Coalition partners:

> I think it's a shame that we had such a strict rule about how many special advisers we have, not least because we have this extra function, which is the cross-Coalition function. (Conservative special adviser)

The Coalition has seen a big increase in special advisers in its first three years, with the total number rising from 63 in June 2010 to 98 in October 2013.[6] Much of the increase has been in the Centre, with the PMO increasing by seven (from 15 to 23) and the Deputy Prime Minister's Office by six.[7] By 2013, four secretaries of state had gone up from two to three special advisers (the Foreign Secretary, the Home Secretary, and the Secretaries of State for Education, and Work and Pensions).

The cap of two advisers per Cabinet minister has also been avoided by the appointment of additional advisers as temporary civil servants. As noted in chapter seven, this happened during the 1997–2010 Labour Government, where there were reported to be as many as 20 temporary civil servants (usually called political advisers or 'pads') who acted like special advisers:

> Generally they are policy advisers to the Secretary of State—largely because they have already reached their limit of political appointments. Occasionally they would be described as 'secret spads' because they didn't formally count and weren't on the radar, but worked in exactly the same way with the same level of ministerial patronage, trust etc. I would say there were at least 20 pads at any one time—probably more at some points. Most main departments had at least one. (Former Labour special adviser)

Similar appointments have happened under the Coalition, where a minister like Michael Gove has recruited three or four policy advisers in addition to his three special advisers. In July 2013 the Coalition Government proposed formalising this kind of arrangement by allowing all Cabinet ministers greatly expanded ministerial support, with the plans announced by Cabinet Office Minister Francis Maude for extended ministerial offices, quickly known in Whitehall as EMOs.[8]

IV. EXTENDED MINISTERIAL OFFICES

The proposal is not as novel as it might appear. It was first suggested in a report of the Treasury and Civil Service Committee back in 1986, when the Committee

---

[6] Of the 68 special adviser *posts* listed by the Cabinet Office in June 2010, five were recorded as vacancies.

[7] The number of special advisers supporting the Deputy Prime Minister rose from seven in June 2010 to 19 in October 2013, but six of those were recruited in late 2011 specifically to provide additional support for the dozen Liberal Democrat junior ministers scattered around Whitehall departments.

[8] Cabinet Office, *Civil Service Reform Plan: One Year On* (July 2013). The proposals for extended ministerial offices are right at the end of the report. More detailed guidance about EMOs was published in December 2013: for the full text, see *Civil Service World* (3 December 2013).

proposed strengthened private offices with ministerial policy units analogous to *cabinets*.[9] Suggestions for adoption of a *cabinet* system have surfaced frequently ever since Fulton (see chapter eight). EMOs are one more variant on this theme. They would have three categories of staff: civil servants in the traditional Private Office role, special advisers and external appointees. The main expansion was likely to be in the third category, with the Civil Service Commission creating a new exception to allow recruitment without competition of chosen individuals as temporary civil servants for up to five years.[10] The previous maximum was two years: the new exception would allow outsiders to be recruited for the whole of a Parliament.

Under Cabinet Office guidance issued in late 2013, ministers would need first to agree the mix of staff and the budget with their Permanent Secretary before seeking the approval of the Prime Minister. There were two twists in the tail for ministers who wanted an EMO. The first was that at least one member of the EMO must focus on implementation, reporting to the Head of the Cabinet Office Implementation Unit. The second was that requests must include 'specific proposals for strengthening the offices of junior Ministers … of a different party'.[11] Where no EMO was planned, junior ministers could put forward their own proposals. This was primarily to strengthen support for the dozen Liberal Democrat junior ministers scattered round Whitehall, who felt isolated and outgunned.[12]

In the remainder of the 2010 Parliament, it seemed unlikely that many ministers would want an EMO. Energetic ministers like Gove had already found ways of recruiting additional advisers. Also, outside experts invited to join as temporary civil servants might be reluctant to risk the job insecurity, because they would be expected to leave when no longer required in the EMO. So the real test for EMOs would lie in the next Parliament.

EMOs will inevitably be compared to *cabinets*, which frequently comprise a mix of outsiders and officials. It is a loose comparison, because *cabinets* come in various different shapes and sizes (see chapter eight). The main risk is the distancing of the minister's office from the department, so that the ministerial team ends up fighting the department rather than working with it. Distancing has happened in Australia and Canada, as well as in the European Commission, as our interviewees confirmed:

> I have spent a lot of time in Brussels and have seen cases there where the *cabinet* and the Directorate become in effect two different organisations, and nothing the Directorate puts forward is trusted. So that would be the risk you run. (Former Permanent Secretary)

---

[9] Treasury and Civil Service Committee, *Civil Servants and Ministers: Duties and Responsibilities* (1986) para 5.28.

[10] Civil Service Commission, 'A New Exception for Extended Ministerial Offices' (15 October 2013).

[11] Cabinet Office, *Guidance on Extended Ministerial Offices* (December 2013).

[12] 'I think it's been a terrible mistake to send people on their own into a department behind enemy lines, as it were, with no support mechanism at all.' Liberal Democrat minister quoted in Robert Hazell and Ben Yong, *The Politics of Coalition: How the Conservative-Liberal Democrat Coalition Works* (Hart Publishing 2012) 204.

The Coalition was evidently aware of the risk, because the Cabinet Office guidance includes strong emphasis on integration of staff within the EMO and with the department:

> The success of the office will be dependent on all staff being fully integrated and working as one to deliver the Minister's priorities, as well as working closely with the rest of the Department. Advice from officials in the Department must go to Ministers unaltered, although as now staff in the Minister's office will often comment on the advice.[13]

The key to the success of EMOs lies in the quality of the people who staff them. Integration with the department will be greatly facilitated if the Principal Private Secretary is head of the EMO. As for other staff, Canada points to the risks of more advisers meaning less in terms of quality. The main quality control for EMOs is that ministers must first consult their permanent secretary and then seek the approval of the Prime Minister. It could go one of two ways. No 10 could yield to the demands of the bigger beasts in Cabinet, exercise no effective quality control and pass the buck back to the Permanent Secretary. Alternatively, the Prime Minister's chief of staff could use the opportunity to insist that there are proper job descriptions and person specifications for any additional posts, and perhaps competition for those posts, as we have proposed in chapter nine. The chief of staff might want to lay down further criteria by which proposals for EMOs will be judged in order to ensure that quality thresholds are met.

But there is only so much which can be achieved by central approval and exhortation. Ultimately the tone will be set by the minister and the head of the ministerial office:

> So whether a *Cabinet* system would work would depend heavily on the personality of the [secretary of state], but you cannot legislate for that. If you have someone like Stephen Byers, for example, who was strongly inclined to shut himself off from official advice and the formal input of the Department, then a *Cabinet* system could be very dangerous. (Former Permanent Secretary)

V. GREATER TRANSPARENCY ABOUT SPECIAL ADVISERS

The other mechanism which might help to ensure quality control is greater transparency. If ministers had to release details of each of their advisers, their role and their qualifications, they might pause before recruiting unsuitable people. In the lists of special advisers published by the government, there are no details about their individual roles. Parliament has started to demand details of their roles and qualifications, and if the Cabinet Office was astute, it could use that as an additional lever to say to ministers: 'We cannot approve this EMO, or that adviser, because there will be trouble with your Select Committee.'

---

[13] Cabinet Office Guidance for departments on EMOs, November 2013.

The UK has gradually published more about special advisers and compares well with other countries in this respect (see chapter nine), although more could be done. Pressure for greater transparency has come from the media, from Parliament and from the Committee on Standards in Public Life. In its 2003 report *Defining the Boundaries*, the Committee recommended that:

> An annual statement should be made to Parliament setting out: (i) the total number of paid special advisers employed in the year; (ii) their names; (iii) the Ministers for whom they work or have worked; (iv) their particular roles and areas of responsibility; (v) the total salary cost by department; (vi) comparison figures for earlier years.[14]

As we found when compiling our database (see appendix one), there has not been a wholly complete series of annual statements, and the lists have not been consistent in the information provided. There is now a statutory duty on the Minister for the Civil Service to publish an annual report about the number and cost of special advisers.[15] The Coalition Government undertook to release quarterly lists of special advisers, and almost achieved this, with three lists published in 2011 and three in 2012. But such frequent publication was burdensome and in 2013 it reverted to annual publication.

The Cabinet Office lists give no information about the roles of individual special advisers. This is something which has been picked up by the House of Commons Public Administration Select Committee, which recommended:

> To aid transparency and accountability, information about ministers' special advisers should appear on departmental websites, including advisers' names and a description of the policy areas in which they work and the types of tasks they undertake, alongside the equivalent information about ministerial portfolios ... this would help Parliament to hold ministers to account for the work of their special advisers.[16]

The Government did not agree, saying that: 'It is for the appointing Minister to decide on what he or she wants special advisers to focus. This will typically be relatively fluid but should be assumed to match the Minister's own responsibilities and priorities.'[17] This was a missed opportunity by the Cabinet Office to raise the quality threshold. Given the importance of special advisers, it is perfectly reasonable to expect their details to be published on departmental websites, along with their roles. It would help to clarify which special advisers focus on the media and which on policy, as well as their main priorities. The Government's reluctance may have been because it wanted special advisers to remain invisible, or it may be part of a wider reluctance to give them job descriptions because of some ministers' inability to specify what they want their special advisers to do.

---

[14] Committee on Standards in Public Life (chair Sir Nigel Wicks), *Defining the Boundaries* (2003) R21.
[15] Constitutional Reform and Governance Act 2010, s 16.
[16] Public Administration Select Committee, 'Special Advisers in the Thick of It' (2012) HC 134 [75].
[17] ibid [8].

A. More Transparency about Roles, Less about Salaries

In one respect, the Coalition Government has gone beyond the recommendations of the Committee on Standards in Public Life and the Public Administration Select Committee by publishing the individual salaries of special advisers. This has since given rise to tensions, with special advisers putting in claims to catch up with other more highly paid advisers. Disputes over pay have been a vexed issue since the formal introduction of special advisers.[18] The pay of special advisers is fixed on their appointment—there are no annual increments and no promotion. But over time people grow and develop, and take on more responsibility, even if the job title does not change. It is not surprising if they seek pay increases to reflect that, and publication of individual salaries has added fuel to the flames of their resentment.[19]

Pay is set by the Special Advisers Remuneration Committee, whose role is to determine special advisers' salaries, decide the annual pay increase, consider appeals against pay decisions and requests for individual pay increases, and act as guardian of the pay system.[20] So a mechanism is in place to determine the pay of individual special advisers and to hear claims for an increase. Although many special advisers do not have job descriptions, an assessment and job evaluation is carried out for anyone seeking a pay increase.

There is the basis here for a new deal which might be of benefit to all sides: first, to roll back transparency a bit and put publication of the pay of special advisers on the same basis as their equivalents in the Senior Civil Service (SCS)—namely, to publish their Pay Bands (SCS1, 2 or 3), but no more than that. This would give sufficient indication of their level of seniority and experience; but, second, and more important, to increase transparency by publishing details of special advisers' roles. That is what the Public Administration Select Committee has called for, and the Government has given no convincing reason why their roles should not be disclosed. Special advisers complained to us about some ministers' lack of clarity in what it was they wanted. Having job descriptions would help to sharpen up ministers' thinking, sharpen up their accountability and demystify what special advisers do. It is another respect in which they are unnecessarily depicted as people who live in the dark. As a further response to the Public Administration Select Committee, the Government could agree to notify the appropriate departmental select committee whenever a new special adviser is appointed, with their job description and their qualifications for the appointment. The Public

---

[18] Rodney Lowe, *The Official History of the British Civil Service: Reforming the Civil Service, Volume I: The Fulton Years, 1966–81* (Routledge 2011) 220–24.

[19] See most recently Toby Helm, 'Civil Service Unions Attack High Salaries for Cabinet Advisers' *The Guardian* (16 March 2014).

[20] Its members in 2013 were Danny Alexander (Chief Secretary to the Treasury), Theresa May (Home Secretary), Francis Maude (Cabinet Office Minister) and Sir Bob Kerslake (Head of the Civil Service).

Administration Select Committee (rightly) rejected pre-appointment hearings, but recommended instead:

> [T]hat ministers should notify the relevant departmental select committee whom they have appointed as a new special adviser ... They should include a proposed job description, setting out the policy areas and types of tasks the special adviser will be expected to carry out, and the special adviser's relevant qualifications for appointment, including why they believe him or her to be of suitable 'standing and experience'. This would enable select committees better to hold ministers to account for the quality and conduct of their special advisers, and would deter ministers from promoting less suitable candidates.[21]

The Cabinet Office should see this as in its long-term interest as well. No 10 and the Cabinet Office need not be the only judges of whether a minister has a suitable ministerial team; select committees could prove to be useful additional scrutineers.

B. Distribution of Special Advisers

One interesting innovation in the proposals for EMOs is the requirement that any bid for an EMO must include specific proposals for strengthening the offices of junior ministers who come from a different party from that of the Secretary of State. And even where the Secretary of State does not plan an EMO, junior ministers of the other party may put forward proposals for extending their own offices. This raises the question of whether junior ministers in general should be allowed special advisers or additional policy advisers recruited as temporary civil servants. Some junior ministers already have special advisers: part of the additional status for 'Ministers attending Cabinet' is to have a special adviser.[22] In 2013, half a dozen ministers in this category had a special adviser (in the Cabinet Office, the Department for Communities and Local Government, the Foreign and Commonwealth Office, the Department of Energy & Climate Change and the Department for Business, Innovation & Skills, where two junior ministers had one each).

Our interviewees were divided about whether junior ministers needed special advisers. Some felt that this could cause difficulties within the department, with junior ministers developing alternative power centres, rather than loyally supporting the secretary of state.

Set against this, there is the experience in Australia, where all junior ministers have political staff (non-Cabinet ministers have six, parliamentary secretaries

---

[21] Public Administration Select Committee (n 16) [82]–[83].

[22] Recent Prime Ministers have created a new top tier amongst ministers of state of ministers not formally in the Cabinet, but entitled to attend. They typically number up to six ministers. They were first allocated special advisers under Blair.

two) and the fact that almost 20 junior ministers in the UK already have special advisers, without report of adverse consequences.[23] The Coalition was right to focus on the needs of junior ministers from the 'other' Coalition party, because Liberal Democrat junior ministers have felt particularly under-resourced. But in the spirit of experimentation which lies behind EMOs, it is to be hoped that some bids will include proposals to strengthen the offices of junior ministers, whether or not they come from a different party. To a small extent, this can happen now. In some departments the Secretary of State has been willing to share his special advisers with his junior ministers, so that the special advisers supported the whole ministerial team. However, that has not been general practice. In most cases the special advisers acted as a communication channel between the secretary of state and junior ministers, but they were not available to provide additional support.

C. The No 10 Policy Unit

Of the 100 or so special advisers in 2013, there were around 40 special advisers in the Centre (defined narrowly as the Prime Minister and the Deputy Prime Minister), with 22 supporting the Prime Minister. There have been particular difficulties with the No 10 Policy Unit. David Cameron started with a very small Policy Unit of just five advisers, partly because of his determination to have fewer special advisers than the outgoing Government. The previous Delivery Unit and Strategy Unit were both disbanded (see chapter four). This soon led to criticisms of a weak centre. In February 2011, No 10 acknowledged:

> There is a capacity issue. Under the Labour Government, there was a policy unit that shadowed departments. We did not continue with that because we did not have enough special advisers. We had used our numbers because of the Coalition. The policy unit was therefore very small … This meant that the capacity to work with departments to make sure that everything was in good order was very limited.[24]

People whom we interviewed in departments also complained that they did not always know whom to go to in No 10. So, in spring 2011, a new Policy and Implementation Unit of 11 people was formed. Six were outsiders from the private sector and five came from Whitehall, but they were all formally designated as civil servants.[25] Yet, in time, criticism was renewed that the Unit was too weak,

---

[23] The six ministers attending Cabinet, who have one each, and the 12 Liberal Democrat junior ministers who share half a dozen special advisers between them.

[24] Nicholas Watt, 'Cameron's New Backroom Team Aims to Move Story on from U-turns and Cuts' *The Guardian* (18 February 2011).

[25] Because the new Unit worked jointly with the Prime Minister and the Deputy Prime Minister, it was thought unacceptable for it to be staffed with overtly political advisers. For a full list of its members and their backgrounds, see Hazell and Yong (n 12) Appendix 7.

this time because it was composed of civil servants.[26] So in spring 2013, a third shake-up took place, with Jo Johnson MP brought in to head a Policy Unit of eight advisers, with an advisory board of half a dozen MPs as a link to the Conservative backbenches.

We asked our interviewees about the ideal model for the No 10 Policy Unit. A record of the different models since 1979 is in Table 2.1. Most agreed that the ideal model was a mix of special advisers and civil servants:

> My strong view is that what you need at the centre is a mix of civil servants and political appointees; you need a good blend of both. John Major in his small way had a nice mix; it was political and civil servants, they worked well together. (Former Cabinet Secretary)

There was less agreement about the ideal size, with numbers ranging from eight to 20. To match every Whitehall department, the Policy Unit would need at least 15 people. But our interviewees were agreed that the quality of the people was far more important than the quantity and that the Policy Unit did not need one person per department:

> Prime Ministers should only have a few priorities if they want to achieve anything. So there should be really heavyweight figures for each of the four or five priorities that the Prime Minister has. Then you can have younger, less significant figures, or civil servants, covering three or four departments. So if the Prime Minister doesn't really care about DEFRA, energy, DfID or whatever, you can have people handling a number of those together. But if he's really interested in health reform, or education, then you need to have big figures doing just that. (Former senior adviser, No 10)

The other reason for keeping the Policy Unit small is so that its members can genuinely claim to speak with the voice of the Prime Minister:

> Small size was, I think, crucial to effectiveness. The whole team had sufficient contact with the Prime Minister to give them credibility throughout Whitehall and to ensure they understood what was in his mind. There was no need for internal competition for access to him or for power struggles for leadership on particular issues. (Former member of John Major's Policy Unit)

> But the advantage of [a small] policy unit is, when they call up a cabinet minister and say, 'Tony wants', people have a pretty good idea whether they do represent what Tony wants … when you have very junior people from the Policy Unit, who maybe meet the Prime Minister once a year or twice a year, saying, 'Tony wants', the Cabinet ministers don't always know … Then that leads to complaints that Number 10 speaks with many voices. (Former adviser, No 10)

Another common complaint was that No 10 wanted to drive the detail of a policy without sufficient knowledge or understanding of the front line (see chapter four). One solution might be to recruit into the Policy Unit more special advisers

---

[26] Criticism came mainly from the Conservative press. Typical was Nick Wood, 'The Nerve Centre of No 10 is Pathetically Weak: It's Time to Ditch the Civil Servants and Bring Back the Political Heavyweights' *Daily Mail* (2 April 2012).

with prior experience of working in Whitehall departments. That is easier mid-term than for a new government entering office.

VI. 'POLITICISATION' AND THE CIVIL SERVICE

Implicit in some of the criticism of Cameron's Policy and Implementation Unit is the assumption that civil servants cannot perform 'political' roles. We also found some small evidence of this in our interviews, where a couple of ministers who had served in the last Conservative Government commented on the difference they found when they came back in 2010, with officials being unnecessarily fussy about touching anything which might be 'political'.

This is a category error which needs challenging. People forget how many civil service roles require day-to-day involvement in politics in many different forms. This is particularly the case for the officials who work in No 10 and the Whips' Office, for all the officials who work directly with ministers, especially their principal private secretaries, and for officials in particular departments, such as the officials in the Northern Ireland Office who negotiated with the political parties in the run-up to the Belfast and St Andrews Agreements. Part of the fascination of working in Whitehall is involvement in the political process, and part of the unique skill and experience of civil servants lies in their understanding of how Parliament and politics work.

One of the justifications for introducing special advisers into Whitehall is that they can perform the more political tasks, thus freeing the civil service from any involvement in the political side and from any taint of politicisation.[27] But there is a risk for the civil service of gradual de-skilling, of losing their close involvement in politics and their understanding of the political process. Civil servants in the past have not been so fearful of getting involved in the political side of their ministers' work. Robin Butler was working beside Thatcher at the Conservative Party Conference in Brighton when it was bombed by the IRA,[28] and other principal private secretaries have found that serving their ministers efficiently inevitably brings them into contact with the party political side. This doesn't necessarily involve politicisation. The distinction was neatly put by one of our interviewees: 'Effective civil servants, particularly those who work close to the minister, have to

---

[27] The *Code of Conduct for Special Advisers* opens: 'The employment of special advisers adds a political dimension to the advice and assistance available to Ministers while reinforcing the political impartiality of the Civil Service … Special Advisers are employed to help Ministers where the work of Government and the Governing Party overlap and where it would be inappropriate for permanent civil servants to become involved' (paras 1 and 2).

[28] Illustrating the commitment of senior civil servants. 'By about 2.40 am the [conference] speech was finished. Meanwhile, I got on with some Government business. At 2.50 am Robin Butler asked me to look at one last official paper—it was about the Liverpool Garden Festival … At 2.54 am a loud thud shook the room.' Margaret Thatcher, *The Downing Street Years* (HarperCollins 1993) 379.

be very politically attuned. That doesn't mean to say they have to be politically aligned.'

The fear of 'politicisation' lies in assuming that civil servants who so assiduously serve their ministers must also share their political beliefs. But those same officials go on to serve other ministers from other parties. Sir Robin Butler was a Private Secretary to Ted Heath and Harold Wilson, Principal Private Secretary to Margaret Thatcher, and went on to become Cabinet Secretary to John Major and then Tony Blair. The acid test of civil service impartiality is: would this behaviour impair an official's ability to serve ministers of a different party with equal commitment and equal impartiality?

The problem is one of perception: it is widely assumed, by politicians and by civil servants, that an individual cannot change his or her behaviour when assuming different roles. But in other professions, this happens all the time. Barristers can be defence counsel one day and prosecuting the next, with different obligations in each role. So, in the public service, it should be possible for people to switch careers or change roles, as long as they assume the obligations that go with the new role. This does happen, and people have even switched from being a civil servant to being a special adviser, or vice versa. In the course of our research, we have come across a dozen special advisers—both Conservative and Labour —who subsequently became civil servants.[29] But it is uncommon, and there is a worry about the negative impact on perceptions of civil service impartiality if it became more common. With more outsiders brought in to strengthen ministerial offices, such moves should be encouraged, not discouraged. It enables special advisers to go on working on government policy if that is what they are good at, and it brings additional talent into Whitehall.

VII. BIRTH OF A NEW PROFESSION

Running through all the chapters in this book is the argument that special advisers matter. They matter for positive, not negative reasons. Officials and ministers both recognise they are now indispensable to the way Whitehall works. Yet they are still treated as a transient phenomenon. The individuals may move on, but special advisers as a profession are here to stay. This final section starts by thinking through the consequences of treating them as a professional cadre which needs greater recognition and support because of the importance of their potential contribution. It discusses the need for greater ownership of special advisers during their time in Whitehall and the possibilities for greater career progression while still working as special advisers. It then sets out a summary of all our recommendations before closing by linking the effectiveness of special advisers to wider debates about ministerial effectiveness.

---

[29] Examples include Peter Levene, Howell James, Michael Barber, Justin Russell and Will Cavendish.

Special advisers are a profession with a high turnover. Half of all special advisers stay in Whitehall for three years or less. The role is very precarious. They have little job security, they work very long hours and the job is a blind alley in terms of professional development, with little training and no promotion. That is one of the reasons for high turnover: with no possibilities for promotion, if special advisers want to progress in their careers, they have to leave.

One way of improving the possibilities for promotion and support and supervision for special advisers would be to allow a bit more progression in this mini-profession. It is a fiction that all special advisers are equal. Of the list published in October 2013, 25 special advisers—one-quarter—were in the higher pay bands (PB3 and PB4), earning salaries between £70,000 and £140,000.[30] They are senior in terms of pay, but only two—the Chiefs of Staff—are formally senior in terms of responsibilities. As we suggested in chapter nine, more could be done by other senior special advisers in looking after their fellow special advisers: in support and supervision, mentoring, training and appraisal. Having a recognised cadre of senior special advisers would help develop a bit more career progression for those willing to assume greater responsibilities. This need not undermine the flexibility and fluidity which is the great strength of special advisers; it would be for individual special advisers to decide if they wanted to progress in this way, with the support of the Deputy Chief of Staff (see below).

It would also help in developing a mini-career structure if working at the centre was regarded as a step up from working as a special adviser in a Whitehall department. This might help to reduce complaints about 'teenyboppers in No 10' who don't understand the realities of life in front-line departments. It would also help to recognise the greater seniority of most special advisers working in the centre, where three-quarters of the higher-paid special advisers are concentrated. Such a career progression will always be hard for an incoming government, unless it can recruit a lot of former special advisers. It started to happen under Blair, where from 2001 to 2007 a dozen advisers had worked in departments and at the centre (see Figure A2.1 in Appendix 2). They also had longer service, with an average tenure of six years.

The brief tenure of most special advisers may also be one of the reasons why no one takes care of them or 'owns' them. The civil service tend not to see them as theirs, and indeed positively avoid treading on what they see as ministers' political territory. Ministers are formally responsible, but, as we noted in chapter seven, when under pressure, they find it difficult to exercise that responsibility. The political parties don't see them as theirs either, because they are working in the civil service, paid out of public funds and seldom seen in party headquarters. Special advisers by their nature fall between the two worlds, but they shouldn't be allowed to fall down the gap between the two.

---

[30] Salaries generally reflect pay levels before becoming a special adviser, not higher levels of responsibility (for example, special advisers coming from the private sector will expect higher salaries than those coming from the voluntary sector).

As stated at the beginning of this chapter, it is 40 years since special advisers started working as an identifiable cadre in Whitehall. But in terms of support arrangements, special advisers are still treated as a temporary and transient phenomenon. The occasional scandals have exposed the fact that no one is willing to take responsibility when things go wrong. However, more serious is the lack of anyone who takes positive responsibility to ensure that things go right in terms of special advisers' recruitment, careers and professional development. We made recommendations in this and the previous chapter for some basic improvements in all three areas. Improvements are starting to happen. For convenience, our recommendations are summarised in the table below.

Table 10.1: Recognising special advisers as a new profession

Greater professionalism
Special advisers are a mini-profession. They would be more effective if they were more professionally managed in terms of their selection, support and supervision, and development of their professional skills.
Recruitment
Special adviser posts should be more open to competition. Ministers should remain free to choose whom they recruit, but they should be encouraged to interview more than one candidate. If they want to advertise, they should be allowed to do so and should be supported by the civil service (in government) and by the party (in opposition) in shortlisting and interviewing.
All special adviser posts should have a job description setting out the main duties and a person specification identifying the skills and experience required.
The Chief of Staff should use the Prime Minister's veto to raise the quality threshold and require details of the job description, person specification and degree of competition for each post before approving an appointment.
The Chief of Staff could maintain a register of people who are interested in being special advisers and who had undergone an initial sift and interview to ensure their suitability.
Support and supervision
Every new special adviser should be paired with a more experienced current or former special adviser as their mentor, to whom they could turn for help and advice.
There should be a Deputy Chief of Staff charged with the support, supervision and appraisal of all special advisers. In a coalition, there would be a Deputy Chief of Staff for each coalition party.
The Deputy Chief of Staff could nominate senior special advisers to conduct appraisals on their behalf.

(Continued)

Table 10.1: *Continued*

Induction and training
Induction training should be mandatory for all new special advisers. It should cover how Whitehall works, how special advisers work within that structure, the Codes of Conduct, their obligations as temporary civil servants and where to seek advice and support. Within departments there needs to be separate induction training about the work of the department.
The Cabinet Office should make additional modular training available (where possible online) so that special advisers recruited subsequently could access it as and when they want.

Transparency
The Cabinet Office has a statutory duty to publish an annual report about the numbers and cost of special advisers. There is no need to publish individual salaries; pay bands would suffice.
Departments should publish on their websites advisers' names and brief descriptions of their functions. Ministers should notify the relevant select committee whenever a new special adviser is appointed, with his or her job description and qualifications. This would also help to ensure a minimum quality threshold.

VIII. THE POTENTIAL OF THIS NEW PROFESSION

This book has been about the effectiveness of special advisers, but behind every page has been the wider debate about the effectiveness of ministers. Ministers (and Prime Ministers) often leave office wishing that they had made more of a difference. Some blame themselves, others the lack of support from their colleagues or from Parliament, and others the inertia of the Whitehall machine. Many different solutions are propounded, including endless proposals for civil service reform. These range from the Coalition Government's specific proposals in its Civil Service Reform Plan, including extended ministerial offices, to wider proposals for a Parliamentary Commission or a Royal Commission on the Future of the Civil Service.[31]

Civil service reform is always on the agenda, but is notoriously difficult, because of its size and complexity, all the different interests involved and lack of agreement about how 'responsive' the civil service can be before it loses its core values of objectivity and impartiality.[32] In this wider and increasingly polarised debate, one

---

[31] The proposal for a Parliamentary Commission came from the Public Administration Select Committee (chair Bernard Jenkin MP): *Truth to Power—How Civil Service Reform Can Succeed* (September 2013). Lord Browne, the Government's non-executive director, suggested a Royal Commission: Civil Service World, *Special Report—Civil Service Accountability* (2 December 2013).

[32] The Civil Service Commission opposed Francis Maude's proposals to allow ministers greater choice in selecting their Permanent Secretary. Institute for Government, *Permanent Secretary Appointments and the Role of Ministers* (December 2012).

smaller-scale solution never considered is improving the quality and effectiveness of special advisers. It is only a partial solution, but unlike these wider reforms, it is a solution directly within the control of ministers, both individually and collectively.

For ministers to be more effective, one of the simplest things that they could do is to recruit better-quality special advisers. It is no coincidence that most of the special advisers we listed at the beginning of this chapter as having made a difference were high-quality policy experts or people with a lot of experience. But the haphazard recruitment processes disclosed in chapter nine suggest that individual ministers cannot always be relied upon to make good choices. If there is to be a sustained, across-the-board improvement, the Prime Minister, supported by his Chief of Staff, will need to give a lead in raising the overall quality threshold.

Through his power of approval and veto, the Prime Minister could help to raise the overall quality standard. We do not pretend that this is easy. Prime Ministers do not always have sufficient authority with their Cabinet colleagues to intervene in this way. But if they want to try to ensure greater ministerial effectiveness, then setting about improving the effectiveness of their special advisers is a very good place to start.

Appendix 1

Methodology

MAX GOPLERUD

IN CHAPTER THREE, it was noted that there were 626 special advisers employed from 1979 to 2013 and various descriptions of their length of service were provided. Whilst this certainly matches the available data, identifying the number of and finding the relevant information on special advisers was surprisingly difficult. This appendix briefly outlines our procedures for gathering information on special advisers, as well as highlighting some of the difficulties involved. The first section provides an overview of the main database, while the second and third sections address the methodology of the survey and the interviews.

In general, we attempted to rely on official government sources (written answers to parliamentary questions and data releases issued by the Cabinet Office or by departments). However, these are somewhat incomplete.[1] For example, whilst an MP normally posed a question such that the Prime Minister gave a full 'snapshot' of special advisers in post around July of each year, this did not occur in 2002 and thus there simply is no centralised, complete list of special advisers for that year.[2] Moreover, 'transitional' years, specifically 1997 and 2010, also tend to lack official information on the special advisers in post before the general election occurred and the government changed.

To flesh out these existing sources, we relied on periodicals (*Civil Service Yearbooks, Dod's Parliamentary Companion, Vacher's Quarterly*) that serve as directories of key members of the government and the civil service. These normally provide good coverage of special advisers in post. However, ambiguity over special advisers' roles means that these sources sometimes provide inaccurate or incomplete information. Finally, we augmented these sources with academic texts,

---

[1] We also had to deal with more easily solved issues of misspelling of names, name changes because of marriage and so on.

[2] Another issue with the 'snapshot' nature of this data is that the number of special advisers in post at any one point is generally lower than the number of persons who were employed across Whitehall in a given year, as there is inevitably turnover for reasons discussed elsewhere in the book. Thus, numbers generally have to be 'adjusted' to give a rough guess of the number of special advisers working at any single point in time in the year. The usual method employed was to subtract the number of special advisers who left in a given year from the total number employed.

ministerial biographies and newspaper articles.[3] The problem with the latter set of sources is that journalists may describe persons as 'special advisers' who are not actually classed as such in the official records.[4] The increase in people putting their own career information into the public domain further muddies the waters as special advisers or potential special advisers in our project may have described themselves in ambiguous terms on pages such as LinkedIn (eg 'senior policy adviser'). Therefore, we tried to avoid wherever possible relying on self-reported duration of service, status etc.

The implication of this is that for some special advisers, the information on their tenure will not be wholly accurate: for example, if someone started in December 1998, our database may list them as starting in 1999 unless a fortunately timed *Hansard* entry happens to exist. Further, because of the wording used by many sources (eg, 'this special adviser served in 1999'), there may be slight issues with some numerical analysis—a special adviser who started in September and left the following June served for 'two years' under our coding scheme. Part-time special advisers also presented a coding challenge; recorded sources neither universally nor consistently reported this information. The final coding scheme did not distinguish between the two in the dataset as it was difficult to find a consistent and defensible way of differentiating them. A relatively small number of special advisers were part time, but this does include some of the longest-serving ones, eg, Katherine Ramsay.

Obviously this is not ideal, but it was impossible to find more fine-grained information that would allow coverage of all individuals and their periods of employment. Rather than having data that was in different forms (yearly, quarterly or the exact dates), the database incorporated all of the data in a form that was comparable and gave quite accurate coverage. Despite these caveats, our strong impression is that the data is very nearly complete and is the best available without systematically interviewing every ex-special adviser.

The main reason for these coding problems was that the formal status of special advisers has itself been quite fluid. Furthermore, over the course of our research, we located a 'penumbra' of individuals who performed similar functions to special advisers, but whom the official data did not class as official special advisers. For example, whilst special advisers are generally paid positions, some receive no remuneration from the government (as their salary is paid from another organisation, eg, a political party, or, for instance, they are wealthy individuals working part time for free); these people appear in the official records as 'official' special advisers. Yet there are some officials who provide unpaid advice in a similar

[3] In terms of the formal inclusion rules, we took *Hansard* to be a definitive source that they were a special adviser at the time claimed and then relied upon two additional sources to warrant inclusion, with priority given to the periodicals.

[4] See the discussion in chs 7 and 10 on the blurring of lines between temporary civil servants and special advisers to illustrate this point. As an illustration of this point, some temporary civil servants describe themselves as 'special advisers' on LinkedIn, whereas some special advisers refer to themselves as 'policy advisers' (a title more commonly associated with temporary civil servants).

fashion who are not listed in official data releases (eg, Lord Birt under Labour) and sometimes they are deliberately described as not being special advisers in the official *Hansard* references.[5] These have not been included in our data.

In addition (and also not included in our data), there are a number of party-funded advisers ('political advisers' or 'pads') as well as temporary civil servants, both of whom work in departments alongside the normal ministerial team. These people are not special advisers using the formal definition (they are not subject to the *Code of Conduct for Special Advisers* and have different sorts of contracts) and their existence was mostly detected via interviews or accidental discovery. The Register of Interests of Member's Staff and Research Assistants reports some, but its coverage is incomplete and the House of Commons Library has not kept old copies of the Register. Key examples of political advisers who were not special advisers are the Political Secretaries (providing liaison between 10 Downing Street and the governing party) that served under the Conservative and Labour Governments, for example, John Whittingdale and Joe Irvin.[6] To obtain a rough indicator of their prevalence, the survey that was done of ex-special advisers (see below) asked about such people ('are there people who perform tasks similar to special advisers but are not classed as such?'), with 20 per cent reporting 'Yes'.

It also became clear from the interviews that some special advisers did not necessarily serve the people to whom they were said to be assigned in official records. A number of special advisers were assigned to ministers who had very little interaction with them, to the extent that the ministers were, when interviewed, unable to remember their existence or explicitly said they worked for a different minister. Generally, this was not usually an attempt to avoid the informal cap on two special advisers per minister (as certain ministers were clearly willing to break this) and perhaps reflects internal party politics in a way that no formal source could ever attempt to capture. A prominent example of this would be special advisers assigned to the Chief and Financial Secretaries of the Treasury, who sometimes worked for their listed minister, but often were involved with assisting the Chancellor. See appendix two for a more detailed discussion of unusual assignments of special advisers.[7]

It is perhaps inevitable that a role like a special adviser has these sorts of ambiguities as its purpose is to provide the minister with a degree of flexibility beyond the normal formal structures. Yet, as a number of regulatory regimes govern the behaviour of special advisers (for example, the *Model Contract* and the *Code of Conduct*; see chapter seven for an in-depth discussion), it is also unsurprising that there are other more flexible positions and roles (eg, 'political advisers') that exist to serve ministers. These flexible arrangements are not new and probably have existed long before special advisers were systematised in 1974.

[5] HC Deb 6 May 2003, vol 404, col 559W: 'Lord Birt is an unpaid adviser not a special adviser.'
[6] To make matters more confusing, many political secretaries were special advisers before being appointed to this non-special adviser role, as is the case with both cases listed above.
[7] Andrew Blick, *People Who Live in the Dark* (Politico's 2004) 196.

The Coalition Government's proposals for Extended Ministerial Offices (EMOs—on which, see chapter 10)[8] seem likely to increase the problem of separating out special advisers from those who perform similar tasks. As chapter ten notes, there is a lack of transparency in the available data on special advisers; the suggestions in that chapter would help resolve that problem, as well as allowing future researchers to determine more clearly who formed part of the ministerial office.

I. SURVEY METHODOLOGY

A second source of data came from a survey that we conducted of all special advisers from the Conservative and Labour Government cohorts. The survey design followed closely the work of Eichbaum and Shaw's work in New Zealand,[9] and Edward Page's work in the UK.[10] Of the 297 Labour special advisers, we were able to find biographical information on about 280. Some simply lacked an Internet presence; some had died. For the survey, we contacted 249 Labour special advisers by email and received 107 responses (36 per cent of the total cohort). These results informed the discussion in the book and were broadly in line with the information found in the manual search for information on background (career and university) that formed the basis of chapters three and eight. The survey of Conservative special advisers was more challenging due to the fact that some had stopped serving nearly 30 years ago, but we successfully contacted 93 ex-special advisers. There were 38 responses (20 per cent of the cohort). However, the manual data gathering was more successful; see chapter three for specific figures.

II. INTERVIEW METHODOLOGY

The project also gathered qualitative data from 102 semi-structured interviews conducted by members of the project team. In order to attempt to get a representative picture of special advisers, the interviewees were carefully selected to cover a range of backgrounds. Table A1.1 gives the distribution of interviewees (special advisers and ministers) by government.

---

[8] For example, Francis Maude's recent proposals discussed in ch 10.

[9] We are grateful to Chris Eichbaum and Richard Shaw for providing us with copies of their survey instruments. See Chris Eichbaum and Richard Shaw, 'Minding the Minister? Ministerial Advisers in New Zealand Government' (2007) 2 *Kotuitui: New Zealand Journal of Social Sciences Online* 95.

[10] The LSE GV314 Group, 'New Life at the Top: Special Advisers in British Government' (2012) 65 *Parliamentary Affairs* 715.

Table A1.1: Number of interviewees by government

Government	Spads	Ministers
Conservative	8	7
Labour	19	15
Coalition	12	5
TOTAL	**39**	**27**

The smaller number of Conservative special advisers interviewed is both a function of the smaller number of special advisers appointed under the Conservative Governments (181 versus 297 under Labour) and the difficulty of locating persons decades after they served. The responses of the Conservative interviewees were, however, generally in line with information from other sources, so we think that the sample is reliable.[11] In the case of the Coalition, the interviewers attempted to contact roughly equal numbers of Conservative and Liberal Democrat special advisers. For Labour, interviewers covered special advisers from both the Blair and the Brown administrations (and some who had served both). There was also a concerted effort to ensure the inclusion of female special advisers. For all interviewees, an initial list was drawn up based on various characteristics of service (eg, to a junior minister, for a long (short) period of time, to a single minister etc) and then the interviewers attempted to contact the suitable persons.

The interviewing team selected ministers and special advisers to cover a variety of departments, including the territorial offices (the Scottish, Welsh and Northern Ireland Offices) and the Cabinet Office. The vast majority of ministers interviewed employed special advisers by virtue of being a secretary of state; however, the team spoke to a few ministers of state who employed special advisers. A number of interviews attempted 'triangulation' of the relevant stakeholders, ie, interviewing (separately) a minister, their special adviser and officials who worked with them.

Finally, 23 civil servants and 13 external stakeholders (journalists, lobbyists, interest groups etc) were interviewed for the project. Because of the long tenure of civil servants, these tended to span both Conservative and Labour Governments and sometimes also the Coalition.

We also carried out a group interview in June 2013 at the Institute for Government to test some of our initial findings and recommendations. This group interview involved nine special advisers, five from the Conservative Governments of 1979–97 and four from the Labour Governments of 1997–2010.

---

[11] See especially an unpublished doctoral thesis by Stephen Hanney, 'Special Advisers: Their Place in British Government' (Brunel University 1993).

Appendix 2

Further Work on the Distribution and Tenure of Special Advisers

MAX GOPLERUD

THIS APPENDIX PROVIDES a quantitative analysis of special advisers to complement the more qualitative analysis in the majority of the book. It first examines special adviser tenure, ie, how long they serve in government, and then looks at the distribution of special advisers, ie, how they are assigned amongst ministers and departments. All the data relates to governments since 1979, namely the 1979–97 Thatcher and Major Governments, the 1997–2010 Blair and Brown Governments and the Coalition Government between 2010 and 2013.

Chapter three provided an overview of special adviser tenure. This appendix digs deeper and explores whether certain characteristics of special advisers correspond to longer tenure and whether certain events increase the likelihood of special advisers leaving office. The analysis here is mainly descriptive: a fleshed-out statistical analysis of the data, eg, including survival analysis, is beyond the scope of this project. Following a division used elsewhere in the book, this chapter mostly divides departments between the 'Centre' (No 10 and the Cabinet Office) and all other departments. It is possible, therefore, to divide special advisers according to whether they have worked only in the Centre (OC), have never worked in the Centre (NC) or have worked in both (BC), with membership of the final group necessarily implying that the special adviser is one of the smaller group who have worked for more than one minister and/or department (the Prime Minister and the Centre being counted as a minister and a department for the purposes of this analysis). Figure A2.1 shows the distribution of special advisers by area over time.

As Figure A2.1 shows, the number of special advisers in the BC group increases gradually over time because some special advisers, when they leave, either follow their minister or are employed by a new minister (generally following a reshuffle). The large surge in the BC group around 2007 is due to the fact that Gordon Brown retained a large number of special advisers upon his move from No 11 to No 10. The data on length of service also confirms that those in the BC grouping are more likely to remain as special advisers for long periods of time; their median tenure is six years, versus three for the other groups, and over half of those who serve more than 10 years fall into the BC grouping.

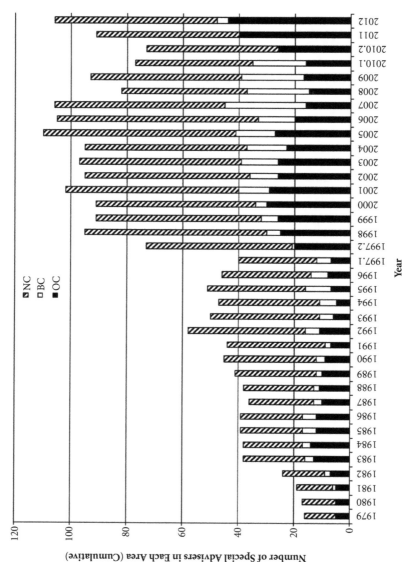

Figure A2.1: Special advisers by 'area' over time

Interestingly, it appears that these special advisers are switching *minister* and department, with 80 per cent serving more than one minister, versus only 25 per cent of those classed as OC or NC. This suggests that there are some special advisers who are perceived to be 'fixers'. If there is a problem in a department or a minister needs a safe pair of hands, certain names (such as John Hoskyns or Dan Corry) are likely to be suggested. Moreover, these fixers are likely to have already served one spell as a special adviser and therefore return to Whitehall, with nearly 40 per cent of those in the BC group having two distinct periods of service, versus only five per cent of advisers in the other groups. An extreme case of these fixers would be those three special advisers who served in the Thatcher or Major Governments and returned to assist the Coalition: Patrick Rock, Andrew Dunlop and Jonathan Caine.

Different factors apply in the case of the number of special advisers entering and leaving government. As discussed elsewhere, a special adviser's appointment formally terminates when their minister leaves the Cabinet or changes department, and special advisers who work during the general election campaign must also resign their appointment in order to engage in more direct party-political activity.[1] Figure A2.2 below shows the number of persons who started in government from 1979 to 2010, excluding 1979 (when a new Conservative Government came in) and 1997 (when a Labour Government took over) because the necessary turnover of the entire cohort in these years skews the graph.[2]

Figure A2.2 distinguishes between special advisers according to whether they started work in Whitehall in their corresponding minister's first year either in government or in that department (a 'synchronised' start) or not.[3] The graph predictably shows that the years following general elections (marked with a '-G') and change in premier show a large number of special advisers starting with ministers who are themselves relatively new in their portfolio. If one notes that a general election provides a convenient excuse for a reshuffle, this makes sense.

Overall, if one excludes 1979 and 1997, roughly half of special advisers joined their minister in a new department at the same time. Moreover, the majority of special advisers and ministers will be new to the relevant department, notwithstanding the fixers discussed above and ministers who lead the same department twice—such as Michael Heseltine at the Department of the Environment. Together, these points complement the recommendation in chapter nine for more formalised inductions for special advisers; it is odd that ministers are fairly comprehensively briefed upon their arrival in a new department, yet special advisers who are themselves fresh to the department are left to fend for themselves.

---

[1] See Cabinet Office, *Model Contract for Special Advisers* (2010), www.gov.uk/government/uploads/system/uploads/attachment_data/file/62452/special-advisers-model-contract_0.pdf; and the Constitutional Reform and Governance Act 2010.

[2] Coalition special advisers are excluded as it is premature to analyse their patterns until the full term is completed.

[3] This means that some cases of a minister waiting a number of months to appoint a special adviser are classed as 'synchronised' even though that is not exactly right.

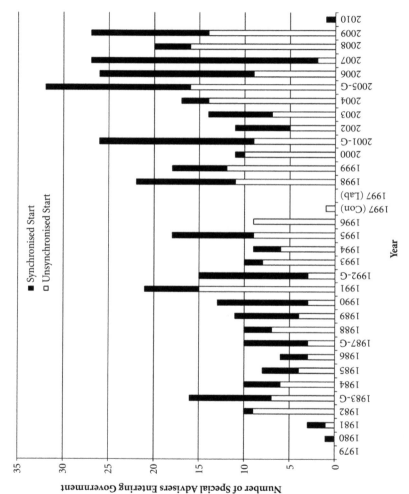

Figure A2.2: Number of special advisers entering government

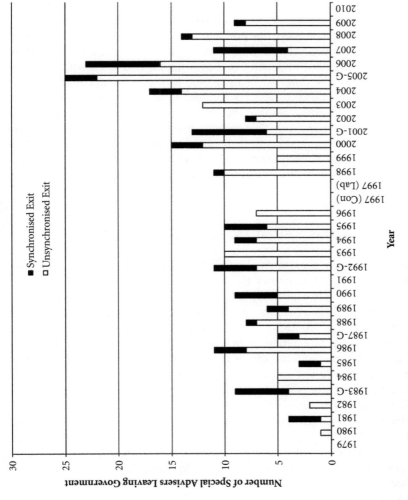

Figure A2.3: Number of special advisers exiting government

Figure A2.3 shows the figures for special advisers leaving their post, excluding the year 2010 for the same reasons as 1997 is excluded in Figure A2.1. As might be expected, the graph shows a rise in special advisers leaving government around the time of general elections or premier changes. Some special advisers may wish to serve in the election campaign or indeed run for office themselves.[4] Alternatively, the election may serve as a natural 'break' in a special adviser's career: they have worked until the end of the term and may find it time to move on. Large reshuffles that follow elections or premier changes also contribute to these numbers.

The data may also support the problem over retaining advisers mentioned in chapter three. Under Labour, the number of unsynchronised exits began to climb during the 2000s, suggesting that ministers found it difficult to retain special advisers for the duration of their time in a department. As during the Conservative Government, there were roughly equal numbers of synchronised and unsynchronised exits, meaning that many special advisers left government whilst their minister remained. This suggests that whilst the personalised nature of special advisers does tie them to their ministers, many will leave due to other factors. It is perhaps a recognition of this fluidity that more support for special advisers, eg, pension arrangements and severance pay, appear to have been formalised over time.

I. DEPARTMENTAL AND MINISTERIAL ANALYSIS

This section looks at departmental and ministerial patterns of special adviser assignment. Table A2.1 examines the departments that had the most special advisers. As one might expect, No 10 and the Treasury (HMT) have had the most, though the Treasury under Labour had on average more special advisers in post per year than No 10 under the Conservatives. This was mostly due to Brown's desire to operate a 'rival' policy unit in the Treasury. As discussed elsewhere, he avoided the informal cap of two special advisers by having additional advisers assigned to 'junior' ministers and listed under the 'Council of Economic Advisers'. Whilst the other departments listed have high numbers of special advisers, this may reflect ministerial churn rather than explicit size. For example, the Department of Work and Pensions (DWP) under Labour had a large number of special advisers, but they spent a fairly short length in the Department on average.

Outside of those large departments, there are a number of departments that differ quite markedly from the norm. Specifically, some departments with much more 'technocratic' operations require special advisers with particular skill sets. As Table A2.2 shows, the Lord Chancellor's Department (LCD), which later became the Department of Constitutional Affairs (DCA)—and the Chief Whip's Office had special advisers who served for a very long duration. It is telling that,

---

[4] See Appendix 3; or Max Goplerud, 'The First Time is (Mostly) the Charm: Special Advisers as Parliamentary Candidates and Members of Parliament' [2013] Parliamentary Affairs.

in these departments, the average special adviser serves for longer than over half of their cohort (noting that the median tenure for special adviser is three years). Appointments of special advisers to the Chief Whip in the Commons (CWOC) appears to have reverted to a more normal pattern under Labour (but note that it still ranks 12 out of 65 departments assigned special advisers on the metric used in Table A2.2) and the DCA and parts of the Home Office were merged into the Ministry of Justice. The adviser to the Chief Whip in the Lords (CWOL),

Table A2.1: Top departments by number of special advisers

Party	Dept	No of spads	Avg per year	Avg length in dept	Period
Labour	PM	98	27.7	4.0	1997–2010
Conservative	PM	48	9.6	3.8	1979–97
Labour	HMT	34	10.1	4.1	1997–2010
Conservative	HMT	24	4.1	3.3	1979–97
Conservative	DoE	23	4.1	3.3	1979–97
Labour	CO	23	3.8	2.1	1997–2002 and 2004–10*
Labour	HO	22	4.0	2.5	1997–2010
Labour	DWP	21	3.8	1.8	2001–2010
Conservative	DTI	20	3.9	2.9	1983–97
Labour	FCO	19	3.7	2.7	1997–2010

*No advisers are recorded in 2003. Advisers listed in the Cabinet Office include those working for non-departmental ministers like the Chancellor of the Duchy of Lancaster whose portfolio varies.

Table A2.2: Top departments by average special adviser length of service

Party	Dept	No of spads	Avg spad length in dept	No of ministers	Avg minister length in dept
Conservative	CWOL	1	6	3	2.3
Labour	LCD*	1	6	1	6
Conservative	CWOC**	4	5.5	6	4
Labour	DCA	2	5	1	5
Labour	CWOL	3	4.3	4	3.3

*The LCD was reorganised into the DCA in 2003; the one special adviser started in 1998 and served the entire period of the Labour administration.
**Under the Conservatives, a special adviser only appeared in the CWOL in 1992 and served until 1997.

however, remained unusual in terms of longevity of appointment for the entire period examined. A key explanatory factor is that service in those departments equipped the serving special advisers with skills that an incoming minister's personal choice of adviser would almost certainly lack. Interviews also suggest that incoming ministers in these departments were quite happy to keep the existing special adviser for exactly this reason.

Turning to ministers, Prime Ministers always have the most special advisers. Table A2.3 lists the five ministers–department combinations that had the most special advisers after the Prime Minister. Unsurprisingly, the Treasury captures most of this list. However, the data confirms the discussion in chapter 3 that 'big beasts' of the Cabinet are generally given leeway to appoint a larger number of persons than other ministers.

Table A2.3 also illustrates that Gordon Brown at the Treasury kept his special advisers for remarkably long periods of time—each serving on average five years with him. Most of these were concentrated in the Council of Economic Advisers, but there were exceptions such as Sue Nye or Ian Austin. This places Brown as Chancellor as the minister with the second longest-serving special advisers on average.

Finally, the common viewpoint is that special advisers are almost exclusively assigned to a secretary of state who is a member of Cabinet. This is broadly accurate, but it is worth analysing the exceptions. To explain the tables, each summarises the number of assignments of a special adviser to a minister in a department in a given year. For example, Alistair Darling moved from the Treasury to the Department of Social Security (later the Department of Work and Pensions) in 1998. One of his special advisers (Andrew Maugham) moved with him; thus, the database reports two assignments for that special adviser in 1998. Alternatively, if a special adviser changes minister in a given year (Jonathan Caine

Table A2.3: Ministers with the most special advisers

Government	Name of minister [dept]	Total persons	Avg no of spads employed per year	Avg years with minister
Labour	Brown, Gordon [HMT]	16	7.9	5.4
Labour	Blunkett, David [DfEE]	10	5.8	2.9
Conservative	Heseltine, Michael [DoE]	9	2.6	2.3
Conservative	Lawson, Nigel [HMT]	9	2.8	3.1
Labour	Darling, Alistair [HMT]	8	3.5	2.6

worked for both Owen Paterson and Theresa Villers in 2012 at the Northern Ireland Office), this is also coded as two assignments. Table A2.4 provides the number of assignments over the period in each category, while Table A2.5 splits this information by party in power. For example, it shows that 83.3 per cent of recorded special adviser assignments for the Conservatives were attached to a Secretary of State who attended Cabinet.

The tables show that not many ministers of state or ministers not attending Cabinet employed special advisers. To explain the more anomalous categories, the Chief Whip's Office are the main departments where special advisers served a minister who did not attend Cabinet. The practice of the Chief Whip in the Commons attending Cabinet emerged under Blair, since all holders after the first (Nick Brown) attended Cabinet, as noted by the fall in Table A2.5 (3.9 per cent to 0.5 per cent). The practice with the Chief Whip in the House of Lords is more variable, with their attendance in Cabinet appearing to depend on their relationship with the Prime Minister. For example, Lord Bassam (2008–10) did not attend Cabinet, whilst Lords Carter of Coles (1997–2002) and Grocott (2002–07) did.

The ministers of state attending Cabinet who employed special advisers were usually located in the Cabinet Office or the Treasury, and probably received permission to do so due to their influential portfolio, though some interviewees in the Treasury report that special advisers listed under their name actually worked for Gordon Brown. Other ministers of state who employed special advisers appear

Table A2.4: Special adviser assignments by ministerial rank

Attending Cabinet	Parliamentary Under-Secretary of State*	Minister of State	Secretary of State**	Total
Yes	0	188	2,441	2,629
No	4	99	42	145
Aggregate total	4	287	2,483	2,774

*Three of these four entries are attributed to Emily Thomas, who was an unpaid special adviser to Lord Sainsbury whilst he was Parliamentary Under-Secretary of State in the Department of Trade and Industry (DTI). His allowance of a special adviser, presumably formalised as such to ensure that she had appropriate access to the Department, was probably a function of his status within the Labour Party. Thomas later became a special adviser to Alistair Darling at the DTI and the Treasury. The other entry (David Ruffley, adviser to Charles Wardle at the Home Office in 1992) is an example, discussed in the main text, of special advisers being assigned to junior ministers.

**Secretary of State is coded as being the most senior minister in a given department, even if their formal name (eg, Chancellor of the Exchequer) is different. This is also applied to non-'line' departments (eg, the Chief Whip's Office) in order to form a standardised hierarchy. The position of Deputy Prime Minister (in the Cabinet Office) is also coded as a Secretary of State; this includes John Prescott and Nick Clegg.

Table A2.5: Special adviser assignment by party and ministerial rank

Attending Cabinet	Government party and rank (% of total assignments)								
	Conservative (n = 881)			Labour (n = 1,489)			Coalition (n = 404)		
	PUSS	MOS	SOS	PUSS	MOS	SOS	PUSS	MOS	SOS
Yes	0.0	5.3	83.3	0.0	7.5	89.7	0.0	7.4	91.8
No	0.1	7.4	3.9	0.2	2.1	0.5	0.0	0.7	0.0

to have held influential or high-profile portfolios—some of which later became separate departments, for instance, the Department for Transport.

For the remainder of those ministers who did not attend Cabinet, a large number were located in the Department of the Environment under the Conservatives, partially explaining the partisan difference observed in Table A2.5. This Department was unique insofar as a series of special advisers for about a decade starting in 1985 were assigned exclusively to junior ministers, according to *Hansard*[5] and other sources. The data suggests that there was only one special adviser (at a time) assigned to do this role, but five persons overall were involved over the period. These special advisers co-existed alongside those attached to the Secretaries of State, each of whom had approximately two special advisers per year. This helps to explain why it ranks just below the Treasury in terms of total special advisers employed.

A possible explanation for the unusually high number of advisers in the Department of the Environment comes from a combination of ministerial 'churn' and the fact that it was a large department with a number of high-profile port-folios (the Department had been formed in 1970 by the amalgamation of the Departments of Transport, Housing and Local Government, and Public Works).[6] The corresponding junior ministers (ministers of state) were reshuffled quite regularly. The three posts combined had approximately 30 ministers over the

---

[5] For example, HC Deb 26 July 1990 vol, 177, col 382W assigns Richard Marsh to the junior ministers, whilst noting that David Pearce and Patrick Rock worked for the Secretary of State (Chris Patten).

[6] Transport had been hived off again into a separate department in 1976, but was merged again with the Department of the Environment in 1979 to create the Department for Environment, Transport and the Regions (DETR) under the Deputy Prime Minister. After the 2001 election, the environment and wildlife and countryside portfolios were detached and merged with the Ministry of Agriculture, Fisheries and Food (MAFF) to form the Department for Environment, Food and Rural Affairs (Defra) and the remaining parts of the department became the Department for Transport, Local Government and the Regions (DTLR). Transport was split off to form its own department again in 2002, and the rest of the DTLR followed John Prescott to the 'Office of the Deputy Prime Minister', which in 2006 became the Department for Communities and Local Government. As a supporting point, a relatively large number of special advisers were assigned to non-Cabinet ministers of state in the DETR.

decade in consideration, with many serving in post for around a year at a time.[7] Thus, it may be that the Secretary of State in conjunction with the Prime Minister took a decision to assign a special adviser to these posts in order to ensure that there was some degree of continuity and experience that was available to the incoming junior ministers. Moreover, the churn in the Secretaries of State (eight over that decade) may have also contributed to this.

Overall, the picture of special adviser assignments—to one minister in one department for a median of three years—discussed in chapter three is broadly right. Yet, this appendix has shown that under those aggregate figures, there is a large amount of heterogeneity with regards to their assignment and patterns of service. This supports the themes elsewhere in the book that suggest that some special advisers serve in fluid ways, dependent on structural and personal factors that are difficult to characterise in broad strokes.

---

[7] David Butler and Gareth Butler, *British Political Facts* (Palgrave Macmillan 2011).

Appendix 3

The Post-government Career of Special Advisers

ANNA SELLERS

THIS APPENDIX SEEKS to shed light on where special advisers go after they leave government and to what extent their subsequent careers reflect trends towards the 'professionalisation' of politics and a revolving door between the public and private/voluntary sectors.

I. METHODOLOGY

This appendix analyses the careers of all special advisers after leaving their posts with the Conservative and Labour Governments from 1979 to 2010.[1] Special advisers from the Coalition are excluded as the majority are still in post. Special advisers who served under more than one Prime Minister are coded under the first one they served.

The text here follows all known careers to get a complete picture.[2] As many individuals participated in multiple occupational sectors (and are coded accordingly), there is inevitably overlap. It was not feasible to code the order of post-special adviser careers. In the graphical presentation, percentages are derived from *all careers* coded, as this gives a clearer presentation of the balance between the various sectors. Table A3.1 explains the coding scheme.

---

[1] See ch 2 for a further justification of the decision to start from 1979 versus 1974. Information on those special advisers serving from 1974 to 1979 is limited, with a higher proportion of 'unknown' codings. Other sources express similar concerns about finding data on older special advisers. House of Commons Library, 'Party Political Broadcasts' (House of Commons Library 2013) 8.

[2] Sources used were extensive. The most common sources were LinkedIn, Debrett's People of Today, and the UK Parliament website; the information is current as of June 2013. Further data is available upon request from the author or the Constitution Unit. It was impossible to find information on 11 per cent of special advisers and they are excluded from the following analysis. This figure is similar to that in ch 3: see Appendix 1 for more details.

Table A3.1: Coding categories for post-government careers of special advisers

GOV-PB	Government-Public Body: includes roles with local authorities and their executive agencies and commissions, non-departmental public bodies, regulatory bodies and regional public sector bodies, the NHS, temporary commissions, enquiries and advisory panels for central government
GOV-CS	Government-Civil Service: includes roles in Whitehall with a central government department
MP	Member of Parliament
MPFB	Member of Parliament-Frontbench: includes becoming a secretary of state, minister of state, shadow secretary of state, shadow minister of state, parliamentary under-secretary of state, parliamentary private secretary and official spokesperson. This is a wider definition than is often given to the term 'frontbench'. It was felt necessary to adopt such an all-encompassing definition in order to make a firm separation from those who remain purely 'backbench' MPs
LO	Member of the House of Lords
LOFB	Frontbench member of the House of Lords. The same criteria used in the MPFB category was applied
ER	Elected representative: includes a Member of Scottish Parliament (MSP), a Member of the Welsh Assembly (AM) or a Member of the European Parliament (MEP)
ERFB	Frontbench elected representative: the same criteria used in the MPFB category were applied
CO	Local councillor
BUS	Business: includes roles taken with investment banks, consultancies, major corporations, freelance consultants or posts in an association that represents business interests such as the Confederation for British Industry
AC	Academia
ME	Media
TT	Think tank
NPS	Non-profit sector: roles with NGOs and charities
UN	Trade unions
POL	Party-political employment: includes roles such as parliamentary researcher, party central staff and roles working for a political campaign group such as No2AV
IGO/FG	International governmental organisation/foreign government: includes positions in the World Bank, the European Union, the United Nations and any foreign governments
PA/COMMS	Public affairs/communications practitioner
OTHER	Those individuals who went on to a role that did not fit into any of the sectors created

Notes:

— The two categories used in chapter three, TECH and OTHER, have been merged in the analysis undertaken in this appendix.

— To elaborate on the definition of 'public affairs', a former special adviser is deemed to have become a 'PA practitioner' if he or she was employed by a public affairs or communications firm. This is a reasonably strict definition, but it is consistent with the other categories that are defined by the nature of the employer, rather than trying to directly ascertain what roles the employee performed inside the relevant organisation.

II. FINDINGS AND ANALYSIS

The results of the data collected are summarised in Figure A3.1.[3] The following section analyses the more noteworthy findings. To be clear, we have used two kinds of measures in the text: percentages of *all careers coded*; but on occasion, percentages of *all special advisers coded*.

A. Elected Representatives (MPs, Peerages, Other Elected Representatives) and 'Success'

It has been observed that governments are now dominated by career politicians 'who have made politics their occupation and have no other professional aim than to remain in politics',[4] with an increasing number of MPs who have held 'politics facilitating' roles, including that of special adviser, prior to their election.

How far is this confirmed by the data? Examination of the elected representatives (ER) category reveals that almost 10 per cent of former special advisers were elected MPs at some point after leaving post. Further data segregation shows 42, or 90 per cent of the 46 became frontbenchers, indicating many former special advisers have been 'successful' as MPs. It must be mentioned here that the frontbenchers category includes the position of Parliamentary Private Secretary (PPS). On this count, only four former special advisers who were elected MPs never held *any* frontbench position and were only backbench MPs. Goplerud has found that closer to 80 per cent became actual frontbench MPs, ie, held positions higher than PPS.[5]

---

[3] Summation of roles is 904, which means that roughly there were two roles found for each of the 478 former special advisers in the data set. When calculating percentages, 'unknowns' were included and therefore 478 was used as the denominator. For instance, on 46 occasions a former special adviser was elected as an MP. This means that 46 of 478 or 9.6 per cent of special advisers *at some point* were elected MPs after leaving post.

[4] Uwe Jun, 'Great Britain: From the Prevalence of the Amateur to the Dominance of the Career Politician' in Jens Borchert and Jürgen Zeiss (eds), *The Political Class in Advanced Democracies* (Oxford University Press 2003) 164.

[5] Max Goplerud, 'The First Time is (Mostly) the Charm: Special Advisers as Parliamentary Candidates and Members of Parliament' [2013] *Parliamentary Affairs* 1. Goplerud uses Allen's

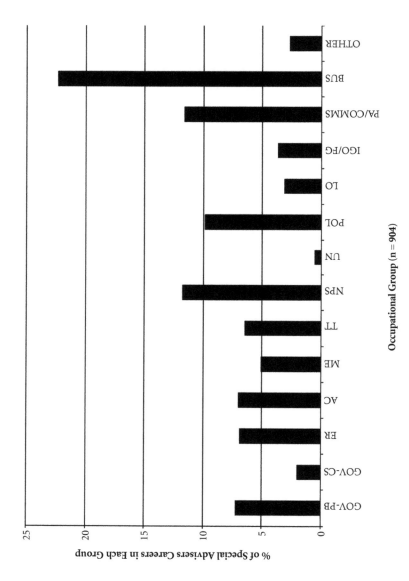

Figure A3.1: Roles taken by former special advisers by occupational sector 1979–2010

The data also reveals that the proportion of former special advisers who became MPs at some point is more than twice as much for those who served a Conservative government than for those who served a Labour government (15 per cent of former special advisers who served a Conservative government versus six per cent of former special advisers who served a Labour government). This finding is, at first glance, surprising, considering that both parties were in government for significant stretches of time. Goplerud notes, however, that the number of Labour special advisers who run for office does not appear to have peaked yet, as Labour only left office in 2010. He suggests that the difference between the parties is likely to continue to even out over the next few elections as more former Conservative special advisers 'give up' on becoming MPs and the younger former Labour special advisers decide to run or are successful in being selected.[6]

The data therefore confirms the frequently made observation that many former special advisers who become MPs are likely to eventually become ministers, and often high-ranking ministers. But it also reveals that the proportion of former special advisers who become MPs is relatively small—only 12 per cent of special advisers stood for Parliament after leaving Whitehall. Yet, the fact that the latter achieve high levels of success shows that being a special adviser is clearly an 'instrumental' profession, and a powerful one at that.

While the proportion of former special advisers in the Commons may not be large, this figure has risen consistently since 1979. As Figure A3.2 shows, the 2010 election returned the highest number of ex-special advisers ever in the House of Commons—33 out of 650. This is in contrast to the five former special advisers who entered Parliament in 1987.[7] These findings, of course, need to be put into context: the greater proportion of former special advisers in the Commons may be a side-effect of the proliferation of special advisers in Whitehall rather than an indication that a bigger proportion of special advisers are becoming MPs.

---

five-level coding scheme ranking the various governmental offices that MPs can hold where Level 1 is backbench, Level 2 is PPSs, Level 3 includes parliamentary under-secretaries of state, opposition spokespeople, junior whips and advocate generals, Level 4 includes ministers of state, shadow ministers and whips, and Level 5 includes Cabinet ministers, the Shadow Cabinet, the Chief Whip and party leaders. Goplerud finds that 80 per cent held positions in Level 3 and higher, while 84 per cent held positions in Level 4 and above.

[6] ibid.
[7] The graph comes from data used in ibid.

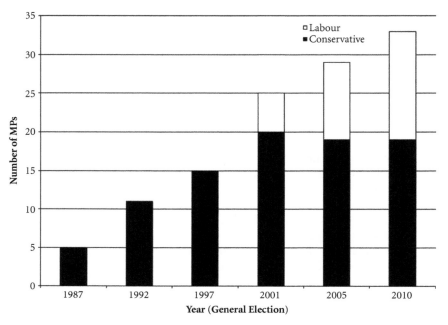

Figure A3.2: Number of ex-special advisers who became MPs between 1983 and 2010 by party

It is worth noting that the idea that former special advisers who are elected to public office are successful can also be seen in the fact that five former special advisers became an elected representative outside of Westminster and that three of these were frontbenchers. Amongst these five are Iain Gray MSP, who served as the Scottish Labour leader from 2008 to 2011, and Rod Richards, former MP and AM, who was Leader of the Welsh Conservative Party in 1999.

As to why many former special advisers have had 'successful' careers as MPs, Lord Adonis, a former Secretary of State for Transport and a former special adviser to Tony Blair, compared the role to an apprenticeship for ministerial office.[8] One former special adviser who became an MP, and later a minister, said that:

> Having held office locally, having been a special adviser, I think it would be very hard to describe a better apprenticeship, for being both a Member of Parliament and a Minister and a Cabinet Minister. Because you have, in all respects you have seen how the system works.

---

[8] Peter Riddell, Zoe Gruhn and Liz Carolan, 'The Challenge of Being a Minister: Defining and Developing Ministerial Effectiveness' (Institute for Government 2011).

Adonis endorses this argument:

> [F]ar from decrying the reign of ex-SpAds ... we should welcome the fact that at least some ministers come to office with an apprenticeship worth the name, beyond service in the House of Commons.[9]

This apprenticeship notion echoes a suggestion by Paul Cairney that being a special adviser is an 'instrumental' occupation to becoming an MP, ie, 'a means to an elected end'.[10] It also accords with Cowley's argument that the increased frequency of MPs having been a 'political worker' explains the greater speed at which these politicians reach parliamentary success—that is, attain a ministerial position—after election.[11]

The argument is therefore that the skills and connections that special advisers attain in post (ie, during their apprenticeship) are viewed as attractive ministerial qualities by senior party officials.[12] But we should be careful: it may that those who were elected might have been elected even if they *had* not been special advisers: David Miliband, for instance, might have elected as a Labour MP regardless of his earlier role as Head of the Policy Unit.

A small number of special advisers have become peers. The data indicates that six per cent became members of the House of Lords, but only 39 per cent of those individuals became frontbenchers. This suggests that a majority of former special advisers from 1979 to 2010 who became peers did not become successful in the House of Lords, despite (presumably) acquiring the same skills, contacts and knowledge that facilitate success in a political post. This is arguably not only because peerages are often awarded to those in recognition of service rather than to those who actively seek political careers in the House of Lords, but also because of the limited number of ministerial positions that are awarded to peers in the first place. Indeed, Cowley and Melhuish argue that there is a 'glass ceiling' in the House of Lords: of the 137 peers who held ministerial posts examined in their study, only 21 actually became members of the Cabinet.[13] They explain that 'the Lords is an alternative game, but because those who play know that they cannot win, the ambitious may decide that the game is not for them'.[14] A comparison reveals that the proportion of former special advisers who served a Conservative government who became peers is only slightly more than the proportion of former special advisers who served a Labour government. Of 181 former special

---

[9] ibid.

[10] Paul Cairney, 'The Professionalisation of MPs: Refining the "Politics-Facilitating" Explanation' (2007) 60 *Parliamentary Affairs* 212, 214–24.

[11] Philip Cowley, 'Arise, Novice Leader! The Continuing Rise of the Career Politician in Britain' (2012) 32 *Politics*, 31–38.

[12] Goplerud (n 5).

[13] Philip Cowley and David Melhuish, 'Peers' Careers: Ministers in the House of Lords, 1964–95' (1997) 45 *Political Studies* 21, 33.

[14] ibid.

advisers who served Conservative administrations, seven per cent became peers and of 297 former special advisers who served a Labour government, five per cent became peers.

B. Career Political Actors

The data indicate that 14 per cent of all former special advisers joined public bodies—that is, public sector organisations such as non-departmental public bodies and executive agencies, temporary commissions, inquiries or advisory panels, local bodies or their executive agencies or commissions, or the NHS and its regulatory bodies. The data further reveals that four per cent of all former special advisers became civil servants in Whitehall departments. These findings offer some evidence towards the notion that a significant proportion of former special advisers remain in the political class after leaving post.

Almost one-fifth of all former special advisers took roles in party-political organisations and the party-political employment sector was the fourth most frequently joined sector. We saw in chapter three that many special advisers tend to work in party-political organisations beforehand, but as we shall see, these individuals generally tend to abandon the sector after leaving government. This makes sense, if we understand career moves as stepping stones.

III. PUBLIC AFFAIRS PRACTITIONERS, THE BUSINESS SECTOR, THINK TANKS, THE NON-PROFIT SECTOR AND OTHER OBSERVATIONS

Figure A3.1 shows that approximately 12 per cent of post-special adviser careers involved working as a public affairs (PA) practitioner. The more interesting finding is that the proportion of former special advisers who have worked as a PA practitioner at some point after leaving post has risen substantially between 1979 and 2010. Information disaggregated by premiership is shown in Figure A3.3 below. Of the 101 special advisers working for the Thatcher administration, only 16 individuals, or 16 per cent, became PA practitioners at some point after leaving post, whereas of the 237 special advisers who served during Blair's premiership, 59 or nearly 25 per cent per cent became PA practitioners at some point.[15] So it seems that going on to PA/lobbying, whether for a PA firm or in-house, has been an increasing trend.

What are the reasons for this trend? One reason may be that in earlier periods special advisers tended to focus on policy, while special advisers from more recent governments included more 'spin doctors' or what political commentator

---

[15] These proportions may be higher as it only includes those for whom information could be found.

Hugo Young described as 'information peddlers whose cardinal faculty ... is an understanding of the definition of truth: that it consists exclusively of what is politically convenient'.[16] These individuals may be more inclined to become a PA practitioner after leaving post than, say, an academic who served as a special adviser.

However, it is not just a matter of supply: there is also demand. The lobbying industry itself has grown. Organisations are paying more attention to their interactions with government and are increasingly seeking advice and assistance on how best to do so. Former special advisers are seen as particularly well suited to assist with these interactions because they will, in theory, via contacts and insider knowledge, give clients or their employing organisation an advantage in their contact with government. So another reason for the increasing number of ex-special advisers in this area is probably the greater demand.

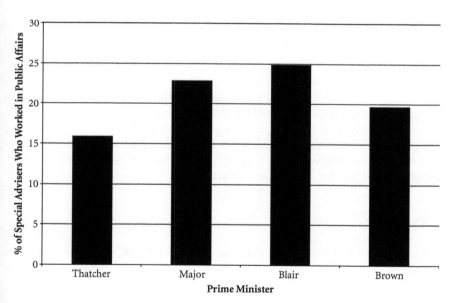

Figure A3.3: Proportion of former special advisers of each Prime Minister who served between 1979 and May 2010 who became a PA practitioner

---

[16] Hugo Young, 'The Blairites Have Wrecked the Best of the Civil Service' *The Guardian* (28 February 2002).

The business sector is the sector to which the most former special advisers migrate. Almost half of all former special advisers (202 individuals) went into the business sector at some point after leaving post. This trend applies across all premierships and under certain premierships overwhelmingly. The fact that this sector can offer greater remuneration than most other sectors is no doubt a factor in this.

A. Non-profit Sector

The non-profit or voluntary sector is the second most popular sector for ex-special advisers, with slightly over one-fifth going on to work in it at some point. More interestingly, a comparison between parties reveals that more former Labour special advisers joined the non-profit sector than former Conservative special advisers. This would seem to corroborate the observation by some commentators that more Labour supporters join the voluntary sector than Conservative ones.[17] However, there are other possible explanations. Again, there is the matter of demand. The voluntary sector has grown over the last 15 years. Snowdon found that between 1997 and 2005, the combined income of Britain s charities nearly doubled, from £19.8 billion to £37.9 billion. This rise coincided with the relaxation of the rules regulating lobbying activity by charities, a development that Snowdon argues led to a politicisation of the third sector.[18]

There was probably also increased interaction between the voluntary sector and government under Labour. Thus, there were not only more jobs available in this sector for former Labour special advisers after leaving post than there were for their earlier Conservative counterparts, but there were also more roles suited for individuals with insider knowledge of government.

B. Think Tanks

A small contingent of former special advisers join think tanks (six per cent of post-special adviser careers). Data disaggregated by party shows the partisan links of some think tanks; for instance, the connection between Labour and the Institute for Public Policy Research (IPPR) is often discussed and 15 out of the 44 Labour special advisers who joined think tanks worked for the IPPR. Demos and the Smith Institute were also popular for Labour advisers, and are also known for their partisan links.[19]

---

[17] Fraser Nelson, 'Gordon Brown's Secret Army Could Defeat the Coalition's Welfare and Education Reforms' *Daily Telegraph* (25 October 2012); Ian Griggs and Stephen Cook, 'Analysis: Are Charities a Nest of Scheming Labourites?' (*Third Sector Online*, 17 December 2012).

[18] Christopher Snowdon, 'Sock Puppets: How the Government Lobbies itself and Why' (Institute of Economic Affairs 2012) 12, www.iea.org.uk/sites/default/files/publications/files/Sock%20Puppets.pdf.

[19] Matt Chorley, 'Politics? Nothing that a Bit of Thinking Can't Cure' *The Independent* (30 January 2011); Toby Helm and Christopher Hope, 'The Top Twelve Think Tanks in Britain' *Daily Telegraph*

Previous observations of links between the Conservative Party and the Centre for Policy Studies (CPS) are also corroborated by the data as, of the 15 former special advisers who served Conservative governments who went on to join think tanks at some point, five held roles with the CPS after leaving post. It has been suggested that employing such individuals gives certain think tanks an unfair advantage in influencing policy, particularly if the special adviser's party is still in government.[20]

However, Mulgan has conversely argued that the political environment for think tanks in the twenty-first century is one where 'more pragmatic governments place a higher premium on what works, are more willing to copy good ideas from elsewhere, and may be less constrained as to the types of solutions they adopt'. As a result, 'it is now possible for a right-wing think tank to influence a Labour government as it would be for a think tank of the left to influence a ... Conservative one'.[21] This may indicate that it may not be as controversial as it once was for bodies such as the IPPR or the CPS to employ special advisers before or after their time in post.

IV. THE EVOLUTION OF THE POST-SPECIAL ADVISER CAREER SINCE 1979

Analysing differences between special advisers' careers depending on when they served in government (by premier) reveals an evolution over time. First, as previously noted, the business sector has been, amongst special advisers under all Prime Ministers, the sector joined most frequently. It is interesting to note that this proportion increased amongst special advisers in John Major's premiership (from 45 per cent under Thatcher to 56 per cent under Major), but then dropped slightly amongst special advisers from Blair's premiership (40 per cent), which would seem to confirm the traditionally close ties between the Conservative Party and the business sector.

The data also shows that the proportion of former special advisers from amongst each premiership who joined academia at some point after leaving post has declined since 1979: from 21 per cent under Thatcher to seven per cent under Brown. Interestingly, the proportion of former special advisers amongst each Prime Minister's administration(s) who have gone into the party-political employment sector at some point has been relatively consistent between Prime Ministers (16 per cent), with the exception of those who served under Brown (36 per cent). Arguably this higher proportion is the result of the regrouping of the Labour Party which occurred following the 2010 general election (it conducted a

---

(24 January 2008); Justin Bentham, 'The IPPR and Demos: Think Tanks of the New Social Democracy' (2006) 77 *Political Quarterly* 166.

[20] Jon Slater, 'Meshed in Web of Power', www.tes.co.uk/article.aspx?storycode=2118244.

[21] Geoff Mulgan, 'Thinking in Tanks: The Changing Ecology of Political Ideas' (2006) 77 *Political Quarterly* 147, 154.

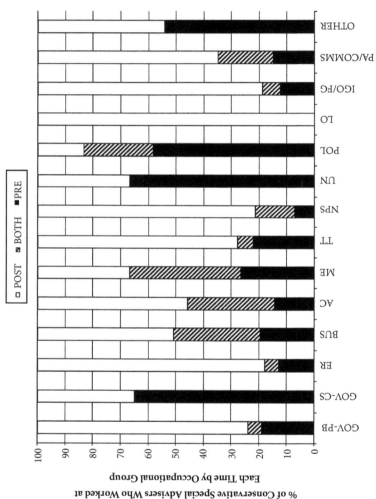

Figure A3.4: Conservative career links

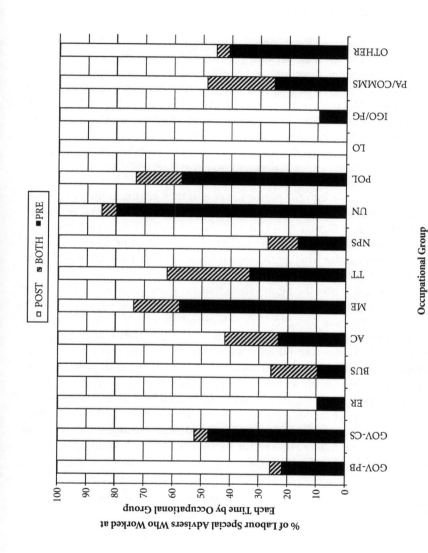

Figure A3.5: Labour career links

policy review and elected a new leader, all of which one would expect requires employing a greater number of individuals in these types of roles).[22]

A. A Revolving Door or Career Ladder?

A trend that has concerned some commentators is the revolving door in Whitehall, 'the movement of individuals between positions of public office and jobs in the private sector, in either direction' and the potential that this has to influence policy making.[23] Pre- and post-special adviser occupations are frequently cited as examples of this revolving door. One example is the move of Anji Hunter, formerly a special adviser to Blair, to British Petroleum in 2001,[24] despite the fact that the government is the key buyer in the energy sector.[25]

The findings in this appendix suggest that the revolving door between special advisers and the private sector is alive and well in at least one direction. However, for the term 'revolving' to be accurate, special advisers would have had to come from the private sector into the public sector and then return to the private sector. A comparison of pre- and post-special adviser roles indicates that this is not necessarily the case.[26] Figures A3.4 and A3.5 show the information on career links for Conservative and Labour special advisers, respectively. The figures show for each occupational group whether the special advisers worked in that sector before or after (or both) their time in Whitehall.

For the business sector, the figures show that the existence of a revolving door is stronger amongst the Conservative special advisers, with 30 per cent of those who worked in business doing so both before and after their time in Whitehall, compared to only 15 per cent of Labour advisers. Yet, the fact that more special advisers enter the business sector only afterwards suggests that many former special advisers have found that the skills and contacts they acquire in post were useful to gain jobs subsequently with consultancies and lobbying companies. This, in turn, suggests less a revolving door amongst special advisers than a career ladder.

The idea of a career ladder is supported by noting that special advisers whose previous occupation had been in party-political organisations (writ broad to include unions) tend to leave that sector afterwards to work in other more lucrative areas, eg, public affairs or business. Conversely, some sectors have higher rates

---

[22] Patrick Wintour, 'Labour Policy Chiefs Meet to Fill in Ed Miliband's "Blank Piece of Paper"' *The Guardian* (22 June 2011).
[23] 'Cabs for Hire? Fixing the Revolving Door between Government and Business' (Transparency International UK 2011) 5, www.transparency.org.uk/our-work/publications/10-publications/132-cabs-for-hire-fixing-the-revolving-door-between-government-and-business.
[24] Terry Macalister and Michael White, 'BP Stops Paying Political Parties' *The Guardian* (1 March 2002).
[25] 'Cabs for Hire' (n 23) 7.
[26] I am grateful to Max Goplerud for the analysis of the career links between pre- and post-special adviser roles. The coding scheme in these figures mirrors the one employed in ch 3, though it uses the same underlying data as the rest of this appendix.

of retention. Academics and think-tank employees show a greater tendency to return to their previous profession. It is difficult to know definitely, but it seems that many of these special advisers performed more policy-focused work and thus returned to that work after leaving Whitehall—Ian Heggie and Stuart Wood (see the case study in chapter four) are paradigmatic Conservative and Labour examples. This retention also holds relatively true for special advisers working in the media, though that appears to have shifted during the Conservative to Labour period.

Finally, the approximately 40 per cent who were PA practitioners before becoming special advisers include some of the senior communications special advisers. Most prominent under the Blair administration; some returned to their jobs after leaving government. One example is David Hill, former Director of Communications in Downing Street, who worked for Bell Pottinger before becoming a special adviser and who returned to this role upon leaving post.[27] Interestingly, and perhaps illustrating something about the world of public affairs, Jonathan Caine also worked for Bell Pottinger after his service as a special adviser under the Conservative Governments before returning to service as a special adviser for the Coalition.

V. ETHICAL ISSUES

There is considerable debate as to how far movements from public to private or voluntary sector bring benefits. In the US, Hugh Heclo has written about what he calls the 'in-and-outer system',[28] the political appointment of outsiders to the executive branch of government, and the movement of these individuals 'in-and-out' of the public and private sector. He argues that, because temporary political executives move between the amorphous boundaries of the public and private sector, they are 'in a unique strategic position to understand these two worlds and their interconnections' and can subsequently bring 'into government outside perspectives that are unavailable to permanent officials and that they will return to non-governmental organizations with new appreciations that are otherwise inaccessible to private groups'.[29]

In Britain bringing such 'new appreciations' into the private sector is not usually perceived as a benefit. Instead, former special advisers moving into the private sector are seen as potentially harming the public interest by distorting the policy-making process. Sir Christopher Kelly, then Chairman of the Committee on Standards in Public Life, explained, while giving evidence to the PASC in March

---

[27] Public Administration Select Committee, *Lobbying: Access and Influence in Whitehall* (2008) 32.
[28] Hugh Heclo, 'The In-and-Outer System: A Critical Assessment' (1988) 103 *Political Science Quarterly* 37.
[29] ibid.

2012 as part of its inquiry into the Business Appointment Rules, that there are two possible ways in which the revolving door can hurt the public interest:

> [T]here are real questions to answer about whether the phenomenon of the revolving door involves instances where people's behaviour before leaving employment is altered in a way that is not in the public interest in anticipation of future employment or, post-public office, commercial or other organisations are given unfair advantages over others as a result of the knowledge or contacts of people they employ post-office.[30]

The debate on how to regulate movement out of the public sector receives a lot of political and media attention. The Special Advisers' Code of Conduct, most recently revised in June 2010, requires special advisers upon leaving government to 'obtain prior approval before accepting an outside appointment in circumstances set out in the rules'.[31] The Code states:

> Special advisers are subject to the Business Appointment Rules. Under the Rules, they are required to submit an application to the Head of their former Department for any appointments or employment they wish to take up within two years of leaving the Civil Service. Applications submitted by special advisers are considered by the independent Advisory Committee on Business Appointments (ACoBA). Decisions on applications are taken by the Head of Department based on advice from the Advisory Committee.

It was not until 2011, however, that all special advisers leaving office were required to submit such an application. Previously, all ex-ministers and senior civil servants had to notify ACoBA of plans to take up new roles, but special advisers only had to do so if their salaries were at or above senior civil service pay-grade 'SCS3' (although all did have to notify top officials in their department).[32] As a result, of the large numbers of special advisers who left post following Blair's departure as Prime Minister in 2007, only two, Jonathan Powell and Elizabeth Lloyd, 'went through the ACoBA system'. The remainder either rejoined their previous employer and were therefore exempt from seeking clearance or were not senior enough to go through the ACoBA notification procedure.[33]

Some argue that the current regulatory system is not robust enough as ACoBA's advice is not binding and the ban on lobbying lasts only two years.[34] ACoBA's

---

[30] Public Administration Select Committee, *Business Appointment Rules* (2012) HC 404 Ev, 6 March 2012 Q10.

[31] House of Commons Library, 'Special Advisers' (House of Commons Library 2013); 'Cabs for Hire?' (n 23). The Code was given statutory underpinning by the Constitutional Reform and Governance Act 2010.

[32] PubAffairs, 'What Is Public Affairs?' (2011), www.publicaffairsnetworking.com/whatis_pa.php. SCS3 is the highest pay grade in the Senior Civil Service before Permanent Secretary. Director Generals are usually in the SCS3 pay grade. The delayed introduction of such regulation is not atypical regarding special advisers. Indeed, formal regulation of special advisers did not begin until Major's premiership. Andrew Blick, *People Who Live in the Dark* (Politico's 2004) 249.

[33] Public Administration Select Committee (n 27) 32.

[34] Andy Denwood, 'Call to Limit Businesses Profiting from Political Ties' *BBC News* (26 July 2011); 'Cabs for Hire?' (n 23) 14. Denwood quoting Dr Liz David-Barrett also suggests that if 'people have worked in very high risk departments ... there should be a lifelong ban in the associated industry'.

limited resources have also been criticised, with the Committee on Standards in Public Life noting that in April 2012 ACoBA employed only 4.5 staff members in a joint secretariat serving both ACoBA and the House of Lords Appointments Commission.[35]

Conversely, however, some find the system in certain instances to be overly restrictive and complicated. For instance, one former special adviser said that, despite his professional experience only having been in one particular industry, after leaving post he 'could not have gone to work directly for anybody in [that same] industry for six to nine months'. The concern is that these restrictions will deter experienced and talented individuals from joining the public sector in the first place. The same special adviser argued:

> [T]he notion that you're going to get highly experienced people from think tanks and academia and industry to go and do a year or two inside at the Department of State, and not getting paid a huge amount of money at a very sure noted risk of you losing your job, who are then unable to go back into their career profession for a period of time, anything up to two years, is for the birds frankly.

The challenge is therefore achieving both transparency in monitoring as well as robustness in preventing abuse in post-special adviser careers, while not being so restrictive as to discourage those from the private sector becoming special advisers because of the risk of reduced employment prospects afterwards. Sir Christopher Kelly describes this as finding 'a proportionate approach that takes a balance between people's right to earn a livelihood and the public interest'.[36]

VI. CONCLUSION

This appendix has, for the first time, examined where special advisers go when they leave government across several different premierships. There are a number of salient points which arise from this study. A relatively high proportion become PA practitioners at some point, but this is a more recent trend. High proportions of special advisers from amongst all premierships since 1979 have gone into the business sector. And the number of special advisers who enter politics as an MP or peer is in fact quite small—something that is masked by the prominence of the political offices held by many former special advisers.

One of the more interesting findings is that a high proportion of former special advisers have joined the non-profit sector. This feeds into the media discussion of the so-called revolving door between the private sector and government. While more concern has been raised over the business sector's influence on policy

---

[35] 'Response to the Government's Consultation on Proposals for a Register of Lobbyists' (Committee on Standards in Public Life, April 2012) 5, www.public-standards.gov.uk/our-work/other-reports-statements-and-publications.

[36] Public Administration Select Committee (n 30) Ev 4.

through former public officials, including former special advisers, joining these organisations, the research presented here indicates that the non-profit sector also plays an active part in the in-and-outer system that has emerged in Whitehall. The lack of attention paid to the influence of the non-profit sector on government is arguably the result of the perception that commercial organisations have more money to spend on influencing government policy and thus have greater potential to do so effectively.[37]

However, former special advisers who join the non-profit sector are just as likely to be seeking to influence government.[38] The relatively large proportion of former special advisers joining this sector further ensures that this is the case as they bring with them their insider knowledge, skills and contacts from Whitehall.[39] There has, however, been a growing awareness in the last few years of the non-profit sector's interaction with government. Indeed, in January 2012, Mark Harper MP, minister in the Cabinet Office, said that the Government was particularly interested to hear views on whether organisations like NGOs and charities, which do not lobby for others for money but are advancing agendas, should be covered by a statutory register of lobbyists.[40]

With regards to the professionalisation of politics and the revolving door in Westminster, the findings presented here support the idea that the careers of former special advisers have contributed to these trends. More specifically, the findings regarding the rise in the proportion of former special advisers in the House of Commons and the high proportion of those who do not remain backbenchers offer some support to the concept of the career politician in Parliament and that the special adviser post is a politics-facilitating occupation.

Meanwhile, the data on think tanks, the party-political employment sector and various public bodies and the civil service suggest that the professionalisation of politics over recent decades has not just occurred in Parliament and given rise to the career politician, but has also happened in the growing political class in the 'Westminster Village' and has seen the emergence of what we might call the *career political actor*, meaning special advisers who come from or subsequently enter public affairs, think tanks, interest groups, Party HQ or the civil service. These changes are not just a matter of supply, but also of demand.

Finally, findings on those joining the business sector and non-profit sector suggest that some semblance of Heclo's in-and-outer system has been established in London. However, the fact that more special advisers join these sectors after leaving government than come from them suggests that the revolving door has taken the form of a career ladder on this side of the pond—a previously unconfirmed notion.

---

[37] Public Administration Select Committee (n 27) 6, 32.
[38] ibid.
[39] ibid.
[40] House of Commons Library, 'Lobbying: July 2013 Update' (House of Commons Library 2013) 4.

Appendix 4

Biographies

Table A4.1: Biographies of special advisers mentioned in this book

Name	Career: Ministers served as special adviser (own political career shown in bold)
Adonis, Andrew	Tony Blair (PM), 1998–2005. **Minister of State (DTp), 2008–09; Secretary of State (DTp), 2009–10**; now Lord Adonis of Camden Town
Austin, Ian	Gordon Brown (HMT), 1999–2005. **Minister of State (DEFRA), 2008–10; Shadow Minister of State (DCMS, DCLG, DWP), 2010–**
Bailey, Shaun	David Cameron (PM), 2012–
Balls, Ed	Gordon Brown (HMT), 1997–2004. **Economic Secretary (HMT), 2006–07; Secretary of State (DCSF), 2007–10**
Balogh, Thomas	Harold Wilson (PM), 1964–68; later Lord Balogh of Hampstead
Barber, Michael	David Blunkett (DfEE), 1997–2000
Barnes, Peter	Peter Lilley (DSS), 1993–97
Barwell, Gavin	John Gummer (DoE), 1995–97
Beckett, Margaret	Judith Hart (ODM), 1974. **Shadow Minister of State (DSS, HMT), 1984–92; Shadow Leader of the Commons (LOC), 1992–94; temporary Leader of the Opposition, 1994; Secretary of State (BIS, LOC, DEFRA, FCO), 1997–2001, 2006–07; Minister of State (DCLG), 2008–09**
Burke, Tom	Michael Heseltine, Michael Howard, John Gummer (DoE), 1991–97
Cable, Vince	John Smith (DT), 1979. Shadow Chancellor of the Exchequer (HMT), 2003–10; Secretary of State (BIS), 2010–
Caine, Jonathan	Peter Brooke, Patrick Mayhew (NIO), 1991–95; Owen Paterson, Theresa Villiers (NIO), 2010-
Cameron, David	Stephen Dorrell (HMT), 1992–93; Michael Howard (HO), 1993–94. **Shadow Minister (DCLG), 2004; Shadow Secretary of State (DfE), 2005; Shadow Leader of the Opposition (PM), 2005–10; Prime Minister (PM), 2010–**

(Continued)

Name	Career: Ministers served as special adviser (own political career shown in bold)
Campbell, Alastair	Tony Blair (PM), 1997–2003
Cavanagh, Matt	David Blunkett (HO), 2004; Gordon Brown (HMT), 2005–06; Des Browne (MOD), 2006–07; Gordon Brown (PM), 2007–10
Corry, Dan	Margaret Beckett (DTI), 1997–98; Peter Mandelson (DTI) 1998; Stephen Byers, 1999–02; Ruth Kelly (DfES), 2005–06; Gordon Brown (HMT, PM), 2006–10
Coulson, Andrew	David Cameron (PM), 2010
Cradock, Percy	Margaret Thatcher, John Major (PM), 1984–92
Cummings, Dominic	Michael Gove (DfE), 2011–
Dunlop, Andrew	George Younger (MOD), 1986–88; Margaret Thatcher (PM), 1988–90; David Cameron (PM), 2012–
Evans, Huw	David Blunkett (HO), 2001–2004; Tony Blair (PM), 2005–2006
Foster, Christopher	John MacGregor (DTp), 1992–93
Gray, Iain	Alastair Darling, Douglas Alexander (SO), 2003–07
Hall, Peter	Michael Heseltine, Michael Howard, John Gummer (DoE), 1991–94
Hazarika, Ayesha	Harriet Harman (LOC), 2007–09
Healy, Anna	Mo Mowlam (NIO), 1997–98; Jack Cunningham (CO) 1998–99; Lord Macdonald (DETR) 2001; John Prescott (CO, ODPM) 2001–03; Harriet Harman (LOC) 2007–10; now Baroness Healy of Primrose Hill
Heggie, Ian	Norman Fowler (DTp), 1979–81
Hellawell, Keith	Jack Cunningham, Mo Mowlam (CO), 1998–2000; David Blunkett (HO), 2001–02
Henricson-Bell, Torsten	Alistair Darling (HMT), 2009–10
Hill, David	Tony Blair (PM), 2003–07
Hilton, Steve	David Cameron (PM), 2010–12
Hodge, Dorothea	Baroness Amos (LOL), 2005–07
Hoskyns, John	Margaret Thatcher (PM), 1979–82; David Howell, Tom King, Nicholas Ridley, John Moore (DTp), 1982–86
Hunter, Anji	Tony Blair (PM), 1997–2002
Hyman, Peter	Tony Blair (PM), 1997–2003
Irvin, Joe	John Prescott (DETR), 1997–2001; Gordon Brown (PM), 2007; Political Secretary (not a special adviser), 2008–10

(Continued)

Name	Career: Ministers served as special adviser (own political career shown in bold)
Jackson, Sue	Ann Taylor, Hilary Armstrong, Jacqui Smith (CWOC), 1998–2007; Jacqui Smith (HO), 2007–08; Lord Bassam (CWOL), 2009
Jacobs, Michael	Gordon Brown (HMT, PM), 2004–10
James, Howell	David Young (CO, DE, DTI), 1985–87
Kaldor, Nicholas	James Callaghan, Roy Jenkins, Denis Healey (HMT), 1964–68, 1975–76; later Lord Kaldor of Newnham
Kemp, Alan	Michael Heseltine (DoE, DTI, CO), 1991–96
Letwin, Oliver	Keith Joseph (DES), 1982–83; Margaret Thatcher (PM), 1983–86. **Shadow Minister of State (HMT), 1999–2001; Shadow Secretary of State (HO, HMT, MWP); Minister of State (CO), 2010–**
Levene, Peter	Michael Heseltine (MOD, DoE, DTI), 1984, 1991–95; John Major (PM), 1992–97; now Lord Levene of Portsoken
Linden, Sophie	David Blunkett (DfEE, HO), 1997–2004
Livermore, Spencer	Alan Milburn, Andrew Smith, Paul Boateng, Gordon Brown (HMT), 1998–2007; Gordon Brown (PM), 2007
Macrory, Henry	David Cameron (PM), 2010
Marsh, Richard	Michael Portillo, Michael Spicer, David Trippier, George Young (DoE), 1990–91; Virginia Bottomley, William Waldegrave (DH, CO, MAFF, HMT), 1991–95
Maugham, Andrew	Alistair Darling (HMT, DSS, DWP, DTp, SO, DTI), 1997–2009
McBride, Damian	Gordon Brown (HMT, PM), 2005–08
McFadden, Pat	Tony Blair (PM), 1997–2001. Minister of State (BERR, BIS), 2007–10; Shadow Secretary of State (BIS), 2010
Miliband, David	Tony Blair (PM), 1997–2001. Minister of State (DfES, CO, DCLG), 2002–06; Secretary of State (DEFRA), 2006–07; Secretary of State (FCO), 2007–10
Miliband, Ed	Alastair Darling, Alan Milburn, Andrew Smith (HMT), 1997–2000; Gordon Brown (HMT), 2001–05. Minister of State (CO), 2007–08; Secretary of State (DECC), 2008–10; Leader of the Opposition, 2010–
Moore, Jo	Stephen Byers (DTI, DTLR), 1999–2002
Morgan, Sally	Political Secretary (not a special adviser), 1997–2001; Tony Blair (PM), 2001–05; now Baroness Morgan of Huyton
Murphy, Nicola	Andrew Smith, Paul Boateng, Des Browne (HMT), 2001–06

(*Continued*)

Name	Career: Ministers served as special adviser (own political career shown in bold)
Nicholson, Chris	Edward Davey (DECC), 2012–
Nye, Sue	Gordon Brown (HMT, PM), 1997–2010; now Baroness Nye of Lambeth
Oliver, Craig	David Cameron (PM), 2011–
O'Shaughnessy, James	David Cameron (PM), 2010–11
Owen, Ed	Jack Straw (HO, FCO), 1997–2005
Parsons, Anthony	Margaret Thatcher (PM), 1982–83
Pearce, David	Michael Heseltine, Chris Patten (DoE), 1989–92; John MacGregor (DTp), 1992–94
Pearce, Nick	David Blunkett (DfEE, HO), 1999–2003; Gordon Brown (PM), 2007–10
Powell, Jonathan	Tony Blair (PM), 1997–2007
Purnell, James	Tony Blair (PM), 1997–2001. **Minister of State (DWP), 2006–07; Secretary of State (DCMS, DWP), 2007–09**
Ramsay, Katherine	Tom King (DTp), 1983; Nicholas Ridley (DTp, DoE, DTI), 1983–90; William Waldegrave (DH), 1990–92; John Major (PM), 1992–97
Raymond, Katherine	David Blunkett (HO, DWP), 2001–2005; Gordon Brown (PM), 2007
Richards, Ed	Tony Blair (PM), 1999–2003
Richards, Paul	Patricia Hewitt (DH), 2005–2006; Hazel Blears (MwP, DCLG), 2006–09
Richards, Rod	David Hunt (WO), 1990
Ridley, Adam	Geoffrey Howe (HMT), 1979–83; Nigel Lawson (HMT), 1983–85; Earl Gowrie, Richard Luce (CO), 1984–85
Rock, Patrick	Michael Howard, William Waldegrave, John Gummer, Chris Patten (DoE), 1987–93; Michael Howard (HO), 1993–97; David Cameron (PM), 2011–
Ruffley, David	Kenneth Clarke (DES), 1991–92; Michael Howard, Michael Jack, Peter Lloyd, Robert Shirley, Charles Wardle (HO), 1992–94; Jonathan Aitken, Kenneth Clarke, Michael Portillo (HMT), 1993–96. **Shadow Minister of State (DWP, HO), 2005–10**
Ryan, Conor	David Blunkett (DfEE), 1997–2001; Tony Blair (PM), 2005–07
Scott, Derek	Tony Blair (PM), 1997–2003
Seward, Matthew	Lord Williams, Baroness Amos (LOL), 2001–04; David Blunkett (HO), 2003–04

(*Continued*)

Name	Career: Ministers served as special adviser (own political career shown in bold)
Silva, Rohan	David Cameron (PM), 2010–
Smith, Adam	Jeremy Hunt (DCMS), 2010–12
Sterling, Jeffrey	Patrick Jenkin, Cecil Parkinson, Norman Tebbitt, Leon Brittan, Paul Channon, David Young, Nicholas Ridley (DI, DTI), 1982–90; now Lord Sterling of Plaistow
Strauss, Norman	Margaret Thatcher (PM), 1979–81
Straw, Jack	Barbara Castle (DHSS), 1974–76; Peter Shore (DoE), 1976–77. **Home Secretary 1997–2001; Foreign Secretary 2001–06; Leader of the Commons 2006–07; Lord Chancellor 2007–10**
Stroud, Philippa	Ian Duncan Smith (DWP), 2010–
Taylor, John	David Waddington (HO, LOC), 1990–91
Thomas, Emily	Lord Sainsbury (DTI), 2004–06; Alistair Darling (DTI, HMT), 2007
Turley, Anna	David Blunkett (DWP), 2005; Hilary Armstrong (CO), 2006–07
Vadera, Shriti	Gordon Brown (HMT), 1999–2007; now Baroness Vadera of Holland Park
Walters, Alan	Margaret Thatcher (PM), 1981–84, 1989
Westlake, Sheridan	Eric Pickles (DCLG), 2010–
Whelan, Charlie	Gordon Brown (HMT), 1997–99
Whittingdale, John	Norman Tebbitt, Leon Brittan, Paul Channon, David Young (DTI), 1984–1987; Political Secretary (not a special adviser), 1988–90. **Shadow Secretary of State (DTI, DCMS, DEFRA), 2001–05**
Williams, John	John Hutton (CO, DWP, BERR, MOD), 2005–09
Young of Graffham, Lord	Keith Joseph (DI, DES), 1980–82; Patrick Jenkin (DI), 1981–82. **Secretary of State (MwP, DE, DTI), 1984–89**

Table A4.2: Biographies of ministers mentioned in this book

Name	Career
Baker, Kenneth	Secretary of State (DoE), 1984–86; Secretary of State (DES), 1987–89; Secretary of State (HO), 1990–92
Bassam of Brighton, Lord	Chief Whip (Lords), 2008–10
Blair, Tony	Prime Minister, 1997–2007

(*Continued*)

Name	Career
Blunkett, David	Secretary of State (DfEE), 1997–2001; Secretary of State (HO), 2001–04; Secretary of State (DWP), 2005
Brown, Gordon	Chancellor of the Exchequer (HMT), 1997–2007; Prime Minister, 2007–10
Brown, Nick	Chief Whip (Commons), 1997–98; Secretary of State (MAFF), 1998–2001; Minister of State (DWP), 2001–03; Chief Whip (Commons), 2008–10
Byers, Stephen	Secretary of State (DTI), 1998–2001; Secretary of State (DTLR), 2001–02
Carter of Devizes, Lord	Chief Whip (Lords), 1997–2002
Castle, Barbara	Secretary of State (DHSS), 1974–76
Clarke, Kenneth	Minister of State (DE, DTI), 1986–88; Secretary of State (DH), 1988–90; Secretary of State (DES), 1990–92; Secretary of State (HO), 1992–93; Chancellor of the Exchequer (HMT), 1993–97; Secretary of State (MOJ), 2010–12; Minister of State (CO), 2012–
Clegg, Nick	Deputy Prime Minister (CO), 2010–
Darling, Alistair	Chief Secretary (HMT), 1997–98; Secretary of State (DSS), 1998–2001; Secretary of State (DWP), 2001–02; Secretary of State (DTp), 2002–06; Secretary of State (SO), 2003–06; Chancellor of the Exchequer (HMT), 2007–10
Dorrell, Stephen	Financial Secretary (HMT), 1992–94; Secretary of State (DNH, DH), 1994–97
Duncan Smith, Iain	Secretary of State (DWP), 2010–
Fallon, Michael	Minister of State (BIS, DEn), 2012–
Fowler, Norman	Secretary of State (DTp), 1979–81; Secretary of State (DHSS), 1982–86; Secretary of State (DE), 1987–89
Gove, Michael	Secretary of State (DfE), 2010–
Grocott of Telford, Lord	Chief Whip (Lords), 2002–08
Heseltine, Michael	Secretary of State (DoE, MOD, DTI), 1979–85; Deputy Prime Minister (CO), 1995–97; now Lord Heseltine of Thenford
Hewitt, Patricia	Secretary of State (DTI), 2001–05; Secretary of State (DH), 2005–07
Howe, Geoffrey	Chancellor of the Exchequer (HMT), 1979–83; Secretary of State (FCO), 1983–89; Leader of the Commons, 1989–90; now Lord Howe of Aberavon
Hunt, David	Minister of State (DoE), 1989–90; Secretary of State (WO, DE), 1990–94; Minister of State (CO), 1994–95; now Lord Hunt of Wirral

(*Continued*)

Name	Career
Hunt, Jeremy	Secretary of State (DCMS, DH), 2010–
Hutton, John	Secretary of State (DWP, BERR, MOD), 2005–09; now Lord Hutton of Furness
Jenkin, Patrick	Secretary of State (DHSS, DI, DoE), 1979–85; now Lord Jenkin of Roding
Kelly, Ruth	Secretary of State (DfES), 2005–06; Secretary of State (DCLG), 2006–07; Secretary of State (DTp), 2007–08
Knight, Jim	Minister of State (DWP), 2009–10; now Lord Knight of Weymouth
Lamont, Norman	Financial Secretary (HMT), 1986–89; Chief Secretary (HMT), 1989–90; Chancellor of the Exchequer (HMT), 1990–93; now Lord Lamont of Lerwick
Lawson, Nigel	Financial Secretary (HMT), 1979–81; Secretary of State (DEn), 1981–83; Chancellor of the Exchequer (HMT), 1983–89; now Lord Lawson of Blaby
Luce, Richard	Minister of State (CO), 1985–90; now Lord Luce of Adur
Macdonald of Tradeston, Lord	Minister of State (DETR, CO), 1999–2003
Major, John	Chancellor of the Exchequer (HMT), 1989–90; Prime Minister, 1990–97
Mandelson, Peter	Minister of State (MwP), 1997–98; Secretary of State (DTI, NIO), 1998–2001; Secretary of State (BERR, BIS), 2008–10; now Lord Mandelson of Foy
Maude, Francis	Minister of State (HMT), 1990–92; Minister of State (CO), 2010–
McCartney, Ian	Secretary of State (MwP), 2003–05; Minister of State for Trade, 2006–07
Pickles, Eric	Secretary of State (DCLG), 2010–
Portillo, Michael	Minister of State (DoE), 1990–92; Chief Secretary (HMT), 1992–94; Secretary of State (DoE, MOD), 1994–97
Prescott, John	Secretary of State (DETR), 1997–2001; Deputy Prime Minister (CO, ODPM), 2001–07; now Lord Prescott of Kingston upon Hull
Prisk, Mark	Minister of State (BIS, DCLG), 2010–
Sainsbury of Turville, Lord	Parliamentary Under-Secretary of State (DTI), 1998–2006
Shore, Peter	Secretary of State (DoE), 1976–79
Thatcher, Margaret	Prime Minister, 1979–90; later Baroness Thatcher of Kesteven

(Continued)

Name	Career
Walker, Peter	Secretary of State (MAFF, DEn, WO), 1979–90; now Lord Walker of Worcester
Wardle, Charles	Parliamentary Under-Secretary of State (HO), 1992–94; Parliamentary Under-Secretary of State (DTI), 1994–95
Whitelaw, William	Secretary of State (HO), 1979–83; Leader of the Lords, 1983–86; later Viscount Whitelaw of Penrith
Willetts, David	Minister of State (BIS), 2010–

Glossary

The table below lists the structure of the Senior Civil Service, in order of decreasing rank.

Table G.1: Glossary

Name	Description
Better Government Initiative	A group set up by the academic and former special adviser Sir Christopher Foster to make recommendations on improving the operation of government.
Cabinet Office	An office providing support to the Prime Minister (and under the Coalition the Deputy Prime Minister) and responsible for government efficiency, transparency and accountability.
Cabinet Secretary	Usually the most senior civil servant in the country, the Cabinet Secretary heads the Cabinet Office and supports the Prime Minister and the Cabinet Office
Central Policy Review Staff (CPRS)	A unit in the Cabinet Office that examined issues or developed policies from a medium to long-term perspective. It reported to the Cabinet. It was established in 1971 and was abolished in 1983.
Chief of Staff	Usually—but not always—the most senior special adviser in No 10 or the Deputy Prime Minister's Office, often responsible for leading and/or coordinating operations in the relevant office.
Committee on Standards in Public Life (CSPL)	An advisory committee established in 1994 by the then Conservative Government to advise on standards of conduct of all holders of public office.
Delivery Unit	A unit created under Blair that attempted to monitor the ability of the British government to implement its policies in key areas.
Diary Secretary	Secretary based in a minister's private office responsible for the ministerial diary arrangements.
Extended Ministerial Office (EMO)	Proposed by the 2013 *Civil Service Reform Plan— One Year On* Report. It will consist of a mix of existing civil servants fulfilling the traditional private office role, special advisers and external appointees. Members of the office—including civil servants— would be personally appointed by the minister and be directly accountable to them.

(Continued)

Name	Description
Government Communications Network	A network of all the civil servants working in communications in government departments and non-departmental public bodies. This body was previously known as the Government Information (and Communications) Service.
Minister of State (MOS)	A more junior government minister, ranked immediately below the Secretary of State, usually with a specific portfolio, eg, Minister for Housing.
Ministerial Code	The primary 'rulebook' for government ministers
National School of Government	Previously the Civil Service College. The main training establishment for civil servants. Abolished in 2012.
Parliamentary Private Secretary (PPS)	An MP appointed by a government minister to act as his or her unpaid assistant, and to be his or her eyes and ears in the House of Commons.
Parliamentary Researcher	Staff attached to a specific MP, located in Parliament and paid for out of staffing allowances.
Parliamentary Under-Secretary of State (PUSS)	The most junior in the ministerial hierarchy, ranking below Secretary of State and Minister of State. They usually have a specific portfolio, eg, Parliamentary Under-Secretary of State for Planning.
Permanent Secretary (Perm Sec)	The most senior civil servant in a government department. Called Permanent Under Secretary (PUS) in the Foreign and Commonwealth Office.
Policy advisers ('pads')	Individuals employed by a minister and who work in a government department. They are normally on fixed-term contracts and can perform similar work to special advisers. NB: they are referred to by the same acronym as political advisers—pads—but are different in that policy advisers are appointed to government, and not to shadow ministers.
Policy and Implementation Unit	A group set up in 2011 under the Coalition Government, reporting jointly to the Prime Minister and the Deputy Prime Minister, consisting of a mix of civil servants and outsiders.
Policy Unit	A group that may consist of a mix of special advisers and civil servants who provide policy advice principally to the Prime Minister. The first one was established in 1974.
Political advisers ('pads')	Labour Party terminology, referring to individuals employed by a political party who advise ministers or shadow ministers. These are analogous to special advisers for the Opposition in that they are generally the personal appointment of the shadow minister.

(*Continued*)

Name	Description
Political Secretary	Chief liaison between Downing Street and the governing political party; works in No 10. The Political Secretary is paid for out of party funds and has traditionally not been classified as a special adviser.
Press Officer	A career civil servant whose job is to help ministers present departmental policy publicly and engage with the media.
Principal Private Secretary	A civil servant who heads up a senior minister's private office. Sometimes abbreviated to PPS, though this more commonly refers to a Parliamentary Private Secretary.
Private Office	Ministerial office staffed by civil servants responsible for such tasks as liaising with departments and officials on behalf of the minister, handling correspondence and organising the minister's diary. Usually headed by a Principal Private Secretary or a Private Secretary, depending on the minister's seniority in government.
Prospective Parliamentary Candidate (PPC)	A political party's official candidate for a general election.
Public Administration Select Committee (PASC)	The Select Committee of the House of Commons that examines the quality and standards of administration within the civil service.
Secretary of State (SoS)	The most senior government minister in a department; some departments have different names for this role, eg, Chancellor of the Exchequer in the Treasury.
Select Committee	A committee of MPs (or peers in the House of Lords) set up by the relevant House of Parliament who check and report on the work of government departments.
Short Money	State funding given to opposition parties in the House of Commons, based upon numbers of seats and votes won at the last election, and usually used for research and staffing support for frontbench spokesmen. There is an equivalent fund—Cranborne Money—in the House of Lords.
Special Advisers' Code of Conduct	A code published by the Cabinet Office that sets out the status of special advisers and gives guidance on how they should operate.
Submission (Brief)	Usually a written note (or email) to a minister on a specific policy or issue. A submission makes recommendations on the issue; a brief provides briefing material for the minister to use at a meeting, parliamentary debate etc.

(*Continued*)

Name	Description
Temporary, or time-limited civil servants	People who are appointed without open competition to fill a short-term need in the civil service. They are generally limited to a maximum of a two-year contract; for longer, the approval of the Civil Service Commission is required. Special advisers are a class of temporary civil servant, but may differ in that they are personally appointed by the minister (leaving with him or her, or after elections) and are able to be politically partisan.

Table G.2: The structure of the Senior Civil Service

Current Title	Previous Title
Cabinet Secretary & Head of the Civil Service	(unchanged)
Permanent Secretary	(unchanged)
Director General	Grade 2
Director	Grade 3
Deputy Director	Grade 5, Assistant Secretary or Head of Division
Assistant Director, Team Leader, Policy Manager etc	Grade 6 and 7 or Senior Principal, Principal

Source: http://www.policy.manchester.ac.uk/resources/civil-servant/

Table G.3: Acronyms

Acronym	Full title
BERR	Department of Business, Enterprise and Regulatory Reform (predecessor of BIS)
BIS	Department for Business, Innovation & Skills
CO	Cabinet Office
CPRS	Central Policy Review Staff
CSPL	Committee on Standards in Public Life
CWOC	Chief Whip of the Commons
CWOL	Chief Whip of the Lords
DCA	Department of Constitutional Affairs
DCLG	Department for Communities and Local Government

(Continued)

Acronym	Full title
DCMS	Department for Culture, Media & Sport
DCSF	Department for Children, Schools, and Families
DE	Department for Employment
DECC	Department of Energy & Climate Change
Defra	Department for Environment, Food and Rural Affairs
DEn	Department of Energy
DES	Department for Education and Science
DETR	Department for the Environment, Transport and the Regions
DfE	Department for Education
DfEE	Department for Education and Employment
DfES	Department for Education and Skills
DfID	Department for International Development
DFT	Department for Transport
DH	Department of Health
DHSS	Department of Health and Social Security
DI	Department for Industry
DIUS	Department for Innovation, Universities and Skills
DNH	Department for National Heritage
DoE	Department of the Environment
DPM	Deputy Prime Minister
DSS	Department for Social Security
DTI	Department of Trade and Industry
DTLR	Department for Transport, Local Government and the Regions
DTp	Department for Transport
DWP	Department for Work and Pensions
EMO	Extended Ministerial Office
FCO	Foreign and Commonwealth Office
GIS, GICS	Government Information Service, Government Information and Communications Service
HEO	Higher Executive Officer
HMT	HM Treasury
HO	Home Office
LCD	Lord Chancellor's Department

(*Continued*)

Acronym	Full title
LOC	Leader of the Commons
LOL	Leader of the Lords
LSE	London School of Economics
MAFF	Ministry of Agriculture, Fisheries and Food
MOD	Ministry of Defence
MOJ	Ministry of Justice
MoS	Minister of State
MwP	Minister without Portfolio
NIO	Northern Ireland Office
ODPM	Office of the Deputy Prime Minister
PAD, pad	Political adviser, policy adviser
PASC	Public Administration Select Committee
Perm Sec	Permanent Secretary
PM	Prime Minister
PPC	Prospective Parliamentary Candidate
PPS	Parliamentary Private Secretary. May also refer to the Secretary of State's Principal Private Secretary
PUSS	Parliamentary Under Secretary of State
SEO	Senior Executive Officer
SO	Scotland Office
SoS	Secretary of State
SPAD, SpAd, Spad or spad	Special adviser
WO	Wales Office

Bibliography

BOOKS AND JOURNAL ARTICLES

Aberbach, JD, Putnam, RD and Rockman, BA, *Bureaucrats and Politicians in Western Democracies* (Cambridge, MA, Harvard University Press 1981).

Aberbach, JD and Rockman, BA, 'Mandates or Mandarins? Control and Discretion in the Modern Administrative State' (1988) 48 *Public Administration Review* 606.

——, 'Conducting and Coding Elite Interviews' [2002] *Political Science & Politics* 673.

——, 'The Past and Future of Political-Administrative Relations: Research from Bureaucrats and Politicians to in the Web of Politics—and Beyond' (2006) 29 *International Journal of Public Administration* 977.

——, 'The Appointments Process and the Administrative Presidency' (2009) 39 *Presidential Studies Quarterly* 38.

Adonis, A, *Education, Education, Education* (London, Biteback 2012).

Alford, J, 'The Limits to Traditional Public Administration, or Rescuing Public Value from Misrepresentation' (2008) 67 *Australian Journal of Public Administration* 357.

Annesley, C and Gains, F, 'The Core Executive: Gender, Power and Change' (2010) 58 *Political Studies* 909.

Aucoin, P, 'New Public Management and the Quality of Government: Coping with the New Political Governance in Canada' (presented at the Conference on 'New Public Management' and the Quality of Government University of Gothenburg, 13 November 2008).

——, 'Canada' in C Eichbaum and R Shaw (eds), *Partisan Appointees and Public Servants: An International Analysis of the Role of the Political Adviser* (Cheltenham, Edward Elgar 2010).

——, 'New Political Governance in Westminster Systems: Impartial Public Administration and Management Performance at Risk' (2012) 25 *Governance* 177.

Aucoin, P and Jarvis, M, *Modernizing Government Accountability: A Framework for Reform* (Ottawa, Canada School of Public Service 2005).

Aucoin, P, Smith, J and Dinsdale, G, *Responsible Government: Clarifying Essentials, Dispelling Myths and Exploring Change* (Ottawa, Canadian Centre for Management Development 2004).

Aucoin, P, Turnbull, LB and Jarvis, MD, *Democratizing the Constitution: Reforming Responsible Government* (Toronto, Emond Montgomery Publications 2011).

Barber, M, *Instruction to Deliver: Fighting to Transform Britain's Public Services* (London, Methuen 2008).

Bell, S and Hindmoor, A, 'The Governance of Public Affairs' (2009) 9 *Journal of Public Affairs* 149.

Bell, S, Hindmoor, A and Mols, F, 'Persuasion as Governance: A State-Centric Relational Perspective' (2010) 88 *Public Administration* 851.

Bellamy, C, 'The Whitehall Programme and After: Researching Government in a Time of Governance' (2011) 89 *Public Administration* 78.

Bennister, M, *Prime Ministers in Power: Political Leadership in Britain and Australia* (Basingstoke, Palgrave Macmillan 2012).

Benoit, L, 'Ministerial Staff: The Life and Times of Parliament's Statutory Orphans' in *Restoring Accountability—Research Studies, Volume 1: Parliament, Ministers and Deputy Ministers* (Ottawa, Commission of Inquiry into the Sponsorship Program and Advertising Activities 2006).

Bentham, J, 'The IPPR and Demos: Think Tanks of the New Social Democracy' (2006) 77 *Political Quarterly* 166.

Berlinski, S, Dewan, T and Dowding, K, 'The Length of Ministerial Tenure in the United Kingdom, 1945–97' (2007) 37 *British Journal of Political Science* 245.

——, 'The Impact of Individual and Collective Performance on Ministerial Tenure' (2010) 72 *Journal of Politics* 559.

Bevir, M and Rhodes, RAW, 'Prime Ministers, Presidentialism and Westminster Smokescreens' (2006) 54 *Political Studies* 671.

Blackstone, T and Plowden, W, *Inside the Think Tank: Advising the Cabinet 1971–1983* (London, Heinemann 1988).

Blair, T, *A Journey* (London, Hutchinson 2010).

Blick, A, *People Who Live in the Dark: The History of the Special Adviser in British Politics* (Oxford, Politico's 2004).

Blick, A and Jones, GW, *Premiership: The Development, Nature and Power of the Office of the British Prime Minister* (Exeter, Imprint Academic 2010).

——, *At Power's Elbow: Aides to the Prime Minister from Robert Walpole to David Cameron* (London, Biteback 2013).

Blunkett, D, *The Blunkett Tapes: My Life in the Bear Pit* (London, Bloomsbury 2006).

Blunkett, D and MacCormick, A, *On a Clear Day* (London, Michael O'Mara 1995).

Bogdanor, V, 'The Civil Service' in V Bogdanor (ed), *The British Constitution in the Twentieth Century* (Oxford, Oxford University Press for The British Academy 2004).

Borchert, J, 'Professional Politicians: Towards a Comparative Perspective' in J Borchert and J Zeiss (eds), *The Political Class in Advanced Democracies: A Comparative Handbook* (Oxford, Oxford University Press 2003).

Borchert, J and Zeiss, J (eds), *The Political Class in Advanced Democracies: A Comparative Handbook* (Oxford, Oxford University Press 2003).

Borzel, TA, 'Networks: Reified Metaphor or Governance Panacea?' (2011) 89 *Public Administration* 49.

Boston, J and Nethercote, JR, 'Reflections on "New Political Governance in Westminster Systems"' (2012) 25 *Governance* 201.

Bourgault, J, 'Canada's Senior Public Service and the Typology of Bargains: From the Hierarchy of Senior Civil Servants to a Community of "Controlled" Entrepreneurs' (2011) 26 *Public Policy and Administration* 253.

Bovens, M, 'Two Concepts of Accountability: Accountability as a Virtue and as a Mechanism' (2010) 33 *West European Politics* 946.

Bowles, N, King, DS and Ross, F, 'Political Centralization and Policy Constraint in British Executive Leadership: Lessons from American Presidential Studies in the Era of Sofa Politics' (2007) 2 *British Politics* 372.

Brans, M, 'Comparative Public Administration: From General Theory to General Frameworks' in BG Peters and J Pierre (eds), *The Handbook of Public Administration* (London, Sage Publications 2003).

Brodie, I, 'In Defence of Political Staff' [2012] *Canadian Parliamentary Review* 33.

Burch, M and Holliday, I, 'The Blair Government and the Core Executive' (2004) 39 *Government and Opposition* 1.

Burnham, P, Lutz, K, Grant, W and Layton-Henry, Z, *Research Methods in Politics*, 2nd edn (Basingstoke, Palgrave Macmillan 2008).

Butler, D and Butler, G, *British Political Facts* (Basingstoke, Palgrave Macmillan 2011).

Campbell, A, *The Blair Years: Extracts from the Alastair Campbell Diaries* (London, Arrow 2008).

——, *Power and the People: The Alastair Campbell Diaries Volume Two* (London, Arrow 2011).

Campbell, C and Peters, BG, 'The Politics/Administration Dichotomy: Death or Merely Change?' (1988) 1 *Governance* 79.

Campbell, C and Wilson, G, *The End of Whitehall: Death of a Paradigm?* (Oxford/ Cambridge, MA, Blackwell 1995).

Carroll, L, *Through the Looking Glass* (Plain Label Books 2007 [1871]).

Chapman, R, *The Civil Service Commission 1855–1991: A Bureau Biography* (London, Routledge 2004).

Cohen, MD, March, JG and Olsen, JP, 'A Garbage Can Model of Organizational Choice' (1972) 17 *Administrative Science Quarterly* 1.

Communications Review Group, *An Independent Review of Government Communications* (London 2004).

Connaughton, B, '"Glorified Gofers, Policy Experts or Good Generalists": A Classification of the Roles of the Irish Ministerial Adviser' (2010) 25 *Irish Political Studies* 347.

——, 'Ireland' in C Eichbaum and R Shaw (eds), *Partisan Appointees and Public Servants: An International Analysis of the Role of the Political Adviser* (Cheltenham, Edward Elgar 2010).

Constitution Unit, *Being a Special Adviser* (London, Constitution Unit, 2014).

Corry, D, 'Economics, Government, Policy and Politics: Reflections from the Front Line'. Bernard Corry Memorial Lecture. Queen Mary, University of London. London, 22 October 2008.

——, 'Power at the Centre: Is the National Economic Council a Model for a New Way of Organising Things?' (2011) 82 Political Quarterly 459.

Craft, J, 'Institutionalized Partisan Advisors in Canada: Movers and Shapers, Buffers and Bridges'. Dissertation. Simon Fraser University, 2012.

Curran, J and Seaton, J, *Power without Responsibility: Press, Broadcasting and the Internet in Britain*, 7th edn (London, Routledge 2009).

Dahlström, C, Peters, BG and Pierre, J (eds), *Steering From the Centre: Strengthening Political Control in Western Democracies* (Toronto, University of Toronto Press 2011).

Daintith, T and Page, AC, *The Executive in the Constitution: Structure, Autonomy, and Internal Control* (Oxford, Oxford University Press 1999).

Darling, A, *Back from the Brink: 1000 Days at Number 11* (London, Atlantic Books 2012).

Denham, A and Garnett, M, '"What Works"? British Think Tanks and the "End of Ideology"' (2006) 77 *Political Quarterly* 156.

Derlien, H-U, 'Mandarins or Managers? The Bureaucratic Elite in Bonn, 1970 to 1987 and Beyond' (2003) 16 *Governance* 401.

Diamond, P, 'Governing as New Labour: An Inside Account of the Blair and Brown Years' (2011) 9 *Political Studies Review* 145.

——, *Governing Britain: Power, Politics and the Prime Minister* (I.B. Tauris 2014).

Dierickx, G, 'Politicization in the Belgian Civil Service' in BG Peters and J Pierre (eds), *Politicization of the Civil Service in Comparative Perspective: The Quest for Control* (London, Routledge 2004).

Donoughue, B, *Downing Street Diary: With Harold Wilson in No. 10* (London, Jonathan Cape 2005).

——, *Downing Street Diary Volume Two: With James Callaghan in No. 10* (London, Jonathan Cape 2008).

Dorpe, K Van and Horton, S, 'The Public Service Bargain in the United Kingdom: The Whitehall Model in Decline?' (2011) 26 *Public Policy and Administration* 233.

Dowding, K, 'The Prime Ministerialisation of the British Prime Minister' (2012) 66 *Parliamentary Affairs* 617.

——, 'Beneath the Surface: Replies to Three Critics' (2013) 66 *Parliamentary Affairs* 663.

Duggett, M and Desbouvries, M, 'The Civil Service in France: Contested Complacency?' in A Massey (ed), *International Handbook on Civil Service Systems* (Cheltenham, Edward Elgar 2011).

Dull, M and Roberts, PS, 'Continuity, Competence, and the Succession of Senate-Confirmed Agency Appointees, 1989–2009' (2009) 39 *Presidential Studies Quarterly* 432.

Dull, M, Roberts, PS, Keeney, MS and Choi, SO, 'Appointee Confirmation and Tenure: The Succession of U.S. Federal Agency Appointees, 1989–2009' (2012) 72 *Public Administration Review* 902.

Durant, RF, 'Getting Dirty-Minded: Implementing Presidential Policy Agendas Administratively' (2009) 69 *Public Administration Review* 569.

Durose, C, Combs, R, Eason, C, Gains, F and Richardson, L, '"Acceptable Difference": Diversity, Representation and Pathways to UK Politics' [2012] *Parliamentary Affairs*.

Dutil, P, 'Working with Political Staff at Queen's Park: Trends, Outlooks, Opportunities' (Institute for Public Administration of Canada, 2006).

Eichbaum, C and Shaw, R, 'Enemy or Ally? Senior Officials' Perceptions of Ministerial Advisers Before and After MMP' (2006) 58 *Political Science* 3.

——, 'Ministerial Advisers and the Politics of Policy-Making: Bureaucratic Permanence and Popular Control' (2007) 66 *Australian Journal of Public Administration* 453.

——, 'Ministerial Advisers, Politicisation, and the Retreat from Westminster: The Case of New Zealand' (2007) 85 *Public Administration* 609.

——, 'Minding the Minister? Ministerial Advisers in New Zealand Government' (2007) 2 *Kōtuitui: New Zealand Journal of Social Sciences Online* 95.

——, 'Conclusion' in C Eichbaum and R Shaw (eds), *Partisan Appointees and Public Servants: An International Analysis of the Role of the Political Adviser* (Cheltenham, Edward Elgar 2010).

——, 'Introduction' in C Eichbaum and R Shaw (eds), *Partisan Appointees and Public Servants: An International Analysis of the Role of the Political Adviser* (Cheltenham, Edward Elgar 2010).

——, 'New Zealand' in C Eichbaum and R Shaw (eds), *Partisan Appointees and Public Servants: An International Analysis of the Role of the Political Adviser* (Cheltenham, Edward Elgar 2010).

—— (eds), *Partisan Appointees and Public Servants: An International Analysis of the Role of the Political Adviser* (Cheltenham, Edward Elgar 2010).

Elcock, H, 'The Proper and Improper Use of Special Advisers' (2002) 17 *Public Policy and Administration* 1.

Elgie, R, *Political Institutions in Contemporary France* (Oxford, Oxford University Press 2003).

——, 'Core Executive Studies Two Decades on' (2011) 89 *Public Administration* 64.

Ellinas, A and Suleiman, E, *The European Commission and Bureaucratic Autonomy: Europe's Custodians* (Cambridge, Cambridge University Press 2012).

Fawcett, P and Gay, O, 'The United Kingdom' in C Eichbaum and R Shaw (eds), *Partisan Appointees and Public Servants: An International Analysis of the Role of the Political Adviser* (Cheltenham, Edward Elgar 2010).

Fleischer, J, 'Power Resources of Parliamentary Executives: Policy Advice in the UK and Germany' (2009) 32 *West European Politics* 196.

Flinders, M, 'The Enduring Centrality of Individual Ministerial Responsibility within the British Constitution' (2000) 6 *Journal of Legislative Studies* 73.

——, 'Devolution, Delegation and the Westminster Model: A Comparative Analysis of Developments within the UK, 1998–2009' (2011) 49 *Commonwealth & Comparative Politics* 1.

Foley, M, 'Prime Ministerialisation and Presidential Analogies: A Certain Difference in Interpretive Evolution' (2012) 66 *Parliamentary Affairs* 655.

Foster, C, *British Government in Crisis, or, The Third English Revolution* (Oxford, Hart Publishing 2005).

Fox, R and Korris, M, 'A Fresh Start? The Orientation and Induction of New MPs at Westminster Following the 2010 General Election' (2012) 65 *Parliamentary Affairs* 559.

Frey, JH and Fontana, A, 'The Group Interview in Social Research' (1991) 28 *Social Science Journal* 175.

Gains, F, 'Elite Ethnographies: Potential, Pitfalls and Prospects for Getting Up "Close and Personal"' (2011) 89 *Public Administration* 156.

Gains, F and Stoker, G, 'Special Advisers and the Transmission of Ideas from the Policy Primeval Soup' (2011) 39 *Policy & Politics* 485.

Gauja, A, 'Democracy within Parties: Candidate Selection Methods and their Political Consequences' (2012) 65 *Parliamentary Affairs* 478.

Goodsell, CT, 'Relations between Political Appointees and Career Officials: Principal-Agent or Moral Equals?' (2006) 36 *Presidential Studies Quarterly* 323.

Goplerud, M, 'The First Time is (Mostly) the Charm: Special Advisers as Parliamentary Candidates and Members of Parliament' [2013] *Parliamentary Affairs*.

Grant, P and Jary, C, *Understanding British Government* (National School of Government 2011).

Greer, SL, 'Whitehall' in R Hazell (ed), *Constitutional Futures Revisited: Britain's Constitution to 2020* (Basingstoke, Palgrave Macmillan 2008).

Greer, SL and Jarman, H, 'What Whitehall? Definitions, Demographics and the Changing Home Civil Service' (2010) 25 *Public Policy and Administration* 251.

Gruhn, Z and Slater, F, 'Special Advisers and Ministerial Effectiveness' (London, Institute for Government 2012).

Haines, J, *Glimmers of Twilight: Harold Wilson in Decline* (London, Politico's 2004).

Hamburger, P, Stevens, B and Weller, P, 'A Capacity for Central Coordination: The Case of the Department of the Prime Minister and Cabinet' (2011) 70 *Australian Journal of Public Administration* 377.

Hamburger, P and Weller, P, 'Policy Advice and a Central Agency: The Department of the Prime Minister and Cabinet' (2012) 47 *Australian Journal of Political Science* 363.

Hanney, SR, 'Special Advisers: Their Place in British Government' (Department of Government, Brunel University 1993).

Harris, P, and Fleisher, CS (eds), *The Handbook of Public Affairs* (London, Sage Publications 2005).

Hay, C, 'Interpreting Interpretivism Interpreting Interpretations: The New Hermeneutics of Public Administration' (2011) 89 *Public Administration* 167.

Hay, C and Richards, D, 'The Tangled Webs of Westminster and Whitehall: The Discourse, Strategy and Practice of Networking within the British Core Executive' (2000) 78 *Public Administration* 1.

Hazell, R and Yong, B, *The Politics of Coalition: How the Conservative-Liberal Democrat Government Works* (Oxford, Hart Publishing 2012).

Headey, BW, *British Cabinet Ministers: The Roles of Politicians in Executive Office* (London, Allen & Unwin 1974).

Heclo, H, 'OMB and the Presidency: The Problem of Neutral Competence' [1975] *Public Interest* 80.

——, *A Government of Strangers: Executive Politics in Washington* (Washington DC, Brookings Institution 1977).

——, 'The In-and-Outer System: A Critical Assessment' (1988) 103 *Political Science Quarterly* 37.

Heffernan, R, 'There's No Need for the "-isation": The Prime Minister is Merely Prime Ministerial' (2012) 66 *Parliamentary Affairs* 636.

Hennessy, P, *Whitehall* (London, Fontana 1990).

——, *The Prime Minister: The Office and its Holders since 1945* (London, Allen Lane 2000).

——, *Whitehall* (London, Pimlico 2001).

——, 'From Blair to Brown: The Condition of British Government' (2007) 78 *Political Quarterly* 344.

Heseltine, M, *Life in the Jungle: My Autobiography* (London, Hodder & Stoughton 2000).

Hibbing, JR, 'Legislative Careers: Why and How We Should Study Them' (1999) 24 *Legislative Studies Quarterly* 149.

Hondeghem, A, 'Changing Public Service Bargains for Top Officials' (2011) 26 *Public Policy and Administration* 159.

Hood, C, 'It's Public Administration, Rod, But Maybe Not as We Know it: British Public Administration in the 2000s' (2011) 89 *Public Administration* 128.

Hood, C and Lodge, M, *The Politics of Public Service Bargains: Reward, Competency, Loyalty—and Blame* (Oxford, Oxford University Press 2006).

——, 'From Sir Humphrey to Sir Nigel: What Future for the Public Service Bargain after Blairworld?' (2006) 77 *Political Quarterly* 360.

Horton, S, 'Contrasting Anglo-American and Continental European Civil Service Systems' in A Massey (ed), *International Handbook on Civil Service Systems* (Cheltenham, Edward Elgar 2011).

Howarth, D, 'Reaching the Cabinet: A British Cursus Honorum?' (SSRN Working Papers, 2013).

Huber, JD, Shipan, CR and Pfahler, M, 'Legislatures and Statutory Control of Bureaucracy' (2001) 45 *American Journal of Political Science* 330.

Hyman, P, *1 Out of 10: From Downing Street Vision to Classroom Reality* (London, Vintage 2005).

Institute for Government, 'Oiling the Machine: Thoughts for Special Advisers Working in Government' (London, 2010).

Jarman, H and Greer, SL, 'In the Eye of the Storm: Civil Servants and Managers in the UK Department of Health' (2010) 44 *Social Policy & Administration* 172.

Jones, N, *Sultans of Spin* (London, Gollancz 2000).

——, *The Control Freaks: How New Labour Gets its Own Way* (London, Politico's 2002).

Jun, U, 'Great Britain: From the Prevalence of the Amateur to the Dominance of the Career Politician' in J Borchert and J Zeiss (eds), *The Political Class in Advanced Democracies* (Oxford, Oxford University Press 2003).

Kassim, H, Peterson, J, Bauer, M, Connolly, S, Dehousse, R, Hooghe, L and Thompson, A, *The European Commission of the Twenty-First Century* (Oxford, Oxford University Press 2013).

Kaufman, G, *How to Be a Minister* (London, Faber & Faber 1997).

Kaufman, H, *The Forest Ranger: A Study in Administrative Behavior* (Baltimore, Johns Hopkins Press for Resources for the Future 1960).

Kavanagh, D and Seldon, A, *The Powers Behind the Prime Minister: The Hidden Influence of Number Ten* (London, HarperCollins 2008).

King, A, 'The Rise of the Career Politician in Britain—And its Consequences' (2009) 11 *British Journal of Political Science* 249.

King, A and Crewe, I, *The Blunders of our Governments* (London, Oneworld Publications 2013).

King, S, *Regulating the Behaviour of Ministers, Special Advisers and Civil Servants* (London, Constitution Unit 2003).

Kjaer, AM, 'Rhodes' Contribution to Governance Theory: Praise, Criticism and the Future Governance Debate' (2011) 89 *Public Administration* 101.

Lalonde, M, 'The Changing Role of the Prime Minister's Office' (1971) 14 *Canadian Public Administration/Administration publique du Canada* 509.

Langer, AI, *The Personalisation of Politics in the UK: Mediated Leadership from Attlee to Cameron* (Manchester, Manchester University Press 2012).

Laughrin, D, 'Working Effectively for Ministers' (Ashridge Public Sector Learning Guide 2009).

——, 'Swimming for their Lives: Waving or Drowning? A Review of the Evidence of Ministerial Overload and of Potential Remedies for it' (2009) 80 *Political Quarterly* 339.

Lawson, N, *The View from No.11: Memoirs of a Tory Radical* (London, Corgi Books 1993).

Lee, JM, Jones, GW and Burnham, J, *At the Centre of Whitehall: Advising the Prime Minister and the Cabinet* (Basingstoke, Macmillan 1998).

Lewis, DE, 'Testing Pendleton's Premise: Do Political Appointees Make Worse Bureaucrats?' (2007) 69 *Journal of Politics* 1073.

Light, PC, *Thickening Government: Federal Hierarchy and the Diffusion of Accountability* (Washington DC, Brookings Institution: Governance Institute 1995).

——, 'A Government Ill Executed: The Depletion of the Federal Service' (2008) 68 *Public Administration Review* 413.

Lindquist, E, 'From Rhetoric to Blueprint: The Moran Review as a Concerted, Comprehensive and Emergent Strategy for Public Service Reform: From Rhetoric to Blueprint' (2010) 69 *Australian Journal of Public Administration* 115.

Lindquist, E and Tiernan, A, 'The Australian Public Service and Policy Advising: Meeting the Challenges of 21st Century Governance' (2011) 70 *Australian Journal of Public Administration* 437.

Lodge, M, 'Public Service Bargains in British Central Government: Multiplication, Diversification and Reassertion' in M Painter and BG Peters (eds), *Tradition and Public Administration* (Basingstoke, Palgrave Macmillan 2010).

Lodge, M and Hood, C, 'Into an Age of Multiple Austerities? Public Management and Public Service Bargains across OECD Countries' (2012) 25 *Governance* 79.

Lowe, R, 'Grit in the Oyster or Sand in the Machine? The Evolving Role of Special Advisers in British Government' (2005) 16 *Twentieth Century British History* 497.

Lowe, R, *The Official History of the British Civil Service: Reforming the Civil Service, Volume I: The Fulton Years, 1966–81* (Oxford, Routledge 2011).

Maley, M, 'Conceptualising Advisers' Policy Work: The Distinctive Policy Roles of Ministerial Advisers in the Keating Government, 1991–96' (2000) 35 *Australian Journal of Political Science* 449.

——, 'Australia' in C Eichbaum and R Shaw (eds), *Partisan Appointees and Public Servants: An International Analysis of the Role of the Political Adviser* (Cheltenham, Edward Elgar 2010).

——, 'Strategic Links in a Cut-Throat World: Rethinking the Role and Relationship of Australian Ministerial Staff' (2011) 89 *Public Administration* 1469.

Mallory, JR, 'The Minister's Office Staff: An Unreformed Part of the Public Service' (1967) 10 *Canadian Public Administration/Administration publique du Canada* 25.

Mandelson, P and Liddle, R, *The Blair Revolution: Can New Labour Deliver?* (London, Faber & Faber 1996).

Mann, S, 'Book Review: Maranto, R. (2005). *Beyond a Government of Strangers: How Career Executives and Political Appointees Can Turn Conflict to Cooperation.* Lanham, MD: Lexington Books' (2009) 29 *Review of Public Personnel Administration* 197.

Manning, R, 'Development' in A Seldon (ed), *Blair's Britain, 1997–2007* (Cambridge, Cambridge University Press 2007).

Marsh, D, 'Understanding British Government: Analysing Competing Models' (2008) 10 *British Journal of Politics & International Relations* 251.

——, 'The New Orthodoxy: the Differentiated Polity Model' (2011) 89 *Public Administration* 32.

Marsh, D and Rhodes, RA, *Policy Networks in British Politics* (Oxford, Clarendon Press 1992).

Marsh, D, Richards, D and Smith, M, 'Unequal Plurality: Towards an Asymmetric Power Model of British Politics' (2003) 38 *Government and Opposition* 306.

Marsh, D, Richards, D and Smith, MJ, 'Re-assessing the Role of Departmental Cabinet Ministers' (2000) 78 *Public Administration* 305.

——, *Changing Patterns of Governance in the United Kingdom: Reinventing Whitehall?* (Basingstoke, Palgrave 2001).

Marshall, J, 'Handbook for Ministers' (London, National School of Government 2010).

McBride, D, *Power Trip: A Decade of Policy, Plots and Spin* (London, Biteback 2013).

McElwee, M, 'The Great and Good? The Rise of the New Class' (London, Centre for Policy Studies 2000).

McNally, T, '*Downing Street Diary: Volume Two.* By Bernard Donoughue.' (2009) 20 *Twentieth Century British History* 415.

Meyer, C, *DC Confidential* (London, Phoenix 2006).

Mintrom, M, 'Policy Entrepreneurs and the Diffusion of Innovation' (1997) 41 *American Journal of Political Science* 738.

Mitchell, JE, 'Special Advisers: A Personal View' (1978) 56 *Public Administration* 87.

Mountfield, R, '"Politicisation" and the Civil Service', 2002. Retrieved from *http://www.policy.manchester.ac.uk/media/projects/policymanchester/civilservant/politicisation.pdf.*

Mulgan, G, 'Thinking in Tanks: The Changing Ecology of Political Ideas' (2006) 77 *Political Quarterly* 147.

Mulgan, R, 'Politicization of Senior Appointments in the Australian Public Service' (1998) 57 *Australian Journal of Public Administration* 3.

——, '"Accountability": An Ever-Expanding Concept?' (2000) 78 *Public Administration* 555.

——, 'How Much Responsiveness is Too Much or Too Little?' (2008) 67 *Australian Journal of Public Administration* 345.

——, 'Where Have All the Ministers Gone?' (2010) 69 *Australian Journal of Public Administration* 289.

Mullin, C, *A View from the Foothills* (London, Profile Books 2010).

Oborne, P, *The Rise of Political Lying* (London, Free Press 2005).

——, *The Triumph of the Political Class* (London, Simon & Schuster 2007).

Page, E, 'Comparative Public Administration in Britain' (1995) 73 *Public Administration* 123.

——, 'Joined-Up Government and the Civil Service' in V Bogdanor (ed), *Joined-Up Government* (Oxford, Oxford University Press 2005).

——, 'Middle Level Bureaucrats: Policy, Discretion and Control' in JCN Raadschelders et al. (eds), *The Civil Service in the 21st Century* (Basingstoke, Palgrave Macmillan 2007).

——, 'Has the Whitehall Model Survived?' (2010) 76 *International Review of Administrative Sciences* 407.

Page, E and Jenkins, WI, *Policy Bureaucracy: Government with a Cast of Thousands* (New York, Oxford University Press 2005).

Page, E and Wright, V, *Bureaucratic Elites in Western European States* (Oxford, Oxford University Press 1999).

——, 'Conclusion: Senior Officials in Western Europe' in E Page and V Wright (eds), *Bureaucratic Elites in Western European States* (Oxford, Oxford University Press 1999).

——, 'Introduction' in E Page and V Wright (eds), *Bureaucratic Elites in Western European States* (Oxford, Oxford University Press 1999).

Paun, A, 'United We Stand? Coalition Government in the UK' (London, Institute for Government 2010).

——, 'Supporting Ministers to Lead' (London, Institute for Government 2013).

Paun, A and Harris, J, 'Permanent Secretary Appointments and the Role of Ministers' (London, Institute for Government 2012).

Peters, BG, *Comparing Public Bureaucracies: Problems of Theory and Method* (London, University of Alabama Press 1988).

——, 'Back to the Centre? Rebuilding the State' (2004) 75 *Political Quarterly* 130.

——, *The Politics of Bureaucracy*, 6th edn (Abingdon, Routledge 2009).

——, 'The United States' in C Eichbaum and R Shaw (eds), *Partisan Appointees and Public Servants: An International Analysis of the Role of the Political Adviser* (Cheltenham, Edward Elgar 2010).

Peters, BG and Pierre, J, 'Conclusion: Political Control in a Managerialist World' in BG Peters and J Pierre (eds), *Politicization of the Civil Service in Comparative Perspective: A Quest for Control* (London, Routledge 2004).

——, *Politicization of the Civil Service in Comparative Perspective: A Quest for Control* (London, Routledge 2004).

——, 'Politicization of the Civil Service: Concepts, Causes and Consequences' in Peters BG Peters and J Pierre (eds), *Politicization of the Civil Service in Comparative Perspective: A Quest for Control* (London, Routledge 2004).

Pfiffner, JP, 'Political Appointees and Career Executives: The Democracy-Bureaucracy Nexus in the Third Century' (1987) 47 *Public Administration Review* 57.

Philp, M, 'Delimiting Democratic Accountability' (2009) 57 *Political Studies* 28.

Pitts, DW and Fernandez, S, 'The State of Public Management Research: An Analysis of Scope and Methodology' (2009) 12 *International Public Management Journal* 399.

Plowden, W, *Advising the Rulers* (Oxford, Basil Blackwell 1987).

Podger, A, 'What Really Happens: Department Secretary Appointments, Contracts and Performance Pay in the Australian Public Service' (2007) 66 *Australian Journal of Public Administration* 131.

Poguntke, T and Webb, P, *The Presidentialization of Politics: A Comparative Study of Modern Democracies* (Oxford University Press 2005).

Pollitt, C, 'Institutional Amnesia: A Paradox of the "Information Age"?' (2000) 18 *Prometheus* 5.

——, 'Bureaucracies Remember, Post-bureaucratic Organisations Forget?' (2009) 87 *Public Administration* 198.

——, 'Not Odious But Onerous: Comparative Public Administration' (2011) 89 *Public Administration* 114.

Powell, J, *The New Machiavelli: How to Wield Power in the Modern World* (London, Bodley Head 2011).

Prescott, J, *Prezza: My Story: Pulling No Punches* (London, Headline Review 2008).

Price, L, *The Spin Doctor's Diary: Inside Number 10 with New Labour* (London, Hodder & Stoughton 2005).

——, *Where Power Lies: Prime Minister v the Media* (London, Simon & Schuster 2010).

Purnell, J and Lewis, L, 'Leading a Government Department: The First 100 Days' (London, Institute for Government, 2012).

Pyper, R, 'The UK Coalition and the Civil Service: A Half-Term Report' (2013) 28 *Public Policy and Administration* 364.

Pyper, R and Burnham, J, 'The British Civil Service: Perspectives on "Decline" and "Modernisation"' (2011) 13 *British Journal of Politics & International Relations* 189.

Raadschelders, JCN, 'The Study of Public Administration in the United States' (2011) 89 *Public Administration* 140.

Rawnsley, A, *Servants of the People: The Inside Story of New Labour* (London, Hamish Hamilton 2000).

——, *The End of the Party* (London, Viking 2010).

Rhodes, RAW, *Understanding Governance: Policy Networks, Governance, Reflexivity and Accountability* (Buckingham, Open University Press 1997).

——, 'Understanding Governance: Ten Years On' (2007) 28 *Organization Studies* 1243.

——, *Everyday Life in British Government* (Oxford, Oxford University Press 2011).

——, 'One-Way, Two-Way, or Dead-End Street: British Influence on the Study of Public Administration in America since 1945' (2011) 71 *Public Administration Review* 559.

Rhodes, RAW and Dunleavy, P, 'From Prime Ministerial Power to Core Executive' in RAW Rhodes and P Dunleavy (eds), *Prime Minister, Cabinet, and Core Executive* (New York, St Martin's Press 1995).

Rhodes, RAW and Wanna, J, 'The Limits to Public Value, or Rescuing Responsible Government from the Platonic Guardians' (2007) 66 *Australian Journal of Public Administration* 406.

Rhodes, RAW, Wanna, J and Weller, P, *Comparing Westminster* (Oxford, Oxford University Press 2009).

Richards, D, *New Labour and the Civil Service: Reconstituting the Westminster Model* (Basingstoke, Palgrave Macmillan 2008).

Riddell, P, *Honest Opportunism: The Rise of the Career Politician* (London, Hamish Hamilton 1993).

——, *The Unfulfilled Prime Minister: Tony Blair's Quest for a Legacy* (London, Politico's 2006).

——, *In Defence of Politicians (in Spite of Themselves)* (London, Biteback 2011).

Riddell, P, Gruhn, Z and Carolan, L, *The Challenge of Being a Minister: Defining and Developing Ministerial Effectiveness* (London, Institute for Government 2011).

Riddell, P and Haddon, C, 'Transitions: Preparing for Changes of Government' (London, Institute for Government 2009).

Roberts, PS and Dull, M, 'Guarding the Guardians: Oversight Appointees and the Search for Accountability in U.S. Federal Agencies' (2013) 25 *Journal of Policy History* 207.

Robertson, G, 'The Changing Role of the Privy Council Office' (1971) 14 *Canadian Public Administration/Administration publique du Canada* 487.

Rose, R and Mackenzie, W, 'Comparing Forms of Comparative Analysis' (1991) 39 *Political Studies* 446.

Rouban, L, 'Politicization of the Civil Service' in BG Peters and J Pierre (eds), *Handbook of Public Administration* (London, Sage Publications 2003).

——, 'Politicization of the Civil Service in France: From Structural to Strategic Politicization' in BG Peters and J Pierre (eds), *Politicization of the Civil Service in Comparative Perspective: The Quest for Control* (London, Routledge 2004).

——, 'Public Management and Politics: Senior Bureaucrats in France' (2007) 85 *Public Administration* 473.

Saint-Martin, D, 'The New Managerialism and the Policy Influence of Consultants in Government: An Historical-Institutionalist Analysis of Britain, Canada and France' (1998) 11 *Governance* 319.

Sausman, C and Locke, R, 'The British Civil Service: Examining the Question of Politicisation' in BG Peters and J Pierre (eds), *Politicization of the Civil Service in Comparative Perspective: A Quest for Control* (London, Routledge 2004).

Savoie, D, *Governing from the Centre: The Concentration of Power in Canadian Politics* (Toronto, University of Toronto Press 1999).

——, *Breaking the Bargain: Public Servants, Ministers, and Parliament* (Toronto, University of Toronto Press 2003).

——, *Court Government and the Collapse of Accountability in Canada and the United Kingdom* (Toronto, University of Toronto Press 2008).

——, 'The Rise of Court Government in Canada' (2009) 32 *Canadian Journal of Political Science* 635.

Schröter, E, 'The Politicization of the German Civil Service: A Three-Dimensional Portrait of the Ministerial Bureaucracy' in BG Peters and J Pierre (eds), *Politicization of the Civil Service in Comparative Perspective: The Quest for Control* (London, Routledge 2004).

Schuck, P, 'Is a Competent Federal Government Becoming Oxymoronic?' (2009) 77 *George Washington Law Review* 973.

Scott, D, *Off Whitehall: A View from Downing Street by Tony Blair's Adviser* (London, I.B. Tauris 2004).

Seldon, A, *Blair's Britain, 1997–2007* (Cambridge, Cambridge University Press 2007).

Sellers, A, 'An Examination of the Careers of Special Advisers after Leaving Post and the Emergence of a New Policy Actor in Whitehall' (MSc thesis, LSE 2011).

Shaw, R and Eichbaum, C, 'Ministers, Minders and the Core Executive: Why Ministers Appoint Political Advisers in Westminster Contexts' [2012] *Parliamentary Affairs*.

Shepherd, RP, '*Power: Where is it?* by Donald J. Savoie' (2011) 54 *Canadian Public Administration* 308.

Shergold, P, 'What Really Happens in the Australian Public Service: An Alternative View' (2007) 66 *Australian Journal of Political Science* 367.

Smith, M, 'The Paradoxes of Britain's Strong Centre: Delegating Decisions and Reclaiming Control' in C Dahlström et al (eds), *Steering from the Centre: Strengthening Political Control in Western Democracies* (Toronto, University of Toronto Press 2011).

Smith, MJ, *The Core Executive in Britain* (New York, St Martin's Press 1999).

——, 'Tsars, Leadership and Innovation in the Public Sector' (2011) 39 *Policy & Politics* 343.

Smithers, A, 'Schools' in A Seldon (ed), *Blair's Britain, 1997–2007* (Cambridge, Cambridge University Press 2007).

Snowdon, C, 'Sock Puppets: How the Government Lobbies Itself and Why' (London, Institute of Economic Affairs, 2012).

Sossin, L, 'Speaking Truth to Power? The Search for Bureaucratic Independence in Canada' (2005) 55 *University of Toronto Law Journal* 1.

Spence, D, *The European Commission*, 3rd revised edn (London, John Harper Publishing 2006).

——, 'The President, the College and the Cabinets' in *The European Commission*, 3rd revised edn (London, John Harper Publishing 2006).

Stone, B, 'Administrative Accountability in the "Westminster" Democracies: Towards a New Conceptual Framework' (1995) 8 *Governance* 505.

Suleiman, E, *Politics, Power and Bureaucracy in France* (Princeton, Princeton University Press 1974).

Svara, JH, 'Introduction: Politicians and Administrators in the Political Process—A Review of Themes and Issues in the Literature' (2006) 29 *International Journal of Public Administration* 953.

Thatcher, M, *The Downing Street Years* (London, HarperCollins 1993).

Theakston, K, *The Civil Service since 1945* (Oxford, Blackwell 1995).

Theakston, K and Fry, G, 'Britain's Administrative Elite: Permanent Secretaries 1900–1986' (1989) 67 *Public Administration* 129.

Tiernan, A, *Power without Responsibility: Ministerial Staffers in Australian Governments from Whitlam to Howard* (Sydney, UNSW Press 2007).

——, 'Advising Australian Federal Governments: Assessing the Evolving Capacity and Role of the Australian Public Service' (2011) 70 *Australian Journal of Public Administration* 335.

Tiernan, A and Weller, P, *Learning to be a Minister: Heroic Expectations, Practical Realities* (Carlton, Melbourne University Press 2010).

Vacher's Quarterly June 2013 (Dod's Parliamentary 2013).

Walcott, C and Hult, K, 'White House Structure and Decision Making: Elaborating the Standard Model' (2005) 35 *Presidential Studies Quarterly* 303.

Waller, P, 'Workings of Whitehall—An Insight into the Civil Service and How Policy is Developed' (Whitehall & Industry Group 2012).

Webb, P and Poguntke, T, 'The Presidentialisation of Politics Thesis Defended' (2012) 66 *Parliamentary Affairs* 646.

Whitehall & Industry Group, 'Searching for the X-Factors: A Review of Decision-Making in Government and Business' (2011).

Wildavsky, A, *Speaking Truth to Power: the Art and Craft of Policy Analysis* (New Brunswick, NJ, Transaction Books 1987).

Wilson, GK and Barker, A, 'Bureaucrats and Politicians in Britain' (2003) 16 *Governance* 349.

Wilson, H, 'Appendix V: The "Political Advisers" Experiment' in *The Governance of Britain* (London, Weidenfeld & Nicolson 1976).

Baron Wilson of Dinton, 'Government: A Suitable Case for Treatment?' (2011) 89 *Public Administration* 93.

Wilson, R, 'Portrait of a Profession Revisited' (2002) 73 *Political Quarterly* 381.

Wolf, PJ, 'Neutral and Responsive Competence: The Bureau of the Budget, 1939–1948, Revisited' (1999) 31 *Administration & Society* 142.

Wolmar, C, *Broken Rails: How Privatisation Wrecked Britain's Railways* (London, Aurum 2001).

Wood, BD and Waterman, RW, 'The Dynamics of Political Control of the Bureaucracy' (1991) 85 *American Political Science Review* 801.

Wright, T, 'Doing Politics Differently' (2009) 80 *Political Quarterly* 319.

Yeung, K, 'Regulating Government Communications' (2006) 65 *Cambridge Law Journal* 53.

Yong, B, 'New Zealand's Experience of Multi-Party Governance' in A Paun and R Hazell, (eds), *Making Minority Government Work: Hung Parliaments and the Challenges for Westminister and Whitehall* (London, Institute for Government 2009).

Young, D, *The Enterprise Years: A Businessman in the Cabinet* (London, Headline Book Publishing 1990).

Zaring, D, 'Against Being Against the Revolving Door' [2013] *University of Illinois Law Review* 507.

GOVERNMENT AND PARLIAMENT REPORTS

UK

Cabinet Office, 'Ministerial Code' (July 2001).

——, *The Government's Response to the Ninth Report of the Committee on Standards in Public Life* (Cmd 5964, 2003).

——, 'Departmental Evidence and Response to Select Committees' (July 2005).

——, *Ministerial Code* (May 2010).

——, *Code of Conduct for Special Advisers* (June 2010).

——, 'Model Contract for Special Advisers' (June 2010).

——, 'The Cabinet Manual' (October 2011).

——, 'The Civil Service Reform Plan' (June 2012).

——, 'Special Adviser Data Releases' (July 2012).

——, 'Civil Service Reform Plan: One Year On' (July 2013).

——, 'Cabinet Office Staff and Salary Data as at 31 March 2013' (June 2013).

——, 'Consultation Principles' (October 2013).

——, 'Special adviser data releases: numbers and costs, October 2013' (October 2013).

——, 'Extended Ministerial Offices—Guidance for Departments' (November 2013).

Cabinet Office (Office of the Advisory Committee on Business Appointments) 'Sixth Report 2002–2004' (July 2004).

Cabinet Office (Office of Public Service), 'Report of the Working Group on the Government Information Service' (November 1997).

Civil Service, *Civil Service Code* (November 2010).

Civil Service Commission, 'Recruitment Principles' (April 2012).

——, 'Appointment to Senior Roles in the Civil Service by the Use of Exceptions' (December 2012).

——, 'Recruiting Permanent Secretaries: Ministerial Involvement' (December 2012).

——, 'Exception Relating to Extended Ministerial Offices' (October 2013).

Committee on Standards and Privileges, *Premature Disclosure of Reports of the Foreign Affairs Committee* (HC 1998–99, 607).

Committee on Standards in Public Life, *Reinforcing Standards: Review of the First Report of the Committee on Standards in Public Life* (Cmd 4557, 2000).

——, *Defining the Boundaries within the Executive: Ministers, Special Advisers, and the Permanent Civil Service* (Cmd 5775, 2003).

——, 'Response to the Government's Consultation on Proposals for a Register of Lobbyists' (April 2012).

Committee on the Civil Service, *The Report of the Committee on the Civil Service* (Cmd 3638, 1968).

Constitution Committee, *The Cabinet Office and the Centre of Government* (HL 2009–10, 30).

——, *The Accountability of Civil Servants* (HL 2012–13, 61).

Foreign Affairs Committee, *The Decision to Go to War in Iraq* (HC 2002–03, 813-I).

House of Commons Library, 'Members' Office Costs—The New System' (House of Commons Library 2001).

——, 'Parliamentary Pay and Allowances: Current Rates' (House of Commons Library 2001).

——, 'The Whip's Office' (House of Commons Library 2008).

——, 'Social Background of MPs' (House of Commons Library 2010).

——, 'Special Advisers' (House of Commons Library 2010).

——, 'Members 1979–2010' (House of Commons Library 2010).

——, 'Limitations on the Number of Ministers and the Size of the Payroll Vote' (House of Commons Library 2012).

—— 'The Ministerial Code' (House of Commons Library 2012).

——, 'Lobbying: July 2013 Update' (House of Commons Library 2013).

——, 'Members' Pay and Expenses—Current Rates from 1 April 2013' (House of Commons Library 2013).

——, 'Short Money' (House of Commons Library 2013).

——, 'Civil Service Statistics' (House of Commons Library 2013).

——, 'PIL: Ministers in the Coalition Government: 2010–Present' (House of Commons Library 2014).

Independent Parliamentary Standards Authority, 'MPs' Scheme of Business Costs & Expenses' (April 2012).

Institute for Public Policy Research, *Accountability and Responsiveness in the Senior Civil Service: Lessons from Overseas* (London, Cabinet Office 2013).

National Statistics, 'Civil Service Statistics 2000' (2000) Office for National Statistics, 'Civil Service Statistics, 2012' (October 2012).

Political and Constitutional Reform Committee, *The Impact and Effectiveness of Ministerial Reshuffles* (HC 2013–14, HC 255).

Public Administration Select Committee, *Special Advisers: Boon or Bane?* (HC 2000–01, 293).

——, *'These Unfortunate Events': Lessons of Recent Events at the Former DTLR* (HC 2001–02, 303).

——, *The Attendance of the Prime Minister's Strategy Adviser Before the Public Administration Select Committee* (HC 2005–06, 690).

——, *Politics and Administration: Ministers and Civil Servants* (HC 2006–07, 122-I).

——, *Lobbying: Access and Influence in Whitehall* (HC 2008–09, 36-I).

——, *Outsiders and Insiders: External Appointments to the Senior Civil Service* (HC 2009–10, 241).

——, *Business Appointment Rules* (HC 2012–13, 404).

——, *Special Advisers in the Thick of it* (HC 2012–13, 134).

——, *Truth to Power: How Civil Service Reform Can Succeed* (HC 2013–14, 74).

——, *Special Advisers in the Thick of it: Government Response* (HC 2013–14, 515).

Public Service Committee, *Ministerial Accountability and Responsibility* (HC 1995–96, 313-I).

'Records of the Prime Minister's Office: Correspondence and Papers, 1979–1997' (National Archives, 10 October 1980).

Tee, M, 'Review of Government Direct Communication and COI' (Cabinet Office, 18 March 2011).

Treasury and Civil Service Committee, *Civil Servants and Ministers: Duties and Responsibilities* (HC 1985–86, 92).

——, *The Role of the Civil Service* (HC 1993–94, 27).

Canada

Commission of Inquiry into the Sponsorship Program and Advertising Activities, *Restoring Accountability—Recommendations* (Ottawa, Commission of Inquiry into the Sponsorship Program and Advertising Activities 2006).

Furi, M, 'Public Service Impartiality: Taking Stock' (*Public Service Commission of Canada*, July 2008).

Office of the Conflict of Interest and Ethics Commissioner, 'Conflict of Interest Act: Summary of Rules for Ministerial Exempt Staff' (Information for Public Office Holders, 2012).

——, 'Conflict of Interest Act: Summary of Rules for Public Office Holders' (Information for Public Office Holders, 2012).

——, 'Conflict of Interest Act: Summary of Rules for Reporting Public Office Holders' (Information for Public Office Holders, 2012).

Privy Council Office, *Accountable Government: A Guide to Ministers and Ministers of State* (Ottawa, Government of Canada 2008).

——, *Accountable Government: A Guide for Ministers and Ministers of State* (Ottawa, Government of Canada 2011).

Smith, A, 'The Impact of Individual and Collective Performance' (Ottawa, Library of Parliament 2006).

——, 'Ministerial Staff: Issues of Accountability and Ethics' (Ottawa, Library of Parliament 2008).

Treasury Board of Canada Secretariat, 'Demographic Snapshot of the Federal Public Service, 2010' (*Office of the Chief Human Resources Officer*, 2010).
——, 'Appendix A: Exempt Staff Position Structure' (Policies for Ministers' Offices— January 2011).

Australia

Code of Conduct for Ministerial Staff (Minister for the Public Service and Integrity, 2008).
Commonwealth of Australia, 'Annual Report 2010–11' (Members of Parliament (Staff) Act 1984 Annual Reports, 2011).
——, 'Annual Report 2011–12' (Members of Parliament (Staff) Act 1984 Annual Reports, 2012).
Henderson, A, 'Review of Government Staffing' (Senate Standing Committee of Finance and Public Administration, 2009).
Horne, N, 'The Members of Parliament (Staff) Act 1984 Framework and Employment Issues' (Parliament of Australia 2009).
Senate Select Committee for an Inquiry into a Certain Maritime Incident, *Report on A Certain Maritime Incident*. Commonwealth of Australia, Canberra, 2002.

Other

OECD, *Ministerial Advisors: Role, Influence and Management* (Paris, OECD Publishing 2011).

NEWSPAPER ARTICLES

Alleyne, R, 'Government Politicising the Civil Service by the Back Door with Expert Advisers' *Daily Telegraph* (20 February 2013).
'Andy Coulson Resigns: As it Happened' *The Guardian* (21 January 2011).
Aston, H, and Swan, J, 'Control Freak Peta Credlin Accused of Pulling Coalition Strings' *Sydney Morning Herald* (4 December 2013).
Barker, A and Pickard, J, 'Concern over Career Politicians' Dominance' *Financial Times* (14 May 2010).
Boffey, D, 'Controversial New Adviser's "Tactless" Jibes Stir up Trouble for Michael Gove' *The Observer* (14 October 2012).
Brecknell, S, 'Special Report: Civil Service Accountability' *Civil Service World* (2 December 2013).
Brogan, B, 'Tony's Cronies Pack into Lords' *Daily Telegraph* (1 May 2004).
Budd, A, 'Obituary: Sir Alan Walters' *The Guardian* (6 January 2009).
Cameron, S, 'Advisers Have Corroded Trust in Whitehall' *Financial Times* (7 April 2003).
Castle, B, 'Mandarin Power' *Sunday Times* (10 June 1973).
Chakelian, A, 'Back to Front: From SpAd to Worse?' *Total Politics* (28 May 2013).
Chapman, J, 'What Emails Did Ed Send to Smear Plotter? More Disturbing Questions for Labour Leader in our Serialisation of Spin Doctor's Explosive Memoir' *Daily Mail* (20 September 2013).

Chorley, M, 'Politics? Nothing that a Bit of Thinking Can't Cure' *The Independent* (30 January 2011).

Coates, S, 'Labour Paid £1m of Government Cash to Left-Wing Think-Tank' *The Times* (31 May 2007).

Crampton, C, 'The Pulling Power of IPPR' *Total Politics* (6 January 2011).

Crowe, D and Hepworth, A, 'Business Declares War over Ministerial Staffers "Costing us Billions"' *The Australian* (21 September 2012).

Curtis, P, 'Q&A: Ministerial Special Advisers' *The Guardian* (2 September 2010).

Cusick, J, '"Dump F***ing Everyone": The Inside Story of How Michael Gove's Vicious Attack Dogs are Terrorising the DfE' *The Independent* (15 February 2013).

Doward, J, 'Michael Gove Advisers Face Claims of Smear Tactics Against Foes' *The Observer* (2 February 2013).

'Education Department "Deleted Email Exchanges" with Michael Gove Adviser' *The Guardian* (3 March 2012).

Ganesh, J, 'A False Economy' *Prospect* (23 February 2011).

'Guide to 10 Downing Street' *The House* (April 2012).

Helm, T, 'Are Dark Arts Spinning Out of Control in Michael Gove's Department?' *The Observer* (2 February 2013).

——, 'Michael Gove's Officials Act to Clean up Abusive @toryeducation Twitter Feed' *The Observer* (16 February 2013).

—— 'Civil Service Unions Attack High Salaries for Cabinet Advisers' *The Guardian* (16 March 2014).

Helm, T and Hope, C, 'The Top Twelve Think Tanks in Britain' *Daily Telegraph* (24 January 2008).

Kirkup, J and Prince, R, 'How Shriti the Shriek Became Baroness Vadera' *Daily Telegraph* (24 September 2009).

Kite, M, 'Gordon Brown Aide Damian McBride Resigns over "Smear Campaign" Emails' *Daily Telegraph* (11 April 2009).

Macalister, T and White, M, 'BP Stops Paying Political Parties' *The Guardian* (1 March 2002).

Martin, D, 'How Cameron Put 26 Aides on Public Payroll: PM in New Row over Civil Service "Jobs for the Boys"' *Daily Mail* (9 November 2010).

Mason, R, 'Douglas Alexander Accused of "Divisive" Leak by Former Spin Doctor' *The Guardian* (22 September 2013).

Montgomerie, T, 'Trust the Brain Trusts' *The Guardian* (7 June 2008).

Moore, C, 'This is the Moment to Revive the Conservative and Liberal Democrat Coalition, Not to Break it Apart' *Daily Telegraph* (4 May 2012).

Nelson, F, 'Gordon Brown's Secret Army Could Defeat the Coalition's Welfare and Education Reforms' *Daily Telegraph* (25 October 2012).

Oborne, P, 'The Eunuchs of the Cabinet' *The Spectator* (15 December 2001).

Routledge, P and Hoggart, S, 'Major Hits Out at Cabinet' *The Guardian* (25 July 1993).

Seymour, R, 'Cameron: Care Bear, or Lame Duck?' *The Guardian* (2 October 2010).

Sherman, J, 'Ministers "Must Be Allowed to Choose Officials"' *The Times* (17 June 2013).

——, '"Political Reform" Plans Stir Civil Service Anger' *The Times* (9 July 2013).

'Shriti Vadera: A Orofile of the Business Minister Nicknamed "Shriti the Shriek"' *Daily Telegraph* (15 January 2009).

Slater, J, 'Meshed in Web of Power' *Times Educational Supplement* (22 July 2005).

Sutherland, K, 'In the Know, But Out of Sight' *Times Higher Education* (8 October 2004).

'Think Tanks' *The Guardian* (30 September 2013).

Watt, N, 'Cameron's New Backroom Team Aims to Move Story on from U-turns and Cuts' *The Guardian* (18 February 2011).

———, 'Ed Miliband Says He Urged Gordon Brown to Sack Damian McBride' *The Guardian* (22 September 2013)

Wintour, P, 'Blair: Media is Feral Beast Obsessed with Impact' *The Guardian* (13 June 2007).

———, 'Labour Policy Chiefs Meet to Fill in Ed Miliband's "Blank Piece of Paper"' *The Guardian* (22 June 2011).

———, 'Dominic Cummings: Genius or Menace?' *The Guardian* (11 October 2013).

Wood, N, 'The Nerve Centre of No10 is Pathetically Weak: It's Time to Ditch the Civil Servants and Bring Back the Political Heavyweights' *Daily Mail* (2 April 2012).

Young, H, 'The Blairites Have Wrecked the Best of the Civil Service' *The Guardian* (28 February 2002).

WEBPAGES AND BLOGS

'Adam Smith, Jeremy Hunt, and the Fall of the "Spad"' (*Channel 4 News*, 24 May 2012), www.channel4.com/news/adam-smith-jeremy-hunt-and-the-fall-of-the-spad.

'Andrew Adonis Announced as New Director of the Institute for Government' (Institute for Government, 15 July 2010), www.instituteforgovernment.org.uk/news/article/144/andrew-adonis-announced-as-new-director-of-the-institute-for-government.

'Nick Barber: The Special Adviser Who Wasn't' (*UK Constitutional Law Group*, 25 October 2011), http://ukconstitutionallaw.org/2011/10/25/nick-barber-the-special-adviser-who-wasn%E2%80%99t.

Barker, A, 'Exit Coulson, Enter Cummings' (*Westminster Blog [FT]*, 27 January 2011), http://blogs.ft.com/westminster/2011/01/exit-coulson-enter-cummings/#axzz1bi6ctNNP.

Barrington, R, 'The Lobbying Bill: A Missed Opportunity' (*Huffington Post*, 23 July 2013), www.huffingtonpost.co.uk/robert-barrington/the-lobbying-bill-a-misse_b_3638508.html.

BBC Democracy Live, 'The Rt Hon Jack Straw: Great Offices of State', July 2012, http://news.bbc.co.uk/democracylive/hi/house_of_commons/newsid_9688000/9688423.stm.

'Brown Unveils Huge Cabinet Revamp' (*BBC News*, 28 June 2007), http://news.bbc.co.uk/1/hi/6247502.stm.

'Cabs for Hire? Fixing the Revolving Door between Government and Business' (*Transparency International UK*, 2011), www.transparency.org.uk/our-work/publications/10-publications/132-cabs-for-hire-fixing-the-revolving-door-between-government-and-business.

'A Career of Controversy: Keith Hellawell' (*BBC News*, 10 July 2002), http://news.bbc.co.uk/1/hi/uk/2120044.stm.

'Clayton H. Riddell Graduate Program in Political Management' (Carleton University), http://carleton.ca/politicalmanagement014.

Cole, B, 'Ian McDonald: Face of the Falklands' (*Channel 4 News*, 1 February 2007), www.channel4.com/news/articles/uk/ian+mcdonald+face+of+the+falklands/263753.html.

Denwood, A, 'Call to Limit Businesses Profiting From Political Ties' (*BBC News*, 26 July 2011), www.bbc.co.uk/news/uk-politics-14193449>

'Dr Tim Leunig' (London School of Economics, 2012), www.lse.ac.uk/economicHistory/whosWho/profiles/tleunig@lseacuk.aspx.

Griggs, I and Cook, S, 'Analysis: Are Charities a Nest of Scheming Labourites?' (*Third Sector Online*, 17 December 2012), www.thirdsector.co.uk/Communications/article/1164484/Analysis-charities-nest-scheming-Labourites.

Hall, I, 'Spads Moving on from Whitehall All Face "Revolving Doors" Committee' (*Public Affairs News*, 9 March 2011), www.publicaffairsnews.com/fileadmin/templates/images/PAN%20March%202011.pdf.

Levitt, R and Solesbury, W, 'Policy Tsars: Here to Stay But More Transparency Needed' (King's College London 2012), www.kcl.ac.uk/sspp/departments/politicaleconomy/research/tsarsreport/Tsars-Final-Report-Dec-2012.pdf.

Lock, D, 'Special Advisers and Public Allegations of Misconduct 1997–2013' (London, Constitution Unit 2013), www.ucl.ac.uk/constitution-unit/research/special-advisers/special_advisers_and_public_allegations_of_misconduct_1997_-_2013.pdf.

McClory, J, 'Special Advisers: The Great Cull or Stealthy Rise?' (Institute for Government, 13 April 2011), www.instituteforgovernment.org.uk/blog/2395/special-advisers-the-great-cull-or-stealthy-rise.

'Nuclear Review "was Misleading"' *BBC News* (15 February 2007), http://news.bbc.co.uk/1/hi/uk_politics/6364281.stm.PubAffairs, 'What is Public Affairs?' (2011), www.publicaffairsnetworking.com/whatis_pa.php.

'Obituary: Lord Biffen' (*BBC* News, 14 August 2007), http://news.bbc.co.uk/1/hi/uk_politics/6945600.stm.

'Permanent Secretary "Stonewalls" MPs over Jeremy Hunt' (*BBC News*, 26 April 2012), www.bbc.co.uk/news/uk-politics-17858198.

'Political Advisor to Mary Creagh MP (Wakefield)' (*w4mpjobs*, 11 September 2013), www.w4mpjobs.org/JobDetails.aspx?jobid=42064.

Singleton, D, 'David Cameron Rebuked by Gus O'Donnell over Special Advisers' (*PR Week*, 3 March 2011), www.prweek.com/news/1058054.

'Stephen Harper's First Shuffle' (*CBC News*, 4 January 2007), www.cbc.ca/news/background/parliament39/cabinet.html.

'The UK Government' (*Good Relations Political Communications*, April 2013), www.goodrelationspolitical.co.uk/wp-content/uploads/2013/03/GRPC-UK-Gov-April-2013.pdf.

Index

comparative experience:
  assessment, 166–8
  Australia, 156–60, 167, 196, 202–3
  Canada, 152–6, 167, 196
  ministerial *cabinets,* 162–6, 167
  New Zealand, 160–2
  numbers of advisers/political staff, 153–4,
    157, 196, 198
  survey, 151–68
  transparency, 200
  Whitehall model, 151
conduct *see* misconduct of special advisers
Conservative governments *see* Coalition
  government; Major administration; Thatcher
  administration
Constitution Unit, 11, 146, 187
core executive model, 27–30
Corry, Dan, 22, 47, 139n40, 219
Coulson, Andy, 1, 58, 111, 124, 178
Council of Economic Advisers, 99, 140, 224
Cowley, Philip, 235
Cradock, Percy, 24
Cummings, Dominic, 58–9, 178, 185

Darling, Alistair, 47, 225
database, 6, 200, 212
Davey, Ed, 37
Davies, Gareth, 22
defence procurement, 194
Delivery Unit, 21–2, 24, 65, 81, 203
Demos, 238
Diamond, Patrick, 80–1, 82
Directors of Communications, 132, 186,
  187, 243
discipline:
  accountability theory and practice, 134
  forms of misconduct, 130
  ministers' duty, 129, 134, 190
  problem with special advisers, 130–2
  regulatory framework, 132–4
discrimination legislation, 194
Donoghue, Bernard, 19
Downing Street (No 10)
  see also Cabinet Office; specific departments
  communication with, 179
  overload, 78
  policy-making and
    interaction, 91, 98–100
    special advisers, 88
  political involvement of civil service, 205
  Political Secretaries and, 213
  quality, power and risks, 83
  setting government direction, 78–9
  special advisers, 77–84
    arrogance, 177
    finding right levers, 82
    impact, 83–4
    numbers, 77

  origins, 113–15
  policy-making, 88
  step change, 79–80
  strategy, delivery and media, 79–80
  structure, 20
  ways of working, 83
Dunlop, Andrew, 54, 219

education: special advisers, 40–2
effectiveness:
  age and, 37–9, 175
  defining, 169–70
  effective special advisers, 170–4
    building relationships, 173–4
    challenging conventional wisdom, 173
    clear political objectives, 172
    clear priorities, 172
    close relationships with ministers, 170–1
    drive and determination, 172
    good on policy detail, 173
    media sense, 173
    'perfect' advisers, 171
  improving
    greater professionalism, 191, 206–10
    induction and training, 186–8, 207, 209
    options, 179–80
    recruitment, 109, 181–5
    support and supervision, 188–90, 207, 208
    transparency, 199–202
  ineffective special advisers
    briefing against other ministers, 176–7
    bullying and arrogance, 177–8
    examples, 174–9
    freelancing, 175, 176
    giving instructions to officials, 175–6
    inexperience, 175, 185, 207
    overstepping the mark, 175
    poor communication, 179
    restricting access to officials, 176
  media special advisers, 125–7
  policy-making, 96–7
  Policy Unit, 203–5
  responsibility and, 145–8
  role rather than salaries, 201–2
Eichbaum, Chris, 29, 161–2, 214
election manifestos, 24, 66, 71
employment conditions:
  adviser profiles and, 56–7
  Australian political staff, 159
  contracts, 133, 135, 146
  job descriptions, 85, 145–7, 182, 183,
    199, 201
  pay, 201, 207
  performance appraisal, 147–8, 189
  support and supervision, 188–90, 208
  training, 147–8, 159, 186–8, 209
environmental policy, 194
Euroscepticism, 115

Lightning Source UK Ltd.
Milton Keynes UK
UKHW020827111120
373193UK00005B/218